PUBLIC LIKE A FROG

Entering the Lives of Three Great Americans

Praise For The Book

"Jean Houston gives back to contemporary society the powers of the Mysteries not by expounding ancient myths but by examining modern lives lived to mythic proportions. Her essays on Dickinson, Jefferson, and Keller are more than biographies of great lives; they are biographs of the 'yearned' in every soul."–Normandi Ellis, author of *Awakening Osiris* and *Return to Egypt*

"This book shines with the brilliance of four geniuses: the three of whom Dr. Houston writes and Jean herself, who brings the three to life so convincingly that one feels one is having breakfast with them."–Barbara Jo Brothers, M.S.W., B.C.S.W., editor of the *Journal of Couples Therapy* and Adjunct Professor at Tulane University School of Social Work

"Jean Houston's genius as a creative teacher shines through on every page of this remarkable book. For those who have despaired of finding new paths for inner work, Jean has cut a fresh road to the goal of seeing one's life with transformed vision."–Jeremy Tarcher, publisher

"Jean Houston has an unparalleled ability to symphonize science, art, world culture and myth, philosophy and psychology, religious and spiritual disciplines into new forms that are both world and mind growing."–The Honorable William R. Bryant, Jr., Republican Leader Emeritus, Michigan House of Representatives

"Jean Houston has pioneered a new form–book as experiential workshop. Her evocative accounts of Emily Dickinson, Thomas Jefferson, and Helen Keller put these heroic lives to a vivid, new, and practical use. Bravo!"–Marilyn Ferguson, publisher of *Brain/Mind* and author of *The Aquarian Conspiracy*

"This stunning book allows us to understand from the inside and to bring alive in ourselves what it means to write like Emily Dickinson, think like Thomas Jefferson, and experience the world like Helen Keller. A quantum leap in education, this book is a model for the textbooks of the future. It should be in every classroom."–Gay Luce, author of *Longer Life, More Joy: Techniques for Enhancing Health, Happiness, and Inner Vision*

Entering the Lives of Three Great Americans

by
JEAN HOUSTON

QUEST BOOKS
The Theosophical Publishing House

Wheaton, IL U.S.A./Madras, India/London, England

The Theosophical Publishing House
P.O.Box 270
Wheaton, IL 60189-0270

A publication of the Theosophical Publishing House
a department of the Theosophical Society in America

*This publication made possible with
the assistance of the Kern Foundation.*

Library of Congress Cataloging-in-Publication Data

Houston, Jean.
    Public Like A Frog: entering the lives of three great Americans / Jean Houston.
        p. cm.
    Includes index.
    ISBN 0-8356-0694-5 : $14.00
    1. Celebrities--United States--Biography. 2. Success--Biography.
I. Title.
CT215. H73 1993   93-14025
920.073--dc20   CIP

                9 8 7 6 5 4 3 2 1 * 93 94 95 96 97 98 99

Printed in the United States of America by Versa Press

Contents

PART TWO: THOMAS JEFFERSON

PART THREE: HELEN KELLER/ANNIE SULLIVAN

Foreword

MYSTERY SCHOOL:
A PARTICIPANT'S
HEART VIEW
by The Hon. William R. Bryant, Jr.
Republican Leader Emeritus
Michigan House of Representatives

*O*ur births and deaths, and more particularly, our rebirths are at once intimate and private—and excruciatingly public. How does a caterpillar feel as it experiences entering into chrysalis? And the tadpole? Is it embarrassed suddenly to start growing appendages, especially to be the first one in the pond? Do others laugh or sneer or shy away or shun, or do they somehow know and give a sacred nod and smile?

Our lives are public, whether or not we flaunt them or seek the public eye. Everything we do, or fail to do, in what is increasingly and inescapably recognized to be a quantum universe of awesome relationality and complexity sets off karma-like ripples throughout the pond which is the universe. The specifics of quantum physics are fathomable by only a few, although its themes resonate with those of ancient mystics and modern poets, with spiritual teachings, with the intuitive musings of millennia. Science and mysteries from the depths of mind here join, conspiring to excite us toward a better, richer truth.

Our transformations are required by the best combination of genetics and environment. We seem somehow to be seeded with a truth that calls us to come forth. Whenever we can fight away exasperating fears, we have the chance to be born again. We are meant to live and die and live again—even within the confines of a single lifespan. We do so in ways which are seen and felt by all fellow creatures, and Earth and cosmos cry in agony and laugh in joy each time. We are sorely public in our metamorphoses, like tadpoles and frogs.

A tadpole, we have surmised, may be benefitted by a community of others who do not laugh or shy away or shun as its limited tadpoleness grows new possibilities, until it emerges to breathe the spirit of air atop a sacred mountain log. To go all this alone would not be impossible, but it would surely be different and somehow less. How much better it must be to know that one's transformation is one's own possibilities unfolding, without taint or fear of inappropriateness. How much more likely are we to gain the lofty heights of human possibility if we do so in the company of others who are also growing, wriggling, crawling, hopping, and climbing, knowing that entelechy—the possibilities encoded in each of us—is calling others, too, to be reborn.

Enough of frogs. In order to traverse well the pits and pratfalls of midlife passage, or earlier, to find out who we could or are meant to be, or later, to extend more usefully into wisdom's time, we can choose from an infinite variety of means. Some may climb mountains, or fall off; some may fall into love, or out. Others seek constructive and transformational growth as individuals in a dedicated learning community, and of these, some seek a Mystery School.

Since 1985 I have felt the possibility and reality of growth and renewal. And I found a Mystery School. The deep explorations into the lives of the three Americans who are the subjects of this book draw on themes and techniques which were part of the curriculum of a year's study in a learning community led for the past ten years by Jean Houston. I have attended her Mystery School for seven of those years.

But all this still says little about what Mystery School is, from a participant's heart view. So it is my considerable task to try to explain.

Allow me to give you some of the basics. Mystery School consists of nine weekends in the course of a year. In its ten years, well over two thousand participants have taken part in its mind and spirit expanding experiences. Mystery School engages body, mind, and spirit in a positive, high play evocation of creativity and knowing, evoking a sense of contact with the Creative Spirit beyond the local self. The school is in certain of its theses built upon, but goes boldly beyond the archetypal psychology of Carl Jung, the mythography of Joseph Campbell, and the typologies of Abraham Maslow of higher level needs and peak experiences. All world culture, art, religion, music, dance, psychophysical movement, poetry, and myth are thematic looms on which the strands of Mystery School work is woven.

Each year of Mystery School has a major focus. Reading and experiential homework are assigned. Depth journaling and one day a week fasting are encouraged. Sessions consist of lectures, discussions, storytelling and joke telling, dance, drama, ritual, high play, and experiential processes. Conducted in a peaceful mountain setting, Mystery School is a community of ordinary, extraordinary people who come together from all parts of the country to dance and dream themselves into their highest human possibility.

Why the name *Mystery School*? It could be called the Graduate School in Human Potential, or The Sacred University of the Depths, or Archetypal School, or Spirit School. It is, in fact, all of these. *Mystery* refers to that which is hidden—perhaps that which one explores only by following clues which reveal, in a nonlinear way, new truths. That fits. Further, the sacred schools of past civilizations—of Egypt and Eleusis, of Pythagoras and Rumi—were called Mystery Schools as well. The linkage of the modern Mystery School with its sacred precursors of the past deepens and extends its scope and patternings.

Why did I go to Mystery School? It started in October of 1985 when my wife Lois asked if I wanted to go to a week-long Jean Houston workshop in Chicago. I did, and we went. The theme of the workshop was the Arthurian legend. In one exercise, Jean Houston asked us to visualize ourselves in the ancient British Isles, in a pre-Iron Age tribal village, and to let the experience flow and see what happened. I experienced a profound visualization of being a young boy in the village, standing around the bonfire among the huts, then, bored, running off to the woods, and later walking south to the sea with my mentor—all of it involving incredible sensory acuity. I knew the landscape and the characters intimately. After that, I had to attend Mystery School. It called me, and I would have swum oceans to get there.

That first year, 1986, I ecstatically kept the required daily journal. Stories, poems, and drawings poured out of me in joyful release. I experienced a new sense of being alive and growing, and with my wife's own growing, she and I rediscovered each other, our marriage became vastly more satisfying, and our lives began to fill with new possibility. In each of the years since 1986 but one, I have attended Mystery School. In the year I stayed home, I wrote two books and listened over and over again to the tapes of the school. I keep signing up because I feel uncomfortable being away from the study, the dancing, the celebration, the tears, the periodic contact with the depths, and the very special community of sacred learning that awaits me there.

I was in Mystery School in 1990 when Emily Dickinson, Thomas Jefferson, and Helen Keller were among those serving as focal points for entering and plumbing the depths. I recall each easily and with love—with relish and mustard, if you will. Their lives came alive among us. One member of the community, a sculptress, brought each great American to life during the weekend before our eyes, in that highly-charged, creative space. The moist clay bust of Emily Dickinson especially, to me and to many who were there, seemed to come alive, to move—ever so slightly, mind you—to quake at being so called forth, so honored, known, and loved.

Emily was the first of the weekends devoted to the particular subjects of this book. Preparing for that weekend, I dove into her poems of solitary spirit and delicious longing. Wormholes in her tiny physical universe of home and hearth were easily seen as sufficient to give her access to the lofty realms beyond, to senses of wonder and awe we can, with due benefit, both celebrate and emulate. It was a weekend filled with the wonder of innocence and of death, of the celebration of children and the crushing formality of fundamentalist ways and religion. I felt like I was suffocating in a box, or sent careening into chasms of deep psyche. I was charmed by the strangeness and sweetness of Emily. I smelled her garden and her cookies and tasted the warm, sweet cornbread she made. I heard the children laughing and pointing at Emily smiling on them from her upstairs window. Her little universe—limitless—extended and blended with mine. I found myself writing poetry in her style—not feeling I was imitating her, just feeling sensuously close to her. I felt our skin as one and gazed out her window at the children giggling and playing beyond the fence below. Smiling and sighing with her, I wrote in love—

> *Really, children, how you titter*
> *Into the dappled, sunlit day*
> *One would think you had no better*
> *Lessons to learn than how to play*

Thomas Jefferson was next, requiring two brimfull weekends. While Emily Dickinson's weekend was centered on the co-creation of the universe of mind, Jefferson's theme was the co-creation of nation, state, and civilization. I was overwhelmed by the wholeness of his sensibilities of both heart and mind, his complexity, his neverending quest for newness, form, sense, rightness. I refused to read his autobiographies, concluding that there was too much to be able to fathom satisfactorily in such short time. Instead, I read his Bible—the one from which he removed all the passages not directly attributable to Jesus. I was blown away, dumfounded, amused, and dramatically uplifted by the audacity and the persistence of the project and the beauty of the creation.

We were blessed during the weekends by Jefferson's seeming presence, by the breadth of his experience, by the character molded by hardship, loss, and gain. We examined, under Jefferson's tutelage, the value of our own toughest times—honoring the trials as well as the triumphs met. We rediscovered letter writing, a Jeffersonian passion, not in the hopes of duplicating his tireless dedication to probing inquiry, to supporting and to spurring others on, but simply to remind ourselves of the value of the letter, the honor we do to our own caring words by sending them to others, near or far away. Taking a shaman's role, I sent such a missive to a doctor friend in Australia, and lo, a healing came to him.

Later that year, we turned inward again, to the study of Helen Keller and Annie Sullivan, Helen's Teacher and mentor—creator of the universe Helen knew. What strength I drew from both! What incredible responsibility we all have as we affect, forever, the universe of all. What immense integrity lived in Annie; what abiding genius and sheer guts in Helen. I was quite taken by both the ideas and the highly stylized handwriting of the flowered intellect of Helen. I found myself feeling thoughts as if from her and Annie about education, intended for us today. As I wrote, I had the sense of knowing something of the depth of Helen's mind in the silence and darkness of her vast cosmos, and I wrote in Helen's hand and voice:

> Teacher gave me light, the world, Heaven, in the very same way all need to learn, regardless of what senses they have or have not, in full or in part. For, indeed, it is the same mind that is to be reached and teased and delighted into knowledge and usefulness.

At the weekend itself, I was pulled into sensory perception, one sense at a time, learning, treasuring each anew. Through the glory of Helen's mind, we experienced our own soul's birthday while celebrating hers. Taking hands with her, we were led into ourselves and out again, to see the patterns formed in our childhood which grew and spiraled outward toward where and what we are called to be. In heeding that call, we—like Helen—are not assured of success, nor of love or happiness, only that we will arrive at life's end knowing that we did well with what we were given, and knowing that along the way, we honored the truth of both our interdependence and our separateness.

Each of the weekends was full of concepts, feelings, experiences rich beyond our dreams. Each called us to our edges, to the living brink of the possible. We tadpoles heard the frogs. The more we were nudged toward our edges, the more we felt the sense of walking the perimeter fence, of prowling the outer limits of both self and community. Mystery School teaches ways and means of honoring and entering, of becoming adept at the exploration and harvesting of our depths of mind. Through its work, we are given multiple perspectives on ourselves and on the world at large, experiencing symbolic and archetypal lenses from every culture and tradition. As we are guided through these lenses, we come to realize that each person has unique potential, colored and coded by an individual genetic and experiential template. And yet, at the same time, the deep archetypal patterns we each inhabit are shared simultaneously by millions or billions of others throughout time. Each life, we learn, is a part of a larger One.

Mystery School is more highly spiritual than any religion. This is partly true because of its ecumenism, its absolute openness to truth wherever and whenever it may be derived. Persons who seek in the school a religion or a guru will be disappointed. Its scope is wildly ecumenical. Its focus is not practice in Eastern mystical disciplines, a *via negativa* dedicated to a stripping away of the illusions of Maya in order to attain a sense of oneness. Its roots are, rather, in a joyous and Western *via positiva*—a means of repatterning the mind by the addition of new knowledge and multiple experiences.

Participants come to Mystery School because they feel the call, because they yearn so badly for growth they can taste it, because they ache to be where ecstasy is allowed and encouraged, where hugs are real and huge, where everything is safe, where they can sing and dance and be the fool, the mad priest, the wild woman, the poet, the poem, the song, the dance—where they can engage in high play and meet new intellectual challenges, where their quirks and quarks are honored and celebrated. Mystery School students range in age from eighteen to eighty and represent all disciplines from artists to engineers, doctors to dancers, priests to politicians, therapists to theoretical physicists, givers of workshops to workers in shops—men and women of all races and ethnic groups, and all religions and none. They are people who care, people who are committed to living at their edges, to stretching themselves and their society, who are avid to be pushed and tried and to go beyond.

Mystery School is also Jean Houston—a woman of high intellect and deep thinking, with a most complete classical education and an uncanny ability to call up pieces of her amazingly well-stocked mind when they are most relevant and useful. She has an unparalleled ability to symphonize science, art, world culture and myth, philosophy and psychology, religious and spiritual disciplines into new forms that are both world and mind growing. She is the most dramatic person I have known, the best storyteller, and a wonderful stand-up comedian. She is open and nonjudgmental and is far more demanding of herself than of others. Her gifts are sacred psychology, process, and the creation of spontaneous ritual. She believes in love and in fallibility, including her own. She teaches her students not to claim that they know the one and only truth, except the glorious truth of human possibility. She believes that all individuals deserve to be nurtured to full flowering.

In her work outside of Mystery School, Jean is a visionary and a healer of individuals and of cultures in transition. I have seen her work in Africa, healing a brilliant young shaman who had allowed his powers to become so twisted and cynical after touring the United States that he was unable to do good for anyone. Jean healed him merely by talking to him as no one had ever talked to him. She knows herself what it is to be a shaman, to allow a higher power to possess one and to use that power for good—honestly, and with love. She sees through those who are charlatans and hucksters, ripping people off with New Age drivel or playing on fear instead of engaging in loving play. But then she laughs about them and forgives them, as she does everyone.

Most of all, Jean is a deepener of ideas and processes. Inevitably, wherever I think she may be headed with some train of thought, she is headed vastly deeper, into far less personal, more universal, meatier territory. Believing as she does in the creative power of the mythic and symbolic realm of mind, she models for her students the efficacy of such a stance, carrying herself and her students to depths or heights unimagined and unanticipated.

More so than any of Jean's previous books, *Public Like a Frog* offers readers an opportunity to enter the Mystery School experience. The text of this book is drawn from Mystery School lectures and discussions and its processes were lived by the people who came to those weekends. The three shining Americans who walk in these pages lived lives designed to instruct. It is wise for us to attend to them; we thus attend to both ourselves and our posterity. What follows are not biographies, bound within; rather, they are intense journeys into the very heart of the life of this country. Each American honored here lived a life of genius, each is beloved, each is archetypal in the clarity and beauty and strength of what was lived. To enter the psyche of peak performing human beings brightly lights our own lives. The key is to get inside, to dive deeply into the minds of these who came before, who left their marks on us and on our land. They knew something from which we may learn worthwhile, yeasty lessons, and, in the process, we may be moved to plumb our own depths and to unravel our own mysteries.

Let the pages of the book pull you in. All you can do is die and live again, public like a frog.

Acknowledgments

Since going public, like a frog, I would like to croak an appreciative word of thanks to the following fellow amphibians who have joined me in the Mystery School venture of living and working in several worlds at once:

Peggy Rubin for the ongoing duets from the pools of our minds. Bill Bryant for his bright and brash foreword and for the great splashing hops he makes into the Mystery School pond that create ever widening circles of meaning for us all. Betty Rothenberger for her ability to dive into the morass of tapes and transcripts and make them into magic. Emmy Devine for leaps and dances of body and spirit that cause us to remember our forebears and who we may yet become. Judith Morley for spontaneous soliloquies, brilliant banters, and poetry made practical for participants. Marvin Sussman for navigating us through squalls on the academic ponds. Kris Ayalla Jeter for seeking out and setting up high croakers for our round table discussions. Randall Hayward for fancies and phantasms and the bringing together of hitherto divided and distinguished worlds. Mickey Houlihan and Paul Briggs for sonic wonders and wonderful sounds. Fonda Joyce for being chief frog and business manager. Donna Liers for keeping the swamps at bay and never toadying to anyone. Anne Georges for providing heartful nourishment for body and soul. Scott Fray for tadpole joy and froggy arty facts. John White for catching flies and searching out better ponds to play in. The many Mystery School participants, each on their own lily pad of life, who manage somehow to sing together the great song that brings music to the night. Roslyn Targ, agent of the process and great supporter of literary amphibians. And Brenda Rosen, editor and cook extraordinaire, who captures us all and serves us up in a rare feast of ideas.

Introduction

elcome to the Mystery School. With this volume we begin a new series of books devoted to presenting material which grew out of our presentations in the Mystery School.

What is a Mystery School? It is my twentieth-century version of an ancient and honorable tradition going back millennia wherein men and women gather to explore the mysteries of who we are, what we are here for, and what we may yet become. Once upon a time there were such schools in Egypt, Greece, Turkey, Persia, Afghanistan, India, China, Tibet, Ireland, England, France, Hawaii, the Americas, as well as in many other places on the planet where the sacred called to the secular to illumine the mystery of existence.

The central questions of all Mystery Schools are, "How do we place the local self in service to the higher Self? How do we prepare to live a fuller life, one that can enhance not only our own life, but that of our family, our community, our planet as well?" In our modern Mystery School each session tries to answer these questions and to find ways to incorporate our discoveries into our lives. Thus we harvest what is available (or can be imagined) of the knowledge and traditions, rites and ritual of these ancient studies, imbuing them with new realities and discoveries. The weekends of the Mystery School are designed to provide rich experiences embracing sacred psychology, history of consciousness, music, theater, the world's cultures and societies and peoples, philosophy, theology, poetry, high and low comedy, the new science, cosmology, metaphysics, and innovative ideas, to provide a multifaceted, multi-level Time out of time.

Mystery School is both experiential and experimental. We stretch our bodies with psychophysical exercises, explore realms of psyche and spirit, create personal and community expressions of art and high play, and journey through dimensions of consciousness. Joined by a staff of eminent creative artists, some of whose comments are recorded in this volume, we learn the movements, music and dance as well as the arts of many ages and cultures. We participate in rituals, ceremonies, and high drama. We empower one another and embrace transformation. Virtually all of the exercises and processes involve restructuring of mental, physical, and psychological life to enable the activation of many of our extraordinary human potentials. Needless to say Mystery School is intellectually vigorous, psychologically challenging, and spiritually demanding. It requires a commitment to be open and available to the deep inner self. It is also frequently hilarious and zanily satiric. The work itself is mystifying, stimulating, depth-sourcing and soul-charging, and always celebrational.

Mystery School shows you that you are deeper, richer, and stronger than you know. You are the mystery, and the job of the school is to train you in your depths. But it is not for everyone. There is homework, study and preparation; there are practices to enable you to build bridges between your everyday life and your depth life. We therefore try to provide a charged place of amplified space and time—a temple, a hothouse, a summoned community—where you may safely carry out your journey of transformation.

Each month we focus on a different aspect of the year's central theme. For example, one year we studied and enacted the stages of the mystic path, using as texts Evelyn Underhill's *Mysticism* and William James' *Varieties of Religious Experience*. Each step on the mystic path was illustrated with my lectures, as well as literature, music, drama, ritual, and story. Francis of Assisi became the exemplar of the stage of Illumination; Joan of Arc relived for us the stage of Voices and Visions; Don Quixote became the embodiment of the stage of Purification; the ancient texts and legends surrounding the Sophia, the feminine wisdom principle, served to illustrate the Dark Night of the Soul; Hildegard of Bingen gave us a luminous doorway into the stage of Union and Ecstatic Knowing.

Mystery School in other years has included intensive weekend studies of the world's great myths. One series was devoted to the Godseed, an exploration of the gnostic Jesus (published by Quest as *Godseed: The Journey of Christ*). In the same series we studied the Grailquest, the Arthurian journey of Percival and Gawain; and *The Hero and the Goddess*, which dealt with the journey of initiation of Odysseus (now published as a book with that title by Ballantine.) We also entered into the mystery plays of Demeter and Persephone, of

Psyche and Eros, of Isis and Osiris, of the ancient Hindu epic, the *Ramayana,* and of the ecstatic Sufi mystic Jalaloddin Rumi and his search for the beloved. We have explored the biographies of great individuals, such as we offer in this book, have investigated the mysteries and the mythologies of the Americas, have journeyed into the myths of the future, and in 1993 entered upon an intensive two-year program in exploring extraordinary human capacities. Each of the great scenarios of the journey of the soul provided participants with a dramatic opportunity to live a larger story, thus engaging the pattern and passion for extraordinary growth.

Each weekend of Mystery School deals with new material with little repetition except in the overall intent and the development of certain exercises. Each month, then, my associate Peggy Rubin works with me closely, helping to develop the lectures and exercises which in many cases constitute a small book. This monthly regimen keeps us constantly reading and studying regardless of where we are working and teaching throughout the world. Thus while giving a seminar on human possibilities in southern India based on the life of Gandhi, we might be getting up at 4 A.M. to prepare the Mystery School to be given the following week in New York on Native American myths and ceremonials. Last week in Bangladesh we were training UNICEF teams and working with the leaders of that country to develop a new vision of what their society could be, while in our pre-dawn labors, we were preparing a Mystery School session on heightened sensory acuity. We find that our global experience always enhances the meaning and the methodology of our Mystery School sessions, while the material we develop in Mystery School is often applicable to our work in international human development. This correlation is both an ancient as well as a natural one, for the essential task of the Mystery Schools has always been to develop the possible human in the possible society, and some of the most remarkable social artists in history have developed their calling in one or another kind of mystery school.

The transcript of each session of Mystery School is typed up by my much valued colleague and friend Betty Rothenberger, with each session running complete with lectures and experiential processes to well over 250 pages. To date there are about 100 such books of transcripts on my shelf, some of which are slowly but surely being rewritten, amplified, and published. The volume you hold in your hands grew out of the Mystery School transcripts of 1990, which dealt with the biographies of great individuals. In the case of *Public Like a Frog*, Quest editor Brenda Rosen was midwife to the book, helping to call it forth, shape its design and flow, and putting her own extraordinary resources of heart and mind into its becoming.

In preparing the lectures I gave at Mystery School which were adapted for *Public Like a Frog*, I drew on the work of many wonderful historians and biographers, often extending their ideas and interpreting the famous lives they wrote about in ways that facilitated their use as Mystery School subjects. In particular, I am indebted to Cynthia G. Wolff's luminous study of the life and work of Emily Dickinson and to Jane Langton's superb presentation of Dickinson's poetry. My thinking about Jefferson was shaped both by my own reading of his letters and papers and by important studies by Saul K. Padover, Dumas Malone, and Alf J. Mapp, Jr. In the case of Helen Keller, the remarkable and comprehensive biography of Joseph P. Lash provided an important jumping off point for my own speculations.

As the material which follows has been edited and largely rewritten from the original transcripts of the Mystery School sessions, we have tried to retain the flavor of the sessions by keeping the colloquial use of speech as well as the odd turn of phrase in the lectures I gave, and most especially in the exercises. Often the exercises are given spontaneously, created on the spot to fit the framework of the session. Thus the reader will note the cadence and curiosities of spoken speech, even where the exercises have been adapted from the actual exercises done at the Mystery School. Needless to say there were many more exercises and processes given for each session. Here, however, we offer in the interest of space only four such processes for each of the biographies. Hopefully, we have given readers ones that they might find most useful for their own development.

The first in this series of three Mystery School books presents material coming out of sessions dealing with spiritual biography in relation to the mysteries of the Americas. In our work we discovered that the history, culture, and landscapes of the Americas are coded with mysteries which, if explored, can yield perspectives on human possibilities that can literally re-enchant the world. As voyagers into new continents of mind, body, and spirit, we can learn especially from the American experience of discovery ways to see familiar things from a deeper point of view. What is it about the Americas that has lured so many, for good or ill, to trek and meander, sail to, wander through, and traverse endlessly back and forth in beauty and in shame, searching for a thousand different kinds of riches? For that matter, what is it that drives all of us to the "discovery" of new realms—physical, mental, emotional, and spiritual? To answer in Native American words, we seek the heart of the Great Mystery by learning to experience the truth of our personal Medicine, as well as our community and global Medicine.

Part of the mystery of America is that we are probably the oldest modern nation on Earth. By that I mean that we were the first to move through the full consequences of the industrial revolution, the urban revolution, the cross-ethnic and multi-cultural revolution, the democratic revolution, the technological revolution, the atomic revolution, the media and information revolution, the outer space revolution, and now, the inner space revolution. Regardless of when our ancestors arrived here, we are an old people in terms of the expectations of the modern world. We are fast becoming post-moderns.

We recall the eighteenth-century country gentlemen who helped found this country with their premises of enlightened reason and their visions of a just but limited social order that would check and balance itself. We remember too, the genial and genius-minded pragmatists like Benjamin Franklin who primed both a nation's conscience with hardy maxims and its ambitions with practical designs, widgets, and labor-saving devices. If the Washingtons, Hamiltons, Jeffersons, and Adamses seeded the soul of America, the Franklins certainly helped seed its head and ego.

These forebears made the first planting, but its fruit has been harvested and shipped over the world like our excess wheat. Part of the mystery of America is that we have become the paradigm of nations, beginning as the visionary land of opportunity, which fulfilled humankind's millennia-old dreams of the golden age returned in a new land beyond the Western waters, and in which the democratization that had been promised only in paradise would be realized in historic space and time. This is a critical point, and one that we often forget—that America was built on the expectations not just of a several hundred years of frustrated Europeans, but on the radical eschatological hopes of millions of people over thousands of years. The hopes of history and the psychospiritual imagination of many peoples and cultures came to fruition in the very founding of America. From the point of view of the psychodynamics of the planet itself, this is an enormously heavy fact of our existence as a nation, and perhaps it explains the relative blessedness of our country, our remarkable good fortune in the canon of nations. Traveling as much as I do, sometimes as much as a quarter-million miles a year, and working in human and cultural development in many countries, I always return to America grateful for living in a nation that has not been recently ravaged by war or political or religious persecution.

Compared to other countries, the opportunities here are immense, the chances to re-invent the world unparalleled. Certainly our problems are grave—economic inequality, homelessness, racial tensions, the refusal until recently to learn from the vast wisdom and knowledge of the Native peoples of this land, a government that is too big for the small problems of life and too small in spirit for the big problems. Then too there is the possibility that we found our manifest form too quickly to allow for the full flowering of the genius seeded in the nation's psyche by the dreams and visions of the millions who landed on these shores as well as by the residing spirit already implanted here by the Native peoples. I suspect that the flowering of this psyche was hampered by the brutal rejection of the spirit, wisdom, and integrity of the Native peoples and also by the settling of America by so many puritanical sectarian groups whose religion gave them an image of themselves as born-guilty creatures who dared not probe their inner states lest they discover themselves to belong to hellish realms. These things, along with the outward looking of the prevalent frontier psychology and the galloping pluralism of peoples, ideologies, cultural and social styles, inhibited the tapping of the deeper strata of the nation's psyche, and the uncovering of the possibilities that were there for art, religion, myth, culture, and consciousness. Thus we recognize the great number of complex short-term solutions we find to social and economic problems, but we recognize also the long-term failure of these because of their psychologically simplistic base. The dominant social paradigm of reality perceived largely in economic and technological terms is deficient in that it is bound only by the objective, external dimension of things, and thus contains no internal limiting factor, no psyche as it were. But the external environment is itself strictly limited in its resources, and so each solution yields ten new problems, and our "successes" become world-eroding failures.

I think of the case of American rice that I encountered in Bali. Now Bali is an enormously fertile country, its staple diet based on rice. The Balinese have many rituals and ceremonials based on the planting and harvesting of their twice-a-year crop of rice. Much of the social and religious calender is based on these rituals, and the Balinese psyche has been geared to the intricate interplay between agricultural rhythms and spiritual celebration. Along comes American rice, with economic incentives from American agronomic firms to plant. it. It will yield, the Balinese are told, three crops a year! So for a number of years, Balinese farmers plant this American rice. However, they soon discover that it requires an enormous amount of chemical fertilizers to force the crop. They buy and spread these chemical fertilizers. Almost immediately the snails and other water creatures that grow in the rice paddies die off. Then the ducks (another staple of the Balinese diet) begin to die also for there are fewer and fewer snails and water creatures to eat. Because one now has to plant and harvest three times a year, there is not sufficient time left over for ceremonials, taking part in sacred dance and dramas, making batiks and carvings the way one had done before the coming of American rice. People begin to complain about the taste of the rice, saying that it has no soul, no life left in it. Where did the soul of the rice go? That does it, and before long, the rice planters return to the Balinese rice that needs far less fertilizer but a great many more songs, dances, dramas, chants, and dreams to call forth its growth. It needs culture, not chemicals; psyche, not high tech solutions.

What this story of the unhappy experiment with American rice tells us is that clearly the natural continuum of people and nature, as well as the richness of human psychological and spiritual processes, have been ignored and derided during the recent reign of quantity. Clearly, too, the national absorption in the prodigies of technology not only inhibited the development of a sensorium attuned to more subtle inward dimensions of the real, but also encouraged a dangerous interface and modelling of human personality with mechanistic forms. Shaped and manipulated by the technological environment; modified and treated by education, social plans, and therapies still based for the most part on obsolete and inhibitory mechanistic models, many people have come to think of themselves as prosthetic extensions of the technological process, instead of understanding that technology is a prosthesis of the human process. To some, technology would seem to be the metaphysic of the twentieth century.

The inadequate use of the psyche—both personal and national—and its resulting compounding of catastrophe tells us that it is time to change the metaphysic. That will mean entering into the time of our second planting—not of the variations based on "American rice," but on the rich and subtle cultivation of the human psyche. It is the time of re-seeding, not just of ourselves, but of the complex weave of nations and cultures, both new and old, which are implicated and influenced by the changes that we experience.

But something else is going on that may give us the key to our future and to this re-seeding. This is the fact that as we dig in the soil of our national psyche, we discover that it is rich with the potency of thousands of years of imaginings and expectations. The ground is still charged with the psychodynamic power, pulse, and psyche that brought so many people teeming to these shores to be re-charged, re-aligned, re-awakened. This depth of the psyche, joined to the opportunities that reside here, joined to the radical challenge of our time, gives us an open moment for human and cultural advancement rarely, if ever, known. How do we discover it? In the present book I propose that we begin to find it in the lives of three great Americans who, each in his or her own way, were connected to this psychic depth of America, who found in this sacred source the powers to reinvent society (Jefferson); language, art, and perception (Dickinson); and human possibilities (Keller). I sincerely doubt if any of these extraordinary people could have been grown on other soils, could have found the required nourishment and opportunity in other lands. Their lives are uniquely American ones, and certain patterns in their ways of being strangely similar.

Each was highly educated, both formally and as life-long learners. Each was hypersensitive and developed both inner and outer sensory acuity to the highest degree, having highly original perceptions as to the nature of things. Each was given to passionate broad sweeps of vision and purpose, but discovered God in the details as well. Each would find epiphany in a flower, eternity in a grain of sand. They expressed these passions and perceptions in their writings, but most especially in their letters which they wrote assiduously. They were phenomenal communicators, and it was in the very act of communication that they honed their thought and purpose. And yet when it came to voice, all three were hampered or inhibited.

Jefferson had a small voice that would not carry; Dickinson did not wish to meet and talk with many people after the age of thirty; while Keller could speak only with difficulty. And yet in their lives they actively dismantled the old orders of things and fought the great forgetting that afflicts us all. They traded old ways of being for new ones and gave us lessons in what it means to live richly the lives we are given: what it means to unpack the mind and find a still greater mind residing there. The personal particulars of their lives became the stuff of the personal universals, the broader contexts and wider formulations which they would put forth for reality at large.

Each loved with a fine intensity and yearning, was devastated by death and rejection, and yet continued on the path in spite of it all. Each was devoted to Nature above all things and was capacious in the desire to reside with Her forever. Each loved a home, and made of them houses for their souls. Each was wounded in body or in spirit, and each used these wounds to fire them to higher purpose, richer possibilities. Each had a unique relationship to spiritual matters. No orthodoxy for them, but rather a contentious turn of mind to ordinary religion, offended by its narrowness and exclusivity. So we find them madly chasing spirit past the churches and into the fields of nature, social justice, and the beyond within. Each in his or her own way caused the world to turn a corner, and so, in the discussion and exercises based on their lives, we let them lead you as archetypal guides, numinous persons, who live still in the American psyche, who yet quicken us with examples of greening lives—lives that call us into the Great Mystery. For Mystery School work is for those of you who are committed to inner growth for yourselves so that you can help to join with others to generate a force strong enough to green the mind and body and soul of this planet. With the help and inspiration, then, of these three luminous Americans, perhaps we too can begin to re-vision, as they did, our world, and, like them, to devote ourselves to the task of sacred stewardship on its behalf.

I created the Mystery School principally to help evolve a moral force for good in the world; I wanted to help engender a passion of purpose and deep commitment to live truly and beautifully in high service to others. I can only hope that through this series, the community of those who are in accord with these premises will bring some of the excitement, inspiration, and experience of the Mystery School to you who know that "These are the times, and we are the people."

How to Use This Book

*T*his book is intended to enable groups of people to create shared experiences as co-voyagers in living biography as sacred psychology. In the pages that follow, you will enter the lives of three great Americans and, by seeing the world through their eyes, experience your own uniqueness as well as your interconnection with all lives. The notes that follow are offered as guidelines for these living biography sessions. They are similar to preparatory notes that I offer in some of my other books dealing with transformational journeys. The group that meets together to experience these exercises must devote careful attention to the preparation and conducting of these sessions. Included also are recommendations for those who will be journeying alone.

THE NATURE OF THE GROUP

As the import of these experiences can be trivial or profound, it is necessary that the intention of the group and of its members be clear from the beginning. The group should consist only of those who freely choose to participate and who feel well motivated to do so. The community that composes the members of the group may take any form: family, friends, colleagues, students, clients, parishioners, and so forth. In general, the experiences should be undertaken by intelligent, resourceful people who are mature enough to have had sufficient life experience to appreciate the historical and psychological scope of the human drama they will be required to go through. Galloping narcissists, psychic exhibitionists, and "poor me" whiners may offer more challenge and distraction than you need.

Working in groups helps to eradicate one of the worst tyrannies that afflicts Homo sapiens—the tyranny of the dominant perception. This is reflected in such smug statements as "If it's good enough for me, it's good enough for you" and "Why can't you respond like everyone else does?" The participants in a living biography exercise will stimulate, support, and evoke each other. In their diverse reactions, they will prime a diversity of responses within and between themselves. While consensus and commonalties are quite important, our differences are equally enriching: "Thank God," we say to ourselves, "I need not be limited to my own experience but may share in yours." As we recognize the enormous richness of experience in others, we can drop simplistic judgments and projections and stand in awe before this wild abundance of human variation.

By pursuing the living biography adventure as part of a group, we also bypass one of the most insidious of human failings—the potential for sloth. Self-discipline and good intentions have a way of evaporating without some consistent external commitment. The practices and procedures in this book challenge the deeply entrenched patterns of mind, body, and psyche, and so allies are needed to help one remount the slope of thought and acquire new ways of being. Resistance to change is natural, maybe even healthy, but one of the few ways to overcome it is through regular participation in the mutually helpful, empowering, and celebrating company of co-journeyers. This is why those who are voyaging alone need to tell at least one person close to them of their undertaking.

The group of co-voyagers should probably number not fewer than five nor more than twenty-five, although I have conducted groups of over five hundred through similar processes. There should also be an odd number of participants, since some of the experiences are performed by couples while one member of the group is acting as Guide.

At its initial meeting the group should assign members to take responsibility for obtaining and preparing the setting or settings (indoors or out-) for each of the exercises. This includes providing appropriate music and record, tape or CD players, art supplies, musical instruments, paper, drawing and other art materials, as well as bringing food for closing celebrations after each exercise. The setting is to be treated as sacred space. Special attention must be taken that during the sessions there be no intruders, wandering dogs, curious children, or ringing telephones. (Let me modify that. Wandering dogs have often played a welcome role in many of my seminars and have become much loved members of all of my Mystery School sessions. Generally, they know how to act appropriately and provide needed love and wordless understanding.)

Prior to each meeting every member of the group should read the relevant material from this book. The text should be read in such a way that the reader dialogues with it, taking note of images and ideas that emerge so that these may feed the group discussion. The group discussion of this material should in most cases be the subject of the first part of the meeting, so as to explore the meaning of its content in the lives and understanding of the members. The purpose of the text is only to evoke a depth sensibility of historical and personal patterns, not to describe and dissect times past. Another part of the discussion session (which can be led by a member of the group or by the Guide) might be devoted to a sharing of reflections concerning the changing patterns of viewpoint and awareness that members have observed in themselves since the last meeting. Many have found it extremely valuable to keep a journal of their experiences, often decorating the cover of their journals with images or drawings that evoke both the spirit and content of their personal journey.

After the discussion has ended, there should be a break of at least fifteen minutes before the group comes back together to share the experiences of the particular biography that they are entering. A good way to do this is to leave the space in which the discussion was held and reenter it after a while as sacred space, silently, with full awareness of a commitment to making the exercise meaningful. Each member of the group will spend some time centering and bringing his or her consciousness to an awareness of the experiences about to unfold. Each should make a kind of internal commitment to take responsibility for his or her own personal experience and, at the same time, be respectful to the needs of others and of the group as a whole.

THE GUIDE

Ideally the Guide is a person who has already participated in similar transformational processes with another group, though this need not be the case. At the initial preparatory meeting the group will decide on who the Guide or Guides will be and how they will function. The Guide can be the same for all sessions, or the role can rotate. Living biography groups must avoid the error: Guide equals Leader. The role of the Guide is to be understood by everyone as that of one who assists, one who enables. As enabler, the Guide serves the needs of the voyage into sacred psychology and of the co-voyagers.

The person who is to be Guide will prepare for the session by reading the historical and psychological material with great care and, wherever possible, will do extra reading about the life and times of the famous American whose life is being entered. Also, prior to each exercise, the Guide will engage in a period of relaxation, deep breathing, and meditation. This meditation should be used by the

Guide especially to become conscious of, and to eliminate, ego hungers and power drives, as well as any other improper attitudes or tendencies that would be exploitive or manipulative of the co-voyagers. Each Guide will determine his or her own needs, and prepare the meditations accordingly. It must be remembered that the role of the Guide is a most ancient one, which found one of its most accomplished forms in the hierophants of the ancient Mysteries. In this tradition the Guide is the midwife of souls, the evocateur of growth and transformation. In becoming Guide, then, one knows oneself to be part of a continuity stretching across millennia. It is a role of the greatest challenge and responsibility, and therefore one invests it with High Self.

The Guide needs to have the capacity to be at once part of the experience and observer of the voyage of the travelers. She, or he, must be able to judge sensitively the amount of time needed for each part of the journey and to use the experiences flexibly. The experiences described are not cast in stone and would probably gain much from the suggestions and additions of the group and the Guide.

The Guide will have read the exercise materials aloud several times before the group meeting, sensing the nature of the journey and allowing his or her voice and timing to reflect that experience. The voice must not be intrusive, lugubrious, or overly dramatic, but it must remain clear and in relation to the experience. Wherever music is part of the experience, the Guide must rehearse so as to carefully integrate the timing of the reading and the music.

The Guide will always have one or more "soul catchers" present. These are members of the group selected because of their ability to be sensitive to the needs of others. Thus, even while going through the experiences themselves, they will have a part of their consciousness available to help others should this be required. It must be stated, however, that part of helping others may be in knowing when to let someone alone and not intrude unnecessarily on his or her experience. The soul catcher will also have the task of guiding the Guide through the experience shortly after the group journey has ended if the Guide so desires.

TREADING GENTLY

In working with this material, it is most important that members of the group refrain from acting as therapists or theologians. Professional therapists and theologians may find this very difficult, but it is imperative that they practice their profession only during regular working hours. Comments I have heard, despite repeated pleas to refrain from making them, have included, "You really are blocked," "I can see some enormous anger stored up there," and even "You clearly are spiritually immature." Such remarks are inappropriate here even if they seem accurate, and you intend them to be helpful. Acceptance of people for who and what they are in the present moment is critical to the practice of sacred psychology. Each person is perfectly capable of interpreting his or her own experience and can invite the comments of others if desired.

One of the great advantages of sacred psychology is that it invites the participant to move into high witness, to tap into forgotten wisdom, and to practice nonobtrusive spiritual intimacy with others. One is always in a place to see the other as God-in-hiding, and to be so seen oneself. Many of the processes given in this book allow for the practice of deep empathy maintained in a variety of ways—the gentle holding of the hand of your partner while she or he is describing experience or reflections; eye-to-eye contact whenever appropriate; and, above all, careful and compassionate listening that knows when to speak out of one's deepest wisdom and when to maintain silence, communicating understanding and respect by eye or gesture alone. The sharing of powerful experience and reflection that accompanies the processes of this book especially when done by a group requires that people enter into a state of mutual trust. Thus after the sharing I have found it to be a good and satisfying thing to express words of appreciation to each other for the sharing and the trust given. One might say, for example, "I am honored that you shared so deeply of your experience with me."

Please, please, keep in mind that there is no such thing as doing any exercise wrong. This is a journey of the soul, and each person will have his or her unique way of approaching it. In fact, whenever possible, CHEAT! Do the exercise differently, or add other ideas or images or actions with which to enhance the process.

TIME AND SPACE AND THE PLACES IN BETWEEN

The set of exercises outlined in each biography can be performed over different time periods—even over the period of a very long day, although some have found this too compacted and intense. Others, however, have found this condensed sequence extremely powerful for the immediate continuity it provides for all stages in the living biography process. A two-day period, like a Saturday and Sunday, is perhaps the best time within which to enter and experience the life of a great American described in this book. Then, the following weekend, one could enter the life of the next great American.

Thus the best procedure is probably that of meeting once a week for five weeks. The first meeting should last a few hours and is devoted, as I have described, to preparation—assigning responsibilities and choosing the Guide or Guides. This is followed by the three weekend-long meetings, each devoted to entering one living biography. In a fifth meeting, the co-voyagers reflect together on the sequence as a whole and on the understandings they have gained. This pattern of five meetings can also be held over five consecutive days.

It is extremely important that each member of the group make a firm commitment to the other members to be on time and to see the entire sequence through to its completion. To leave it suddenly is to open oneself to further fissures and frustrations in the ecology of the self. Completed, however, the process has proved to be a most potent and revealing therapy, providing the orchestral dynamics with which to integrate the structures of one's being with the energy and genius of the human past. What emerges is the possible human as a living reality, ready and willing to enter into the next spiral of human development.

IF YOU ARE JOURNEYING ALONE

If you are entering these living biographies by yourself, you need to make a serious commitment to engage and complete all of the processes. Then, it seems important that you perform whatever are your most effective modes or rituals of preparation. Buy a new notebook for journaling. Make sure you have art materials for drawing, pens and pencils for writing. Create a very special sacred space where you will work; it is best if this space has a boundary of some kind, so that you cross a threshold to enter it. This prevents the energies of everyday life from bleeding through and diverting your attention.

Make sure there is music available for you there—your favorites as well as some of the kinds of music suggested throughout this book. The musical selections listed at the beginning of each process are meant only as suggestions for the types of music you might want to use.

Set specific times for doing this work. As journeying solo can be more challenging than journeying with a group, it probably is not advisable to attempt to complete the stages of this journey during the course of a long weekend. If you decide to do this work on a weekly basis, then make an agreement with yourself about those times; try not to let more than a week go by between sessions. Dedicate that time to complete immersion within the living biography you are entering.

You may wish to decorate the front of your journal with appropriate images. If it seems helpful, you might even decorate your space and dress in a costume appropriate to the period of the biography.

Write out a contract with yourself to embark upon this journey through sacred psychology and to complete it. Set the time span that you allow yourself for the entire sequence. Sign and date the contract. You might even wish to set a forfeit should you not comply with the terms of the contract. This could be the giving up for a time of special foods or entertainments that you enjoy. Or, on a more constructive note, the giving of a service to friends or community, offering unexpected help to surprise and delight.

Then tell someone who cares about you and will support your inner work that you're making a transformational journey. Ask if you may call upon this person occasionally to ask for assistance or a second opinion or a shoulder to lean on. Have this friend witness and sign the contract you have made.

In my experience it has proven to be good practice to work with at least one other person in making this journey. Another voice, another life story, a companion for the road helps train us in that most valuable of human skills—working and playing and growing together with mutual and equal honor. I also realize that, for many people, this is not easy or practicable. But at least tell someone what you're doing, and invite her or him to participate in the process, to see that you keep your side of the bargain.

The most important thing that you have to do in voyaging solo is to prerecord the scripts for the Guide on tape. This will give you greater freedom and spontaneity in doing the exercises. A cautionary note here. Please do not use an overly dramatic or peculiar voice when you make the tapes or you'll end up not trusting that person on the tape! Also, be sure to leave yourself pauses of sufficient length wherever they're called for so that you have enough time to do the exercises properly. If you prefer not to make your own tapes, I have made a set of tapes of the exercises and processes in this book, which are available from the publisher at a moderate cost.

Where processes require working with other people, there are suggestions at appropriate places in the text for solo journeyers. But, as a general rule, using your imagination is key. Wherever a partner or partners are needed you can always imagine or visualize them being present and then enact the interaction and/or dialogue with them by writing in your journal. In fact, try to create an ongoing process of dialogue, interchange, and persuasion by devising new ways of working with your journal. It is a marvelous thing to experience yourself as a participant in a great and fruitful life. Record the images and feelings that will inevitably come of this experience. Create, if you can, art with your learning and your feelings. Most especially write poetry or Jeffersonian letters. But also draw and paint, work in clay and other materials. It makes no difference whether you think you have no special gift for writing or for painting—just let your imagination loose. Free your hand to move as it wants, directed by your inner knowing and seeing. You may be surprised and pleased with the results.

LET US BEGIN THE JOURNEY

Thus warned and primed, let us begin. We are about to take a depth experiential look at the lives of three great Americans. This will be an exploration in prolepsis: To gain the future, one casts back into and recovers the past. To participate in such lives is to experience evolution entering into time, calling us to awaken to a citizenship in a universe larger than our aspirations and richer and more complex than all our dreams. The exultation of this work is in its celebration of the larger cycle, in the divine intoxication of the larger life experienced as one voyages into Eternity—or, as Emily Dickinson expressed it:

> *Exultation is the going*
> *Of an inland soul to sea*
> *Past the houses—past the headlands—*
> *Into deep Eternity—*
>
> *Bred as we, among the mountains,*
> *Can the sailor understand*
> *The divine intoxication*
> *Of the first league out from land?*

Emily Dickinson

INTRODUCTION

I dwell in Possibility -
A fairer House than Prose -
More numerous of Windows -
Superior - for Doors -

Of Chambers as the Cedars -
Impregnable of Eye -
And for an Everlasting Roof
The Gambrels of the Sky -

Of Visitors - the fairest -
For Occupation - This -
The spreading wide my narrow Hands
To gather Paradise -[1]

The little Belle of Amherst, wren small, with bright eyes the color of sherry left by the guest at the bottom of the glass, coils of rich auburn hair covering her wildly original brain, rewove both world and time and gathered Paradise. Rarely leaving her home after the age of thirty, she traveled the aeons as well as the acres of the worlds further and deeper than anyone in her time. Her life, as Alan Tate has remarked "was one of the richest and deepest ever lived on this continent . . . . All pity for [her] starved life is misdirected."[2]

No frustrated little frump was she, but a poet of massive passion who took her power in her hand and went against the world. Her love life was immense and almost entirely taken up with the adoration and illumination of "this remarkable world." So intense is her obsession with the world's beauty—the slant of light on a winter day, the still brilliance of a summer noon, the sound of the wind before the rain—that she cracks open our perceptions, this "half-cracked" poetess of Amherst, and shocks our insights into being. She gives us new mind when we were content with our old one. She forces us to value ourselves as givens—givens in brain and body before and beyond any educational additions. Our brains are peers of God, she tells us:

> *The Brain - is wider than the Sky -*
> *For - put them side by side -*
> *The one the other will contain*
> *With ease - and You - beside -*
>
> *The Brain is deeper than the sea -*
> *For - hold them - Blue to Blue -*
> *The one the other will absorb -*
> *As Sponges - Buckets - do -*
>
> *The Brain is just the weight of God -*
> *For - Heft them - Pound for Pound -*
> *And they will differ - if they do -*
> *As Syllable from Sound -*

Emily's syllables were volcanic, life releasing magma that poured new landscapes into literature. And yet her high craft and compound vision required that she shape her intensities into forms that would astonish while achieving marvels of pith and precision.

1 CHILDHOOD

Let us visit her now—this Vesuvius at home. You come into Amherst, Massachusetts, and turn left on Seelye Street; then go right on Main. The driveway is at the end of a yellow picket fence. The house is somewhat hidden by a high hedge of cedars. Behind that hedge is the house itself, a brick mansion built by her grandfather early in the nineteenth century with a full complement of wings and porches, old majestic trees, and emerald lawns. It is an affluent, satisfied, apple-of-the-eye kind of house—the kind of total home in which one could live forever and from which one could rebuild the world.

You catch sight of Emily's own garden and it is wondrous strange—not just for the rare and ebullient blossoms it nurtures, but for the curiosa it contains, calla lilies and pomegranates, and things that only grow in other climes. How did Emily ever manage to coax these inhabitants of other shores to root in New England soil? The same way she coaxed Eternity to take up housekeeping in her own mind. Indeed you feel yourself brushed by eternity as you enter that house.

It is a nested place, and more than one world is present here. There is a sea and mermaids in the basement and frigates in the upper floor. The smell of Emily's gingerbread baking breathes through the house, and her jellies bubble over the wood stove. A practical woman Emily—one who can do many things, cook, bake, garden, nurse, sew, and mend. We climb the stairs and find her room—the room that was for her, freedom—the room in which she married Eternity. There it is—the best and biggest bedroom in the house, a sunny, merry corner room overlooking the comings and goings of Amherst on Main Street. From this window you can see life whole—gossipy neighbors, bees and birds, circuses and caravans, and let us not forget cattle fairs, the nocturnal passage of lovers and drunks, the grim regularity of the hearse going by, the playing children, the pompous visitors making their stately way to the door, and always, always the cycling of the seasons, the eternal dialogue between death and the resurrection of nature.

We look around the room. Her white dress hangs in the closet, her neat iron bed stands in a corner. Her books lie on the shelves—Elizabeth Barrett Browning's "Aurora Leigh," a woman poet's narrative poem of a woman poet's life, also Shakespeare, the Bible, George Eliot, Emerson, Carlyle, Charlotte and Emily Bronte, and a big much-thumbed lexicon. There is Emily herself with wild eyes and precise careful hands fashioning poems at her small table. There she sits in this white-curtained, high-ceilinged room, writing poems about volcanoes, earthquakes, deserts, suicide, passions, wild beasts, power, madness, separation, demons, dooms, dreams, and death. There she binds with a darning needle batches of her poems into bundles, where one day after she leaves us, they will be discovered by her sister Lavinia, slowly but surely published, and the world will have turned a corner. But for now, an adamant anonymity.

I'm Nobody! Who are you?
Are you - Nobody - Too?
Then there's a pair of us!
Don't tell! they'd advertise - you know!

How dreary - to be - Somebody!
How public - like a Frog -
To tell one's name - the livelong June -
To an admiring Bog!

But then she will tell us in a letter, "I'm so amused at my own ubiquity."

This house has muchness in it; this house contains its generations, moving as something more than ghosts throughout its rooms. There's grandfather, Samuel Fowler Dickinson, a manic Puritan, once a distinguished and wealthy lawyer, but fired by religious passions, hell bent to devote all his life and substance to the creation of a seminary college for missionaries—the future Amherst College. His mad excesses of devotion will cause the family to lose the Homestead for years, drive all but one son as far away across the continent as they can get. See him stalking the halls, a flaming zealot for religion and education, convinced he was the one to bring the kingdom of God upon the earth, the city upon the hill, at Amherst. From here he was convinced he would start the fierce piety raging that would accomplish the conversion of the whole world to evangelical Puritanism and Trinitarian theology. As the promised moneys fail to come, he boards the workers on the college in his own house, sends his own horses and laborers to draw the brick, and even goes himself, rather than that the work should stop. He loses his status, his wealth, his power, and his final bitter days in Amherst are "an unrelieved nightmare of despondency and humiliation." This partnering of God one way or another goes very deep in the Dickinson family of God-intoxicated or God-furious folk.

The years of Grandfather blink out, and other years and faces take their place: Emily's father, Edward Dickinson—a man who from his father's experience has become phobic for failure, a complex man fascinated by the ways of power and driven to exert his formidable energies and intelligence to become a recognized success in law and business, a leading citizen of Amherst, the leader of the parade—any parade. When the railroad came by from New London to be set up for the first time, who was the strutting peacock leading the railroad down the track? Edward Dickinson. But ultimately he is a pinched and lonely man, his dry unemotional manner in stark and chosen contrast to the booming juiciness of his spirit-ridden father. However, like all Dickinsons, he has his whimsies too—such as the time that he leapt out of bed in the middle of the night to ring the church bells so that all citizens could wake and come see the display of northern lights that were riddling the horizon.

There is mother, Emily Norcross Dickinson, diffident and withdrawn, a sallow silent soul who will provide the comforts of home, cakes of new maple sugar, polished apples, anxious good will for her children, but then disappear into the shadows. One can barely see her—her life shines so faintly. Emily tells us that her life is tranquil but trifling. "My mother does not care for thought. She reads a little—sleeps much. . . and reminds one of Hawthorne's blameless Ship—that forgot the Port."

The shadows shift; the children come—firstborn Austin, followed by Emily in 1830, completed by Lavinia—vital, independent children who found much comfort and support in each other—each in some way married to the other—and but for a few short years, never more than a few feet away from each other until the day they died. It is, in the main, a lonely household, "bound" as Lavinia tells us, "to those to whom you gave loyalty and devotion, but with whom you did not share your thoughts."

We see the whole family now passing through the doors, friendly and absolute monarchs, each in his or her own domain. We watch the children grow from infancy. There is little touching of them and small communication. Father is distant, aloof except for his sonorous reading of the Bible; Mother withholds speech. The words that are exchanged are precious, jewels to be hoarded and never squandered. Starved for language, Emily becomes an imagizer, valuing seeing over speaking. Speaking and writing are second best. Here is Emily at fourteen writing to her bosom friend, Abiah Root: "I long to see you, dear Abiah, and speak with you face to face; but so long as a bodily interview is denied us, we must make letters answer, though it is hard for friends to be separated. . . .Do write me soon, for as I cannot see you, I must hear from you often, very often." Again and again her letters are filled with longing for sight—"I grow too eager to see you. . . .It has been a long week dear, for I have not seen your face. . . . Shall I indeed behold you. . .I would whisper to you in the evening of many and curious things—and by the lamp eternal read your thoughts and response in your face, and find what you thought about me. . . .our eyes would whisper for us, we would not ask for language."[3]

The house moves to another house for some years, but it brings itself along. It carries the mighty cast of a nursery culture—utterly safe, safe enough even to make a career of being a child. "How to grow up, I don't know," says Emily. "I wish we always were children." When she is grown, she has one prayer: "Dear Lord, make me a child." In many ways Emily stays a child, a cunning, knowing little fighter against the size and importance of the big folks and the big male God. She thumbs her nose against the whole overgrown and decaying lot of them. Her many nursery rhymes tell us how wise a child she was and how widely she observed the genius of childhood and the unfairness with which it is treated. Later when as a spinster woman she went unseen and unesteemed by the prosy conscience of her society, she took comfort in her child, knowing that:

> *They shut me up in Prose -*
> *As when a little Girl*
> *They put me in the Closet -*
> *Because they liked me "still" -*

Still! Could themself have peeped -
And seen my Brain - go round -
They might as wise have lodged a Bird
For Treason - in the Pound -

As adolescents, brother Austin reproved her for being "too loud" in her use of language. He tired of her living in metaphor. Young Emily responded in a parody of obligingness, "I'll be a little ninny, a little pussy catty, a little Red Riding Hood." With the innocent stance of a child she blasphemes freely:

What is -"Paradise"-
Who live there -
Are they "Farmers"-
Do they "hoe"-
Do they know that this is "Amherst"-
And that I - am coming - too -

Do they wear "new shoes" - in "Eden"-
Is it always pleasant - there -
Won't they scold us - when we're homesick -
Or tell God - how cross we are -

You are sure there's such a person
As "a Father"- in the sky -
So if I get lost - there - ever -
Or do what the Nurse calls "die"-
I shan't walk the "Jasper" - barefoot -
Ransomed folks - won't laugh at me -
Maybe - "Eden" a'n't so lonesome
As New England used to be!

Very early in childhood, Emily begins her war with God:

Of Course - I prayed -
And did God Care?
He cared as much as on the Air
A Bird - had stamped her foot -
And cried "Give Me"-

Emily's Father in heaven is an archetypal Yankee, a thrifty deity who is no fun. He is the playground bully flexing his religious muscles, beating his divine chest and lording it over the smaller children. She on the other hand would do a much better job if she were God. That's why they have to keep her out of heaven.

Why - do they shut Me out of Heaven?
Did I sing - too loud?
But - I can say a little "Minor"
Timid as a Bird!

Wouldn't the Angels try me -
Just - once - more -
Just - see - if I troubled them -
But don't - shut the door!

Oh, if I - were the Gentleman
In the "White Robe" -
And they - were the little Hand - that knocked -
Could - I - forbid?

As a child in childhood and as a childlike woman she gloried in her small size and the capacity to turn her apparent insignificance into creative power, as many heroic children do. Indeed, when you look at the structure of so many children's stories, they are about little children—Hansel and Gretel, Jack and the Beanstalk—being sent out into the middle of the world to rescue the cosmos. They discover within themselves phenomenal powers, extraordinary craft and cunning. A wonderful current example of this is to be seen in some of the books of Madeleine L'Engle, such as *A Wrinkle In Time, A Wind in the Door*, and *A Swiftly Tilting Planet*. In each book she tells luminous tales of a family whose children, either separately or together, are partnered by cosmic powers to help save the universe! L'Engle seems to be saying that it is the child's state of wonder and astonishment, his or her fresh perception before the world, that gives them the extraordinary power of a God mind.

And that is why in all nursery stories, child characters discover that they have been abandoned in a universe that has closed down, and they save this abandoned universe by the power and by the immense but innocent availability of their stupendous minds and souls. All great nursery and children's stories have essentially that theme. The extraordinary thing about Emily is that she never grew out of it; instead, she turned childlike innocence into the highest crafted poetry and the most imaginative letters, which she sent winging their way to startled recipients. That is why even today we are sometimes shocked by her imagery, appalled by her audacity, because she simply didn't give up the child's power.

I was the slightest in the House -
I took the smallest Room -
At night, my little Lamp, and Book -
And one Geranium -

In 226 poems she uses the word *little,* and in many more refers to *slight, low,* and *small,* but then, she outwits all giants.

> *I took my Power in my Hand -*
> *And went against the World -*
> *'Twas not so much as David - had -*
> *But I - was twice as bold -*
>
> *I aimed my Pebble - but Myself*
> *Was all the one that fell -*
> *Was it Goliah - was too large -*
> *Or was myself - too small?*

Nineteenth-century Emily is writing at much the same time that others are turning out the great classics of the genius of childhood. Consider, for example, *Peter Pan*, the story of a boy who refuses to grow up; *Alice in Wonderland*, the delicious antics of a small girl who is manipulated by but remains unafraid of a world of absurd and paradoxical grownups; and, of course, *Huckleberry Finn*, the story of a boy who refuses to be civilized, and who by following his adolescent bliss, repudiates and shows up the adult society of his time for the sham it really is. These kinds of themes were especially common in American children's literature from about the mid-nineteenth century through the early twentieth century.

In a recent study, Jerry Griswold analyzes the structural themes of a dozen books for and about children from the Civil War to 1914, showing how each tells essentially the same story. The central character is almost always an orphan fallen upon hard times who still retains a few happy memories of an earlier time before being orphaned or abandoned. The central characters' assurance of the golden age that once was gives them the courage to act and be in remarkable ways. Thus each child takes on his or her own "Hero's Journey" and often becomes part of another kind of family or a different social class. Huckleberry Finn runs away from his brutish drunken father to launch himself down the deep river with Jim, a runaway slave. Rebecca has to leave the well named Sunnybrook Farm to live instead with her dour and icy Aunt Miranda. Little Mary, the heroine of *The Secret Garden*, is taken to Misselthwaite Manor where she encounters the secret garden and meets a young boy who is her spiritual partner. And, of course, in Frank Baum's great classic of 1900, Dorothy is carried away on a tornado from dreary, bleak Kansas to the wonderful land of Oz where she acquires several extraordinary new friends. In their new home or reality, the children face serious and sometimes life threatening antagonism; the Wicked Witch of the West is the daunting foe of Dorothy; the grim aunt constantly throws cold water on the chronic good cheer of Pollyanna;

Huck and Jim are taken advantage of by the fake nobility they meet on the river. Still, through courage, cunning, indomitable spirit and sometimes purity of heart, the child hero wins out over his or her antagonist, and a new order of reconciliation or even redemption prevails. Thus Little Lord Fauntleroy is recognized and honored for who and what he is by his arrogant grandfather; Rebecca inherits her grim aunt's estate; Dorothy kills the Wicked Witch by throwing water on her and wins wonders for herself and her companions; the Prince and the Pauper are revealed as their true selves. All are returned to their true state enhanced and exalted, and the world is the better for their journey.[4]

The nineteenth century is the time of the great philosophical admiration of childhood. Some of this admiration finds its source in the radical re-casting of human life and experience unique to that era. We must remember that for most people, until the nineteenth century, the world looked pretty much as it had for millennia. With the nineteenth century came the biggest shake-up in history; the Industrial Revolution brought with it a fundamental restructuring of our relationship to space and time. Whereas prior to this time, most of our ancestors never went more than a dozen miles from their own homes, now tides of travellers swept across the world on railroads and steamships. The movement from country into town and city affected the lives of many who sought work in the new factories, where they were caught up in an entirely new sense of time. Whereas before, time was cyclical, solar, and sensible, getting you up when the cock crowed, and putting you to sleep with the sun's descent, now in the world of cities and factories, both solar and biological rhythms were replaced by the piercing whistle of factory time and the long night of artificial illumination. These essential changes in space and time created equally immense psychological changes. Traditional relationships to kith and kin were sundered. Suddenly people were no longer part of labor and nature—this, of course, was Karl Marx's big complaint—but became wage servants, abstracted from the tools of production. The nineteenth century was the era of enormous systematic abstraction from a world that up until now had been both sensual and consensual, tribal givens in the eternal round of soil and sanctity. And yet at the same time, the century also meant the coming of universal suffrage, and with it the desirability of going "public like a frog" as well as the necessity of acquiring a public education in order to get anywhere in this brave new world.

Faced with such massive changes, many countered with a romantic rediscovery of Nature over and against the felt tyranny of what William Blake referred to as the "gray Satanic mills." Nature became a transcendent force that redeemed one's humanity from the growing mechanization of the world. This need for compensation, for finding balance on the opposite side of the equation, was as necessary then as now. Now we compensate for the high tech of televi-

sion, computers, and satellites by the "high touch" of 12-Step programs, alternative medicine, growth seminars, voluntarism, and other
ways of participating more directly in the redirection of one's life and
well-being. The nineteenth-century equivalent of this was replacing
objectivity and analysis with the conscious and often sentimental
appreciation of Nature, childhood, self-reliance, and the sense of a
spiritual dimension inhabiting the things of this world. We see all of
these in the Transcendental movement, initially a group of young
New England Unitarian ministers and writers like Emerson, Thoreau,
and Margaret Fuller whose writings were much read by Emily, and
who saw God in Nature and God in the self reflecting the God in
Nature. Among these cross-currents grew Emily, a true romantic, passionately dedicated to the redemption of Nature through poetry and
the recreation of the world through her own god-like feeling.

Both the Romantic and the Transcendentalist movements
were literary, artistic, and philosophical answers to the exponential
change that occurred in the world of the nineteenth century. In both
movements one consciously returned to the source and reconsidered
one's roots in nature and spirit. Another answer was based on the
perception that the world had suddenly become so much more complex that people simply needed a much longer time to prepare for it.
Of course, one way to prepare oneself for life in a complex world was
having a much longer childhood—not going to work at the age of six
or seven; not moving almost immediately from childhood to an adult
state, which is what most of us did until very recently. And so we
have, as one of the great psychological events of the nineteenth century, the epiphany of childhood through stories, poems, and philosophical forays into its mysteries.

Emily is living out of this epiphany before it becomes overt.
She decides to make herself a prefigural event, to stay in childhood,
to deepen into that state, and to rediscover the original world forgotten in the changes of the nineteenth century. Emily offers perceptions that go against the common sense reality of almost everyone
else. In her own time, there are few who can understand her, for perhaps her unveiling of the world belongs to another era, one that did
not really begin until the twentieth century with its own historic
entry through science into the heart of matter. Like many people of
genius and radical invention, her own era will be baffled by her,
while a later one will celebrate and practically canonize her, using
her unique perceptions and ways of seeing to guide their own.

Early in life Emily learned that the little girl's voice was indispensable for "possibility," as, for example, in all children's stories in
which the child's voice and seeing are indispensable for the solving
of great problems. But the "possibility" that Emily cultivated was not
simply a matter of preserving the rebelliousness and fantasy life of
childhood. Rather, for her, the great eye and ear of childhood, with its
litmus paper mind, held the capacity to know the world and its folly

further and deeper than the matured mind ever could. Metaphori-cally speaking, it is almost as if that part of the head that remains soft and partially opened in young children never really closed in Emily. Thus she remains the great, half-cracked poetess of Amherst.

We can only surmise that Emily's childhood gave her gifts of knowing and perception which she maintained all her life and which were a sure source of her astonishing creativity. Almost two thousand poems remain to us. There may have been many more. You have to go to the love-besotted thirteenth-century Persian poet Rumi to find that prodigality of poetic production. She also wrote thousands and thousands of letters. We have about eleven hundred of them. Most of her letters were destroyed, but she wrote letters every day, all the time, to all for whom she cared, letters tracking the extraordinary ter-rain of the ordinary. This she did while living a very full life at home. Her life and work were a sheer celebration of creativity and of the child's perception grown to its expressive genius.

In much of my work on creativity, we have discovered that if you're going to activate the creative impulse in the adult, it is often essential to reactivate the perceptual capacities of childhood. In my earlier work, we did this by shifting attention. Using altered states of consciousness, employing trance, and playing mind games, we learned to decondition the eye and the ear from the usual ways of seeing so that we could see the world anew. That's one way of work-ing open the doors of perception. Another time honored way is to immerse oneself in nature and to recover what Wordsworth calls the "Intimations of Immortality in Early Childhood." In his great poem of that name, he says that the child's perceptions are essentially the same as the perceptions of God or eternity:

> *There was a time when meadow, grove and stream,*
> *The earth and every common sight,*
> > *To me did seem*
> > *Apparelled in celestial light,*
> *The glory and the freshness of a dream. . .*

Later in the poem he complains:

> *It is not now as it hath been of yore,—*
> > *Turn wheresoe'er I may,*
> > *By night or day,*
> *The things which I have seen I now can see no more.*

Wordsworth is wrong. He is wrong when he declares that "nothing can bring back the hour of splendour in the grass, of glory in the flower."

Emily's life and work testify to the fact that the fresh perception of a child does come back, bearing a fiercer power, a deeper coloration. Why? Because as an adult you have eros, passion, and aesthetic joy. You have a sense of tragedy and knowledge of the shadows that make the sunlight even brighter. You live with the boundaries of your own mortality and the prison of limitations. And this makes your perceptions both fiercer and sweeter. Still, to recover them you have to make that heroic effort to remount the slope of thought. If you are Emily, it's a full time job, one that demands the keeping of the most painstaking records. With Emily we have the records retained through poems and letters to provide us with one of the most interesting case histories ever of someone absolutely agreeing to keep on probing childhood further and deeper, when everybody else said, "No, you can't do it." Her triumph is tantamount to what Johann Sebastian Bach did when, at the end of the Baroque period in music, he said, "We haven't gone far enough with Baroque," and proceeded to evoke within this style a mastery and magnificence that it had not yet known. In a similar manner, Emily kept the freshness of an earlier stage of perception and applied it to the rich language of the adult wordsmith, forcing language to yield treasures of an extraordinary nature.

"I become what I behold!" said that great childlike man Walt Whitman. This gift of identity, of incarnating whatever and whomever one sees, is one of the great virtues of childhood. Emily's dates are 1830 to 1886; Whitman's life precedes and extends beyond hers, as he lived from 1819 to 1896. Both of them, at any point in their lives, could dissolve their identity into whatever they looked at. They were never just looking at a fern; they were also the fern looking back at Emily or Walt. But Walt would always sing the song of himself, sing his body electric, and stand in wonder before his own magnificence. Emily, on the other hand, could drop her margins, but then be fiercer about her integrity. But they both could dissolve their boundaries and fall into identity. A great deal of creativity has to do with the powers of identification, the capacity to take on the existence of another, be it object or person. This Emily Dickinson, with her diaphanous ability to become what she beheld, did supremely well; so well in fact, that she often seemed to hold the gift of identity higher than the gift of poetry:

> *I would not paint - a picture -*
> *I'd rather be the One*
> *Its bright impossibility*
> *To dwell - delicious - on -*
> *And wonder how the fingers feel*
> *Whose rare - celestial - stir*
> *Evokes so sweet a Torment -*
> *Such sumptuous - Despair -*

I would not talk, like Cornets -
I'd rather be the One
Raised softly to the Ceilings -
And out, and easy on -
Through Villages of Ether -
Myself endued Balloon
By but a lip of Metal -
The pier to my Pontoon -

Nor would I be a Poet -
It's finer - own the Ear -
Enamored - impotent - content -
The License to revere,
A privilege so awful
What would the Dower be,
Had I the Art to stun myself
With Bolts of Melody!

With her gifts for incarnation she gained the art to stun not just herself, but anybody who would stand out there under the rain with her long enough.

I must confess that when I was a young girl I didn't like her poetry. I was confused by her strange, macabre, sometimes consciously grotesque rhymes and patterns, and her childlike imagery. But immersing myself in her recently, I find myself stunned, split apart like the lark, made into music, blown through by the bolts of melody.

Great poetry is very hard stuff to wrap one's mind around. You have to stick with it and when you do, you do not necessarily emerge with the poet's perception. You emerge with your own.

PROCESS 1
THE HOUSE OF PERCEPTION/ENJOYING SENSORY IMAGES OF OLD NEW ENGLAND

TIME: ONE HOUR.

• MATERIALS NEEDED:

A table with many interesting things placed on it that have rich sensory aspects, like bark, feathers, handicrafts, cork, sponges, flowers, marble, etc. Also a plate of apples which the Guide will cut up just before the tasting exercise in Part Two.

• MUSIC:

Some richly textured piece of music that is suitable for moving or dancing and which has themes from the nineteenth century woven through it like Aaron Copeland's *Appalachian Spring.*

• INSTRUCTIONS FOR GOING SOLO:

Almost all of the parts of these processes can be done by yourself. You just have to put the Guide's instructions on tape, along with appropriate music. Be careful to allow yourself enough time and pauses in order to get the full benefit of the processes. Prepare for yourself a table with interesting multisensory items and apples. And be sure to chronicle your journey in your journal.

• SCRIPT FOR THE GUIDE:

PART ONE

Close your eyes and breathe steadily and deeply. . . .I want you to imagine that you are approaching a wonderful old New England house of the nineteenth century. It is an ample, satisfied, apple-of-the-eye kind of house with many gables, wings, and porches. It sits on a huge emerald lawn studded with majestic trees. We will call it the House of your Extended Senses, and it is quite special, for in entering it and then cleaning it, you may be able to effect profound changes in how you are able to sense the world. You may even find yourself regaining some of the sensory splendor of childhood.

Going through the door now, you discover that this house has not been kept up for many years. It is full of cobwebs and dust, and debris litters almost every corner of the rooms. It will need a great deal of cleaning up. Almost immediately, you notice in the antechamber that there are all kinds of old-fashioned cleaning equipment: buckets of water, mops, sponges, dustcloths, feather dusters, and large cakes of strong soap. There are also large empty cans—all the things you might need for a clean-up job are right here. Now, rolling up your sleeves, prepare to go to work.

Opening the door to a room on your right, you find yourself in an unsightly mess. As you walk around the room, you finds heaps of accumulated rubbish. The room is lined with many windows through which you can barely see, so darkened and covered are they with dirt and grime. This is the Room of Vision, and its present condition may attest to how much your capacity for seeing has become diminished. So begin now to clean this room up, returning to the antechamber for any equipment that you may need. Work hard and actually use your physical hands to the job. Get rid of the rubbish. Scrub the floor and walls of their grime. Make them bright, shining. . . .Keep working. Put in a lot of elbow grease. (Thirty Seconds.) Alright now, let's polish those windows. Scrub them down. (Thirty Seconds.) You are actually doing real work here, cleaning up your perceptions at their base in the brain. You are working to give yourself back something of the fresh perceptions of a child. Good. . . now fling open the shining clean windows, and remove the dusty drapes. The wind is blowing through now helping you to get the dust out of the room, off of the furniture, and out of the air. Whooosh!

When you have cleaned the room and cleared away all of the debris, walk around in it. Now begin to dance in the sparkling light, feeling the light flood your sight. Look out the window and see the wonderful sights of old New England. When we finish cleaning the other rooms of the senses, we will enjoy a full experience of the sensory delights of nineteenth-century New England.

But for now notice that there is a door at the end of this room, a door that is closed. Open this door now and enter into the Room of Hearing, leaving the door open behind you. You might notice that this room seems very subdued, as if it is clogged with years of deafness. Look at the thick wax buildup on the walls. Baffles of cardboard seem to be everywhere, so that you feel closed in and cut off. Even the ceiling seems caked with accumulations of some gummy sludge that make it seem lower than it should be. So get to it, and clean it up! Scrub it down, scrape off the accumulations and throw them in the trash. Use your real hands and arms. Put some energy into the job. Keep scrubbing, scraping. Push the walls back if they seem too small. Knock down the sludge on the ceiling so that the ceiling becomes higher. Let the whole room expand until it feels the right size. Make it bright and shining, knowing that as you do so, you are improving the quality of your hearing. When you have cleaned the room and cleared away all of the debris, walk around and listen to the sound of your footsteps on the wooden floors. Open the windows and let the fresh air swoosh in, hearing it blow in and letting the strong air currents rid the room of any remaining dust. Hear the wind sighing through the great trees on the lawn, listen to the singing of the birds, the laughing of children playing, the sneeze of a rabbit beneath the window. Move around the room, humming and singing in this freshly cleaned room of sound. Let the room fill with sunbeams and dance to their music.

As you dance, notice that another room opens off of this one. Open the door, and step into the Room of Smell. This is one of the oldest rooms in the house, filled with trunks piled on trunks, with all kinds of clutter, with ancient potpourri from another century, mildewed hangings and furniture, decaying rugs and rubbish. Mice have set up housekeeping here for decades, and their smell permeates the room. Clear it out. Sweep away the clutter. Toss out the ancient mildewed fabrics and furniture. Get rid of those mice. Turn them out of doors and plug up the mouse holes. Bring fresh flowers into the room, and open jars of rose petals. Open the windows, and let the fresh scents of the outside flood the room. Enjoy this room now, breathing in the lovely fragrance coming from the flowers and blown in by the wind. Feel this fragrance filling your whole body, reminding you of the forgotten delight of smelling.

See now another door at the end of the room and, opening it, pass into the Room of Taste. Oh Lord, what a mess! This is a gustatory garbage heap. There is so much refuse deposited here, and it's been here for so long. Clear it out! Get rid of the cigarette butts and the ashes, the left-over cold coffee in cups, the debris from weeks of unwashed dishes, the stale french fries and the moldy bread. Be aware of all the accumulated plaque. Scrape it off, using scouring pads and whatever you need to remove the grit and grime. Clean the windows opening on the garden, letting the winds sharpen your taste buds. Now savor the refinements and subtlety of the cleaned room, the saltiness, the sweetness, the bitter, and the sour. Let these sensations be distinct, and then let your taste buds be filled with all of these in one luscious bite.

When you have finished, notice yet another door at the end of the room. Open this door now, leaving it open as you have the other doors. Now you are in the Room of Touch, your tactile center. The old rubber gloves that lie in a heap on the floor are a testament to your diminished powers of touch. Every surface in the room seems to be covered with calluses, barriers to distinct and sensitive touch sensations. Clean out this room now until the texture of each surface rises up to be felt and enjoyed. Clean it so thoroughly that it becomes sensitive to hot and cold and to all of the temperatures between. Polish it until it is shining with sensation, able to enjoy a tap or a caress, the slippery and the silky, the rough and the nubby. Notice the feel of the wooden window frame as you open the windows, be tickled by the light brush of air moving past you to help clean the room. Walk barefoot on the floor and feel the slippery wood or the carpet or the tile against your feet. Touch the walls and feel their texture. Enjoy all the feelings that are available to your body, which is now alive with sensation.

When you have finished, notice another door and go through it, leaving it open, back into the antechamber, where you will deposit all your rubbish. Notice now that there is a stairway leading to the floor above, and, with your senses refreshed, go up the stairs. At the top of the stairs you find yourself in a very large room. This is the Room of the Sixth Sense, the home of all the senses that you have not encountered below and the place where all these senses come together.

Explore this vast place, becoming aware of its grand perspective and ample proportions. Move around and notice the nooks and crannies. Now begin to clean it up, opening the windows and making yourself at home in this unfamiliar place. . . .Let the light and air circulate and fill the room. After cleaning out so much debris accumulated since your childhood, you may feel refreshed in all your senses, and may even be aware of new senses.

Notice that this room has a balcony, and walk over to that balcony. From the balcony you can look down into all the rooms below, the Room of Sight, the Room of Hearing, the Room of Smell, the Room of Taste, and the Room of Touch. All these clean rooms are connected by the open doors you have left behind you, and you sense the patterns that connect them.

Now, being aware of the gentle, warm breeze blowing through the open windows and doors of your senses, inhale deeply the fresh air of the Room of the Sixth Sense and then, swinging your head down, blow through all five rooms. Actually do this action physically. Bring your head back up to the second-floor room and inhale again. Now, again, circle with your head down and blow like the wind through each room, cleaning and connecting all the rooms and each sense with the other. Keep on doing this, gently and powerfully circling with your head and blowing through the rooms at least a dozen times. . . .

Now fully relax for a minute, and sense your whole body flowing with this new awareness, feel it coursing through your nerves and your blood, your muscles and your flesh. Sense a gentle tingling and exhilaration. and allow yourself to deeply remember this. Promise these rooms that you will keep them clean and come back often.

PART TWO

You have done a great deal of internal work on cleansing your perceptions. Now, in Part Two of this process, we can begin to explore these extended senses with images drawn from the New England of Emily Dickinson's day. You will sense and experience these images as they are offered to you as fully as possible. Consider that from this moment on you are in the New England of the nineteenth century.

Everywhere there are pine trees, their branches heavy with snow. There's the smell of maple sugar cooking on the stoves. There is the smell of wood smoke. There is the sight of steeples, square buildings, and steepled roofs. Sleighs going down the snow-covered streets being pulled by Old Tom. You hear bells as the sleigh passes. There are the crocuses peeping through the snow. There is the sound of wood being chopped. And women in their houses sitting before the fire on their little petit point stools doing needlepoint. The ice wagon goes by. And there are birches in the woods. There are the sounds of wells creaking as the water is drawn up. There are cows mooing. There is the fragrance of freshly baked bread. There is the chewing of a slice of this bread as it has just come out of the oven. It is slathered with freshly churned butter. There is the smell of kerosine from the lamps. There is laundry flapping on the line. Frozen laundry flapping on the line. Grandma's frozen nightshirt etched against the wind like a starched ghost. The sound of butter churning. There is the sound the blacksmith makes with the hammer and the anvil. The smell of jasmine and lavender. The smell of cloves in hot cider on the stove. There are the horses' hooves running down the cobbled streets. There are lamplighters lighting the street lamps at dusk. There is the feel of building fires on the hearth. There is the sound of tubercular cough.

You hear the twittering of bluejays and robins. And the gush of spring brooks that are flowing now with the melt down from the mountains and the streams. Spring brooks bubbling, bubbling. Horse and cow manure in the street. And all shoes having to be wiped at the door because almost all the ladies' shoes and the men's boots contain great wads of horse and cow manure sticking to them.

And ghost stories told at night. The Headless Horseman rides again! Men selling medicine from the carts. There is the feel of the opening of old trunks because it's spring cleaning time and the textures as you put away the the winter clothes. There is the stepping through the muddy ruts in the roads. There is the smell of cedar closets. People reading stories to each other for entertainment. There is the feel of digging and planting your own flower gardens and herb gardens. There is the scratchy sound of pen and ink writing. There is the rubbing of your clothes with chalk in order to take out the ink stains. You hear the whack whack whack of the carpet beater when you take the carpets out in the spring.

There is the feel of carrying and dumping the ashes on the garden in the spring to make it acidic. There is the feel of helping tie your elderly female relative into her corset in the morning. There is the sight and sound of the train coming down the track, belching black smoke and making a tremendous clatter. There is the constant sweeping of floors. The constant whisking of the feather duster.

There is the morning sound of the steam whistle calling the factory workers to work. There is the pulling on the teats of the cow and the sound of milk shooting into the pails as you do the early morning milking. There is the taste of crisp juicy apples. Apple pie. Apple cider. The taste of spice cake. The taste of hot meat pies. Don't forget the bees humming in the meadow. Look at the clouds of butterflies.

So many birds. More birds than ever we could imagine. The morning alive with bird sound. There are the sounds of chickens and ducks. The sound of horses snorting and clip clopping down the streets. Lecturers talking. Oh, how they could talk, talk, talk! On Sundays in the churches the sound of many footsteps walking down the creaking wooden aisles. Trinitarian preachers preaching hellfire and damnation. Asking that we be saved. While down the street the Transcendentalist Unitarian preacher is telling the congregation that we are all part of God and Nature. The rattling of hymn books and the singing of Rock of Ages: "Rock of Ages, cleft for me/Let me hide myself in thee/Let the water and the blood. . . ."

(If this is a group experience, the Guide will then say:)

Now that you've experienced some of the smells, sights, sounds, tastes and touches of old New England, let's hear from you now other images of this time and place. Just call them out so we each can experience them. (Five minutes.)

In a few moments when the music begins I want you to slowly open your eyes and look around the room. You may notice that having cleansed the rooms of perception you will be seeing and sensing things in this room differently. You can move or even dance around the room as you choose. (Music begins.)

And as you do so, notice that the people and the objects in the room begin to come into more dimensionality. Depth perception is deeper. You see more shades and more shapes to things as your eyes attune to greater clarity. Touch things, and notice how textures just seem to rise up under your fingers to be touched. Listen to the range of notes in the music that you now can hear. Really deeply listen. . . . And come over here and take a slice of apple. Smell it and experience the full play of taste and smell sensations. Touch some of the things on this table and see what you notice about your extended capacities for touch. . . .

And stop for just a moment and look at a partner. And feel yourself fall into his or her eyes. And look at the world from these eyes. What is it like to have that kind of eye looking at the world? Looking at the world from your partner's eyes, see some image from their childhood and from a New England childhood with their eyes. . . .Tell each other what you see . . . . And then moving or dancing on.

And this time, if you would, let your hands massage the area of the third eye, in the center of the forehead, said in many traditions to be the place of insight. Emerson describes the work of a poet as that of putting patterns onto the world, of world creation. The poet does not simply see the world, and then use words to describe it. The poet creates the world. With this massaging and honoring of the place of insight, feel yourself capable of creating, as Emily did, any number of new worlds and words to fit them. She used a word, and that word itself drops into the ocean-sea of one's mind and creates a universe. She uses another word, and it drops in and creates another universe. This is the capacity of poets, and it now can be yours. Let yourself now fall into Emily's perceptions. That is, with the full power of the senses as well as the power of insight. And notice the people moving through the room. Notice the many objects in the room also. And let some image of insight come to you. Let it just float in. Ask Emily to touch you with some image, some insight as to the larger meaning of what you are seeing and sensing. And let the eyes go soft. And let some image or words or sense of knowing rise as you shift perception. Invite Emily to present her particular gift of seeing. And let there come into your mind a word or an image or a knowing of seeing the world in this extended manner. And then would you go to your notebook and write down the words and new perceptions and images which you have experienced. (Five minutes.)

Now I'm going to ask you to either lie down or sit up, but get very comfortable. Now I want you to just let that world that's above this building come pouring down into your body.

Let it come pouring down as it must have done for Emily a thousand, thousand times. Let the sense of this larger world pour into you and fill you. The sky. The sun. The clouds. The snow. The rain. The gray, the white, the many colors of nature. The stars. All of reality pouring in. And then, if you would, come back to this world, knowing that you hold a larger universe. And, like Emily, you can create with this universe as well. And when you are ready, write or draw in your notebooks whatever images and words you've seen and known.

2 School Days

We watch the child Emily go to school, and our hearts are in our mouth. Will they ruin her, we wonder. Will they force her brilliant lights to be hidden under the bushel of the four R's—religion, religious reading, religious writing, and religious arithmetic—which, if you can't guess, means showing the geometries of God? Or will she be led astray, as Lewis Carroll so testily put it, by studies in Ambition, Distraction, Uglification, and Derision? Not to worry. Grandfather Dickinson had sowed the seeds of a forward-looking curriculum at Amherst Academy where daughters could be "well instructed." "The female mind," he had written, "so sensitive, so susceptible of improvement should not be neglected. . . .God hath designed nothing in vain."

Science turns out to be the core of Emily's studies, and she is well pleased. "We have a very fine school," she writes a friend. "I have four studies. They are Mental Philosophy, Geology, Latin, and Botany. How large they sound, don't they?" There is a wonderful incident that gives one an idea of how brilliant her mind was even then. She hadn't studied for her Euclid exam. When she was called to the board to demonstrate a Euclidian formula, she drew instead an imaginary theorem and an imaginary series of angles and then proved it. The teacher was so dazzled, he gave her the highest mark. In the same letter, fourteen-year-old Emily declares, "I am growing handsome very fast indeed! I expect I shall be the belle of Amherst when I reach my 17th year."

Her seventeenth year finds her at Mt. Holyoke Female Seminary, where she resides for a year studying chemistry, electricity, physiology, botany, algebra, and Euclid—all well dosed with religious dogma, which she manages to separate out in her mind. Why, we wonder, did Emily get more science and math then in school than we do now? It is because the Amherst Trinitarians thought that there were deep spiritual connections between science and religion. The evangelical ministers who made up the bulk of the teachers at Amherst Academy lectured and preached about God as the master Craftsman and the Supreme Scientist of the Universe. His face was to be discovered through natural laws. Young Emily looked at all this scientific theophany and said, "no doubt—but what about all the annihilation and extinction that the great Artificer plots in his workshop?"

> It's easy to invent a Life -
> God does it - every Day -
> Creation - but the Gambol
> Of His Authority -

It's easy to efface it -
The thrifty Deity
Could scarce afford Eternity
To Spontaneity -

The Perished Patterns murmur -
But his Perturbless Plan
Proceed - inserting Here - a Sun -
There - leaving out a Man -

At Mt. Holyoke the pressure on her was continuous to undergo conversion to this Deity whom she found wildly capricious and less than human. She didn't like Jesus much. She referred to him as "avaricious Jesus looking for souls." The students were divided into those with hope, those who had accepted conversion, and those without hope—the category that Emily valiantly stayed in. Often when many of her classmates were sitting together, and they were asked to stand up if they had given their life to God, she was the only one left sitting. She wrote in a letter, "They thought it queer I didn't rise. . .I thought a lie would be queerer."

After a while she could stand it no more and left Mount Holyoke for Amherst where life bubbled and burned brightly. She writes, "...there is something a going on in Amherst almost all of the time such as shows Conserts Uncle Toms Cabin performed Musters Festivals Fairs Liceums Exhibitions Lectures Commencements and Cattle Shows." By 1855 Father has bought the old Homestead back, but even before that, their home had become the center of the social life of Amherst—and eighteen-year-old Emily is in the thick of it. "Amherst is alive with fun this winter—might you be here to see! Sleigh rides are as plenty as people. . . .Parties cant find fun enough—because all the best ones are engaged to attend balls a week beforehand—beaus can be had for the taking—maids smile like the mornings in June—Oh a very great town is this!"

One's life is continuously touched with courtship and romance: "While I washed the dishes at noon in that little 'sink-room' of ours, I heard a well-known rap, and a friend I love so dearly came to ask me to ride in the woods, the sweet-still woods, and I wanted to exceedingly—I told him I could not go, and he said he was disappointed—he wanted me very much." That was probably referring to a boy she knew who courted her for quite a long period of time, Ben Newton.

She is at the center of secrets: "I am confided in by one—and despised by an other! and another still!" And yet, in one way or another, everybody is available to her. Life is a constant show, a constant opportunity to observe and psychologize the world, a constant training in human hope and human folly: "Our house is crowded daily with the members of this world, the high and the low, the bond and the free, the 'poor in the world's goods,' and the 'almighty dollar'. . . ." Father Dickinson becomes active in politics, is elected to the Massachusetts State legislature, and when Emily is twenty-four, she visits him in Washington after he has been elected to Congress from the Whig Party.

There is little in her girlhood to indicate that soon she will turn her back on all this. And yet in years to come, she rarely leaves her father's house, rarely goes outside the boundaries of her conservatory, her sunny upstairs room, the garden that sloped gently downhill to the east, and the orchard where "the noiseless noise" was. Home was so agreeable, she said, why would anyone want to go away? Nurtured by such a home, she is free to live in the vastness of her own mind, visiting with the enormous populace that resides there:

> *The Only News I know*
> *Is Bulletins all Day*
> *From Immortality.*
>
> *The Only Shows I see -*
> *Tomorrow and Today -*
> *Perchance Eternity -*

So with news from immortality and entertainments from eternity, Emily begins to reside primarily in inner space as she had resided so thoroughly in outer space, fed by her extraordinary access to the imaginal world, the *Mundus Imaginalis*. You might ask, why is it she was allowed these whimsies? Remember that she is living in the middle of the Transcendental movement. The Trinitarians of Amherst do not want to be seen as less au courant than the Unitarian Transcendentalists of Harvard, and so they accept the reality and importance of the inner world—something that fundamentalists have great trouble doing today. They also want to be up-to-date in science. Science at this point has not made the great divide between without and within. God's majesty is portrayed in the geometry of things, but also through the imaginative universe as well.

Remember too, that substantive translations of Eastern literature are being published. These translations of Buddhist and Hindu texts and scriptures receive a great deal of attention by scholars and clerics alike. The sage of Concord, Emerson, was himself deeply influenced by these translations of Eastern thought, with their emphasis on the underlying unity of reality and the practice of inward-turning contemplations. But it is also the time of the sunset of the Romantic movement—of Coleridge, Byron, Keats, Shelley, and Wordsworth writing in English; and in German, of Fichte, Schelling, Schiller, Goethe, and Holderlin. Each of these writers presents in his own way the vision of a world in which inner and outer realities are equal to each other. Immanuel Kant wrote of the Creator having endowed us with both reproductive and the productive imaginations. This gives us the capacity to replicate what we've seen in the outer world (reproductive imagination), but also to create anew from the great original source, patterns of our own minds (productive imagination). Given these currents, the inner world of the imagination gains a remarkable level of social legitimacy in certain circles. Emily, of course, is in the thick of it. She does totally different things with her imaginative faculty than do the Romantics and the Transcendentalists, but she has similar access to its validity and vitality.

She is blessed to have been born at this time, because by the turn of the century, imagery begins to be ostracized by orthodox psychologists. It's only in recent years that we've seen the return of the ostracized and the sanctioning of imagery in therapy and creativity. Emily is living in the time of the validity of inner imagery. When she writes about "Bulletins from Immortality," she is talking essentially about the Transcendental view that we contain the God patterns within our minds. We are reflections of the immensity of these patterns, and join our Maker in the re-invention of the world. Again, this is the passionate statement of the Romantic movement of that time— the romance of Nature set up and over against the graceless smokestacks of the industrial desert.

It is quite possible that if Emily had been let loose in our time she would have been kept on Ritalin or Valium. Her genius would have been drugged, her perceptions blocked, her genius lost. I have known more than a few Emilys in my time. I went to school with a number of them at Barnard College. Frail, wildly poetic, madly imaginative, they were often sent by the college doctor to visit the psychiatrist. Some were twittering birdlike creatures, the girls from someplace else. And several ended their sojourn as strangers in a strange land by taking their own lives. How many of you have known them? You who are therapists or counselors see them in your practice, I'm sure. It may be that part of your practice is to try to keep their original minds alive, expressive, and not repressed.

Occasionally I have tried to empower these people by seeing them as great originals when the rest of the world said they were crazy. Ultimately many of them flowered, perhaps because I insisted that they were not crazy; they were just geniuses. I know a number of stories of people who were sent off to the asylum because they had religious experiences or poetic breakthroughs. Their inward metaphorical space unfolded with such glory, but they were not in the Romantic Age. They were not, like Emily, in the age of the empowerment of inner space, you see.

As Emily withdrew more and more into her mind and inner perceptions, they became almost painfully acute, so that the world passing outside her window had as much effect on her as if she were still living in the midst of it, only more so.

> *Menagerie to me*
> *My Neighbor be -*

"Friday, I tasted life," she writes about one of these occasions. "It was a vast morsel. A circus passed the house—still I feel the red in my mind." These tastes echoed ever after as analogies for everything else she thought about.

Some of us can hardly imagine what it would be like to have those extreme kinds of perceptions that are almost pathological. But highly gifted poets who have access to this dimensionality of inner space do feel things that way. In *The Possible Human* I wrote about a little girl who was having a terrible problem in school. The real problem, it turned out, was that her senses were so acute that she could not stand all the noise. Many people are hypersensitive, and there's nothing mad about it. It makes for great poets. But it is painful, and people try to get you. They say, "You should socialize more. You should be out there. You should ra-ra-ra-ra-ra. . . ." And you can't. You really have to say no, because the nature of your perception is to give you access to inner glory.

For Emily, the steady stream of books and magazines, of Shakespeare and Emerson and Thoreau and Dickens and Mrs. Browning that passed through the Dickinson household made her drunk with stimulation:

> *Strong Draughts of Their Refreshing Minds*
> *To drink - enables Mine*
> *Through Desert or Wilderness*
> *As bore it Sealed Wine -*
>
> *To go elastic . . .*

But before we pursue one of the most hypersensitive and therefore hyperstimulated minds of all time, let us inquire further about what might have driven this girl, who by all accounts greatly enjoyed social occasions and the constant presence of warm friends and family, to remove herself so thoroughly from what once she had known. I believe it has to do with her response to the phenomenon of conversion.

3 Conversion

To begin with, it is hard for us to realize how constant, indeed, how intimate was the presence of death in those days. Most children could not expect to pass the age of eight. "Only one in four," a children's physiology text of the period says, "lives to see twenty-one." The angel of death or variations on the skeletal form of the Grim Reaper was one of the principle forms of art practiced in most New England towns. People went to cemeteries to admire the art of death on the headstones, the way Europeans went to museums. This was an age, remember, in which the medicine being practiced by white men was far far more primitive than that practiced by the Native American healers whom they had driven out of the land. It was the great interim period between the woman's medicine of herbs and salves and natural unguents—gone underground with the witch scare—and a remarkably impotent and harrowing practice by male doctors. There were no antibiotics; all surgery was performed with neither anesthesia nor antiseptics; each muddy, cold, septic and sewage-ridden house—most sewage emptied near to the well—was privy to the inevitable invasion by typhoid, pneumonia, smallpox, cholera, malaria, and above all, consumption, the last of which took off a fair sampling of Emily's close girlhood friends before they reached their twentieth year.

Emily was always going to funerals. It was hard to live at that time without having at least one funeral a month. Childbirth was a disaster, and the arrival of a newborn was almost always met with tentative joy, since chances were, the infant would soon be carried off by some ailment which today would be met with simple treatment. A large percentage of infants died before their first year. "Oh, the baby has colic," we say in an offhand manner about a screaming baby. There was nothing offhand about the baby's ailments then. Children's nighttime prayers were filled with the expectation that they would wake up not in their beds, but rise up in the morning in eternity.

> *Now I lay me down to sleep,*
> *I pray the Lord my soul to keep.*
> *If I should die before I wake,*
> *I pray the Lord my soul to take.*

There were some households in which the parting at night was the time of great affection before the child went to sleep. A child was either shaken hands with, kissed, or looked at with great endearment, because the family wasn't sure that child was going to be awake and alive in the morning.

Part of women's work was to participate in the long watches over the dying, and Emily had more than her share in these. Often there wasn't a month that went by that, if you were a woman, you did not participate in a long watch. You watched the dying person— sometimes for days, sometimes for months on end—but especially during the last days of life, you watched. Emily observed these watches with a certain awe, even a certain macabre fascination. By her own admission she desired to go and attend the death of her friends and watch their faces become so beautiful and unlined and ethereal. She was drawn to the in-between state when a person is not quite dead and not quite alive, when they seem to exist in an immortal place where, perhaps for a few seconds, they would know everything. During those moments she would move closer, hoping that she would catch some of the knowledge of the in-between when the walls between the worlds might suddenly open up. Perhaps, in our terms, such fascination with dying would seem macabre, but in those times, it was not.

Emmy Devine: I don't think fascination with death is macabre in our terms either. I think now that people are beginning again to recognize that being with death is the greatest gift that you can ever receive. That being with a person at the moment of death is a birth, and that it's a tremendous gift. And as more and more people are dying off, people leaving this planet in droves, we're all being given that opportunity. And it's an opportunity that we should all embrace, as Emily did, in order to be birthed into the new time.

Jean: Thank you for saying that. This is especially true with many losing so many friends to AIDS. . . . And that's what's so interesting— that often these kind of diseases that have an inevitability about them, as consumption did then, as AIDS does now, seem to open the dying person to deeper dimensions of themselves that they had not explored during healthier times. They became luminous. Some of the people I've known who have AIDS or died of it have become available to their own spiritual depths in ways that they rarely had been before. As if the breakdown of the immune response had also broken down the walls between their ordinary consciousness and their deeper psyche. As you know, I have been helping AIDS hospice groups and counsellors working with HIV/AIDS patients to create programs that that allow their clients to use the time remaining to them to deepen their spiritual growth.

Peggy Nash Rubin: And people with consumption, you know, are some of the greatest writers in the world. Thomas Mann's *The Magic Mountain* is all about what happens to people who have consumption. The Brontes, all of these people, have lung disorders of one kind or another. And they lived the most wildly involved and engaged lives in the imagination. And Emily herself had lung problems all her life. So I think there is a correlation between what happens with particular kinds of chronic diseases that do take you off, and what opens in your mind then as a result.

Jean: The toxins of tuberculosis have a very definite altered state of consciousness effect on the mind. They suspend the mind from its usual ways of seeing. I mean, if you'd gone on the moors past the Bronte house say in the 1840's where lived Charlotte and Emily Bronte and their brother Bramwell, writers all, you would have heard "cough cough cough cough cough cough cough cough" as they were coughing up *Jane Eyre, Wuthering Heights*. . . . I'm not suggesting that one get these diseases, but it did stimulate an enormous creativity. In fact, there are some who believe that American creativity declined substantially with the ending of consumption!

During the nineteenth century, then, people could share the experience of dying and regard dying as a sacramental event. There was no rationale for all this death, and the sheer inevitability of it gave rise among all folk—the educated as well as the uneducated—to the need for conversion. Conversion, in this case, provided for a state of mind in which one would find hope in utter submission to the inscrutable will of God. Revivals were the great spiritual pastime of the nineteenth century, until after the Civil War, and conversion experiences were their orgiastic form.

In nineteenth-century America, conversion was the communally recognized public rite of passage. With puberty rites largely lost or greatly diminished (witness the attempts Mark Twain makes in *Tom Sawyer* and *Huckleberry Finn* to revive them) conversion, especially, was the way in which to move from youth to maturity.

Now what happened in these revivals? There was always a great deal of jubilant singing. There was a good deal of fiery, charismatic preaching. There was always a tremendous emphasis placed on the great divide, the before and after of which was an immense gulf that lay between your ordinary unredeemed life of sin and unworthiness and a life of flaming certainty, of release from sin, emotional fire, incendiary conviction. What happens in the brain in a conversion experience is that it gets hyperstimulated and overloaded. It gets to a point that it cannot take it any more, and it converts. It flip-flops. One becomes a different person, the person that the collective group spirit requires. One's mind is not the same. In a matter of minutes, one crosses an abyss of beingness and finds oneself on the other side, for better or for worse, a "new" person. This is as true of political conversion as it is of religious conversion.

In conversion, everything in one's identity was shifted, lifted up, and given over to God. The imagery of Jacob wrestling with the angel was often used to illustrate the battle for faith. One experienced "a total loss of independence and autonomy wherein an individual's control over the organization of his or her experience was given over to the Lord. The integrated vision of the world that had united a unique set of memories and values and emotions into a coherent 'self' was replaced by the uniform, divinely dictated vision of a world renewed in Christ's love."[5] But what one gained in emotional enjoyment and certainty, one lost in spiritual autonomy and personal identity. Many people, women especially, became bondswomen to the church and its directors. After conversion, one could find oneself lobotomized as to the normal responses to death and dying. One would accept with meek equanimity the incomprehensible will of the Deity and the horrors of everyday dying. Instead, one would put aside sorrow and grief for the glory of certainty of the resurrection of the dead. Dying was but the supreme way of going home.

In modern terms, the conversion experience can be understood as a radical restructuring of the brain/mind/emotional systems, in which the local self and its individual and independent characteristics go into abeyance—often during the course of the fervor and fever of the revivalist process. As we noted with consumption, a collective fever is created in the revivalist process, during which you lose your local boundaries, beliefs, ways of being. And then, when you are totally displaced, you are replaced by the collective self of the "Christian" soul with its emphasis on meekness, humility, passivity, and utter submission to a certain authority. And love. We must not forget that those calling their listeners to conversion promised them an eternity of living with God's perfect love and companionship. How thrilling, how seductive that must have seemed to the unmarried and the ill-married. One entered into intimacy with the archetype—but again, in the revivalist experience, at what price? This was no deepening into relationship with the Beloved. This was all-out submission to a particular theology and a psychological straitjacket.

In the midst of all of this, Emily from childhood virtually to the day she died, was cajoled, commanded, exhorted to convert, but always she refused, refusing even to go to the revival meetings being held. "I felt that I was so easily excited that I might. . .be deceived and I dared not trust myself." Yet even she felt some indescribable longing for this "golden opportunity." At the age of fifteen she writes, "I feel that I am sailing upon the brink of an awful precipice, from which I cannot escape and over which I fear my tiny boat will soon glide if I do not receive help from above. There is now a revival in college and many hearts have given way to the claims of God." Her refusal was a stupendous act of assertion of her own identity. For as Jane Langton, who has written several marvelous mystery novels with Emily Dickinson critical to their theme, writes in her elegant "Appreciation" of Emily in *Acts of Light*, "It is impossible now to imagine the pressure against which she stood fast, the power and influence ranged against her in a town like Amherst, where the church loomed so large, where the clergyman was a man of supreme importance, where sermons were a matter of daily comment."

And so I say that in Emily's refusal to convert lay the source of the deepening of her genius and her skill with words. She deepened into her own Word instead of capitulating to someone else's. She discovered her own lexicon, her own scripture, instead of becoming just another nameless bondswoman of holy writ. Indeed, she writ her own holy and borrowed the images of the Bible to seed her own scriptures. She firmly refused to be sucked into an ordained and finished word of God, however authoritative and ancient it might be. She danced with the angel rather than fighting with it, and never seemed to stop dancing. And the angel never went away, becoming her partner, not her contender.

PROCESS 2
SELF-BAPTISM

How do we change those attitudes which tend to diminish our perceptions and ideas and narrow our sense of reality? Perhaps it is by uncovering and investigating the ways in which one still holds fundamentalist attitudes. The term *fundamentalism* can mean that one maintains a kind of tunnel vision or a rigid belief system or behavior surrounding certain constructs. One can be said to retreat to a fortress of "truth" concerning certain religious or intellectual or even emotional issues. Thus it often is a habit pattern of mind that tends to put one on automatic and close the door to other ways of seeing and being. It tends to involve conversion, but need not be a dramatic Sunday Meeting kind of experience. Rather it can be very insidious in its very mundaneness, involving a kind of conversion to trivia, to not rocking the boat, to a bored and boring life. It can be an addiction to meaningless work, a commitment to being stuck, a sanctifying of one's mental or emotional sloth.

Emily feared the conversion experience because she saw so many of her friends becoming closed and simplistic after accepting the narrow belief system which the preacher offered. She felt that it reduced their perceptions, narrowed their thought processes, and truncated their very being, while offering them the assurance of salvation and the community of the saved. Thus there were very real emotional rewards for entering the path of conversion. But at what expense!

What Emily Dickinson did, by refusing conversion and discovering instead her own well thought out view of reality was to anticipate some of the most critical and dangerous occurrences in the twentieth century. This is why she speaks more to our time than to her own. For our century has seen so many tragic episodes of political, scientific and religious "conversion" and so many varieties of fundamentalism, which shut up whole peoples in ideological fortresses of "truth," while brutalizing or overrunning those groups or countries not conforming to the approved belief system. From the vision of thousands shouting "Seig Heil" in torchlight celebrations, to the gray fear of millions caught in communist wastelands, to the raging fury of Islamic militants, to the wholesale damnation of all religious groups but their own by certain Christian, Hindu, and Muslim fundamentalists, our century has suffered as no other century has. Also, we must not forget that new methods of brainwashing political and religious prisoners have made the conversion experience a matter of sophisticated manipulation of mind and body. The use of media in the interest of conversion to a myriad of things—religious and political beliefs, the buying of products, entrainment to mindless entertainment—has continued a subtler form of manipulation on a vast scale.

In a time when the world is in desperate need of more ideas and more views of spirit, consciousness, and society, we turn again to Emily. For in discovering her own truth in the face of enormous opposition, she becomes one of those great prefigural events of an heroic consciousness daring to explore the domains of human greatness and inventiveness. In doing this, she anticipates the democratization of human potential and subjective exploration only possible for many at the end of the twentieth century. Emily did this by refusing conversion, saying that while others thought it very queer that she did not stand up for conversion, she thought a lie would be queerer still. But in a sense, Emily became even more fundamental. She explored the very ground of being by falling into nature and falling into her own notions of goddedness and her use of the creative spirit. She self-baptized herself in her own image of her possible human. She chose her belief system as a fully conscious, noncoercive act. Now to do this, she needed a certain amount of emotional fire to serve and sustain her venture. The fires that were lit in Emily's town were fires about the sinful, evil fallenness of our human state. She felt rage over these goings on, but she turned it into creation. Jung once said that creativity has been wrongly applied to an opus—a work of art, a painting, a piece of music or writing—because the ultimate opus for humans is the recreation of ourselves. But following upon Emily, it may well be that the recreative power, the lively and resourceful nub of yourself, is to be found in the deep fire that lies beneath your reactions to your own or others' conversion to a narrow point of view. This fire is the ground of being, the fundamental immensity which supports and sustains all our endeavors. Each one of you is a particular focalization in space and time of this immensity that is yearning at the threshold of existence to find expression in the world. In expressing this immensity, you become god stuff made manifest. In this expression, each one of you is utterly unique, for god stuff always seeks innovation, novelty, new ways of being.

Now some people have more apparent awareness of their uniqueness than others. Emily had the immense good fortune to live in a family of eccentrics in which her uniqueness was appreciated and which gave her time and space to distill and develop it. Most of us have become sort of sloppy and muddled with regard to our own uniqueness. But once one makes a determination to become available to this even more fundamental order of energy, it is like experiencing a kind of kundalini of the soul. It can often involve both spiritual emergence and spiritual emergency at the same time. In her experience of this, Emily called herself a Vesuvius at home. You can agree to be blown out by this energy, and then, as often happens, your life is not your own, as happened in the old fashioned fundamentalist conversions. Or you can agree to partner and wrestle with it like Jacob with the angel. And then you live in the recreated world of your own self-conversion.

TIME: TWO HOURS.

• *MATERIALS:*
For this process it is best to have some body of water nearby—a lake, a waterfall, a stream or brook, a swimming pool, or, failing that, a bathtub, a large container of water, or even, a baptismal font! A pitcher for water is also needed, as is food and music for a concluding celebration.

• *MUSIC:*
Soft background music for the drawing and writing part of the process. If a recording of gospel music or even "Amazing Grace" can be played during this sequence, it would be all to the good. For the wrestling/dancing with the angel sequence, stirring music with a strong beat such as you find in the *Hooked on Classics* series. Ballet music could also work here as could the concluding movement from Bruch's *Violin Concerto.*

• *INSTRUCTIONS FOR GOING SOLO:*
This entire process can readily be done by oneself just by reading and following the instructions. However, for the self-baptizing part, you may want to bring in a friend for witness. If that is not possible, then call upon the trees and the sky and the birds to witness for you. And then treat yourself to some kind of delight or festivity.

• *SCRIPT FOR THE GUIDE:*
Before we go to the water for our process of self-baptism, I want each of you to take a few minutes and write or draw in your notebooks and journals. You will be concerned with discerning some of those narrow beliefs and limitations you hold about yourselves and the world at large that you feel inhibit your life and its possibilities. If, however, you are perfectly happy with your fundamentalist attitudes, then write or draw those in your notebook also.

If there are some among you who feel that once upon a time you underwent conversion to some belief or attitude that you no longer hold, but which still rises up automatically to muffle your experience and censure your explorations, then indicate what that attitude is. If you have difficulty in doing this, then try writing or drawing with your nondominant hand, the more "innocent" hand which is less given to one's usual habits and conditionings. Would you begin to write and draw now. (Ten minutes.)

Now I want you to turn to a fresh page and write or draw the belief system or idea of the self that you would choose as your lure of becoming. If you were to choose your own conversion to some larger ideal or pattern of belief or possibility, what would it be? Perhaps it might be a way of seeing yourself as a child of the all-merciful Creator. Or perhaps as co-creator of your world with your loving spiritual partner. Perhaps you would baptize yourself in the name of a higher consciousness, creativity, and service to humankind. Consider these things and write or draw your own unique perspective on how you would name yourself and what you stand for. (Ten minutes.)

I am now going to read to you Emily Dickinson's own poem of conscious self-baptism:

> *I'm ceded - I've stopped being Theirs -*
> *The name They dropped upon my face*
> *With water, in the country church*
> *Is finished using, now,*
> *And They can put it with my Dolls,*
> *My childhood, and the string of spools,*
> *I've finished threading - too -*
>
> *Baptized, before, without the choice,*
> *But this time, consciously, of Grace -*
> *Unto supremest name -*
> *Called to my Full - The Crescent dropped -*
> *Existence's whole Arc, filled up,*
> *With one small Diadem.*
>
> *My second Rank - too small the first -*
> *Crowned - Crowing - on my Father's breast -*
> *A half unconscious Queen -*
> *But this time - Adequate - Erect,*
> *With Will to choose, or to reject,*
> *And I choose, just a Crown -*

Emily chose a crown. Would everyone now draw their idea of a good looking crown on a fresh piece of paper.

Leave some room on the crown to write something on it. (Two minutes.)

Now let us put our papers to one side and clear the floor. In a few moments some very stirring music is going to be played. It is then that I invite each of you to wrestle and/or dance with your angel. In this you understand that whereas Jacob wrestled for one night, this is symbolic of a match or a dance that lasts your life long. It can refer to your willingness never to stop investigating the ground of your being: to question it, to reach tentative conclusions, and then to question again and again in order to stand like Emily says she did—Adequate, Erect. This attitude implies freedom from belief systems that are not truly one's own but were handed down or embraced without study or mature reflection.

As the music begins, you will wrestle or dance with your angel, whichever mode of being with your angel appeals to you. You will move vigorously through the room as you do this, questioning your emerging beliefs, being challenged by your angel to stand up for what you choose to believe. The dance will last about ten minutes, and in that time I ask you to wrestle, dance, leap, challenge, respond, question, contend, commune with this imagined or real angel who represents your Higher Self and who asks of you that you gain a larger, more vital sense of your new choice of a larger ideal. Begin. (The music begins. Allow ten minutes.)

And now both adequate and erect would you go back to where you have placed the drawings of your crown, but this time, as a result of your wrestling and dancing with the angel, you may have a clearer understanding of what you are choosing. So put a title on the crown that reflects this self-understanding. For example, you might title the crown something like Questioner, Dancer with Angels, Believer in the Lifeforce, Queen, Portrait Painter to the gods, Trickster, Laugher at Life's Jokes, etc. Begin. (Three minutes.)

Now with this new title that you have placed on your crown, let us all go now to the place of self-baptism.

(The Guide leads everyone to the water. Once there, she or he gathers everyone together and says:)

In many cultures baptism is the ancient form of entering a new period of one's life in which one agrees to be free from old and destructive habit and belief patterns. In our variation of this ancient ritual, we will baptize ourselves in front of witnesses to the new life and pattern which we have chosen.

Decide who will go first. Then will that person please dip the pitcher into the water or, if you prefer (and the weather is permitting) take off your shoes and step into the water before dipping the pitcher. (You could also dip the water for self-baptism with your hands, or even immerse yourself completely.) Then will you say words to this effect: "In front of these witnesses and before the Spirit in which I believe, I self baptize myself. . . ." And then state whatever your newly chosen self-understanding or belief or pattern is, such as, "I baptize myself as Student of the Mysteries, Warrior for the Light, Singer of the Darkness, Writer, etc." You can baptize yourself with one title or a number of them, if that seems fitting. Just be clear about it. Then either pour the water over yourself or immerse yourself in it.

After you have done this, will all the other participants standing in high witness say:

Be thou baptized!

Then the one who was baptized will select the next person who will go through the same process.

(After all the participants have been baptized, there should be some kind of festivity or celebration—good food, a picnic perhaps, music, dancing, jokes, and general merriment.)

4 Poet/Goddess/Creator

Because Emily, a hypersensitive poetic and psychological genius who desperately wanted to believe, refused conversion, she had to take on God and reinvent the world—which is just what she did. I know of few other cases in history where one has agreed to so great a challenge, agreeing to wrestle with the angel not for a night but for fifty-five years, and won. It gives a whole new slant to our understanding of the creative act.

Of course you couldn't leave your house much with such an enterprise. It took all your time, space, and focus. So when I read these psychiatric diagnostic accounts written by men—attributing the whole of her work and genius to annals of spinster sexual frustration, I wonder at how distant and compartmentalized science has grown from human understanding. When you rather read Emily from inside out, you are reading woman's fecundity not frustrated but turned to world-making. This is the stuff of goddesses—once and future goddesses. True she still used the Christian imagery of her culture: baptism, confirmation, salvation, but she used it in the service of her own self-conversion to the mind and soul of goddess as Creator.

It is perhaps the most radical kind of choice one can make, the choice to be God. It requires a different psychology, a different way of being, a very different language. It particularly requires a highly conscious relationship to one's own consciousness. You cannot fall asleep, if you have made that choice. It required what she called "the lunacy of light," a dangerous human sanity that was at once a divine insanity. It required the consciousness of the Creator.

Hers was creation in its boldest and sometimes even Biblical sense. For one thing, like a god she named things. Consider how much of her poetry is taken up by giving things names and qualities that exceed all previous knowing of them. See how she renames the seasons, for example, and brings New England color and vitality—and New England grotesque—into a tamed word like *autumn*:

> *The name - of it - is "Autumn"-*
> *The hue - of it - is Blood -*
> *An Artery - upon the Hill -*
> *A Vein - along the Road -*
>
> *Great Globules - in the Alleys -*
> *And Oh, the Shower of Stain -*
> *When Winds - upset the Basin -*
> *And spill the Scarlet Rain -*

That's autumn to the god mind. Look what she does with definitions of strong feelings, like *hope*:

> *Hope is a subtle Glutton -*
> *He feeds upon the Fair -*
> *And yet - inspected closely*
> *What Abstinence is there -*

Or consider what she does in defining *longing*:

> *Longing is like the Seed*
> *That wrestles in the Ground,*
> *Believing if it intercede*
> *It shall at length be found.*

Try her recreation of *remorse*:

> *Remorse - is Memory - awake -*
> *Her Parties all astir -*
> *A Presence of Departed Acts -*
> *At window - and at Door -*

Or of *decay*:

> *Crumbling is not an instant's Act*
> *A fundamental pause*
> *Dilapidation's processes*
> *Are organized Decays.*

And then there is *experience*:

> *Experience is the Angled Road*
> *Preferred against the Mind*

Try *doom*:

> *Doom is the House without the Door -*
> *'Tis entered from the Sun -*
> *And then the Ladder's thrown away,*
> *Because Escape - is done -*

Like a goddess, a divine queen, an Isis revealed stirring the pot, she cooks up a landscape with the power of imagination or revery. Listen to her recite her recipe for landscape building:

> *To make a prairie it takes a clover and one bee,*
> *One clover, and a bee,*
> *And revery.*
> *The revery alone will do,*
> *If bees are few.*

She begins to become exalted with her power. She not only competes with God; she beats him at his own game. Score: Emily 2 - God 1. Here is the poem that does it. She's talking about writing and creation:

> *I send Two Sunsets -*
> *Day and I - in competition ran -*
> *I finished Two - and several Stars -*
> *While He - was making One -*
>
> *His own was ampler - but as I*
> *Was saying to a friend -*
> *Mine - is the more convenient*
> *To Carry in the Hand -*

Another aspect of gods is their drunkenness. Gods are those who live in a state of continuous intoxication over their creations or re-creations. With Emily, the intoxication is caused by her revelation—her re-vealing of Nature.

> *I taste a liquor never brewed -*
> *From Tankards scooped in Pearl -*
> *Not all the Vats upon the Rhine*
> *Yield such an Alcohol!*

And here are some of her greatest lines:

> *Inebriate of Air - am I -*
> *And Debauchee of Dew -*
> *Reeling - thro endless summer days -*
> *From inns of Molten Blue -*

She is just drunk on reality! Everything in Nature roils with significance. A bird's squandered note upon the air causes the universe to quake from the importance of its song. The fact is that Earth is heaven—whether heaven is heaven or not. And what does it matter for one whose closest friend is eternity? Her sense seems to be that since she finds herself caught in time she must try and bring all time into space, as she says in her wonderful words:

> *Behind Me - dips Eternity -*
> *Before Me - Immortality -*
> *Myself - the Term Between -*

She will invest the term between with totality. She will put her circumference around it. What happens when you take on the spirit of creation, and yet are caught in the term between—caught in your own hard shell of mortality? What happens if, like Emily, your mind exceeds the continuum of day-night, day-night? Are you then claustrophobic before the wheeling of the sky, the circling of the seasons? The only thing to do is to put one's circumference around it, to invest all things with what today we could think of as a holonomic knowing. This is a knowing that sees the before, the after, and the between of things, that catches the glint of glory and the shadows skittering in the corner. To me, holonomic knowing, what Emily calls circumference knowing, is the mind wrapping itself around its object like a python, but instead of suffocating it, giving it life.

Interestingly enough, Delphi, before Apollo gained the ascendency there, was the place principally dedicated to the worship of the Great Goddess, and the spirit of the Goddess was often seen in the giant snake, the Python. Then when the Indo-Aryan invaders came down—the Achaeans and the Dorians—they couldn't change the spiritual practices too much. The women priestesses of the older rite remained now as the oracles, each one now addressed as the Pythia, the one who has the snake wisdom of the deep earth, and it was they who offered prophecy in a strange language.

Emily, too, is a kind of nineteenth-century Pythia, uttering a strange language of earth wisdom. Indeed, when the Pythia of Delphi prophesied, people had to listen very closely to figure it out. She was surrounded by priests trying to interpret her. And now here Emily is, the Pythia of Amherst, listening for the oracles of the earth with the full circumferential holonomic mind-wrap of her intelligence, and busting with words such as no one had ever heard—being oracular for all times and all seasons.

And of course she knew, as all Pythias, all goddesses know, that on this earth/heaven everything is connected with everything else—again, a god's knowing. So she writes of the presence of heaven on earth making extraordinary analogies, potent correspondences such as few had ever envisioned. Like the physics of the late twentieth century, she saw that everything is implicate in everything else—stir a flower and bestir a sun—that the normal state of the universe is one of colossal busybodyness in which everything is seeding, pouring, bleeding through to everything and everyone else. And Emily saw this first, before the scientists figured it out. She expressed it in language so acute as to be almost unbearable.

> *Beauty crowds me till I die*
> *Beauty mercy have on me*
> *But if I expire today*
> *Let it be in sight of thee -*

In our society, to a great extent, creativity is limited to a field, painting, music, medicine, science. That's a shame. The work is thought to shape a person. Either you're a painter, an artist, a scientist, and thus it becomes only partially fulfilling, often tragically limiting or crazy-making, because it limits the creative possibility to the confines of a field. Sometimes when someone says, "Oh, she's a very creative person!", you think, "And what else is the matter with her?" There is generally the association of creativity with being cuckoo, and often for a very good reason. What has happened is that the province of the creative field has really yet to be opened in our understanding of it to the whole of the human condition—body, mind and spirit.

Now the term creativity itself is a modern term. Before the Enlightenment, when we were all the God or the Goddess's creatures living in His or Her creation, the word creative in the sense of creativity was almost never used. The notion of "creative production," or even "creative productivity," entered usage only in the year 1803 with the new ego of the nineteenth century—the Promethean ego that went out there and created the steam engine and wrested the forest and re-formed the material universe and got things done. So you might say that as the gods or the sacred receded, and human ego became dominant, creativity was thought to be carried more and more exclusively by the human being. This was particularly a Protestant conundrum more than a Roman Catholic one. As a Protestant of Calvinistic inclination you can never know if you are among the Elect. You do not know really who you are in the scheme of things, and because you do not know, there is little justification for your sanctity except through your work.

So what do you do if you don't have a sacramental system to mediate your sense of continuity with Nature, when you do not have the rituals that reinsert you back in the world and time, when you have no sense of the universe being your familiar friend? What happens is that ego is made to bear a weight of responsibility for which it has not been prepared, and you feel that the only way that you can justify yourself is with a tremendous neurotic drive to be creative or to produce, thereby perhaps justifying yourself to God. In fact, so much—too much—of the North American continent was created by people trying to justify themselves creatively to the God before whom they felt they were ultimately damned.

Emily Dickinson's forebears were possessed by an immense creative neurosis. Her grandfather, you remember, worked all the time to build a college, to put something out there, to justify his existence. And her father, phobic for his father's failure, worked equally as hard to justify his identity in the world. So Emily comes out of a tradition of immense work to prove yourself to God, though being a woman, she turned the normal pattern upside down and took on immense work to disprove herself to God. She reinvents the world over and against that God who requires so much work. She says, "I'll go you one better. I'll wrestle with you. I'll reinvent the world."

The enormous burden that the word *creativity* carries today is owing in large part to our sense of meaninglessness and aimlessness that can only be washed away by the illusion of productivity. How many of you feel that you have justified yourself, that you have had a good day, only when you have been productive? Our sense is that there are no longer any gods out there, and that we are suddenly exclusively responsible for creation. We often feel that we alone bear the creative burden.

In order to remythologize creativity, I think we have to, as James Hillman wrote in *The Myth of Analysis*, bring the gods and the goddesses back in, re-sacramentalize the cosmos.[6] And that means that we cannot confuse the creative and the artistic. The creative is not necessarily the artistic. Creativity is the urge to wholeness, the urge to individuation or to the becoming of what one truly is. And in that becoming, we bring the cosmos into form. It is an urge whose development is empowered by the evolutionary instinct, which demands unfoldment. That demand is ultimately the source of our neurosis and, more, of our pathos. We experience an immense yearning, thinking all the while that it is we who are yearning, but it may not just be ourselves who are in that state. Rather it may be that we are the ones who are yearned through by the cosmos. We are that particular focalization, that lensing in space and time, through which cosmic creation is yearning to express itself.

The evolutionary instinct therefore also demands of us cosmogony—the creation of the cosmos or the unfolding of innovation, novelty, new associations, new patterns within and through you. You are by nature of being human a cosmogenesist. This means then you agree "to cosmose" (a new verb, *to cosmose!*)—to pattern, to order, to cohere, to create. Creativity is the drive of the entelechy, the spiritual drive, the being caught up in a mythical, symbolic realm of the great juicing patterns which are there, burgeoning in us just below the surface crust of consciousness, so that you as a personal particular becomes extended into the personal universal. And that radical uniqueness that is you allows the universe to utterly innovate itself in and through you. You lose your little localness for a while when you do this, but you take the fullness of your own particular historical self down into the place of the great creative patterns where the personal universal is revealed. The god or goddess enters into time. You avail yourself of the infinite; you open the lens of your little localness to your being seeded and sourced by the patterns of creation, of cosmogenesis, yearning to come into time through you.

That is why the phenomenology of the creative experience and of the religious experience is often so similar, if not the same. As part of the same process, in both there occurs the evolutionary drive of the Whole to be realized in the self. It is evolution or entelechy breaking into time in the structure and context of your particular beingness, your particular protein-based focalization of space/time. By accessing this knowing, we allow our psyche to be available for the seeds of goddedness. In this we remember Meister Eckhart's magnificent statement, "Pear seeds bring forth pear trees, nut seeds bring forth nut trees, and God seeds bring forth Gods." In conversion we make ourselves available to one particular form of experiencing sanctity. In creativity we open ourselves to an incredible partnership. And we have the last word; the Pattern does not. We do not become some wind harp upon which the breath of God plays at will.We agree to co-create. And if we do not do a lot of work together, nothing much gets done in this world of ours. In the spirit of Meister Eckhart, I think that what creativity in its ultimate sense is all about is the planting, care, and nurturing of co-creative god-seeds.

This is where Emily Dickinson has something tremendous to tell us. When you engage with and partner creation, your role is equal to God's. Emily was a phenomenal example of someone who was intoxicated with her own God-seededness. She was a profound theologian, quite literally theophanic—diaphanous to her goddedness. She had to re-create the world, bust it apart and restructure it. Those who take on such a task do not look like ordinary creators who merely submit to certain deeper levels of their psyche wherein reside the great collections of imagery and the wonderful patterns and associations with which to embellish their creation. From these they sometimes even experience the automatisms of the creative process—the self-creating works of art that seem to arise spontaneously, and with little conscious direction from themselves, as is the case with many artists, writers, and inventors.

What happened with Emily was a phenomenal example of a person becoming so drunk with creation that she had to go it one better. Falling in love with creation, she held all her powers captive until she could release herself in ecstasy. She did not lose herself in the creative process. Rather, she kept all her craft and powers honed while allowing her well stocked mind, as well as her extraordinary powers of observation, to serve in the creation of a whole new form that enlarged the horizon of human experience.

The utter originality of an Emily Dickinson is that in her poems as in her life she reversed our human inadequacy. She empowered the microcosm and granted it full status with the macrocosm. She restored infinity back into the particular and saw that the partnership became infinity meeting infinity.

PROCESS 3
POEM MAKING

(This process is adapted from an exercise led by poet Judith Morley in the Mystery School.)

The poet's vision is not limited to sight, but includes the inner voice. When we look through the poet's eye, the boundaries of the senses seem to disappear. We hear the sound of rhythms, and those rhythms are a felt sense. We are even given to synesthesias, cross-over senses—the lost sensory system of childhood. The poet's eye is sensitive to light and color, imagery, patterns, metaphor, associations, the reconciliation of opposites, and above all, to absurdities. The poet's eye is equally present to pregnant silence—to what is not heard, not seen, not felt, not touched, but cannot be denied: the Essential Self, the spirit, the soul, the Higher Being. The poet's eye calls, "Come out, come out, wherever you are, so that I can know you, and perhaps even express you." The poet's eye centers within the closed circuit of the head and enters all of outer space.

Poetry is the language of prehistory. It's the language we spoke before we spoke, the language of the soul, of the heart, of the earliest meetings with the Mysteries of the world. Before there was even elementary language, there was an inarticulate cry of emotion. And after a while, syllable by syllable, words came. Denys Thompson supposes that the first words were probably syllabic noises marking the rhythm of the dancing to encourage the fertility of animals and plants.

Let us return to those first inarticulate cries. Imagine that you are living 100,000 years ago. And you wake up on this morning, and what had been a beautiful day is suddenly drenched in snow. The sun is gone. This white stuff is falling. You have no language. Can you express thought without language? What happens? What are the sounds you make? What are these inarticulate sounds you make when you wake up on this morning with snow replacing the sun? Make the sounds that you would make to utter what you feel about this desolate day. Are they different than the sounds you would make today? You have managed to survive the winter on roots and grubs and bugs and dead leaves. A little bit of a carcass, a few bones that were left over. And now a shaft of sunlight comes into the cave and you see something green out there. The year has turned and you are still living. Try saying this without language. You now are beginning to feel a yearning for a fuller manner of expression in this place that you live 100,000 years ago and still you have no language. And the sensations are good ones. It is out of these sounds bearing fullness that poetry is born.

Poetry comes from the word *poiesis* which means "to make, to fabricate, to do, to create." But it also means something else. The word may derive from the Phoenician *phobe* which means "language, mouth, voice," and *ish* which means "the originating being, the organizing principle, God—Ishtar." So, from this derivation, you have *poiesis* meaning "the language of the gods." Julian Jaynes, in his remarkable if eccentric book *The Origins of Consciousness in the Breakdown of the Bicameral Brain*, suggests that prior to the changes in climates and societies some thirty-five hundred years ago, our ancestors heard the internal voice which whispers into the right hemisphere of the brain as admonitions from the gods. We too hear the voice and its admonitions, suggesting that we go to the market, wash the dishes, get the laundry in, though we might identify it as the imperatives of the super-ego. Whether we call it the voice of the gods or the voice of the subconscious or the ruminations of the right hemisphere of the brain appearing as a god-sent voice to the left hemisphere, the voice speaks, and it behooves us to listen.

When we start working in poetry, the most important thing is to catch the first magical line that you hear, for it is this line that comes from the "gods." We will soon do an exercise which encourages us to listen for this magical inner voice. For Emily Dickinson, first lines were often colloquial, the language of the day. Her lines were generally in iambic rhythm, with four stresses to the line, since that's how we talk: ta-DA-ta-DA-ta-DA-ta-DA. If you just read her first lines you know a good deal about her biography. Read aloud some of the following first lines of Emily Dickinson's poems, and you will begin to understand what I mean.

"A coffin is a small domain . . ."
"A little bread, a crust, a crumb . . ."
"A loss of something ever felt . . ."
"A prison gets to be a friend . . ."
"A word made flesh is seldom . . ."
"After great pain, a formal feeling comes . . ."
"Because I could not stop for Death . . ."
"Behind me dips Eternity . . ."
"By my window have I for scenery . . ."
"Come slowly, Eden . . ."
"Death is a dialogue between . . ."
"Faith is a fine invention . . . "
"God is a distant stately lover . . ."
"Going to Him! Happy letter . . ."

"Going to Her . . ."
"He ate and drank the precious words . . ."
"He preached upon 'breadth' till it argued him
    narrow . . ."
"Heaven has different signs to me . . ."
"Her losses make our gains ashamed . . ."
"Hope is a thing with feathers . . ."
"I cannot dance upon my toes . . ."
"I died for beauty, but was scarce . . ."
"Some keep the Sabbath going to church . . ."
"Speech is one symptom for affection . . ."
"Who is it seeks my pillow nights?"
"Why do they shut me out of Heaven?"
"Wild nights - wild nights . . ."
"Witchcraft was hung in history . . ."
"Your riches taught me poverty . . ."
"You're right - 'the way is narrow' . . ."

Another illuminating feature of Emily's poetic method was that she used slant rhymes, rather than true rhymes. One critic, Richard Aldridge, said of Emily's craft, "Slovenly workmanship. A poetic slattern whose intolerable verses could not even be read until a superior art had tossed a rhyme into them." Ridiculous! Emily knew darn well how to rhyme. But she choose not to, because by the miracle of slanting her rhyme scheme, she gave her poems a spine and spirit which they wouldn't have had with a strict rhyme scheme. Instead of being sing-song, the poems make you stop and listen. Listen to some of her "rhyming pairs": *Fields/steal. Pass/countenance. Bee/die. Cloy/necessity. Blossom/bosom. Human/woman. Heaven/even/given.* She would bend sound so as to rhyme *stars* and *eyes.* Or *pearl* and *fool.* She would disregard the consonant *R*, so that something like *come* and *term* would be acceptable, as would *dark* and *spoke.* And sometimes the *L* was silent: *Speak/talk/folk.* Or ignored completely: *Field/cloud.*

A more prescient critic, Joseph Auslander, said of her work, "The poems dart at beauty and truth with such intensity and dancing magic that nothing seems to matter but the life of them. It is strange, living, true poetry. She wrote of her thoughts and feelings more searchingly and surprisingly than any man or woman since."

In addition to her surprising rhymes, there are some other little stylistic tricks that she used. She liked words to do double duty, so that the same word in the same context could be either a preposition or a verb, or a noun or a verb. In this way, you are kept off-balance; you don't know what's coming next. She also would truncate her words into fragments, using only a piece of a word, to fit the essential sense. Can you imagine what happens to consciousness with all of this? When you don't have that nice, tied-down kind of sound, the mind opens up and is tethered to a star. Emily's poesy explodes the music of consciousness and makes you work harder and give more. It fools your expectations and anticipations. When you are involved in a perfect rhyming scheme, you can almost always, with a little practice, anticipate what is coming. You fall into fatuous self-satisfaction with the rhyme. And because the linguistic area of the left brain is so large, when you fool it and break its patterns, it has to fall into the infinite spaces of the right brain, where space and vision and art and the gods reside. Then you enter into that place where there is no time—there is only eternity and the very stuff of pulsing creation. And that is where poets and artists go to discover their creative form. And there you are gifted with the capacities to re-invent or co-create the world. With this as introduction, let us move to the exercise on poem making.

TIME: ABOUT AN HOUR.

•*MATERIALS:*
Writing materials.

•*MUSIC:*
None.

•*INSTRUCTIONS FOR GOING SOLO:*
Follow this process on a tape you have made of the Guide's instructions. Be sure to read your completed poems aloud.

•*SCRIPT FOR THE GUIDE:*

I want you to first start by just breathing very quietly. Just in and out. Gently and quietly. Just go deep into the pattern of breathing, deep into the repetition of the breathing pattern, moving into quietness, and be present in yourself.

And release your shoulders. Let them drop. Just ease, breathe, and relax. Imagine that you can take your breath to the top of your head and, on the exhale, release and relax. Feel that light tingling up there. Release and relax. And breathe that breath behind your eyes. Let it flood your eyes with *chi*, with vital energy—those eyes that are soon about to see both outward and inward simultaneously. Release and relax your eyes. And let that breath flow now from the front of your eyes to the back of your head where the optic rods and cones are, so you'll really be able to see. Release and relax. And let that beautiful energy flood you. Let the energy, your breath, now flow up into your throat, your voice box, so you can let the *chi* nourish your voice so that you may speak. Release and relax. Now let that breath enter your heart space, awaken your heart. Release and relax. And now let that breath enter your spleen. Release and relax, cleansing. And let it enter now your liver. Release and relax. And take a breath now and let it just go from the top of your head way down to the bottom of your feet, like sand in an hour glass. Release and relax.

How good it feels to be so totally relaxed. So aware, so aware of your body space and where you are in this universe. And in a moment I will ask you to gradually open your eyes and notice something in this room or out the window. Notice all the immediate sensory impressions. Before you can get to the soul, you have to go through the senses. So notice what in this room strikes you. And see it and feel it and be touched by it. Sniff it.

So now open your eyes and take in an object and be aware of it. Or look out the window. And that object is going to be something that means something very important to you. If necessary you may move around to find the right object. You have a minute or two. Now turn to a partner and describe in words what your object was. (One minute.)

See if this will prime the pump even more. I want you to tell your partner what your reaction is in glossolalia. Glossolalia can sound like gibberish or nonsense syllables. "Yaska-lamonte pookah myora metusala!" But include all your vowels, your consonants. Change your inflection. Don't think about what you're saying. Let your glossolalia speech just reach out and grab the sensory impression and express it. This is very effective in disinhibiting your speech patterns, your writing blocks, and bringing a freshness of metaphor. This may give you another level of consciousness, of awareness, when we go back to working in English again. All right, begin describing your impressions in glossolalia. (Three minutes.)

And tell your partner your sensory reactions. And this time include where in your body the impressions reside. How your body feels about this information. You have just disinhibited the cerebral cortex through the use of glossolalia so there can be a fresher use of language, grammar, and metaphor. Now I want you to go back to translating what you just said in glossolalia into English. Be very centered in what you're saying and begin to think in what Emily called "narrow" terms. That means to focus it in.

For the next stage of this process would you please

take up your pencils and papers and write your impressions as a poem or a series of poetic metaphors. If anybody has any trouble getting going, if it is not coming out in a poetic consciousness, write a poem in glossolalia. You can choose right now whether to write in glossolalia or in English. But if you do write it in glossolalia, then be sure to translate it into English. The important thing is to just get those impressions out and on paper. The first thoughts, feelings, associations, relationships, sensations. Get them out. Don't be concerned about editing or whether or not it's good. I'm going to give you exactly five minutes to do this. (Five minutes.)

Now I want you to turn to your partner and read your poems to each other as if you're on the stage of a theater. Really read as if you mean it, with intentionality and fine dramatic flair. If any of you first wrote the poem in glossolalia, then read the glossolalia first, followed by the English "translation."

(After everyone has read their poems to their partners, the Guide will say:)

You may wish to make some minor corrections on things that you might have discovered in your poem while you were reading them aloud. So now go back and make your corrections. (Three minutes.)

Now I want you to think about what you wrote, and in one sentence, or two at the most, tell your partner what your poem is about. Think about it. What did you say in your poem? What was the point you were making? What was the observation? What was the crux of it?

The final step to this process is you're now going to turn into Emily Dickinsons. How would Emily have made that thought into a poem? See what you can do about making the thought that you started out with into something by Emily Dickinson. Remember, she usually wrote in iambic rhythm— ta-DA-ta-DA-ta-DA-ta-DA, with an occasional DA-DA thrown in. The first and third line don't necessarily have to rhyme. They could. The second and fourth are likely to be a slant rhyme where either the vowel is a little different or the consonant is a little different. But not identical. Not *boy/toy, spring/wing*, and so forth. Try to get that slight dissonance in there in the rhyme scheme. I'm going to give you about five minutes to transpose the same thought into a poem that Emily might have written. (Five minutes.)

(After the time is over the Guide will invite the participants to read their two poems aloud to the group. Here is an example of poems composed and read at the Emily Dickinson session of the Mystery School.)

Woman participant:

> *Branches, like children dancing in the sand,*
> *Move in and out of sun and shadows.*
> *Playful, caressing air,*
> *Feathery fingers moving on keys of time -*
> *Yesterday, today and tomorrow.*

And then this is the Emily version:

> *Life a dance, a song, a poem,*
> *Darkness moves through time,*
> *Waits to catch the sun off guard*
> *To enfold it in a shroud.*

Jean: I wrote two in the Emily Dickinson nursery rhyme style. First was "The Fern":

> *I came upon myself one day*
> *Midst ferns and feathers thrown.*
> *I lay my life between the fronds,*
> *The greeny spine my rising poem.*

And the second is:

> *The dog lay sodden on the ground,*
> *She'd drunk of April air.*
> *Her biscuits labored in her blood*
> *That she might run with night.*

Why write poetry in Emily's style? One of the values of enjoying leaky margins and having a persona that can become available to another is that you can avail yourself of some of the impetus for the skill of the other. So that if you play with this technique and enjoy the mind and skill of Emily, you can enter more fully into your own creative matrix with discipline and skill. So Emily serves as the teacher who helps you gain the poet's backbone, which keeps you strong in your writing and helps you not to fall into fuzziness. Because poetry is difficult business. Re-naming, re-claiming the world through speech is a re-orchestration of the mind and its perceptions.

5 Love and Death

In a delightful mystery novel, *The Transcendental Murder*, Jane Langton suggests a possible romantic attachment between Emily Dickinson and Henry Thoreau.[7] Although there is not a shred of actual evidence to suggest that they even knew each other, their sentiments were marvelously close. There he was in Concord, a mere sixty miles away, equally intoxicated, equally ravished by Nature: "To have such sweet impressions made on us, such ecstasies begotten of the breezes! . . .There comes into my mind such an indescribably, infinite, all-absorbing, divine, heavenly pleasure, a sense of elevation and expansion. . .I was daily intoxicated, and yet no man could call me intemperate." As Langton suggests elsewhere:

> Thoreau was often surprised to find himself alone in his intoxication, to discover that Concord's sturdy farmers were still sober. He alone was 'self appointed inspector of snow-storms and rain storms,' going about his business early: 'It is true, I never assisted the sun materially in his rising, but, doubt not, it was of the last importance only to be present at it.' [8]

Like Thoreau, Emily Dickinson felt the importance of her solitary witness. "Nature," she said, "plays without a friend."

> *The Sun went down - no Man looked on -*
> *The Earth and I, alone,*
> *Were present at the Majesty -*

Naturally, then, both find themselves never less at leisure than when at leisure and never less alone then when alone. As Thoreau himself remarked, "Why should I feel lonely? Is not our planet in the Milky Way?" Both Emily and Thoreau pour their revelations into writing, he into precise descriptions of Nature as he found it in Walden Pond, Flint Pond, Fair Haven Bay; she into miraculous poetic recreations of sunsets, bird life, bees and butterflies—all manner of Nature's manifold life.

> *We like March - his shoes are Purple.*
> *He is new and high -*
> *Makes he Mud for dog and Peddler -*
> *Makes he Forests dry -*
> *Knows the Adder's Tongue his coming*

And begets her spot -
Stands the Sun so close and mighty -
That our Minds are hot.

Gods, also goddesses like Dickinson, stain the mind with glory.

During the years 1861 to 1863, when Emily was between thirty and thirty-two or -three, something remarkable happened. Torrents of perfection in the forms of madly original letters and magnificently inventive poems poured out of her. In the year 1862, at age thirty-one, she wrote a poem, generally a masterpiece, each day for 366 days of the year! What happened? The popular literary notion, of course, is that she fell in love. There are reams of pages, caches of clinical studies, and whole gardens of unread doctoral dissertations devoted to speculation about who he or they, or, for several feminist critics, she really was. Was there one love or many, or was Emily simply in love with all and everything most of the time? What happened to this woman, self-described as a "wayward nun," to cause her to write some of the most excruciatingly true and poignant love poetry and love letters of her time? What happened to turn her into a cornucopia of invention? Not that this phenomenon has not happened many times before—witness Dante and his Beatrice; Shakespeare and the Dark Lady of the sonnets; Goethe and a telephone book of people. Love and creativity are always linked. Love is an altered state that renews the seeing of the mind, the responsiveness of the body, the energy of all circuits. In a state of being in love, all systems quite simply are on "go," and you have to tell the whole world about it. If you are a person with a very great skill, love bursts the dam of your mastery and pours out of you a prodigality and depth of expression.

The extant material on Emily Dickinson's love life is skimpy, to say the least. There are three letters to someone she calls "Master," and they are wondrous strange. Imagine being the object of Emily Dickinson's Vesuvial affection and receiving a letter like this:

> Master. . .if I wish with a might I cannot repress—that mine were the Queen's place—the love of the Plantagenet is my only apology—To come nearer than presbyteries—and nearer than the new Coat—that the Tailor made—the prank of the heart at play on the Heart—in holy Holiday—is forbidden me. . .would Daisy disappoint you—no—she wouldn't—sir—it were comfort forever—just to look in your face, while you looked in mine—then I could play in the woods till Dark. . .

From this follows a torrent of elegant and sensuous verses enshrining romance and passion. She thinks of herself as the daisy, following the adored sun:

The Daisy follows soft the Sun -
And when his golden walk is done -
Sits shyly at his feet -
He - waking - finds the flower there -
Wherefore - Marauder - art thou here?
Because, Sir, love is sweet!

We are the Flower - Thou the Sun!
Forgive us, if as days decline -
We nearer steal to Thee!
Enamored of the parting West -
The peace - the flight - the Amethyst -
Night's possibility!

Like a daisy she is utterly tropistic for her love—to love him is almost a reflex. We gather that whoever this Master was, he wrote to her in bewilderment why she should love him. Her answer is enshrined in one of the greatest poems ever of the irrational givenness of the one in love, the absolute subjection to the beloved:

"Why do I love" You, Sir?
Because -
The Wind does not require the Grass
To answer - Wherefore when He pass
She cannot keep Her place . . .

The Lightning - never asked an Eye
Wherefore it shut - when He was by -
Because He knows it cannot speak -
And reasons not contained
- Of Talk -
There be - preferred by Daintier Folk -

The Sunrise - Sir - compelleth Me -
Because He's Sunrise - and I see -
Therefore - Then -
I love Thee -

The ardor grows in Emily. She becomes obsessed, smitten, utterly given over to thoughts of him. She even envies "the Fly, upon His pane," and wishes to be with him always:

Forever at His side to walk -
The smaller of the two!
Brain of His Brain -

Blood of His Blood -
Two lives - One Being - now -

She crosses the mid-Victorian line into a dimension of eros left largely
unexpressed by poets of the time. There is no question that some of
her poems of this period are immensely erotic and sexually explicit:

Come slowly - Eden!
Lips unused to Thee -
Bashful - sip thy Jessamines -
As the fainting Bee -

Reaching late his flower,
Round her chamber hums -
Counts his nectars -
Enters - and is lost in Balms.

Or consider this little wayward nun's extraordinary imagery in "Wild
Nights":

Wild Nights - Wild Nights!
Were I with thee
Wild Nights should be
Our luxury!

Futile - the Winds -
To a Heart in port -
Done with the Compass -
Done with the Chart!

Rowing in Eden -
Ah, the Sea!
Might I but moor - Tonight -
In Thee!

Who did she feel so volcanically potent about? When goddesses love, they don't mess about. Some think it was the brilliant
Philadelphia minister and orator Charles Wadsworth, a happily married man whom she met on a number of occasions, who came to her
house twice, twenty years apart, and then died after the second occasion. Emily corresponded with him over the years on spiritual matters. However, we know that she secreted letters to him—perhaps of
a different persuasion—in envelopes addressed to others. Others suspect that the "Master" letters were really addressed to the wonder-

fully handsome and ebullient Samuel Bowles, editor of *The Spring-field Republican*, who was interested in her work, although he didn't understand it. He published a number of her poems anonymously. He, too, was married, but his wife was exhausted after bearing him ten children. It was to him that Emily spoke, we think, of her willing-ness to wait until joined with him in death, in one of the most curious poems in the collection:

> *Title divine - is mine!*
> *The Wife - without the Sign!*
> *Acute Degree - conferred on me -*
> *Empress of Calvary!*
> *Royal - all but the Crown!*
> *Betrothed - without the swoon*
> *God sends us Women -*
> *When you - hold - Garnet to Garnet -*
> *Gold - to Gold -*
> *Born - Bridalled - Shrouded -*
> *In a Day -*
> *Tri Victory*
> *"My Husband" - women say -*
> *Stroking the Melody -*
> *Is this - the way?*

Married men were safe. With them Emily could enjoy the imagination of love, the title divine of wife, without the worry and the bother of ordinary married life with its dirty dishes and daily drudgeries. She remained, however, in a state she described as "Snow" where any actual physical expression was concerned. Indeed, when Bowles came to visit her after a long absence in which he had been very sick, she refused to come downstairs, much to the consternation of her family and sister. Instead, she sent him a note from her place upstairs, "I cannot see you. You will not less believe me. That you returned to us alive, is better than a Summer and to hear your voice below, than News of any Bird." Here is a man she thought about constantly, and here he is in her house, and that's what she does! On another occasion Bowles came to see her, and again, after shooting downstairs an exquisite missive, she refused to descend to see him. Whereupon he shouted up the stairs, "Emily, you damned wretch! No more of this nonsense! I've travelled all the way from Springfield to see you. Come down at once!" Down she came, and her conversation was reported to have never been more witty. So there. It was just that people didn't really make demands. She had so buried herself in myth that people would not cross the archetypal barrier to reach her, until Samuel Bowles says, "You damned wretch!" That got her.

Her love, we gather, was not returned, and she suffered as only Emily could—those who love greatly always suffer in equal measure. Here is a poem to the one she loves but who probably does not return her affections.

> *You left me - Sire - two Legacies -*
> *A Legacy of Love*
> *A Heavenly Father would suffice*
> *Had He the offer of -*
>
> *You left me Boundaries of Pain -*
> *Capacious as the Sea -*
> *Between Eternity and Time -*
> *Your consciousness - and Me -*

Whatever or whoever the object of her fierce affections was, her state of mind and expression was compounded by her adversarial relationship to God. This anger brought out the ghoul in Emily, something that has caused Camille Paglia to refer to her in a recent book as the Madame de Sade of Amherst. As Paglia points out, she dares God to take her on in his most surgical role.

> *Rearrange a "Wife's" affection!*
> *When they dislocate my Brain!*
> *Amputate my freckled Bosom!*
> *Make me bearded like a man!*

She is separated from the beloved by the jealous God, and she responds in a macabre satire of Christ's nailed feet. After telling how God "took away our Eyes and put us far apart," she tells how:

> *They summoned Us to die*
> *With sweet alacrity*
> *We stood upon our stapled feet -*
> *Condemned - but just to see.*

Her Valentines are ingenious, if grotesque, boasts, "The largest Woman's Heart/Could hold an arrow too." She rages at mortality and the fact that "A single Screw of flesh / Is all that pins the soul." Incarnation in human form is, for a goddess, a perpetual torment; the butterfly—the psyche, which is Greek for "soul"—is pinned to the wall by the lepidopterist God. And as for God, in her anger she commits mayhem on him as well. For as the dying once went to "God's Right Hand," she says, "That Hand is amputated Now/And God cannot be found." This is, of course, the dead hand of law, of old Calvinism devoid of moral substance. In another poem she uses the amputated hand in a way reminiscent of Poe: "Of Heaven above the firmest proof/We fundamental know/Except for its marauding Hand/It had been heaven below."

After her experience with love, Emily shows two natures, both of them heated up—one serene, the other very savage. She builds up thunder waves of imagery. Lightning sears saplings; volcanoes eat villages for breakfast. Nature's lips are hissing corals that open and shut, as cities ooze away. Civilization liquifies at nature's touch. She exclaims profanely to the wintry God, "Go manacle your icicle/Against your Tropic Bride." Then blithely, she tries to forgive him: "Heavenly Father. . .We apologize to thee/For thine own Duplicity." People looking for pathology can find in her exactly what they want. Perhaps the most brilliant pathologist of Dickinson's works is the draconian critic Camille Paglia who seeks to prove Dickinson's "unrecognized appetite for murder and mayhem, her sweet tooth for sadomasochistic horror."[9] A vivisectionist of remarkable clinical power herself, Paglia extolls the ways in which Emily rends the body, strewing it in puncture wounds, twisting it upon a rack, leaving it "bursting like a stoven barrel, gushing red in an apoplectic spout." She writes of Emily's style:

> Protestant hymn-measure is warped and deformed by a stupefying energy. Words are rammed into lines with such force that syntax shatters and collapses into itself. . .The structure cramps and pinches the words like a vise. The poems shudder with a huge tremor of contraction.[10]

In a more conventional vein, Emily's love was surely returned by one person, a newly-made widower, Judge Otis Phillips Lord of Salem, when she was forty-six and he sixty-five. He had been a friend of the family for many years, but upon his wife's death, a most passionate correspondence followed. The fact that this exchange of love letters follows so quickly upon the death of his wife (in a time in which the dead are sanctified and memorialized for a very long mourning period) suggests that both parties had felt strongly about each other for some time. Take this letter of 1878: "My lovely Salem smiles at me. I seek his face so often—but I have done with guises," which suggests that she has concealed her love for him for some time. She continues,

> I confess that I love him—I rejoice that I love him—. . .the exultation floods me. I cannot find my channel—the Creek turns Sea—at thought of thee—. . .Incarcerate me in your-

self—rosy penalty—threading with you this lovely maze, which is not Life or Death—though it has the intangibleness of one, and the flush of the other—waking for your sake on Day made magical with you before I went. . .my Darling come oh be a patriot now—Love is a patriot now Gave her life for its. . .country Has it meaning now—Oh nation of the soul thou hast thy freedom now.

Rough drafts of only fifteen letters remain. There were hundreds of others, but they were destroyed. And of the drafts which remain, all were highly edited by her estate, lest the general populace catch onto the unvarnished passion of Emily set free and running wild in the orchards of love. In Judge Lord she "discovered an intelligence and a capacity for passion that could match her own."[11]

Evidently the relationship assumed the proportions of twelfth-century courtly love; full passion of looking and poetic expression was allowed, but, we gather, it was never consummated. Lord obviously wanted a more intimate relationship, but Emily held back, despite the magnitude of her own desire. Here's her letter of holding back from about 1878:

Dont you know you are happiest while I withhold and not confer - dont you know that No is the wildest word we consign to Language?

You do, for you know all things. . . To lie so near your longing - to touch it as I passed, for I am but a restive sleeper and often should journey from your Arms through the happy night, but you will lift me back, wont you, for only there I ask to be. . .

I will not let you cross - but it is all your's, and when it is right I will lift the Bars, and lay you in the Moss - You showed me the word.

I hope it has no different guise when my fingers make it. It is Anguish I long conceal from you to let you leave me, hungry, but you ask the divine Crust and that would doom the Bread.

Another letter from about 1880:

It is strange that I miss you at night so much when I was never with you - but the punctual love invokes you soon as my eyes are shut - and I wake warm with the want sleep had almost filled - I dreamed last week that you had died - and one had carved a statue of you and I was asked to unveil it - and I said what I had not done in Life I would not in death when your loved eyes could not forgive - . . . . How could I long to give who never saw your natures Face -.

Another letter dated April 30, 1882:

> I do - do want you tenderly. The air is soft as Italy, but when it touches me, I spurn it with a Sigh, because it is not you.[12]

How's that for no? It sounds better than yes. Emily's no's were immense yes's. One wonders how different marriages would be if there were some semblance of premarital chastity, and young people had to express their passion in letters to each other. Can you imagine what would happen in terms of the depth and dimensions of relationships? As in the old courtly love, the tension would remain, but there would be another terrain of psychological and spiritual possibilities between women and men to be explored. That's why I'm disappointed by what occurs in so many movies. The boy and girl meet and almost immediately are in bed together. They've barely had time to exchange names. And then the relationship seems to stay not even on a biological level, but vegetates on a botanical plateau— humans turned into stamens and pistils.

In any case, Lord wanted to marry Emily, but she refused. She had lived so long a recluse in her own private domain, it is doubtful she could have ever made a bride. Also she was the nurse and companion for her mother who had suffered a stroke in 1875, was completely incapacitated, and took seven years to die. Camille Paglia makes another case stating that the idea that

> . . .she could or would have tolerated a single day of abridgment of her monastic autonomy is preposterous. Her letters to Lord are contrived and artificial. The voice belongs to her twittering feminine personae, whom she tucks in becoming postures of devotion. The Lord letters are completely blotted out in emotional intensity by those to the one person with whom she was passionately involved: her sister-in-law Susan. By every standard except the genital, the stormy thirty-five-year relationship between the two women must be called a love affair.[13]

But whatever the reason, one after another, the major friendships and passionate relationships of Emily Dickinson's life all confirmed her deepest conviction: where passion is concerned, there must be separation. I think, however, that we cannot avoid the notion that some of her refusal is bound up with her larger refusal to live in the world and culture of the God of her fathers:

> *I cannot live with You -*
> *It would be Life -*
> *And Life is over there -*
> *Behind the Shelf. . .*
>
> *I could not die - with You -*
> *For One must wait*
> *To shut the Other's Gaze down -*
> *You - could not - . . .*
>
> *Nor could I rise - with You -*
> *Because Your Face*
> *Would put out Jesus'-*
> *That New Grace. . .*
>
> *Because You saturated Sight -*
> *And I had no more Eyes*
> *For sordid excellence*
> *As Paradise*
>
> *And were You lost, I would be -*
> *Though My Name*
> *Rang loudest*
> *On the Heavenly fame -*
>
> *And were You - saved -*
> *And I - condemned to be*
> *Where You were not -*
> *That self - were Hell to Me -*
>
> *So We must meet apart -*
> *You there - I - here -*
> *With just the Door ajar*
> *That Oceans are - and Prayer -*
> *And that White Sustenance -*
> *Despair -*

As we know, almost nothing of hers was published in her lifetime—only seven poems in all, and most of those published anonymously. The male editors of magazines would not, could not understand her. At the time of her greatest need, when she was for the period of a year suffering from a disorder in her eyes, and getting no return to her love letters, she read an article in *The Atlantic Monthly* by Thomas Wentworth Higginson, which was written as an encouragement to any "mute inglorious Miltons" who were reading the journal. He was astonished by the "wonderful effusions that landed on my desk." But the most wonderful of all was the letter from Emily that began, "Are you too deeply occupied to say if my Verse is alive?" Higginson wrote back, and their correspondence lasted for the rest of her life. As an adviser, sadly, he failed her. He found her poems too bizarre and advised her not to publish. But at least she had found a willing listener in the literary world. She called him her "Preceptor." She told him that his correspondence to her was like a hand stretched to her in the dark.

What is it like for a vastly creative person who practices her art with diligence never to be seen or known? At a certain point, such a one falls into either numbness or raging pain. You go through life as a mask/masque, but you feel nothing.

> *I tie my Hat - I crease my Shawl -*
> *Life's little duties do - precisely -*
> *As the very least*
> *Were infinite - to me -*
>
> *I put new Blossoms in the Glass -*
> *And throw the old - away -*
> *I push a petal from my Gown*
> *That anchored there - I weigh*
> *The time 'twill be till six o'clock*
> *I have so much to do -*
> *And yet - Existence - some way back -*
> *Stopped - struck - my ticking - through.*

How do you survive with such in-grown passion and despair if you are a genius? You do what Emily finally did. You craft your life to become a myth. In 1881 young Mabel Loomis Todd had been living for two months in Amherst where her husband was appointed head of the College Observatory. On November 6, 1881, she wrote her parents an excited letter about the town's most interesting citizen:

> I must tell you about the character of Amherst. It is a lady whom the people call the Myth. She is a sister of Mr. Dickinson, & seems to be the climax of all the family oddity. She has not been outside of her own house in fifteen years, except once to see a new church, when she crept out at night, & viewed it by moonlight. No one who calls upon her

mother & sister ever see her, but she allows the little children once in a great while, & one at a time, to come in, when she gives them cake or candy, or some nicety, for she is very fond of little ones. But more often she lets down the sweetmeat by a string, out of a window, to them. She dresses wholly in white, & her mind is said to be perfectly wonderful. She writes finely, but no one ever sees her. Her sister, who was at Mrs. Dickinson's party, invited me to come & sing to her mother sometime. . . .People tell me the myth will hear every note—she will be near, but unseen . . . . Isn't that like a book? So interesting.[14]

So interesting it became for Mabel Loomis Todd that she was the one who compiled and edited the first batch of Emily's poems for publication after her death, as well as later editions of new poems as they became available. She also became the mistress of Emily's brother Austin. Emily's sister Lavinia had given Emily's letters to Austin's wife, Susan Gilbert, to whom Emily wrote constantly and for whom, as Camille Paglia noted, she felt Vesuvial affection. Ironically, Susan never got around to doing anything with them. Lavinia felt the urgency and gave them to Mabel Todd, who did a tremendous job. She deciphered Emily's difficult handwriting, pieced together the sequences of poems and letters and, all in all, did the incredible archival work of harvesting Emily's genius and arranging for its publication. Amazingly, she was never permitted to meet the reclusive Emily! Perhaps Emily already sensed her coming destiny in Mabel and maintained for her the mythic stance that would eventually provoke such arduous devotions. Mabel Todd lived a long life of many years in service of Emily. This editorial and publishing service continued in her daughter.

Creating her life as a myth, as an allegory, was so successful that it may have been Emily's greatest poem—a series of Mysteries, which forever invite the reader to participate in them. They were female Mysteries at that, exploring the characteristics and constraints of nineteenth-century womanhood so as to transform and even transcend them. Mysteries are rites of passion, rites of death and resurrection. They are mystical possibilities that pull you towards becoming a person who is larger than your aspirations, richer and more complex than all your dreams. This is the task of the Mystery—to take one beyond the confines of one's little local self into the possibility of the universal self—one who participates in the passion and pathos of the gods.

Emily did that. The ancient mysteries—the Eleusinian Mysteries and Orphic Mysteries, the Mysteries of Isis and Osiris—all have to do with joining your life to Great Life, identifying with archetypal life itself. Within the Mystery tradition we both die and are resurrected with the god. But Emily went one further. She invented her own story of Great Life, her own Mystery, and then lived within the demands of its archetypal structure. She became her own Demeter and Persephone.

Hers is, first of all, the Mystery of an Intelligence that Confounds Local Time and Space—which then refuses confinement in that time and space. She said, "I will transform time and space." We see her practice this Mystery when she gets up in front of the blackboard not knowing her Euclid but then creates her own Euclid and proves the theorem. We also see it when she is the only one who refuses to stand up when everyone else is attesting to their conversion. Most especially we see it in her poetry of transcending time, of erasing space. Witness what she does with time:

> *Long Years apart - can make no*
> *Breach a second cannot fill -*
> *The absence of the Witch does not*
> *Invalidate the spell -*
>
> *The embers of a Thousand Years*
> *Uncovered by the Hand*
> *That fondled them when they were Fire*
> *Will stir and understand -*

Then there are her whimsies with *space*:

> *Perhaps I asked too large -*
> *I take - no less than skies -*
> *For Earths, grow thick as*
> *Berries, in my native town -*
>
> *My Basket holds - just - Firmaments -*
> *Those - dangle easy - on my arm,*
> *But smaller bundles - Cram.*

(Once, long ago, I knew Aldous Huxley. Emily would have loved him and known him for her own. He was six foot five, beautiful like an archangel, with strange opaque eyes misted over by cataract, that barely saw the local world, but seemed to look into the future. When he came to the door to visit me—I was twenty-one—he looked like a luminary drawn by William Blake, like an average man from the future. When I saw him I could understand how he had to write about life as Mystery, because that is what he was. He seemed a graduate student from a higher world taking notes on this one. To me he confounded local time and space.)

A second mystery for Emily is the Mystery of the Eternal Child. She maintains the perceptions and the gifts of childhood after all her contemporaries have lost them. She is neoteny personified, the *puella aeternus*. But like the wise and smirking child, she fathoms all the secrets of her elders. Her genius is to understand the mystery and magic of childhood and to take all steps necessary never to lose it. If we can see the child as that intersection between cosmology and biology, we can appreciate Emily's exaltation in combining the two.

Her War with God also counts as a major Mystery. In this she is not unlike the ancient gnostics who refused to honor the local Johnny-come-lately deity of tribe and nation, and who held out instead for a god worthy of their own imagination and aspirations:

> *The Soul selects her own Society -*
> *Then - shuts the Door -*
> *To her divine Majority -*
> *Present no more -*

Like a gnostic too, she is ever suspicious of the local culture-bound God, saying, "God was penurious with me, which makes me shrewd with Him." Her shrewdness and dislike takes the form of guerilla warfare on God, fracturing his finest concepts, blowing up his follies for all to see. Then with cosmic pen in hand, she rewrites his script, his scripture, and blows a new breath of creation upon the chaos of the world.

There are other Mysteries as well: the Mystery of Excruciating Sensitivity, her nuclear soul filling her body with a kind of radiation sickness, her flesh perpetually on fire with its perceptions. As she tells her preceptor Thomas Wentworth Higginson: "If I read a book and it makes my whole body so cold no fire ever can warm me I know that is poetry. If I feel physically as if the top of my head were taken off, I know that is poetry. These are the only way I know it. Is there any other way?" Her feelings for others could be so intense that she can send a message across the grass to her beloved sister-in-law Susan: "For the Woman whom I prefer, Here is Festival—Where my Hands are cut, Her fingers will be found inside." Even death, she feels, will not desensitize her. Rather, will she drop "Down, and down—/And hit a World, at every plunge."

Emily also lived the Mystery of the Missing Lover. Who was it or who were they who released all that passion in her? Though many have investigated and theorized about it, that is a Mystery to remain unsolved, "No Trace - no Figment of the Thing/That dazzled. . ."

And finally, we have the Mystery of the Muse—the Mystery of Creation itself. How did so much creation happen in one person? This is the Mystery of a person of enormous gifts, born in the right time and right place, and with just the right self-imposed restraints to effect a cataclysm of invention when just the right torch is applied. But that's pedestrian thinking. Emily would scoff at its reasoning. By her own words, she has been godded, enchanted, made magical. The dark Goddess Herself has claimed her for Her own:

> *I think I was enchanted*
> *When first a sombre Girl -*
> *I read that Foreign Lady -*
> *The Dark - felt beautiful -*
>
> *And whether it was noon at night -*
> *Or only Heaven - at Noon -*
> *For very Lunacy of Light*
> *I had not power to tell -*
>
> . . .
>
> *The Days - to Mighty Metres stept -*
> *The Homeliest - adorned*
> *As if unto a Jubilee*
> *'Twere suddenly confirmed -*
>
> *I could not have defined the change -*
> *Conversion of the Mind*
> *Like Sanctifying in the Soul -*
> *Is witnessed - not explained -*
>
> *'Twas a Divine Insanity -*
> *The Danger to be Sane*
> *Should I again experience -*
> *'Tis Antidote to turn -*
>
> *To tomes of solid Witchcraft -*
> *Magicians be asleep -*
> *But Magic - hath an Element*
> *Like Deity - to keep -*

In spite of being unpublished, Emily saw to it that her poems and letters went winging everywhere. She'd write to famous men, and they would be so bemused by her originality that they all would answer her. She daily wrote potent loving letters to her sister-in-law Susan Gilbert, who lived only three hundred feet away. She wrote to the famous novelist Helen Hunt Jackson, author of the popular novel *Ramona*, who alone among her correspondents recognized her genius. Again and again she asked for Emily's poems and urged her to publish. "It is a cruel wrong to your day & generation that will not give them light." In another letter she wrote, "You are a great poet—and it is a wrong to the day you live in, that you will not sing aloud. When you are what men call dead, you will be sorry you were so stingy."[15] She rightly prophesied in the same letter, however, that later generations will know all about her, and her poems will reside in many hearts. Maybe Emily knew this when she wrote:

> *This is my letter to the World*
> *That never wrote to Me -*
> *The simple News that Nature told -*
> *With tender Majesty*
>
> *Her message is committed*
> *To Hands I cannot see -*
> *For love of Her - Sweet - countrymen -*
> *Judge tenderly - of Me*

It all ended, finally, in the Mystery of Death—a theme that looms so large in Emily's thinking and writing. Death was her neighbor. There was a cemetery behind the house where she lived between the ages of nine and twenty-four. And funeral processions were a regular occurrence on the Main Street down from her window. All her life she was forever predicting, anticipating, and looking forward to her own death. Death was the ultimate lover, the final Mystery, the one who would finally seduce her, as she says in one of her grandest poems:

> *Because I could not stop for Death -*
> *He kindly stopped for me -*
> *The Carriage held but just Ourselves -*
> *And Immortality.*
>
> *We slowly drove - He knew no haste*
> *And I had put away*
> *My labor and my leisure too,*
> *For His Civility -*
>
> *We passed the School, where Children strove*
> *At Recess - in the Ring -*
> *We passed the Fields of Gazing Grain -*
> *We passed the Setting Sun -*
>
> *Or rather - He passed Us -*
> *The Dews drew quivering and chill -*

For only Gossamer, my Gown -
My Tippet - only Tulle -
We passed before a House that seemed
A Swelling of the Ground -
The Roof was scarcely visible -
The Cornice - in the Ground -

Since then - 'tis Centuries - and yet
Feels shorter than the Day
I first surmised the Horses' Heads
Were toward Eternity -

Emily died of Bright's disease—kidney failure that included dizziness, hypertension, and dropsy—on May 15, 1886. Her last letter written a few hours before she died to her young relatives went, "Little Cousins. Called Back. Emily." At her funeral she looked wonderfully young and finally at peace. Within a few days, her sister Lavinia opened her box of poems and discovered the priceless treasure hidden there. Emily was launched again into the world and time, and poetry turned a corner. She had wrestled long and hard with God and won. She gave a new ordering to reality and rewrote the priorities. As she says:

I reckon - when I count at all -
First - Poets - Then the Sun -
Then Summer - then the Heaven of God -
And then - the List is done -

But, looking back - the First so seems
To Comprehend the Whole -
The Others look a needless Show -
So I write - Poets - All -

PROCESS 4
SEEING YOUR LIFE AS MYSTERIES

For many years now I've been presenting great myths as Mysteries. We enter into the life of a great mythical figure, which then encourages us to explore the Mysteries of our own life. We then begin to see that our lives have indeed been a series of Mysteries. Have you had Mysteries in your life similar to those we find in Emily? Have you lived the Mystery of an Intelligence that Confounds Local Time and Space? Have you had the Mystery of the Missing Lover? (In this case *missing* may mean that the lover has never showed up or that you have never recognized who or what it was.) Maybe you've been living the Mystery of the Beloved of the Soul, a beloved presence in the archetypal realm like Christ or St. Francis or the god-self within. Have you had a Mystery of a Muse and found yourself caught up in a creative process in which you seem to be the vehicle for some writing or painting or project that feels as if it is writing or painting or producing itself? What have been some of your other Mysteries? And what have you done about them? Have you allowed yourself to go marvelously eccentric? Or have you pretended to be utterly "normal" for too long? Remember that what you call a "normal" person is probably somebody that you don't know very well. To remythologize your life by seeing it as a Passion Play and a series of Mysteries is a phenomenal act of re-invention. This is what Emily Dickinson did, and this is what we will attempt a beginning at doing now.

TIME: NINETY MINUTES TO TWO HOURS.

● MATERIALS:

Each participant should have a journal or notebook for the first part of this process. And for the second part, a room will be set up as a Mystery Temple. That means that it should be a darkened room with ample space within which to move. Candles will be placed throughout the room as described below. The room should also be set up with an altar at one end. Participants will be asked to bring a sacred object to place on this altar. A candle in a beautiful candle holder could be placed in the center of this altar. Fresh flowers to decorate the room would also be a fine idea, as would any other decorations that give a sense of sacrality to the space.

● MUSIC:

Meditative background music from Area One for the first part. The second part should have music that gives a sense of sacred

procession into the Mysteries, like the first part of Vangelis'
Ignacio and, finally, stately but celebrational music such as
Pachelbel's *Canon in D*.

•*INSTRUCTIONS FOR GOING SOLO:*

For this process you will need to follow the instructions in this
book and respond to the question of the Mysteries of your life
by writing in your journal. Perform the concluding process of
entering into the final Mystery by preparing your setting carefully, following the given directions.

•*SCRIPT FOR THE GUIDE:*

PART ONE

To begin would everyone please get a partner and
then sit down together. We are about to enter upon the
enchantments of Emily Dickinson as a guide to our own Mysteries. Drawing from the Mysteries in her life, we will uncover
related Mysteries in our own. We will draw upon the ancient
Mystery tradition wherein one enters into that part of oneself
that is eternal.

Now would each of you touch hands with your partner, breathing slowly and deeply in unison for several minutes,
setting up a resonance of breath, touch, and empathy. (Two
minutes.)

Now decide who will be the first questioner and who
the first answerer. Each of you will now review silently the
Mysteries of your life, those aspects of your life that seem to
transcend ordinary analysis or explanation, but which rather
show you to be a citizen in a universe far more interesting and
complex and magical than the one you were taught to believe
in. I will name the Mysteries of Emily, and as I do, you will
allow whatever thoughts or memories that you have around as
they relate to your own life to rise into consciousness.

(The Guide names the Mysteries of Emily Dickinson
and pauses between each to give the participants time to
reflect on them.)

The Mystery of the Eternal Child. . . The Mystery of
an Intelligence that Confounds Local Time and Space. . .The
Mystery of the Beloved of the Soul. . .The Mystery of the War
with God or War with Fundamentalist or Absolute Principles
. . .The Mystery of the Muse and of Creativity itself. . . And
then, the Mystery of Eternity, of the Beyond Within. . . .

I am now going to give you a series of questions dealing with these Mysteries in your life. The first questioner will
repeat the question after I give it, and the first answerer will

answer. At the end of five minutes, you will switch, and the person who has been answering the question will ask the other the same question. Again there will be five minutes for responding. Then I will ask each of you to write something that is a word or a symbol that came out of your understanding of the questions. At the end of this process we will do something very Emily-like with these words or symbols.

I will repeat this process for each question. If the person who is answering finishes before the five minutes are up, then the questioner will repeat the question so that the answerer may enlarge upon his or her response. It is essential that you who are asking the question maintain your capacity to listen as high witness, with no commentary, no matter what you hear.

The first question will deal with the ways we either had or continue to have the high sensitivity and perceptions of childhood. So the question is: "Tell me, what in your life has reflected the Mystery of the Eternal Child?" Questioner, repeat this question to your partner.

(After five minutes.) Now will the person who has been answering ask the same question of his or her partner: "Tell me what in your life has reflected the Mystery of the Eternal Child?" (Five minutes.)

Now will each of you take a minute and write in your journal or notebook some specific image that sums up the experience of this Mystery. For example, if you experienced as a child the universe in a fig tree, you might write something like "fig tree blazing god in the sun." Find a specific word or words or a symbol or image that comes out of your answer that gives the essence of your experience. (One minute.)

And now the second question deals with an intelligence that confounds local time and space. This refers to knowing things which seemingly you never have been taught, things of the mind or the heart or the spirit that seem to come to you from a higher mind, a deeper spirit. So the question is: "Tell me, what in your life has reflected the Mystery of an Intelligence that Confounds Local Time and Space?"

(After five minutes.) Now will the person who has been answering become the questioner and ask the same question: "Tell me what in your life has reflected the Mystery of an Intelligence that Confounds Local Time and Space?" (Five minutes.)

Find a specific word or symbol or image that comes out of your answer that can be used to give the essence or summation of this Mystery in your life. Try to find as concrete an image as you can. And write it down next to the first image or symbol. (One minute.)

Now for the third question, the one that deals with the missing lover, or with the Beloved of the Soul sensed as that inner beloved with whom one feels a yearning or a communion. This mystery can deal with either a human or an archetypal beloved, or both, as it did in the case of Emily. So the question is, "Tell me what in your life has reflected the Mystery of the Beloved of the Soul?"

(After five minutes.) Now will the person who has been answering become the questioner and ask the same question: "Tell me what in your life has reflected the Mystery of the Beloved of the Soul?" (Five minutes.)

Find a specific word or symbol of image that came out of your answer that can be used to give the essence or summation of this Mystery in your life. Try to find as concrete an image as you can. And write it down next to the previous images or symbols. (One minute.)

Now for the fourth question, the one that deals with one's personal war with the "god" or one's contentions with narrow notions of reality that family or society tried to make you believe. This question therefore deals with absolutist or fundamentalist positions that one refused to agree to. It could be referring to education or politics as much as to theology or morality or other perspectives on reality. So the question is: "Tell me, what in your life has reflected the Mystery of the War with God or War with Fundamentalist or Absolutist Principles?"

(After five minutes.) Now will the person who has been answering become the questioner and ask the same question: "Tell me what in your life has reflected the Mystery of the War with God or War with Fundamentalist or Absolutist Principles?" (Five minutes.)

Find a specific word or symbol of image that came out of your answer that can be used to give the essence or summation of this Mystery in your life. Try to find as concrete an image as you can. And write it down next to the previous images or symbols. (One minute.)

Now for the fifth question, the one that deals with the Mystery of the Muse and of Creativity itself. This mystery refers to times in one's life when a creative project, or writing, or idea or even a way of seeing and understanding things seemed so inspired that you felt yourself to be seized by the very process of creativity itself, in partnership with the Muse. So the question is: "Tell me what in your life has reflected the Mystery of the Muse and of Creativity itself?"

(After five minutes.) Now will the person who has been answering become the questioner and ask the same question: "Tell me what in your life has reflected the Mystery of the Muse and of Creativity itself?" (Five minutes.)

Find a specific word or symbol of image that came out of your answer that can be used to give the essence or summation of this Mystery in your life. Try to find as concrete an image as you can. And write it down next to the previous images or symbols. (One minute.)

Now for the sixth and final question, the one that deals with the Mystery of Eternity. This refers to those times when you have felt yourself part of an immortal life, as if all of time and space and knowledge and experience were contained within you, or you yourself were held within an infinite presence. For some this has been a mystical experience, one of cosmic consciousness, for others an experience of the love that moves the universe. It can take many different forms. So the question is: "Tell me what in your life has reflected the Mystery of Eternity, of the Beyond Within?"

(After five minutes.) Now will the person who has been answering become the questioner and ask the same question: "Tell me what in your life has reflected the Mystery of Eternity, of the Beyond Within?" (Five minutes.)

Find a specific word or symbol of image that came out of your answer that can be used to give the essence or summation of this Mystery in your life. Try to find as concrete an image as you can. And write it down next to the previous images or symbols. (One minute.)

Now would everyone thank their partners for the mysteries they have shared. And after you both have done this, please stand up and stretch before sitting down together again.

I am going to ask you now to look at the images for each of the six Mysteries that you have written down and begin to think of them as stages in the passion play or greater Mystery drama of your own life. Would you now talk with your partner about how you might see these images as reflecting the drama of your life. In this case the Mysteries do not have to be seen as in a series or in any particular order, but rather as emerging at any stage of your life as revealing something of the true Mystery of your existence. You will have ten minutes to pursue this reflection on your images with each other. (Ten minutes.)

Now in the spirit and craft of Emily Dickinson, who made of her life a poem and a Mystery and of her poems a life, I want each of you to use these images and others that may have subsequently occurred to you in writing a poem. You will write a poem, or poetic lines using these images to reflect the Mystery of your life. You might even like to use as a working title, "My Life as Mystery." You have twenty minutes or so to work on the poem. (Twenty to thirty minutes.)

(The Guide will then invite the participant to share with their partners and then with the group the poems of the Mystery of their life which they have written. Here is an example of a poem written during this process at Mystery School:)

Woman participant:

> *Clapping hands in birthday party wonder,*
> *I dive into making Me up as I go along:*
> *Though writing/speaking others mirror clearly,*
> *Zippy brain building now intuition muscles,*
> *While birthing books, with midwife's pride,*
> *Saying Father God NO, Buddha nature heartfelt*
> > *YES,*
> *Seeking Goddess essence, my inner Madonna—*
> *What glee, the Mystery maze of Me!*

PART TWO

(Note to the Guide: This second part of the process may be done in the same or in a different room which has been prepared during the break with candles as well as flowers and a table serving as an altar upon which participants will place their poems and sacred objects. Place four to six candles to mark a threshold about two-thirds of the way across the length of the room. Place four to six candles to mark the edges of the room. Place the remaining candles, one for each participant where they are easily accessible on a table at one end of the room. At the other end of this room stands the altar. It is towards this end that the participants will be moving. After the room is prepared and the candles are lit, the Guide will welcome the participants back and instruct each of them to give the Guide their poems and sacred objects which she or he then places on the altar. The Guide then asks participants to pick up a candle from the table. The Guide then moves to the place in the room where the candles are placed across the threshold and says:)

Will you all please gather at the end of the room. In the ancient Mysteries there was often a ritual walk in which the member of the Mysteries crossed a threshold to a realm of amplified power, sometimes thought to be the place of the god or of the Beloved, sometimes thought to be where the greater Mysteries resided. This ritual was performed in the dark and often with the initiates carrying light. As they walked across the threshold, they knew that they were entering the realm of a Mystery too great to be described. What Mystery was it? Perhaps it was all the other Mysteries combined, perhaps it was the Mystery of death and of immortality. Whatever it was, we know that the celebrants experienced it as something similar to what Emily meant when she referred to a "lunacy of light."

We will soon begin to walk very very slowly, as slowly as each of you can, towards the line of candles. With each step you will be communing with the Mysteries of your life. Think of the candle that you hold as the symbol of the Mysteries of your life, your particular lunacy of light. And as you move very slowly in space, you move very deeply within, to that place known as "the beyond within" which holds all Mysteries known and unknown.

And then, at a certain point, where I stand, as you pass over the line of fire, you know that you are passing into the realm of amplified power and spirit, the realm of the ultimate Mystery that is calling you. Who or what you will find there will be a Mystery known only to yourself. It may be the Beloved of the Soul. It may be the next unfolding Mystery of your life. Once you are there, you will find yourself a place facing the altar upon which lay your poems and sacred objects. There you will sit down, place your candle in front of you, and enter into communion with the Mystery. Know this to be the place of the communion of the self with its deeper meaning, its higher mystery.

Let the walk begin.

(The music begins. During the walk the Guide continues to stand as witness in the center of the line of fire, acknowledging with a nod each person as they cross the line. When all have crossed over, and after some minutes of communion have gone by the Guide continues:)

Know yourself now to have entered upon the greater Mystery of your life. May this Mystery illumine, protect, support, guide, and sustain you in all the days to come. And may you enter from this day forth into living the larger life that is yours.

(The music changes at this point to stately but celebrational music like Pachelbel's *Canon in D*. As the music continues, the participants are invited to perform a dance honoring the Mystery in each other, bowing and exchanging candles as they dance. At the end of this the Guide might say:)

Now blow this lunacy of light into your hearts, that it may kindle a life lived to its fullest in the Mystery of being human.

(At this point, all blow out their candles.)

NOTES

[1]All poetry of Emily Dickinson from *The Poems of Emily Dickinson,* 3 vols., ed. Thomas Johnson (Cambridge, MA: Harvard University Press, 1951, 1955).

[2]Allen Tate, *Six American Poets from Emily Dickinson to the Present: An Introduction* (Bloomington, MN: University of Minnesota Press, 1971).

[3]Throughout the text Emily Dickinson's letters are quoted from *The Letters of Emily Dickinson,* 3 vols., ed. Thomas Johnson (Cambridge, MA: Harvard University Press, 1958). Readers interested in a selection of Emily Dickinson's letters may wish to consult *Emily Dickinson, Selected Letters* (Cambridge, MA: The Belknap Press of Harvard University Press, 1986).

[4]Jerry Griswold, *Audacious Kids: Coming of Age in America's Classic Children's Books* (New York: Oxford University Press, 1992).

[5]Cynthia G. Wolff, *Emily Dickinson* (New York: Penguin, 1989) p. 87.

[6]James Hillman, *The Myths of Analysis: Three Essays in Archetypal Psychology* (New York: Harper & Row, 1983).

[7]Jane Langton, *The Transcendental Murder* (New York: Penguin, 1989).

[8]Jane Langton, "Appreciation," in *Acts of Light,* Burkert and Langton (Boston: New York Graphic Society, 1980), p. 14.

[9]Camille Paglia, *Sexual Personae: Art and Decadence from Nefertiti to Emily Dickinson* (New Haven, CT: Yale University Press, 1990).

[10]Ibid., p. 624.

[11]Wolff, p. 401.

[12]All three letters are quoted in Wolff, p. 402.

[13]Paglia, p. 670.

[14]This letter is quoted in Sandra Gilbert's article, "The Wayward Nun beneath the Hill: Emily Dickinson and the Mysteries of Womanhood," in Suzanne Juhasz, ed., *Feminist Critics Read Emily Dickinson* (Bloomington, IN: Indiana University Press, 1983), pp. 22-44.

[15]Wolff, p. 509.

INTRODUCTION

In studying and thinking about Thomas Jefferson, I would paraphrase a statement once made by Isaac Newton about his own pursuit of knowledge: the more we increase the island of our knowledge about Jefferson, the more we enlarge the shoreline of our wonder. There is so much in his thought, his ideals, and his accomplishment that exceeds all normal human understanding. In his light and in his shadows, too, he is the archetypal American—the American writ large. A wonderful mix of idealism and practicality, of formidable productiveness and deep but sparkling reflections on the nature of the human experiment has made of him the model who can never be copied, the man for all seasons and all years.

Even a summary of some of his achievements exceeds all known summaries of lives. Consider the words of one of his biographers Saul Padover:

> No man in this or any other country in the Western world—excepting Leonardo de Vinci—ever matched Jefferson in the range of his activities, in the fertility of his thinking, and in the multiplicity of his interests. The number of things Jefferson did, or knew how to do, still astonishes. He was a mathematician, surveyor, architect, paleontologist, prosodist, lawyer, philosopher, farmer, fiddler, and inventor. He set up an educational system; he built a university; he founded a great political party; he helped

design the national capital; he was instrumental in establishing America's coinage; he doubled the territory of the
United States; he invented machines and gadgets; he col-
lected scientific materials in the fields of zoology, geology
and anthropology; he wrote a classic essay on poetry; he
codified the legal system of his native State. Everything interested him; nothing was alien to his mind.

One of the principal builders of the American
Republic, Jefferson held nearly every important public
office and enriched them all with his wisdom, humanity and
democratic spirit. He was a member of Congress, Governor
of his State, Ambassador, Secretary of State, Vice President
and President twice. Author of the Declaration of Independence and of Virginia's famous statute for religious freedom,
as well as founder of the Democratic Party, Jefferson may be
considered as a kind of political poet in action.[1]

I'm reminded too of those wonderful words of John F.
Kennedy when he honored a group of White House guests, including
winners of the Nobel Prize. "We have not had such a gathering of
intellect and talent here," he said, "since Thomas Jefferson dined
alone."

However accurate Mr. Padover's summary, his praise would
have embarrassed and even offended Mr. Jefferson, for he would have
probably warned us in his truthful way that if we would but go
deeper, sink the scalpel beneath the veneer of his accomplishments,
the paradoxes would rise. Consider the fact that Jefferson as author
of the Declaration of Independence wrote the words "that all men
are created equal, that they are endowed by their Creator with certain inalienable rights, that among these are Life, Liberty and the pursuit of happiness." This same man was also an owner of many slaves
on his plantations in Virginia. Consider how many times he de-
nounced the institution of slavery as "infamous," and yet when one of
his slaves ran away in 1769, he offered a reward for his capture, and
when his prize cook, a quadroon (which means one-quarter black)
and his dead wife's half-brother, wanted to stay in France where there
was no such thing as slavery when Jefferson was ambassador there,
he persuaded the man to come back with him to Monticello.

As a true paradoxicalist, everybody—liberals and conservatives—can claim him as their patron saint, because in his voluminous
writings, the possibilities for identification with him are infinite. He
was the leader of a view that limited the territory of the early Republic to the given states, the thirteen colonies, yet as President, his was
the hand behind the Louisiana Purchase, which more than doubled
the United States' land mass. His was a radically innovative mind in
both politics and scholarship, but he was also a classical scholar
devoted to ancient Greek and Roman models of art and philosophy.

Indeed, when modern Washington was being planned, he scrapped the innovative architecture and city planning offered in favor of a city that looked back to ancient Athens and Rome—and that is just what we got. He appeared in public to be something of an atheist—he loathed churchmen, having had largely unhappy experiences of them as his teachers as a young boy—but in his private ruminations was passionately devoted to the ethical principles of Jesus and even wrote a new New Testament with all miracles and such deleted.

His private morals were of the highest, the most scrupulous, the most exacting; indeed they seemed to be written on his heart. In France he was shocked by Ben Franklin's extraordinary romantic successes in his late seventies with some of the great women of France. But when confronted, after his wife's death, with the beautiful but married painter Maria Cosway, he probably had an affair with her. There is also the belief, brilliantly explored by Fawn Brodie and others, that he fathered a number of children—maybe five, maybe six—by Sally Hemings, his wife's half-sister, but a slave. He detested England after all of the colonial struggles and revolution but recommended their form of parliamentary government to the European people he loved the most—the French, who also shared his Anglophobia. And his heroes were all English—Bacon, Newton, and Locke.

He was frequently a model of simplicity in clothes and habits; in fact he walked to his inauguration as President from where he was staying in a boarding house. Indeed, when he came back, he assumed his usual place at the end of the table, furthest away from the fire and the first helpings of food. But he also built Monticello, the most elegant house and grounds in America, and apportioned to himself the most lavish of ambassadorial quarters in Paris. Surrounded by the country's aristocrats as his closest friends and associates, he warned against any growth of aristocratic governance and spoke constantly for the the empowerment of the people. He cherished hopes for the "perfectibility of man," yet wrote about general elections, "I have ever observed that a choice by the people themselves is not generally distinguished for its wisdom. . . .The first secretion from them is generally crude. . . ." Clearly he distrusted the popular judgment.

He always saw the broad picture and was consummately aware of patterns of history—that is, both history that was and history that was to come—and yet he kept the most scrupulously detailed notes on every item of his life. No concept was too immense and no detail too small for him to note down and reflect upon. Both his wrists were broken and ill mended, but we have more than eighteen thousand letters and phenomenal numbers of documents extant from him in his own hand. He acted constantly but believed that silence and reflection was the best policy.

As a father he was enormously kind, patient, and appreciative but demanded of his daughters a regimen in some ways equal to his own if they wanted his love. He loved his wife more than anything in the world but kept her pregnant even though she grew weaker with each pregnancy and finally died of childbirth complications after ten years of marriage. His energies and health were phenomenal, but he would suffer from migraine headaches and dysentery after periods of excessive stress that would leave him devastated sometimes for months on end. Frugal in many of his habits, he was the prince of shopping and regarded the whole world as a vast catalog of delights for purchase. Whenever he moved in the course of his work, the packing that attended him was epic. He was happier at his home than anywhere else but was constantly being called away from it while telling everyone that he lived to be home again. He was an addict for facts and a devotee of pure speculation.

What does this all say to us today in the light of modern knowings? It says that here was an artist of the possible, a true creator who balanced polarities in order to bring higher form into the world. As one important student of his, Alf Mapp, has pointed out in *Thomas Jefferson: A Strange Case of Mistaken Identity*:

> By observing Jefferson as his creative imagination is shaped and reshaped, we can detect patterns amid the apparent chaos. Sometimes when he seems to be shifting from left to right and back again with no consistency, he is actually spiralling upward to another plane of understanding and the movements to left or right are purely incidental. . . .We can only look at him from different angles in a great many lights, for his is the iridescence of the butterfly or moth whose wings may be purple from one view, green from another, and bronze from a third. Yet who can say that each perception is not valid or that all are not valid simultaneously? [2]

I will go further and suggest that in looking closely at Thomas Jefferson, we have front row seats on the very nature and practice of creation. We see how the creation of a microcosm—a man—can also be the creation of a macrocosm—a nation; how cosmos—great order—comes from chaos, and how chaos and paradox creates sufficient stimulation to move everything into a whole new dynamic regime. I also believe that what was occurring with and through Thomas Jefferson is resonant with what is trying to occur through each one of us now on the scale of the emerging world order. True, we may not have his felicity of expression, nor the focused passion of a specific just cause, not even the warm sapiential circles of high-minded compatriots all dedicated to working collectively to put their finest efforts to the great task at hand. We may not even know what our task is. But we have something deeper and just as important. We are citizens in a new cosmos in which all of the currents of history are present, trying to reconcile themselves to a point that, I believe, is the end of history as ideology and as dialectical counterpoint to economic or political -isms and -ologies.

We also have the liberation of all peoples, the end of all slaveries, both obvious and subtle, and the birth of an opportunity that exceeds our imagination. And yet, all oppression rises in our time, and factors unique in human history arise around us to compound our folly and confuse our desire. We yearn for meaning and deal with trivia. We are swept in currents over which we have no control. Government has become too big for the small problems of life and too small in spirit for the large problems. The tyranny that threatens to destroy us is not the English battering our shores with unjust demands; it is the tyranny of the unjust demands we have made of Nature and the tyranny of some nations being kept in economic slavery by other nations. We are the ones who have the most profound task in human history—the task of deciding whether we grow or die.

Consider our opportunity: we are a few years, perhaps several hundred months, away from being able to work with microcosms—nanotechnology—to enter into the very structure of cells to release and obviate age and disease. Yet we have no ethics or training for virtual immortality. We are at the point of orchestrating ourselves as gods, physically at least, yet we have no training to be gods. In a few hundred months we may be able to create microcosmic seeds of virtually any kind of machinery, which when put into the appropriate solutions, become whatever we want—computers, television sets, houses, maybe even husbands. Reality has already exceeded even our wildest imaginings, yet there is no law code or court of law in existence, no pattern of behavior, for people who have the powers of gods.

To recall Thomas Paine's words in *Common Sense*, "We have it in our power to begin the world over again. A situation similar to the present hath not happened since the days of Noah until now. The birthday of a new world is at hand." In our time, the challenge is, if anything, more profound. We must begin to think in terms of a whole new order. Most of you will see it in your lifetimes, yet we do not have the social system to sustain even the present imagination. When we look back at capitalism or communism—all the old -isms and -ologies—what we're seeing is the last stand of several very powerful fundamentalisms confronting each other. In the end, they are not going to suffice.

Through Jefferson we address how one creates a Creator—Who or What does it? The very magnificence and, yes, munificence of the life of this man and his extraordinary effect on history suggests a plan, no, more—an artistic venture. It is worthy of myth, and myth it shall be! Let me propose to you, then, a transforming fiction—a whimsical piece of theology, if you will—which serves the story of this creation and its relation to the art of gods. I have proposed that the work of gods lies in their artistic ventures. They create archetypal patterns of imaginal metaplasm as works of art. These could be plans for lives, or music, or patterns of evolutionary emergence, or, the gods only know what. Whatever they are, they are very fluid, very flexible, but with a certain grand style and panache. Occasionally, we catch the breeze of these creations—sometimes even getting into their art galleries in dreams, in visions, in love, and in madness, and seem to see these divine artistic productions. They might be a country, a history, a new sensitivity, or a new feeling.

Once in a while, perhaps, the gods have a problem. Though the other gods can see it and enjoy it, the art gets cloying because it does not have sufficient audience or canvas. The gods are stuck, as we often are here, and so they try to create personas, personalities, beings, whose life probability could help bring artistic creation into time. Sometimes these beings have direct access to divine creativity. The link is not a total givenness, but it's an extraordinary collaboration nonetheless. It's like Mozart, who often composed by listening to the compositions given complete and entire within the cosmic concert hall that he was able to access. To paraphrase Mozart's description of his creative process: "Whence this music comes from I know not, but I thank the good Lord that it is at least Mozartish."

Henry Adams once said that "Almost every other American statesman might be described in a parenthesis. A few broad strokes of the brush would paint all the portraits of the Presidents with this exception. . . .But Jefferson could be painted only touch by touch, with a fine pencil, and the perfection of the likeness depended upon the shifting and uncertain flicker of its semi-transparent shadows." I propose that the archetypal painting of Thomas Jefferson went thus. Some great Maestro or Maestra of the Depths perfected his or her craft for just such a fine portrait. What did they do? How did they go about it?

6 The Genesis of the Man

Let us look now at the genesis of the man Thomas Jefferson. I have proposed that the work of the gods lies in their creation of archetypal patterns as works of art. For Thomas Jefferson, these creators might say, let us give him large spaces—the wilderness of the Blue Ridge Mountains. Let us give him large opportunity, sufficient wealth, sufficient intelligence, sufficient yearning to do what he wants to do. Let us give him at least one model parent to serve as a kind of lure of becoming. Let his parents be diverse in their backgrounds—one a self-made man and the other a member of Virginia's aristocratic families. Above all, let him come into a life and a family in which the massive work of establishing a home in the wilderness has already been done, and the arts and fruits of civilization can be had, yet are still so new as to be deeply appreciated. And so, Thomas Jefferson is born, April 13, 1743.

His father is Peter Jefferson, a hugely strong giant, said to be close to seven feet tall and to weigh three hundred pounds, who goes out and clears a thousand acres upon his betrothal, who can pull two great hogsheads of tobacco up from the ground in a standing position. Peter Jefferson surveyed the wilderness to create the map of Virginia, fought bears, fell in rivers, but also built a vast estate, entertained everyone who came his way—visiting Indians, passels of relatives, farmers, planters, politicians, and wanderers—was at one time or another the sheriff, a Lt. Colonel, and a member of the House of Burgesses, and yet spent his private hours reading Shakespeare, Swift, Pope, and Addison and Steele's *Spectator* papers. He was always improving himself and left this happy model for his son to follow.

The son resembled him in face but not in form, always being far slighter in figure than his huge father. Peter Jefferson taught Tom to read and write, to keep accounts, and to work systematically, but also to ride, to hunt, and to develop endurance. Father told son time and again, "Never ask another to do for you what you can do for yourself." He gave him a hatred of sloth, an obsessive fear of indolence, so much so that Jefferson could write years later to his own daughter reflecting the teaching and example of his father: "Of all the cankers of human happiness, none corrodes it with so silent, yet so baneful a tooth, as indolence. Body and mind both unemployed, our being becomes a burthen, and evry object about us loathesome, even the dearest. Idleness begets ennui, ennui the hypochondria, and that a diseased body. No laborious person was ever yet hysterical. . . .If at any moment, my dear, you catch yourself in idleness, start from it as you would the precipice of a gulph."[3]

Peter Jefferson sent his son to the only school around— small groups of boys studying with the local educated parson. Here he was taught ancient languages which he loved and theology which he detested. One of his teachers, the Reverend Maury, hammered constantly at his boys that the things of this world were as nothing, and the grand purpose of life was to prepare for death and eternity. He also preached the hatred of Indians, the distrust of the common folk, and the abhorrence of democratic institutions. Seven-year-old Tom listened and vowed to think and act upon the opposite—honoring Indians, becoming the country's first demophiliac, and believing wholeheartedly that "The earth belongs to the living."

So then, part of the preparation for greatness is that after having had the influence of an expansive parent-patterner, to be given a teacher who is so outrageous in his close-mindedness that one's own mind is honed in contradistinction to this person-parson. Still the major emphasis on the ancients in young Tom's education was a blessing. He read Homer on his canoe trips down the river and Virgil while lying under an oak tree. For ever after wilderness and great style were always combined in his thinking—the image of his early life and the image of his father.

By contrast, his mother, Jane Randolph, is a dim figure, perhaps because throughout his boyhood, she was always pregnant and always attending upon her growing family of two sons and six daughters, of which Thomas was the eldest son. Psycho-historians like Fawn Brodie suggest some friction between Tom and his mother—but we can never know for certain. Certainly he was fondest of his elder sister Jane, who sang songs to him, told him stories and encouraged him throughout his young life. We know he was devastated by her death when he was twenty-two and she twenty-five and wrote a beautiful epitaph for her in Latin, which reads in translation "Oh Joanna, best of girls. . . ."

The mother was descended from the Adam and Eve of Virginia, William and Mary Randolph, who were the progenitors of the Randolphs, the Carters, the Lees, and now the Jeffersons. (The shock for me in this was that William and Mary Randolph were my great-great-great-great-great-great grandfather and grandmother on my father's side; Thomas Jefferson, I have recently discovered, was my fourth cousin.) These were all people who were interrelated not only by blood, but by privilege. They arrived well-heeled, and most became wealthy. They came over from England with their books, their musical instruments, their culture, and their land grants. They arrived with a tremendous sense of opportunity and hope in the late sixteenth and early seventeenth centuries, leaving the miasma of England's Cromwellian aftermath for the fresh spirit of a new land. And, for the most part, they were prepared to work very hard to create an optimum society of the best of the old world's culture married to the best of the new world's opportunity. They left England as frustrated gentry and became in America visionary aristocrats. There is nothing like a good balance of required hard work, open opportunity, and the continuation of art, philosophy, music and literature to create a special kind of visionary mind—one that can go out and accomplish its visions.

Peter Jefferson died when Tom was fourteen. This means there had been optimal patterning and yet not enough time for Tom to test himself against his father. He recalled that "the whole care and direction of myself was thrown on myself entirely, without a friend or relation to advise or guide me."[4] Further, he had to spend so much of his time in what he later described as the "dull monotony of a colonial subservience." Part of this subservience was having to attend to the enormous amount of details and hosting that went with a plantation owner's life, but it also included the holding of more than a hundred slaves. Even as a very young person, Jefferson had an acute psychological sense of what happened to one's worst instincts if one grew up as a slave holder. Listen now to what he writes about this training in tyranny in his early work, *Notes On the State of Virginia*:

> The whole commerce between master and slave is a perpetual exercise of the most boisterous passions, the most unremitting despotism on the one part, and degrading submissions on the other. Our children see this, and learn to imitate it; for man is an imitative animal. . . .
>
> The parent storms, the child looks on, catches the lineaments of wrath, puts on the same airs in the circle of smaller slaves, gives a loose to his worst of passions, and thus nursed, educated, and daily exercised in tyranny, cannot but be stamped by it with odious peculiarities. The man must be a prodigy who can retain his manners and morals undepraved by such circumstances.[5]

Tom himself had his own personal attendant from the time he was a young boy to the very end of his life, and with these men, the relationship was always very deep, as well as being complex and intense with others of his slaves. He proposed that black men should be educated in various skills as well as arts and literature until the age of twenty-one, and black women until the age of eighteen—suggesting that for their time, they would hold the skills and the culture of the society.

Let us look in now at Tom Jefferson at sixteen. He was six feet two, very slender, with a rather delicate face that always, like his hair, had a reddish tint to it. He blushed very easily, danced gracefully, had the lightness of the walk of a woodman and a surprisingly soft voice. This voice, which was wonderful in private conversations or in small committee meetings, had no power behind it and sounded terrible—harsh and guttural—whenever he tried to make a speech, which he, therefore, rarely did. In this age of impassioned oratory, this deficiency made Jefferson focus even more on the crafting of fine summaries and declarations, which would read like brilliant spoken speech. Get rid of public charisma, his creator/artists might have said, so that Jefferson will have to work harder to hone and refine ideas. Give him a mind that has to contemplate and reflect, reflect and deepen. Also, give him considerable musical talent; have him excel at the violin and practice or play three hours a day—another opportunity to contemplate, reflect, and deepen.

At sixteen, Tom Jefferson was in a formidable state of frustration. This is the required state for innate greatness—the great kick in the pants to move one out of an outmoded condition. He wrote to one of his guardians about how so much of his time was being wasted by so much company coming through. He asked to go away to college to save the family the expense of so much company and to learn, as he wrote, something decent, like mathematics. So off he went to William and Mary College in Williamsburg, there to avoid all the Reverends who were the principal teachers and to find the one teacher who wasn't reverend at all—Dr. William Small, a Scottish mathematician and one of the greatest teachers residing in America. Small had a liberal and capacious mind and was gifted in all of the glories of the Enlightenment period—its literature, philosophy, and burgeoning sciences. He had been a good friend of the scientific luminaries of the time—Erasmus Darwin, James Watt, Joseph Priestley, and even Josiah Wedgewood. He also had a genius for recognizing greatness and saw at once in the tall gangling teenager the makings of a very great man. Small made Jefferson his daily companion.

In some sense Small fathered Jefferson's mind, teaching him the patterns and systems in which things are placed. He brought Jefferson into his own circle of high-minded men—George Wythe, the greatest legal mind in America who became for five years Jefferson's teacher of the law, and Francis Fouquier, the Governor of Virginia Colony, a very expansive man of the world. These three extraordinary older men began by asking Jefferson to play the fiddle at their dinners and then invited him to join their conversation. About these dinners Jefferson wrote, "I have heard more good sense, more rational and philosophical conversation at those dinners than in all my life besides." We see here the pattern of empowerment and deepening of a young person's mind that comes of being included while quite young in a circle of considerate, considering adults.

At the age of nineteen, Jefferson left William and Mary to apprentice for five years with Wythe, years of virtually uninterrupted reading—law, ancient classics, English literature and general political philosophy. In fact, he was being given not so much an apprenticeship for law, as an apprenticeship for greatness.

He took his three greatest heroes, Francis Bacon, Isaac Newton, and John Locke, as lenses through which to see the world. From Francis Bacon he learned to trust his own powers of observation and to question every opinion, even those that were most pleasing to him. He came to believe strongly in Bacon's statement, "Reason and learning applied to the tasks of government could improve society immeasurably." From Sir Isaac Newton he came to trust Nature as the model of harmony from which human beings could find laws to guide them and learned to enhance his acute and constant concern to take notes on Nature, including such homey details as the gathering, cooking and serving of the first peas from the garden, and the time that the first whippoorwill was heard in the spring dusk. You see this concern in his letters, "When did the whippoorwill first sing in your part of the country, Mr. Adams?" He was passionately involved in such details because all things lent their harmony to the whole. From Locke Jefferson took the notion that each human mind was a blank tablet, a *tabula rasa*, until written upon by experience. From this Jefferson gained the hope that virtually all human beings could be lifted up through education and varieties of appropriate and healthy human experience. It was also through Locke's "Second Treatise of Civil Government," that he got the notion that legitimate authority to rule was derived from the consent of the governed and that in the state of nature, all human beings were free and equal. In the Declaration of Independence and his later writings he greatly enlarged upon these notions, and laid the groundwork for a revolution in mind and for a social transformation.

Perhaps our archetypal artists regard lenses like these as a necessary ingredient for greatness. Let a man like Jefferson, these artists might say, at an early age, after he has had some substantial deepening and expansion of his mind, after he's been empowered, get a few lenses through which to see the world. Even if the lenses are inadequate, they will serve to focus energy and comprehension. Then they can be discarded later on for larger lenses. Through the lenses of Locke and Bacon and Newton, Jefferson focused on a country and brought it into perspective in a form that still substantially exists today. Imagine what he would have done with the lenses of Einstein, Freud and Jung, and Prigogine. . . .

By his association with Small and his potent friends, the destinies of Jefferson's life were fixed, or so he himself believed. From Governor Fouquier he developed a taste for elegance and fine living, including fine dining. And so utterly engaged was he by the refined pursuits and intellectual challenge of these men that he seemed relatively immune to the Hogarth-like pastimes that his fellow students pursued in the wenching and wining, cockfighting, gambling, horse racing world of student Williamsburg. His one attempt at a romance was an embarrassing failure. Her name was Rebecca Burwell, and he wrote about this very unfortunate romance to his friend John Page. Here he is, writing in 1762 at the age of nineteen:

> This very day, to others the day of greatest mirth and jollity [it's December 25] sees me overwhelmed with more and greater misfortunes than have ever befallen a descendent of Adam for these thousand years past I am sure, and perhaps after excepting Job since the creation of the world. I am sure if there is such a thing as a Devil in this world he must have been here last night and had some hand in contriving what happened to me.
>
> Do you think the cursed rats, at his instigation, I suppose, did not eat up my pocketbook which was in my pocket within a foot from my head? And not contented with

plenty for the present, they carried away my jimmy work silk garters and half a dozen new minuets I had just got to serve, as I suppose, for provision for their winter. [The rats ate his music scores.] But of this I should not have accused the Devil because, you know, rats will be rats and hunger without the addition of his instigation might have urged them to do this if something worse from a different quarter had not happened. When I went to bed I laid my watch in the usual place, and going to take her up after I rose this morning, [Rebecca's picture was in the watch] I found her in the same place, it's true, but *quantum utatis ab illo*, all afloat in water let in at a leak in the roof of the house and as silent and still as the rats that had eat my pocketbook.

I should not have cared much for this, but something worse attended it. The subtle particles of the water of which the case was filled had by their penetration so overcome the cohesion of the particles of the paper of which my dear picture and watch paper were composed that in attempting to take them out to dry them - Good God! Men's horrid referer! - my cursed fingers gave them such a rent I fear I shall never get over. [6]

This is a man who is intellectually precocious and emotionally immature. He kept asking his friend to write to Rebecca or to speak for him to her. Finally he did get to dance with her. He had been rehearsing for months and months endearments to say to her when they danced in the Apollo Room of the Duke of Gloucester, at the Raleigh Tavern in Williamsburg. But the next day he wrote to Page:

In the most melancholy fit that ever any poor soul was, I sit down to write to you. Last night as merry, as agreeable company in dancing with Belinda [he gave her many names] in the Apollo could make me, I never could have seen the succeeding sun could have seen me so wretched as I now am. I was prepared to say a great deal to her. I had dressed up in my own mind such thoughts as occurred to me in as moving language as I know how, and expected it to have performed in a tolerably credible manner. But good God! When I had opportunity of venting, them, a few broken sentences uttered in great disorder and interrupted with pauses of uncommon length were the two visible marks of my strange confusion. [7]

Jefferson then spent nine months trying to think of how to propose to the girl. But he never saw her that nine months, because he was afraid she would think him too forward. When he finally got around to it, Rebecca married someone else.

Peggy: What do the divine artists/architects have to say about that?

Jean: They say have him fall in love, but don't let him get married too soon. Have him work out of a considerable sentimentality so that he crafts his capacity for loving. Give him sweet sentiment, nurtured in the sea of hope, that comes to an abyss of failure. Let the flame of yearning without consummation stimulate him to extraordinary heights of imagination.

PROCESS 5
MEETING THE DIVINE ARCHITECT OF YOUR LIFE /
COMMITTEES OF CORRESPONDENCE OF THE COSMIC
CONGRESS

Many people today have had very interesting lives, full of challenge and complexity. However, growing up as we do in an age which tends to pathologize rather than mythologize, we often do not see the patterns of possibility, the weave of wonder that fills our lives. Instead, we are always looking for the fault, the trauma, the pathology, and tend to hold our lives in grievance and dwell on negatives. Jefferson grew up in an era as full of opportunity as ours, and with plenty of preachers around who saw the human condition as sick and sinful, but his circle of friends and associates was one which mythologized and celebrated their opportunities and regarded the social pathologies of their time as opportunities to reinvent their country. Since death and natural disasters were for many of them much more frequent than they are for most of us, they tended to be even more appreciative of the good things of their lives. Their letters are filled with affirmations of gratitude for the pattern of challenge and opportunity within the play of their lives, as if some Divine Architect were helping them to realize the fundamental possibilities that were just beneath the surface. This belief both inspired and provided guidance. So for this process let us take on that belief as well, as—if nothing else—a metaphysical fantasy or healing fiction.

We are going to have you imagine that your life had its own designer or Divine Architect. We will begin with the assumption that many of the things that happened to you were in accordance with what the Divine Architect had in mind, so that you might have the kinds of experiences which your soul required, as well as serving a larger purpose for the society in which you live. You will assume the identity of this Divine Architect and therefore be involved in the planning of the qualities and events of your life. In doing this process, you will see how you were divinely designed and may come to look upon yourself as an utterly unique art work of the "gods."

We will do this process as discourses in a Congress of the the Gods where, as a divine designer, you will discuss your own particular artistic creation—your human self. Think of the Congress as an artists' meeting where the godly artisans are talking shop.

This can be a potent exercise, because you'll begin to see a divine aesthetic, an artistry and pattern to your life. From that pattern you may also be able to project something of the future possibilities for your life, as each life has numbers of alternative paths which it might take. When you can discern those several paths, as perhaps Jefferson did, you may feel empowered to work more consciously towards a particular path and to re-imagine and reinvent your life along more interesting lines. In doing this, you may get closer to the "original" artistic plan, what I call the *entelechy* or dynamic pattern and purpose of your life.

In the previous pages I engaged in a metaphysical fantasy to show at least the early life of Jefferson as having been patterned by a Divine Architect. These patterns resulted in an exceptional human being, albeit one with considerable shadows, who nevertheless had the qualities and experiences which enabled him to help create a new society. In this process we are not only going to have you look at your own life in that manner but go even further and try to discover from the microcosm of your life what is trying to happen in the macrocosm or larger life of society.

As an example of how this process works as a spontaneous exercise, the following dialogue is from the transcript of the Jefferson session of the Mystery School, during which I asked my associate in this work, Peggy Rubin, to describe the patterns laid down in her own life:

Jean: If I were to say, Great Artist, what would you lay down for Peggy Rubin? What are the patterns that can enter into time through Peggy Nash Rubin? You have the art form in front of you. Describe it for us.

Peggy: I would pattern her with sufficient time between children in her family so that she would understand aloneness. I would place her in a flat land of vast, verdant riches—and mosquitoes. I would place her in a family where the parents have a burning love for God, but whose understanding of God is different from each other. I would place her in a family where the father's heart has been blasted by disappointment so that she would understand what it is to strive to please. I would place her in a family where the mother had a strange imagination and a world peopled by imaginary friends. I would surround her with people of other skin colors who had the capacity for happiness so that she would feel deeply drawn, yearningly drawn, to people of other races. I would give her teachers who admired and loved her, and teachers who hated her, so that she could learn balance and learn that being hated is not necessarily her fault. I would give her the radio so that words would come to her from a distance, and she would use her imagination to see the scenes she was hearing. I would give her horses to play with so that she would know what it is to ride in the wind.

Jean: Move forward in time a little bit further, just for our benefit.

Peggy: I would have her fall sentimentally in love with a preacher, who spurned her, so that she would learn to be suspicious of preachers. I would have her marry an actor, so that together they could become actors. And then I would have her marry a Jew so that she could understand from inside an entirely different religion. I would have this be a deep and loving relationship with a wise man of vast experience and compassion so that her heart would be utterly opened and her mind would always be avid for learning.

Jean: Thank you Peggy. We will now begin the process of discovering the Divine Architect of our lives in the Committees of Correspondence of the Divine Congress.

TIME: ONE HOUR.

• *MATERIALS NEEDED:*
None.

• *MUSIC:*
For most of this process soft background music from Area One would be appropriate. For the opening of this process however, some elegant eighteenth-century dance music like a minuet would be perfect.

• *INSTRUCTIONS FOR GOING SOLO:*
This exercise is best done with at least one other person. However, if that is not possible, then you should put the script on tape and imagine several other Divine Artists listening to your plans for your creation or, if you prefer, do the process in front of a mirror.

• *SCRIPT FOR THE GUIDE:*

Would you just start to wander in a very elegant eighteenth-century way just among each other. And as you wander, would you gently find and invite two other people to join you so that you have three people. And then would the three people start to walk together, please, in an elegant eighteenth-century manner. Just amble along together, arm in arm, as genteelly as you can.

(Let the eighteenth-century music play as the people continue to walk together.)

Would each of the groups of three form a circle, please. My dear ladies and gentlemen, my dear gods and goddesses, Divine Artists, I welcome you to the first meeting of the Committees of Correspondence of the Cosmic Congress. You are all *grand artistes*. And you are here on this auspicious occasion to design a human being and to share your plans and design for this creation which you are planning to put forward into Earth space and time. And so, as Divine Artists, looking at each other with supreme regard, bowing to each other with great courtesy, as befits gods and goddesses, as befits your station as residents in the Monticello of archetypal space and time, would you now decide who will be the first Divine Architect to discuss his or her plan of creation. Just decide among you who will be the first, and then which god will go second, and which will be third. And you are free, of course, to sit down or to stand or to dance as you choose. But you will present your plan or design in an elegant manner. In fact, I'd like you to address each other as Maestro and Maestra—Maestro for the men; Maestra for the women.

You will be conferring with each other as the great Maestras and Maestros of human life design. And know yourselves now to be these great Divine Architects who also create patterns of art, culture, spirit, and society. But now you need to create appropriate human agents to help bring these new patterns into time. You are no longer your local human selves. You are your Divine Artist, up there in the archetypal, metaplasmic world, sharing the plan of the artistic creation that is your local human self with the other Divine Artists. You can lay down whatever patterns you like, saying as you speak of each pattern you are placing in the life of your creation, "I put this pattern in so that this or that may happen for her, or this or that quality may grow in him," etc. Be as specific as you can with regard to the consequences of each of the patterns for the individual life as well as for the betterment and building of a renewed society through the person you are designing. I will call the time. Each Divine Designer will have about fifteen minutes to discourse before the other gods concerning the nature and plan of his or her artistic creation. Begin.

(After fifteen minutes, the Guide will say:)

Take about a minute to come to a natural ending, and then let the second Divine Architect begin and share with the others the patterns that are being laid down for his or her life. (The Guide will hold the time and say much the same things for each of the Artists. After all three Divine Artists have spoken, the Guide will say:)

Divine Artists and Architects, I'm going to ask you to stretch and shift your divine bodies for a moment, for even gods need to stretch. Now would you please assume again the character of your Divine Architect. And now I'm going to ask you to close your eyes, but allow your hands or foot to stay connected with the other gods in your group. Imagine now that we are journeying together to the spiritual place where the ideal of Monticello continues to endure.

So you're going up a small hill, entering a familiar house, and looking out the windows which give you a view of twenty miles of Blue Ridge Mountains. Here in this archetypal Monticello, you have the panorama of the archetypal Blue Ridge Mountains. And you as Divine Architect see this vast panorama. And then see your creation, your work of art, this human being, placed within this panorama.

And now in your mind's eye let the panorama shift and contain within it the entire array of living things that are part of your human work of art's life—the people, the places, the events, the relationships, the opportunities, the creative challenges, what is going on in the individual life as well as in the lives of the other people who are part of it. And would you now salute the Divine Architects behind the lives of each of the other people who are part of the life of your own creation. Just see the entire range. All the people and events that are there—trees, seas, clouds, cats, dogs, ideas, friends, spouses, teachers, mentors, even worthy adversaries. . . .All are there. And all of them have been designed by great artists in this archetypal world. And you see what your fellow artists had in mind, because you see the whole vast spread of it. But you also see that there is great artistry in the interdependence of it all; each part or person or event or idea is intricately and aesthetically woven with each other part.

And now, feel yourself to be like a movie camera rolling in toward your work of art in that vast panorama. And keep moving in closer and closer and closer so that your eye can even take on a microscopic power. Look at the detail work on that body and mind and spirit. Look at the brush strokes, if you think of it as a painting. Look at the fingerprints or the chisel marks, if you think of it as a work of sculpture. Look at the nails, if you think of it as a work of architecture. And remark in the same way the shape of the mind, the rich palette of colors of the emotions, the vibrational play of the spirit. Note the artistry of the interplay of all of these. Look closely now. And marvel at the detail.

And then move back, to enjoy the panorama again. And take a deep breath and let your body shift so as to be more comfortable. And while you see the panorama, also look at your particular masterpiece, your work of high art. And then feel yourself becoming a Divine Architect for a new kind of planet, a new kind of world. And see how the patterns that you have laid down in this work of art play into the patterns of another, larger work of art. Notice the pattern between the miniature, the human being, and this new world.

And taking a deep breath, and releasing it, find yourself moving out into a realm of the creation of future possibilities. Envision a future of the possibilities for your particular human work of art. Just let the designs for the possible futures appear. Trust that they will. They may appear as images, or words, or feelings, or even some combinations of these. . . . Now choose one of these patterns of possibility, one of these possible futures for this human being.

And now look again at the panorama, but let it now extend to be 360 degrees all the way around, spreading in every direction. And as Divine Architect of this life, see how this choice of one possible future for one individual affects the world in which he or she lives. See that person's future as helping to create the emerging society and world. . . . And see the divine patterns behind that world and how that life is helping those patterns enter into time and space.

And at your own time or space, eyes remaining open or closed as you choose, would you share the vision of the unfolding pattern of that life and that world which you as Divine Artist have patterned. Remember, however, that these patterns are never fixed or absolute, but that Divine Artists always allow freedom for acceptance, rejection, or co-creation by their human partners. And speak to the unfolding pattern of that life, of what it can do and be in the world if the human partner—that is, your human self—agrees to this opportunity for co-creation of new future. And consider too the consequences of this future for the world of space and time in the late twentieth and early twenty-first centuries and what this life can mean to the world. So each of you, speaking as a god or goddess, will say what the vision of the chosen possible future was, and what the human partner needs to do as part of his or her immense opportunity to co-create that unfolding artistic pattern in time and space, both for themselves as individuals and for the world.

Each of you will have ten minutes to speak to this, beginning with the first god or goddess. I will hold the time and tell you when each of the ten minute periods is up. Then the god or goddess who is speaking will come to a natural ending, and the next will speak. Begin.

(After all three have spoken the Guide will say:)

Thank you. This kind of thinking may be what Mr. Jefferson was able to do in his reflections on the relationship of individual life to society. And perhaps it also accounted for some of the most interesting considerations of eighteenth-century artists, social artists, and thinkers. They could be both miniaturists and visionaries of the larger pattern and purpose. Like them, we too have looked down at the patterns of our own singular lives laid down in miniature. We have also looked down at the patterns of self in society. And we are attempting to perceive the great underlying aesthetic purpose—the Pattern that Connects, if you will. If we can have the mindfulness to reflect on these three things—the patterns in miniature, the patterns within the larger design, and the sense of purpose and artistry underlying and uniting the whole, then destiny, or rather entelechy may follow. And what is best of all, we may gain a profound sense of commitment to the divine design and possibilities of our lives.

Mr. Jefferson certainly reflected upon these kinds of things. Many of you have had lives that would be worthy of a biographer, but you probably have not reflected on them in this grand manner. When you think in this way about your life, you are no longer just psychologizing but are mythologizing your life as well. Mythologizing means seeing the connections between local life and planetary life. And that connection is the Great Story that brings the larger life into time.

Thinking mythically allows you to see how your life in its personal particulars is part of the larger life with its personal universals—how your life's patterns are part of a much larger purpose and plan. And by becoming conscious of that larger story, some enormous ignition takes place within you. Often you feel charged to live a larger life, and then the larger life itself becomes attracted to you. Truly that's one of the great secrets. It's out there in the open, but few bother to see it. Life begins to be attracted to you as you work and reflect back and forth on the interrelation between the local patterns and larger patterns of reality, seeing the underlying purpose and artistry of it all.

Then (to speak mythically) Reality says, "Oh, my God! That person is really a hot one! That man or woman is at the point of reflection. I'm going to help that one." In more practical terms, as we reflect on the relation between local and cosmic life, life itself accrues and opportunity comes. If you see your life as just one exhausting experience after another, you descend into the flaccidity of events. But if you engage in this mode of dynamic reflection, you move up into Great Life.

7 Lawyer and Architect

After spending five years preparing himself by pursuing all knowledge fifteen hours a day, Tom Jefferson was at twenty-four the most learned and mentally avid young man in Virginia. A woman writing from Williamsburg at this time said that she "never knew anyone to ask so many questions as Thomas Jefferson." Historian Saul Padover has said that:

> When Thomas Jefferson began to practice law at the age of 24, he was brilliantly prepared and poorly equipped for his profession. . . . It cannot be denied that he was not cut out to be a lawyer; a scholar, a scientist, and inventor, an architect, a botanist, yes—but not a lawyer. His mind was too inquisitive, too speculative, and, above all, too much given to ideas as such, to be happy in jurisprudence.[8]

He was, however, well equipped to change old laws and to devise new ones. He also detested legal language. As he once said, years later, "I was bred to the law, that gave me a view of the dark side of humanity. Then I read poetry to qualify it with a gaze upon its bright side."

Jefferson's law career did not begin at the bottom; it began in the highest appellate court in Virginia, the General Court. This was the place for gentlemen of the greatest erudition, and many of his clients were the river barons, powerful representatives of the leaders who dominated the social, economic, and political life of the colony. A knowledge of classical literature was de rigueur, and one debated before the Governor and the Royal Council in language well-peppered with philosophical and classical allusions. Lawyers quoted Greek and Roman authors, sometimes at great length, while their colleagues took notes on the allusions as well as on the merits of the case. The court became a sapiential circle—a circle of intellectuals having vast entertainment in showing off their classical skills. For this game, Jefferson was, of course, enormously well suited.

Jefferson, however, was a planter as well as a lawyer—an owner of substantial estates, as well as a conciliator and scholar. In 1766 he began keeping his Garden Book, an incredible record of information useful to him as a practical farmer—facts to aid him in projecting the yield of his fields, or how much fodder his cattle consumed. When you study these meticulous records in his small neat hand, you discover that all these practical lists and accounts are invariably interrupted by notations of the blooming of purple hyacinths, bluebells, and wild honeysuckle as well as the aforementioned first green peas of the season and the first sound of the whippoorwill in the gathering night. He turned with graceful ease from interpreting common law to an attempt to work his lands in harmony with the laws of nature.[9]

During this time he visited Philadelphia and consulted a young doctor, John Morgan, who inoculated him against smallpox. Morgan had recently returned from Europe, thrilled over the temples and sculptures of the ancient Greeks and Romans and their neoclassical disciples. He also imported an art collection that included Raphael's work and Palladio's architectural sketches. As Morgan shared these with his young patient, he saw that Jefferson felt an equally intense interest. Jefferson sensed that this kind of art, with its emphasis on perspective, proportion, balance, harmony, and grace, caused the mind to expand, to soar into the places of the highest reason. Jefferson vowed to promulgate classical forms wherever he could. Many of our capital buildings as well as government edifices in almost every state reflect some aspects of Jefferson's passion for the neoclassical revival. He began to dream of building a home on the highest mountain of his estate. In 1769 he levelled the top of a hill, known as Monticello, and having read everything he could about the architecture of the period, began to design his famous home.

It was at Monticello that he became an artist, a poetic philosopher of the Enlightenment, using brick and stone as his media. He was also the architect, builder, engineer, construction foreman, cabinet maker, landscape artist, and interior designer. All his life he made corrections, changes, and adaptations, much as he did with the country—perpetually building and rebuilding the laws, the educational system, the possibilities. It was twenty-five years before Monticello was even reasonably finished. It was his great project and his greatest love, the vehicle and fullest expression of his ever aspiring soul.

After he had finished the basic building, but before he had fully moved all his belongings into the new place, Shadwell, the home of his family where he had been living, burned to the ground. Has a similar thing ever happened to you? Have you ever had such a deep passion for something new that whatever you are leaving behind, whatever had been your container, is destroyed? Jefferson's passion for Monticello was so overarching that Shadwell—his mother's home, the place of his "shadowed well"—burned to the ground, destroying as well all his books and papers and records. It was a staggering loss for a record-keeper; the first twenty-seven years of his life turned into ashes. For many years thereafter, he spent a large portion of his income on buying books to replace his library.

In the wake of this loss, Jefferson moved to Monticello with his huge extended family of thirty-four relatives and eighty-three slaves.

Soon after, in 1770, he fell in love, wooed, and married a young widow, Martha Wayles Skelton, a highly cultivated, high-spirited, and very wealthy young woman of twenty-one. Her father John Wayles was one of the richest of the Williamsburg lawyers and plantation owners. When he died—a year after Thomas and Martha's wedding—he left her forty thousand acres of lands and 135 slaves, which made the young couple two of the largest land-owners in Virginia and enabled a luxurious lifestyle as well as the feast of acquisitions which Jefferson enjoyed all of his life. One of these slaves, Betty Hemings, was the daughter of an African woman and a ship captain. For many years, she had been the mistress of her owner, John Wayles, making some of her children—now slaves in the Jefferson household—the half-sisters and half-brothers of the new Mrs. Jefferson. And therein lies a tale. Betty Hemings' children were enormously interesting, skillful, and beautiful people. Some historians believe that one of them, Sally Hemings, became Thomas Jefferson's mistress for many years after the death of his wife and bore him five or six children.[10]

Tom and Martha were by Jefferson's account, immensely devoted. In his autobiography he describes his wife as "the cherished companion of my life, in whose affections, unabated on both sides, I had lived. . .ten years in unchequered happiness." Martha, Jefferson soon learned, had many prosaic virtues as well as considerable social gifts. She was a fine manager of the ever-expanding household and plantation and as given to meticulous recording of household accounts as he was. Nine months after the marriage, she gave birth to a little girl, also named Martha, who would grow up to be a strong, resourceful woman in her own right, and for much of the time, her father's official hostess. Five other children would be born to them, of whom only Martha and another little girl, Maria, would survive.

Meanwhile Jefferson was turning the entire hilltop into his own private Olympus. He loved to look westward in the winter when he could see a snowstorm, "rising over the distant Allegheny, come sweeping and roaring on, mountain after mountain, til it reaches us, and then when its blast is felt, to turn to our fireside, and while we hear it pelting against the windows, to enjoy the cheering blaze."[11] One could communicate with gods in such a place.

But the world would call—no, more, demand that he come down from the mountain and attend to the affairs of the House of Burgesses, to which he had recently been elected. Election procedures in those days were very simple. You invited your neighbors to come and get drunk at your expense and then asked them to vote for you. Cakes and rum cost Jefferson twenty-five dollars, the sum total of his election campaign costs.

Throughout these years and earlier, the British Parliament had been forcing questionable taxes on the colonies, Stamp Acts, Sugar Acts, taxes on tea, paper, and other goods. The sentiment was moving through the colonies that there should be "no taxation without representation." No power on Earth, declared the Virginia

Burgesses in 1768, "has the right to impose taxes on a people without their consent given by their representatives in Parliament."

George III and his Cabinet were becoming whimsical and arbitrary in the extreme. And many of the Colonies, especially Massachusetts, were experiencing a growing sense of resistance and outrage, as was demonstrated in the spring of 1774, when a group of Massachusetts rebels dressed as Mohawk Indians, threw a considerable cargo of tea overboard to protest new rules about taxation and sale of tea in the Colonies. In retaliation, the British government closed the port of Boston.

The members of the Virginia House of Burgesses soon discovered Jefferson's remarkable felicity of expression and asked him to try his hand on many state papers. His job was assessing and measuring the quality of insult offered by the British government and devising an answer, couched in ceremonial but powerful language, which would explain the colonists' position to the Crown, to the colonists themselves, and to the world at large. He also helped forge a loose but powerful organization, the Committee of Correspondence, designed to serve as a means of communication and ultimately perhaps of union among the thirteen colonies.

8 Writing the Declaration

In Virginia two voices began to rise in ever more verbal opposition to the British Crown: one flaming and oratorical—Patrick Henry—and one subtle and profound—Thomas Jefferson. The subtle voice, Jefferson, prepared a paper which would serve as instructions to the delegates who would be sent from Virginia to the First Continental Congress. This document, *A Summary View of the Rights of British America*, has been described as both a landmark in American history as well as a mirror of Jefferson's own mind. It is the very soul of the destiny of this country and the seed ground for the Declaration of Independence. A masterpiece of English prose, it tells bilious old George III in terms both elegant and blunt that he has no right to impose laws and rules upon an America that was built by pioneers. Listen to some of the words in this remarkable document, and you are listening to the fire in the heart of America that has flamed out the forces of freedom all over the world.

> Can any one reason be assigned why 160,000 electors in the island of Great Britain should give law to four millions in the states of America, every individual of whom is equal to every individual of them in virtue and under-

standing and in bodily strength? Were this to be admitted, instead of being a free people as we have hitherto supposed and mean to continue ourselves, we should suddenly be found as slaves, not of one, but of 160,000 tyrants.

But can his Majesty. . . put down all law under his feet? Can he erect a power superior to that which erected himself? He has done it indeed by force, but let him remember that force cannot give right.

. . . these are our grievances which we have thus laid before his Majesty with that freedom of language and sentiment which becomes a free people claiming their rights, as derived from the laws of nature and not as the gift of their chief magistrate. Let those flatter who fear. It is not an American art. . . . They know that kings are the servants, not the proprietors, of the people.

It is neither our wish nor our interest to separate from her [Great Britain]. We are willing, on our part, to sacrifice which reason can ask to the restoration of. . . tranquility. On their part, let them be ready to establish union on a generous plan. . . . But let them not think to exclude us from . . . other markets. . . . Still less let it be proposed that our properties within our own territories shall be taxed or regulated by any power on earth but our own.

The God who gave us life gave us liberty at the same time. The hand of force may destroy, but cannot disjoin them. This, sire, is our last, our determined resolution.[12]

Though the document was brilliantly prepared, poor Tom Jefferson never got to the Williamsburg Convention to deliver it. He was overcome with dysentery while riding there. He found a messenger by which to send two copies, one to Patrick Henry and the other to Peyton Randolph, the chairman of the assembly. Henry probably never even read it, being as Jefferson said, "the laziest man in reading I ever knew. . . ." He communicated it to nobody. Randolph, however, communicated it to everybody. Jefferson's statement soon became a cause célèbre; it was made into a pamphlet and entered the political world of Europe, the Colonies, and England as a seed crystal in a supersaturated solution. It went through many editions, eliciting much sympathy in England for the Colonies, to the extent that the British Parliament put Jefferson's name on a proscription list.

Then there was Patrick Henry's way of dealing with the British Parliament. There is a wonderful account in Alf Mapp's study of Jefferson of Henry's famous speech, an oration which still stirs the revolutionary embers in all hearers:

Henry got to the floor. At first his speech was halting and deferential, but his words gained momentum as he began to recite the colonists' grievances against London. A peculiar vibrant note of almost hypnotic power crept into his voice as he hurled at his listeners rhetorical questions about the arrogance with which their petitions had been spurned by the King.

Suddenly an Old Testament prophet seemed to inhabit Henry's tall lean figure as he thundered, "We must fight! I repeat it, sir, we must fight! An appeal to arms and to the God of Hosts is all that is left us."

As he lowered his voice it throbbed with a new controlled excitement. "They tell us, sir, that we are weak, unable to cope with so formidable an adversary. But when shall we be stronger? Will it be next week, or next year? Sir, we are not weak if we make the proper use of those forces which the God of Nature hath placed in our power. Three millions of people armed in the holy cause of liberty and in such a country as that which we possess are invincible by any force which our enemy can send against us. The battle, sir, is not to the strong alone. It is to the vigilant, the active, the brave."

Sweeping his audience along on the torrent of his eloquence, Henry cried out, "Gentlemen may cry peace, peace, but there is no peace. The war is actually begun. The next gale that sweeps from the North will bring to our ears the clash of resounding arms."[13]

It was then in high theatrical style that Henry bowed his back and crossed him arms like a manacled slave. "Is life so dear or peace so sweet as to be purchased at the price of chains and slavery? Forbid it, Almighty God!"

Bending his body closer to the earth, and maintaining his pose as a slave, he then said, "I know not what course others may take." Then he rose proudly to his full height and strained against his imaginary ropes while declaiming in a triumphant tone, "But as for me, give me liberty. . . ." All in the Assembly leaned forward, thrilled with excitement. They knew that a momentous peroration approached, one that would influence all future histories. They knew that this was more than a speech, this was the emerging soul of the new nation speaking through its most dramatic mouthpiece. Then, as the word "liberty" resounded through the hall, Henry broke his "ropes," flung out his arms, scattering the bonds of slavery to the four winds. His face was radiant as he then let his left hand fall powerless to his side. Ever the actor, he next took up an imaginary dagger and aimed it at his heart, looking as some witnesses said, like a Roman senator defying Caesar. With dirge like solemnity, he then declaimed his final challenge, "or give me death!" Striking his chest with his right hand, he appeared to plunge the dagger into his patriot's heart.

Patrick Henry returned to his seat, followed by a long, stunned silence. Some felt dizzy. The sentiments of many were finally spoken by Edward Carrington, a man who had been listening through an open window and who broke the silence by exclaiming, "Let me be buried at this spot!"[14] (Strange to say, his wishes were followed exactly more than three decades later.)

With the help of Henry's speech and Jefferson's document, the delegates at the meeting voted to form a standing army, known euphemistically as the Committees of Safety. Meanwhile to the North, the British were pursuing incendiary aims: the shot at Concord had been heard round the world; the Battle of Lexington had taken place and been lost by the Colonists.

Jefferson felt both active repugnance at the notion of fighting—with his gentle aversion to violence (he could never stand the sight of blood)—and great dismay and sadness. In a letter to his old mentor, William Small, he wrote, "This accident has cut off our last hope of reconciliation. It is a lamentable circumstance, that the only mediatory power [the King] should pursue the incendiary purpose of still blowing up the flames."[15]

Jefferson traveled to the Second Continental Congress in Philadelphia through muddy, rutted roads, fording rivers and making notes on everything, flora, fauna, weather. Arriving in Philadelphia, he found himself already famous for his masterly pen. His angular, lean and tanned presence also stood out among the short and paunchy delegates, many of whom, at least if one judges by their portraits, looked like walking puddings. The fact that his face was an exceptionally kind one, radiating good will and intelligence, that he listened deeply to what everyone had to say, and was never confrontational attracted many of the delegates to him. Especially attracted to him was that truculent little bantam rooster, John Adams, who said to him the equivalent of, "My goodness, sir, you're as intelligent as I am!" and paid Jefferson a rare tribute, saying, "He was so prompt, frank, explicit and decisive upon committees and in conversation. . .that he soon seized upon my heart." Everybody loved Jefferson and his writings and asked him to compose sonorous phrases to defy King and Parliament.

Remember that Jefferson was a true son of the American frontier; as such, the thought of any arbitrary authority holding sway over one's life and one's reason, from a distance of over three thousand miles, was intolerable. I have known many frontiers people in my time, people making a hard won life for themselves in Africa, or South America, or Australia, and the thought of government to them is often inimical. "I carved out this wilderness," they sometimes say. "I made this place what it is, and you're telling me I have to agree to the ridiculous demands of men who never worked a piece of land in their life?"

Moreover, Jefferson's historical sense was acute. Even amid the rapidly moving and emotionally rending events that he was living through, he maintained the long perspective of history, seeing the American Revolution in the light of its necessary unfolding from early Anglo-Saxon roots and predicting with extraordinary accuracy the future of the independent country. Perhaps that's why he was always putting himself in a place from which to gain perspective, backwards and forwards in time, living literally and figuratively upon a hilltop, from which he could gaze upon the successive ranges of the Blue Ridge Mountains. The grand prospects of birth and death pursued him. Returning home after the first session of the Second Continental Congress, he saw Jane Randolph, the youngest of his two little daughters, die. As so often happened when he was cast down in sorrow, he left only a stark formal record: "Died this morning, my daughter Jane Randolph, aged two years." In close succession, his cousin and great friend Peyton Randolph—a huge, corpulent man with many chins—went out to dinner with Jefferson, got apoplexy while eating, and died. Around the same time, Dabney Carr, Jefferson's brother-in-law and close friend from school, also died. Perhaps all of these deaths required of Jefferson the balance of new birth, in this case the birth of independence, of liberty, of a new nation.

In January, 1776, Thomas Paine's *Common Sense* appeared. This was perhaps the most thoroughgoing argument against monarchy and tyranny that the world had ever seen. The forty-seven-page pamphlet by a proletarian Englishman with only one year's residence in Philadelphia, by trade a corset-maker, by profession a journalist, and by inclination a propagandist, who had been imprisoned and victimized in England, tolled the death knell of monarchy and placed America as the site upon which a new liberty would ring: "Freedom hath been hunted round the globe. Asia and Africa have long expelled her—Europe regards her like a stranger and England hath given her warning to depart. O, receive the fugitive, and prepare in time an asylum for mankind. . . . We have it in our power to begin the world over again. . . . 'Tis not the concern of a day, a year, or an age; posterity are virtually involved in the contest, and will be more or less affected even to the end of time, by the proceedings now. Now is the seed-time of the Continental union."[16]

Early in its history America was seen as the asylum for a fugitive freedom—no wonder Americans are so taken up with a sense of historical destiny, with the sense that "these are the times, and we are the people." Not one of us can ever get away from the enormous historical sense that comes in with the creation of America. We are born into a sense of being responsible for creating the future, for preparing the ground for the possible human and the possible society. In many ways we inherited this sense of historical destiny from this early appreciation of America as the asylum for freedom, as well as from the sensibility of Paine's *Common Sense* and most certainly from the mind and vision of Thomas Jefferson.

Along with thousands of Americans, Jefferson, as well as Washington and Adams found *Common Sense* irresistible; there is no question that its arguments helped to turn the tide toward revolution. The time had clearly come for an ultimate statement of intention. Jefferson was made chairman of the committee at the Continental Congress charged with preparing a formal declaration of independence. Other committee members were John Adams, Benjamin Franklin, Roger Sherman, and Robert Livingston. All agreed that Jefferson be the author. At first Jefferson refused, asking Adams to prepare the declaration. Nothing doing, said Adams. Jefferson asked why. "Reasons enough," Adams replied. "What can be your reasons?" Jefferson asked. Adams' reply was succinct and to the point: "Reason First: You are a Virginian and a Virginian ought to appear at the head of this business. Reason Second: I am obnoxious, suspected and unpopular. You are very much otherwise. Reason Third: You can write ten times better than I can."[17] Adams' logic was unanswerable, and Jefferson agreed to be the author.

He worked seventeen days on the document, consulting no book or pamphlet, but drawing upon his own mental furnishings, which he said he could call to mind as readily as he might summon the images of familiar objects. He later defined his purpose as follows:

> Not to find out new principles, or new arguments, never before thought of, not merely to say things which had never been said before, but to place before mankind the common sense of the subject in terms so plain and firm as to command their assent, and to justify ourselves in the independent stand we are compelled to take. Neither aiming at originality of principle or sentiment, nor yet copied from any particular and previous writing, it was intended to be an expression of the American mind, and to give that expression a proper tone and spirit called forth by the occasion.[18]

The paragraphs of the Declaration are like music—stately, processional music, carrying with them a kind of mythic power, a sense of cosmic order, the soul of the world herself echoing from the human pen. Its language is almost biblical in its scriptural statement of inevitability.

Jefferson presented his document and listened in an agony of silence as the Congress debated the political and literary merits of his composition on July 2, 3, and 4. Observing his suffering, Benjamin Franklin tried to distract him by telling him a comical story about a hatter, who had so altered his elegantly inscribed sign in obedience to other people's criticisms that eventually it bore only his name and a picture of a hat. Jefferson must have felt that he was undergoing surgery when the delegates excised his favorite historical argument that the American colonies had never owed any more allegiance to Great Britain than the Anglo Saxons had owed to the Germanic lands from which they had sprung. He also suffered over the deletion of a very great passage in which he said that repeated injustices by England had driven the Colonies to this act of separation, which was both undesired and extremely painful. Consider this marvelous passage which should have been in the Declaration:

> These facts have given the last stab to agonizing affection, and manly spirit bids us to renounce forever these unfeeling brethren. We must endeavor to forget our former love for them, and to hold them as we hold the rest of mankind, enemies in war, in peace friends. We might have been a free and a great people together, but a communication of grandeur and of freedom, it seems is below their dignity. Be it so, since they will have it: the road to happiness and to glory is open to us too; we will climb it apart from them, and acquiesce in the necessity which pronounces our eternal separation.[19]

The necessity of such separation was painful to many Colonists, who had great numbers of relatives and friends in England. Eternal separation seemed a cruel—if necessary—step. Also excised was Jefferson's accusation against King George III because he had vetoed attempts to stop the slave trade:

> He has waged cruel war against human nature itself, violating its most sacred rights of life and liberty in the persons of a distant people who never offended him, captivating and carrying them into slavery in another hemisphere, or to incur miserable death in their transportation hither. This piratical warfare, the opprobrium of infidel powers, is the warfare of the Christian king of Great Britain. Determined to keep open a market where men should be bought and sold, he has prostituted his negative for suppressing every legislative attempt to prohibit or to restrain this execrable commerce. And that this assemblage of horrors might want no fact of distinguished die, he is now exciting those very people to rise in arms among us, and to purchase that liberty of which he had deprived them, by murdering the people on whom he also obtruded them: thus paying off former crimes

committed against the liberties of one people, with crimes which he urges them to commit against the lives of another.[20]

This powerful passage was protested by the gentlemen from South Carolina and Georgia and others who feared it might anger other constituents who had grown rich in the slave trade. About this deletion Jefferson wryly observed in his autobiography, "Our northern brethren also I believe felt a little tender under those censures; for tho' their people have very few slaves themselves, yet they had been pretty considerable carriers of them to others."[21] If nothing else, the deletion underscores the ambiguity felt over the slavery issue on the part of many at that time, Jefferson, chief among them. The habits of the past die hard even among "enlightened" minds.

Only John Adams fought for every word of the original document. But that did not prevent the deletion of one-fourth of the original document before it was adopted on July 4. On the day of adoption, John Adams wrote in a famous letter to his beloved wife Abigail that "it will be the most memorable epoch in the history of America. I am apt to believe that it will be celebrated by succeeding generations as the great anniversary festival. It ought to be commemorated as the day of deliverance, by solemn acts of devotion to God Almighty. It ought to be solemnized with pomp and parade, with shows, games, sports, guns, bells, bonfires, and illuminations, from one end of the continent to the other, from this time forward forevermore."[22] Done! John.

Apart from the fact that the Declaration of Independence is one of the greatest literary documents ever written, within it Jefferson sought its deepest purpose in the roots of liberal traditions spread back to England, Scotland, to Geneva, to Holland, to Germany, to Rome, and to Athens. But also, at a fundamental level, it is one of the finest statements ever made of a whole system in transition, because it recognizes and hails the need to break from those archaic traditions and patterns, even those of blood and race, when they threaten to repress the unfolding possibilities of person or nation. It is a statement that the time is ripe for radical renovation, for tapping into those capacities for person and society that rarely have been seen before. The subtext of Jefferson's words is that we are a great people making a great new start, and we have infinite potential. It was a phenomenal statement, and it birthed a phenomenon of human history. Would that we had the likes of a Jefferson today to help guide in words and deeds the present planetary whole system transition.

PROCESS 6
THE DECLARATION OF INTERDEPENDENCE

In the following process we are going to use the Declaration of Independence to reveal some of our own deepest thoughts and beliefs. Following the lines of the Declaration and writing in the classical form of Thomas Jefferson, we may well find ourselves tapping into what is trying to emerge in the global heart and mind. Using the rich ceremonial language of the Declaration, we will call forth from within ourselves some of the new intentions of the human race.

TIME: ONE HOUR.

• MATERIALS:
Each person should have a copy of the excerpts from the Declaration of Independence given below, photocopied either from this or some other book. Also, each participant must have a long piece of paper with which to write his or her own Declaration.

• MUSIC:
Sonorous, evocative music from Areas Two or Three.

• INSTRUCTIONS FOR GOING SOLO:
This process does not have to be put on tape. Just follow the written instructions in this book. Be sure to read your Declaration aloud in a full and sonorous voice.

• SCRIPT FOR THE GUIDE:

Would everyone please pick up a copy of the Declaration of Independence and read aloud from the text with me. As we speak the great opening lines together, please notice the sonorous, scriptural, processional, ceremonial, ritual use of language.

When in the Course of human events, it becomes necessary for one people to dissolve the political bands which have connected them with another, and to assume among the powers of the earth, the separate and equal station to which the Laws of Nature and of Nature's God entitle them, a decent respect to the opinions of mankind requires that they should declare the causes which impel them to the separation. . . .

This is the language of the Enlightenment. It is the language that flows out of the reading of Shakespeare and Locke, of Newton and of Francis Bacon. But it is also the language of America. It is the statement of the imminence of a radical evolutionary event. The language itself becomes even more radical in the next lines which announce the truths and intentions by which the new society is to align itself. This passage is an incredible statement of whole system transition. Read it with me please:

> We hold these truths to be self-evident, that all men are created equal, that they are endowed by their Creator with certain unalienable Rights, that among these are Life, Liberty and the pursuit of Happiness— That to secure these rights, Governments are instituted among Men, deriving their just powers from the consent of the governed, that whenever any Form of Government becomes destructive of these ends, it is the Right of the People to alter or to abolish it, and to institute new Government, laying its foundation on such principles and organizing its powers in such form, as to them shall seem most likely to effect their Safety and Happiness. Prudence, indeed, will dictate that Governments long established should not be changed for light and transient causes; and accordingly all experience hath shown, that mankind are more disposed to suffer, while evils are sufferable, than to right themselves by abolishing the forms to which they are accustomed. But when a long train of abuses and usurpations, pursuing invariably the same Object evinces a design to reduce them under absolute Despotism, it is their right, it is their duty, to throw off such Government, and to provide new Guards for their future security. Such has been the patient sufferance of these Colonies; and such is now the necessity which constrains them to alter their former Systems of Government.

This mighty statement is then followed by the great list of the wrong and tyrannies, "of repeated injuries and usurpations" done by the government and the King of Great Britain to the American colonies.

Let us now read together the passage that begins in the third to the last paragraph of the Declaration:

> We have warned them from time to time of attempts by their legislature to extend an unwarrantable juris-

diction over us. We have reminded them of the circumstances of our emigration and settlement here. We have appealed to their native justice and magnanimity, and we have conjured them by the ties of our common kindred to disavow these usurpations, which, would inevitably interrupt our connections and correspondence. They too have been deaf to the voice of justice and of consanguinity. We must, therefore, acquiesce in the necessity, which denounces our Separation, and hold them, as we hold the rest of mankind, Enemies in War, in Peace Friends.

We, THEREFORE, the Representatives of the UNITED STATES OF AMERICA, in General Congress, Assembled, appealing to the Supreme Judge of the world for the rectitude of our intentions, do, in the Name, and by the Authority of the good People of these Colonies, solemnly publish and declare, That these United Colonies are, and of Right ought to be FREE AND INDEPENDENT STATES; that they are Absolved from all Allegiance to the British Crown, and that all political connection between them and the State of Great Britain, is and ought to be totally dissolved; and that as Free and Independent States, they have full Power to levy War, conclude Peace, contract Alliances, establish Commerce, and do all other Acts and Things which Independent States may of right do.

And for the support of this Declaration, with a firm reliance on the protection of divine Providence, we mutually pledge to each other our Lives, our Fortunes and our sacred Honor.

Let us consider now again the great opening lines: **When in the Course of human events it becomes necessary. . . .**These words, ringing out from our land, which have influenced so many peoples of the world, now speak to us all again, the world over, of our collective danger and dilemma. This archetypal, neoclassical temple of prose cries out once more from its eternal place in the mind of history to be spoken to the peoples and nations of our time in a new kind of Declaration, one that proclaims the Interdependence of us all, if we are to right old wrongs and build a better world. Of course, some of the requirements are different in our time, are they not?

So I am asking you now, **When in the Course of human events it becomes necessary for. . . .** For what? Let me hear some answers from each of you.

(The Guide elicits a number of answers at this point. Here are some of the responses given at the Mystery School session on Thomas Jefferson:)

—People to go beyond nation.

—Men not to kill men.

—People to live without boundaries.

—Undertaking the healing of the planet.

When in the Course of human events it becomes necessary for. . .

—A new economics.

—Us all to work cooperatively.

—Representative government to be held accountable.

When in the Course of human events it becomes necessary for. . .

—All life forms to be recognized as sacred and worthy of protection.

—Eliminating the disease of drugs.

—The development of a loving technology.

—Military power to be relinquished.

—Equality and opportunity for all peoples.

Would you now pick up your long sheet of paper and would you please write in as careful and beautiful handwriting as you can: **When in the Course** [with a capital C on *course*] **of human events it becomes necessary for. . .**

And then let flow out of your mind and your pen what it now becomes necessary to happen. This is your own personal statement and Declaration. I will give you five minutes of clock time to write this part. (Five minutes.)

We turn now in the Declaration to the words, **We hold these truths to be self-evident, that. . .**

(The Guide elicits a number of answers to complete this statement. Here are some of the responses given at Mystery School:)

—All men and all women are created equal.

—Things change.

—Everything is related to everything else.

—Personal sacrifices are honorable, and not foolish.

We hold these truths to be self-evident that. . . What do you deeply believe?

—We have a profound power for interrelatedness.

—All beings are separate and unified, independent and interdependent.

—We are all God Seeds.

—That no one may limit that to which each one of us aspires.

—Love is the universal principle that connects all aspects of living beings, and their environments. Its evolution is our highest value.

I'll remind you of what Jefferson said: **That all men are created equal, that they are endowed by their Creator with certain unalienable Rights, that among these are Life, Liberty and the pursuit of Happiness.**

This says a lot, and it's hard, if not impossible, to improve on it. But we still have to improve, because of the new requirements of our time. (After eliciting a number of statements the Guide will say:)

Let us begin now to write on our paper the words, **We hold these truths to be self-evident, that. . .** In writing "we" here, the reference is to the fullness of all the "we" which each of us contains. I will give you now five minutes of clock time to complete the statement about truths held to be self-evident. (Five minutes.)

Let us now consider the following passage:

> **We, THEREFORE, the Representatives of the UNITED STATES OF AMERICA, in General Congress, Assembled, appealing to the Supreme Judge of the world for the rectitude of our intentions, do, in the Name, and by the Authority of the good People of these Colonies, solemnly publish and declare, That these United Colonies are, and of Right ought to be FREE AND INDEPENDENT STATES. . .**

For our purposes here let us change the words to read: **I, therefore, the Representative of the United State of the World, do solemnly publish and declare that. . .**

That what? What do you solemnly declare from your heart of hearts? This is your opportunity to offer your statement about the world. (The Guide again elicits a number of answers to this point of the Declaration. Here are some of the responses given at Mystery School:)

I do solemnly publish and declare that. . .

—The survival of the planet, its nations and all its creatures are to be held sacred forever.

—All of our elders shall be supported to share their wisdom with us.

—Children are autonomous beings with the right to be treated with dignity and respect.

—All indigenous people shall be protected in their own lands.

I do solemnly publish and declare that . . .

—Governments shall not legislate on religious matters.

—All cultures are distinct and that not one will supersede the others.

—All people have the right to meaningful work and just remuneration for their labors.

(After eliciting responses the Guide will say:) Write these words then please: **I, therefore, the Representative of the United State of the World, do solemnly publish and declare that. . .**

Write your response, leaving room at the bottom of the page for your signature. I will give you five minutes of clock time to write what you wish and to sign your name. (Five minutes.)

(The Guide then invites the participants to read aloud their Declarations. Here are several written at Mystery School:)

Woman participant: When in the Course of human events it becomes necessary for a people to live without self-limiting boundaries, and to treat all sentient beings as sacred, it becomes necessary for that people to identify and dissolve those boundaries and to become the caretakers and stewards for all sentient beings, no matter how great or small. That those people shall then separate and condemn those who force boundaries between people and people, people and other beings, between people and their dreams, or any boundaries that prevent one from fulfilling one's full potential. And that those people should condemn and eliminate all barriers to fulfilling their full potential and purpose.

We hold these truths to be self-evident, that all things are sacred and interrelated and that it is the potential and purpose of each person to become as gods.

I, therefore, the representative of the United State of the Universe, do solemnly publish and declare that all beings, whether animal, mineral, plant, or spirit, be treated with the highest degree of sacredness and interrelatedness, and that all barriers to fulfilling one's highest potential be destroyed and that all efforts be made to become godlike.

Woman participant: When in the Course of human events it becomes necessary for the people of the world to recognize their kinship with one another, to take down, stone by stone, the walls that have separated them, to clear away the fog of lies and deceptions in which they have been persuaded to live, they shall then recognize the community that binds them in one.

We hold these truths to be self-evident, that each person is worthy of and entitled to respect from every other person, and that other creatures also are entitled to respect, and that all the systems in the natural world are entitled to respect.

I, therefore, a representative of the United State of the World, do solemnly publish and declare that I will not again look at another human being without seeing him or her, that I will henceforth be conscious of the place of every being in the great scheme of the universe, and that I will not on my own ascribe insignificance to any part of it.

(The Guide then says:) Would you all please stand up now and face one other person. Decide who will go first. Solemnly, and in full voice, begin to read now your Declaration of Interdependence, first one and then the other.

(After all have finished, the Guide will invite the participants to discuss how they felt as they were writing their Declarations and what they may wish to do now with them. For example, is there any way in which they can act upon these stated beliefs and intentions? Can they draw them out further by continuing to work on them? Do they wish to incorporate ideas they have heard in the Declarations of others?)

9 Making Independence Work

Jefferson tells us in his autobiography that after the Declaration was signed, work began on the Articles of Confederation. These were debated for several weeks more—including such painful discussions and painful details as how to pay the expenses of the war and how to assess each colony its fair share. They had to decide how to count the number of inhabitants in each colony—who was an inhabitant, who or what constituted property, and the riches of each inhabitant. As always, throughout Jefferson's life, the issue of slavery complicated and tortured the negotiations. The number of votes per colony was also at issue. These are the basic discussions which ultimately provided the new nation with a structure which would evolve into its constitution. But every Congressman had an opinion and was loath to let go or to compromise upon it. Hammering out these articles also clarified Jefferson's thoughts about the sense of the Union and what constitutes a majority.

To me what is so fascinating about this particular period of Jefferson's life is that he is always going back and forth between two modes of thinking—inner reflection and visionary creation of the possible society, and the hammering out, over days and days, of the practical details needed to translate the vision into reality. That is the way really creative work has to be done. All too often people on committees, especially those who are working in governments, are so consumed with details, they never work on the vision. Conversely, some do things the other way around. They work on the vision and never consider the details. This country, however, was forged by men like Jefferson who engaged in the supreme dialectic between spending deep reflective time on envisioning—what I call vertical time—and then balancing that with very complex, intricate, horizontal time working out practical considerations. In addition to Jefferson, we know that the Adamses were very much involved in this process, as was Washington, who was a man much given to vertical reflective thought, and yet very much a concrete genius for details. It is rare in human history that so many people were so deeply devoted to the vertical and the horizontal aspects of thought and action at the same time.

The wives of these men were similarly extraordinary. Abigail Adams was herself a remarkable visionary as well as being a lady of enormous spunk who did much to plot the way through the obstacle course of creating a new nation. The letters John and Abigail Adams wrote to each other were letters of co-creating a vision of a possible society and then wondering how they were going to persuade others to see it too, or how it could be accomplished. Here for example is a letter that Abigail, in high martial spirits, wrote John counseling revolution and separation from England:

> Let us separate, they are unworthy to be our Brethren. Let us renounce them and instead of supplication as formerly for their prosperity and happiness, let us beseach the almighty to blast their counsels and bring to Nought all their devices.[23]

Indeed there is much evidence that often John Adams felt that Abigail was his only peer. Consider these words of his:

> I muse, I mope, I ruminate.—We have not Men, fit for the Times. We are deficient in Genius, in Education, in Gravel, in Fortune—in every Thing. I feel unutterable anxiety.—God grant us Wisdom, and Fortitude!
> Should the Opposition be suppressed, should this Country submit, what Infamy and Ruin! God forbid. Death in any Form is less Terrible.[24]

Intense intellectual partnership was true of any number of those couples whose men guided the creation of the new nation. Pioneers and partners in mind and heart, in fortitude and rebellion, their love and commitment to each other and the new country sparked much of the incendiary vision that made America happen. Although we do not have a great deal of information about Martha Jefferson, we know she had a gift for details and that she was a good artist. We also know that being in a state of continuous sickness, she wanted her husband home, but we do not know too much about the partnership in terms of the actual creation of the country. She remains shrouded in mystery since Jefferson, in a fit of privacy, destroyed most of her correspondence to him and we are left only with a few tantalizing fragments.

Jefferson was also deeply sensible of his responsibilities to Virginia, now a state. Having been elected to its legislature, he resigned his position in Congress on September 2, 1776, and took his seat at his state's legislature on October 7. In so doing, he again moved from the macroworld to the microworld, a place in which he could really study and reflect in depth. Almost immediately however, Jefferson received word that Congress had elected him, along with Dr. Franklin and Silas Dean, as members of a joint commission representing the fledgling nation in France. How tempted Jefferson must have been to accept this post. For three days he debated, but then he wrote a painful and poignant letter saying thanks but no thanks. Some writers cite his need to be closer to home as one of his reasons for leaving Congress, and he himself said this was why he could not go to France. We need go no great distance to look for justifications. Certainly Mrs. Jefferson's mental and physical health must have been precarious—all those babies, and so many of them ill and soon dead.

The couple's only son was born in late May, 1777, and died soon after. In addition, as other writers have noted, Jefferson really did believe in the pursuit of happiness as an inalienable right. He took as many opportunities as he could to enhance his happiness by being with his wife and family in his home.

At the same time, his record of work on Virginia's laws and their "many very vicious points which urgently required reformation" is nothing short of remarkable. He wrote and put through a bill for the establishment of courts of justice, "the organization of which," he wrote, "was of importance." This may rank as one of the great understatements in political history. It was as if in these laws for a single state, the patterns of thousands of years were revoked. Jefferson knew that you could not just get rid of a king; you had also to get rid of the king's institutions. So he wrote bills to abolish primogeniture (in which the eldest son inherits everything) and the custom of entails. Entailment was the process by which only the same family could succeed to an estate, with no inheritor being allowed to sell it or bequeath it. This ancient practice was meant to preserve large estates in the same family. Not only did it result in fearful mismanagement, but it locked up the land from use by other people with larger visions. With these changes, the whole millennia-old patrician and patriarchal tradition was ended. No longer would the transmission of property from generation to generation raise up a distinct set of families who perpetuated their wealth. It is curious that such a change could be accepted among a tight little ruling class of men, some of whom—like Jefferson himself—owned fifty-thousand-acre plantations. Yet Jefferson had a peculiar genius that transcended even his intellectual and rational capacities, including a genius for friendship. His sweet-natured, shy warmth greatly attracted people to him. Thus when he represented in his quiet and unaggressive way the possibilities for a new kind of humanity, something very deep was transmitted from his highly developed visionary mind and soul to theirs. And they caught it.

People seemed to know that working with Jefferson, they had the chance to create the world anew. Jefferson enticed them to this perception with such empathy and sympathy that individuals and even institutions were able to release the old patterns of thousands of years. Jefferson's ultimate story is of one person's capacity to love and empower others to the point that they could transcend and release thousands of years of patterning. Jefferson had the capability of calling people forth—of loving them into their greatness. Jefferson's letters reveal the depth of emotion people felt for him. Even testy little John Adams talked about his immense affection for Jefferson. Of course, the Virginia planters and statesmen among whom Jefferson moved were given to immense affections and to tremendous transformational friendships of considerable intensity. Jefferson had a particular genius for such friendships.

Working with George Wythe, his mentor, Edmund Pendle-
ton, and George Mason, he spent the next three years completely
revising the laws of his state, though most of them were not ratified
and enacted until 1785, some years after the Revolutionary War.
When you change laws to make them more humane, you also change
the language to make it human. Thus Jefferson said:

> I thought it would be useful also, in all new draughts, to
> reform the style of the later British statutes, and of our own
> acts of Assembly: which from their verbosity, their endless
> tautologies, their involution of case within case, and paren-
> thesis within parenthesis, and their multiplied efforts at cer-
> tainty by saids and aforesaids, by ors and by ands, to make
> them more plain, do really render more perplexed and
> incomprehensible, not only to common readers, but to the
> lawyers themselves.[25]

Amen. Jefferson brought in a bill to prevent further importation of slaves and had hoped to add an amendment naming the day of
freedom for all slaves and deportation at a proper age. He writes over
and over again that he cannot see any other way of resolving the
problem of slavery except deportation. He writes of the ten thousand
abuses that slaves have undergone, and that he can see no way that
the slaves or former slaves could ever forgive or release them. How,
he wondered, could slaves or former slaves ever live under the same
government with their masters? He saw no other solution to the
black-white problem other than to slowly send black people home to
Africa. Jefferson wrote also about his proposition to abolish slavery
but found that the public mind would not yet bear the proposition.
"Yet the day is not distant," he wrote, "when it must bear and adopt
it, or worse will follow. Nothing is more certainly written in the book
of fate, than that these people are to be free; nor is it less certain that
the two races, equally free, cannot live in the same government." Jefferson led the way to make Virginia the first state to abolish the
importation of slaves in 1778.

The bill that ultimately was passed (after much argument)
and one that meant so much to Jefferson that he wanted it to be cited
on his epitaph, was his "Bill for Establishing Religious Freedom":

> Be it therefore enacted by the General Assembly, that no
> man shall be compelled to frequent or support any religious
> worship, place or ministry whatsoever, nor shall be en-
> forced, restrained, molested or burthened in his body or
> goods, nor shall otherwise suffer on account of his religious
> opinions or belief; but that all men shall be free to profess,
> and by argument to maintain, their opinions in matters of

religion, and that the same shall in nowise diminish, enlarge or affect their civil capacities.

Now this is remarkable in the light of the Jonathan Edwards, Cotton Mather, and the Calvinistic milieu which prevailed in so much of America. After all is said and done, America was settled by a good many religious extremists whose excesses and practices in the name of spirit drove them out of Europe. Jefferson in his earliest days felt himself victimized by the smug, limited parochialism of his clergy teachers, who were all right when it came to ancient languages, but were stifling and repressive when it came to anything else. But there is more, much more, implied by his statement on religious liberty and the separation of church and state. Jefferson believed that so long as church and state were interwoven into the same tapestry of power, a self-governing commonwealth based on justice and freedom was an illusion. In nothing else in Jefferson's life was he more consistent than in his belief in religious liberty:

> Toleration isn't enough. What we need is liberty, fully protected by the law, to believe or not believe as you see fit.

And never was he more consistent than in his hatred of religious tyranny:

> In every country and in every age the priest has been hostile to liberty. He is always in alliance with the despot, abetting his abuses in return for protection of his own.

In his "Notes on Religion" he wrote:

> The care of every man's soul belongs to himself. But what if he neglect the care of it? Well, what if he neglect the care of his health or his estate which more nearly relates to the state? Will the magistrate make a law that he should not be poor or sick? Laws prevent against injury from others, but not from ourselves. God himself will not save men against their wills. I cannot give up my spiritual guidance to the magistrate because he knows no more of the way to heaven than I do, and is less concerned to direct me right than I am to go right.

He also said:

> The rights of conscience we never submitted, we could not submit. We are answerable for them to our God. The legiti-

mate powers of government extend to such acts only as are injurous to others. But it does me no injury for my neighbor to say there are twenty gods or no god. It neither picks my pocket nor breaks my leg. Subject opinion to coercion, whom will you make your inquisitors? . . .

But is uniformity desirable? No more than a face or stature. Introduce the Bed of Procrustes then, and as there is danger that the large men may beat the small, may make us all of a size by lopping the former and stretching the latter, is uniformity attainable? Millions of innocent men, women and children since the introduction of Christianity have been burnt, tortured, fined, imprisoned. Yet we have not advanced one inch towards uniformity.

What has been the effect of coercion? To make one half of the world fools, and the other half hypocrites. To support roguery and error all over the earth.[26]

I believe that this is as radical and innovative a statement as ever was. Since time immemorial, the depth structures of the psyche have only nominally belonged to the individual. They have been kept cut off, mediated by priest and king and shaman, to the point that most people have not known that they even existed within themselves. Free the spirit in each person to pursue its own path, and you release the cosmos within. Free the spirit, and the entelechy within each person is free to emerge, and the rapid increase in evolutionary potential can begin. Every one of us is a radical individualist when it comes to our spiritual sensibility. There are at least five billion religions in the world today, because the God-Self finds itself refracted uniquely in each person ensconced in time and space. I say, as have many others, there are five billion paths to God.

Now you might say there have been other places in the world—India, for example—where a certain kind of freedom to pursue one's spiritual goals remained. That is partially true, but often in such places, the other freedoms needed to develop the human possibility were not available to work in tandem. One thing that Jefferson above all others recognized was that freedom had to be holistically applied, lest the release of one freedom would suppress the development of another. He knew, for example, that if you are going to release the spirit, you are also going to release the desire to learn. Thus Jefferson and his fellow committeemen also worked on ideas concerning the need and method for general education. He presented proposals outlining three grades of education, essentially grade school, high school, and college. In the early grades, the curriculum would encompass reading, writing, arithmetic, drawing, philosophy, language, music, dance, and art. Then high school would take in rich subjects like paleontology, anthropology, studies of other cultures. College would be a deepening of these learnings, with the aim of making one, by the age of fifteen or sixteen, a Renaissance, enlightened man or woman. Jefferson also proposed a new charter for William and Mary, making it a university with an emphasis on science, and put forward a proposal for the establishment of a library. Some of these ideas failed; some passed.

It is no coincidence that James Madison, the principal author of the U.S. Constitution (written after the Revolutionary War and passed in 1787, while Jefferson was in France) began his political career in the same Virginia State Assembly in 1776. The young and modest Madison was an acute observer of the process of writing, proposing, and passing laws, learning his lessons well during this time of hard work on ways to secure and guarantee the rights of humankind as they were conceived and debated in Virginia's legislature. In many ways, Madison was the son of the mind and soul and spirit of Thomas Jefferson.

Of his work in the Virginia Assembly, Jefferson himself said, "I consider four of these bills, passed or reported, as forming a system by which every fibre would be eradicated of ancient or future aristocracy; and a foundation laid for a government truly republican." These four bills essentially reinvented the social cosmos in the following ways: Instead of the traditional aristocracy of wealth, Jefferson envisioned an aristocracy of talent; instead of lawmakers and government officials being drawn from special classes, he saw that they could be drawn from wise and honest officials. Conscience, instead of being taken over by some ancient religious belief, would be free, and being free, could be educated to its own opportunity. Most radically, instead of wealth and privilege determining who should be educated, Jefferson and his fellows proposed that everyone—men, women, slaves, Indians—be educated at the common expense. Here was a clear historical break with the past; here was the evolution of democracy.

On June 1, 1779, Jefferson was elected Governor of the Commonwealth of Virginia, even though he protested, wanting rather, as he said, to "indulge my fondness for philosophical studies." Unfortunately, it was the worst possible time for a philosopher to be king. The American Revolution was at its bloodiest, the British having shifted their attack to the south with most of the assault being on Virginia, which had virtually no fortification and a poorly trained army. After all, its greatest home-grown generals, like Washington, were up north fighting. Furthermore, the money was worthless; most people didn't pay their taxes, and nobody kept accounts.

It was into this model of inefficiency, disorganization and demoralization that peace-loving, efficient, highly organized, incredibly disciplined Thomas Jefferson was jettisoned. Washington coerced him for supplies and men in the north; General Gates pleaded with him for the same in the states to the south, especially the Carolinas which the British were attacking. By 1781 Jefferson found himself watching events which he could not stop—the British sweeping through his state burning and plundering as they advanced. Many of these British troops were commanded by the American turncoat, Benedict Arnold.

Jefferson did his best to enlist soldiers, but the farmers of Virginia would only go if promised a bounty, and then, when they decided that they had seen enough of war, would melt away like ice. After so much work in the service of the design of liberty, Jefferson had to watch as the attacks on liberty took on epic proportions. This is a fascinating commentary on the ways and wiles of history—that those who conceptually bring in a radical new theorem become the ones who are the most tested to sustain that theorem in dramatic, often violent and existential ways. From Christ to Martin Luther King, from St. Joan to Lincoln to Gandhi to the thousands of unsung men and women who have risked their all to serve the turning of the time, too often the most excruciating testing has attended their efforts. It is a terrible truism that those who upset the status quo more often than not get stoned.

There was one gun for every five militiamen, one militiaman for every square mile to be defended, little powder, no containers for cartridges, and no fortresses. The enemy could just walk in. Consider what happened when Benedict Arnold invaded the capitol.

> Richmond had no defenses. Jefferson ordered that public stores be removed. Men worked all night. At one o'clock in the morning of January 6 the governor hurried from the capital to get his wife and young children who were at Tuckahoe out of the reach of danger. He took them eight miles farther up the river, left them with some friends, hurried back to Manchester across the river from Richmond. [Jefferson] had been on horseback for 36 hours, and now his horse fell exhausted within sight of the besieged capital. Jefferson swung the saddle on his back, walked to a farmhouse where he obtained a colt. When he got to Manchester he could see from across the river that the British had taken Richmond. And as watched, fire burst from the capital. Benedict Arnold and his men were burning public buildings and the stores of food and tobacco. Then they left the way they came.[27]

And then, of course, another time he himself was nearly captured. He had awakened to the sound of horses and went out to the East Portico of Monticello to discover what was going on. Captain John Jouett came riding up the steps on what was said to be the "best and fleetest horse in seven counties." Having ridden for almost six hours over rugged mountain paths to reach Monticello, he announced to the startled Jefferson that he'd better leave soon as he was to be captured. What happened next tells a great deal about Jefferson's disposition. Instead of rushing about, as most anyone else would, he asked Jouett in and gave him a glass of his best Madeira. Only then did he ask him to go to the nearby Swan Tavern in Charlottesville and awaken the legislators. Jefferson proceeded to awaken his family and the Speakers of the two houses as well as a number of legislators who were his guests, treated them to a very full and leisurely breakfast, and only then invited them to call a quorum at Charlottesville and adjourn to Staunton, some thirty-five miles west. He then dispatched the ailing Martha Jefferson and their children in a carriage off to safety. He, however, stayed behind to get his papers and books together, have his valuables transferred to the cellar, and prepare for the British invasion. While this was going on, a man rode in warning that the British were fast approaching Monticello. In fact, they were now on the mountain itself. Still unhurried, Jefferson took a telescope and watched the English dragoons overrun the streets of Charlottesville as well as come running up his mountain. This seemed the appropriate moment to leave, so he walked down to a place on the road where his favorite horse was saddled, mounted and took off. Five minutes later, the British soldiers were crawling all over Monticello. They behaved, however, like model guests, their commander, Colonel Tarleton having given "strict order. . .to suffer nothing to be injured." One would like to think that Jefferson's own cavalier attitude to danger was rewarded by a similarly mild response from the powers informing the theater of the world.

Now what did Jefferson do when insoluble problems attacked him from every tangled thicket of red tape, miasma of financial depression, and ambush of hostile armies? Why, he did what Jefferson always did—he went deeper. The occasion was the request that came at this point from a Frenchman, the secretary of the French legation in Philadelphia, "Would you please give me some notes on the state of Virginia?" Now if most of us had been given the task of writing a few notes on the state of Virginia, we would have supplied what was probably wanted—a twenty-page report on broad themes. But Jefferson being who he was, his *Notes on Virginia* turned out to be a masterpiece of highly polished essays on topics ranging from paleontology to history, zoology to theology, anthropology to economics, geography to botany. He consulted no reference books; there were none. He consulted his own remarkable memory and observation and produced a full-scale book designed to tell Europeans and Virginians alike what Virginia and the United States were like—a prophetic treatise on the American dream, written in the midst of the American debacle. As one commentator has remarked:

That Jefferson should have produced a work of such breadth and quality within a period of less than eleven months, seven of which he spent as Governor of a war-torn state and four as an embarrassed retiree preparing a detailed defense against his detractors, a period that brought the severe illness of his wife and death of his daughter, the evacuation of his capital and flight from his home before an invader seeking his capture, not to mention the fall from a horse that broke his arm and confined him for six weeks—that he should have accomplished so much against such odds—is little short of astonishing. Yet such is the case.[28]

Back home at the Gubernatorial ranch however, everybody blamed Jefferson personally for the mess. "Why is this state defenseless?" they cried. It must be that we have Jefferson, a peace-loving man. What we need now is a dictator, not a democrat. Democracy doesn't work in wartime. We need a general at the helm, or, even better, an orator. Yes, let's make Patrick Henry governor. With one of his speeches, all the problems will disappear. The vote to create a dictator was defeated, but only by a few votes.

Then a very young man by the name of George Nicholas in his first term as a legislator made his debut by asking that Jefferson's conduct be officially investigated. It is generally thought that Patrick Henry was behind this move. This resolution was unanimously passed; his every act of the last twelve months was to be closely examined. It was an unprecedented insult, one that Jefferson would bear as a scar for the rest of his life. This was in spite of the fact that he answered all charges meticulously and that when the legislature met to hear the charges, they absolved him of all blame, referring to groundless rumors as the cause of the trouble. Further, they adopted a resolution of thanks for his conduct, ability, and integrity. However, like many people of noble purpose who bring about substantive change, he was unusually thin-skinned when it came to insult and censure. Perhaps such individuals have to be hypersensitive in order to detect and act upon the emerging potential patterns for the new social reality. Jefferson seemed to remember the censure and not the thanks and always recalled his governorship as one of being under a perpetual cloud: "I find that the pain of a little censure, even when it is unfounded, is more acute than the pleasure of much praise." He could never forget that he had stood accused among his peers, he—the kindest and most honest of men. "I'm finished with public life," he told his friends and essentially went off to sulk for more than a year. His friends, James Madison especially, pleaded with him to return, saying that this was not worthy of a man of his calibre. Jefferson's words of reply to Madison are very interesting:

I might have comforted myself under the disapprobation of the well-meaning but uninformed people yet that of their representatives was a shock on which I had not calculated. . . .I had been suspected. . .in the eyes of the world, without the least hint. . .being made public which might restrain them from supposing that I stood arraigned for treason of the heart and not merely weakness of the mind; and I felt that these injuries. . .had inflicted a wound on my spirit which will only be cured by an all-healing grave.

Ironically, after Jefferson retired, the fortunes of the American Revolution changed. The French fleet arrived in Chesapeake Bay in 1781 to utterly rout the British, and to the north, Lord Cornwallis surrendered to General Washington at Georgetown.

Meanwhile Jefferson was back at Monticello, living his ideal life of husband and father, scientist, farmer and scholar, and studious observer of all and everything. His house was now moving toward perfection—a perfection as opposite as could be from the gross imperfections of political life. It was light and airy, with windows facing every direction, and as comfortable a house as had ever been built in America. His French aristocrat friends particularly appreciated the house and the man. Here is how the Marquis de Chastellux, who visited Jefferson at Monticello in the spring of 1782, described his host:

Let me describe you a man, not yet forty, tall, with a mild and pleasing countenance, but whose mind and understanding are ample substitutes for every exterior grace. An American, who without ever having quitted his own country, is at once a musician, skilled in drawing, a geometrician, an astronomer, a natural philosopher, legislator, and statesman. . . .A mild and amiable wife, charming children, of whose education he himself takes charge. . . .Mr Jefferson is the first American who has consulted the fine arts to know how he should shelter himself from the weather. . . .I found his first appearance serious, nay even cold; but before I had been two hours with him we were as intimate as if we had passed our whole lives together; walking, books, but above all, a conversation always varied and interesting.[29]

Then his beloved wife gave birth to their sixth child, and now, worn out by childbirth and fragile health, she began to die. Jefferson sat at her bedside nursing her constantly for the next four months. One day, propped up in bed, she penned a few lines: "Time wastes too fast: every letter I trace tells me with what rapidity life follows my pen. The days and hours of it are flying over our heads like

clouds of windy day, never to return more—eveything passes on. . ."
She paused, too exhausted to continue. Then the handwriting
changes, and it is Jefferson himself who completes the lines from
their shared favorite, *Tristram Shandy*: ". . .and every time I kiss thy
hand to bid adieu, every absence which follows it, are preludes to
that eternal separation which we are shortly to make."

As she died, she made him promise never to marry, never to
give their children a stepmother. On September 6, 1782, Jefferson
recorded in his account book: "My dear wife died this day at 11:45
A.M." Behind this brief notation is the story of wild and overwhelming
grieving. Jefferson's oldest daughter, the sturdy nine-year-old Martha,
called Patsy, became for a month his constant companion. Years later
she wrote this account of what had happened:

> No female ever had more tenderness or anxiety. He nursed
> my poor mother in turn with Aunt Carr and her own sister,
> sitting up with her and administering her medicines and
> drinks to the last. For the four months that she lingered he
> was never out of calling. When not at her bedside he was
> writing in a small room which opened immediately ahead of
> her bed.
>
> A moment before the closing scene he was led from the
> room almost in a state of insensibility by his sister, Mrs. Carr,
> who with great difficulty got him into his library where he
> fainted and remained so long insensible that they feared he
> would never revive.
>
> The scene that follows I did not witness, but the violence of
> his emotion when almost by stealth I entered his room at
> night and to this day I dare not trust myself to describe. . . .
> He kept to his room three weeks, and I was never a moment
> from his side. He walked almost incessantly, night and day,
> only lying down occasionally when nature was completely
> exhausted on a pallet that had been brought during his long
> fainting fit. My aunts remained constantly with him for some
> weeks; I do not remember how many.
>
> When at last he left his room, he rode out, and from that
> time he was incessantly on horseback, rambling about the
> mountains and the less frequented roads and just as often
> through the woods. And on those melancholy rambles I was
> his constant companion, a solitary witness to many a violent
> burst of grief, remembrance of which has consecrated par-
> ticular scenes of that lost home beyond the power of time to
> obliterate.[30]

Three months after he had suffered his tragic loss he wrote his friend the Marquis de Chastellux, saying he was "a little emerging from that stupor of mind which had rendered me as dead to the world as she was whose loss occasioned it." And although none of his letters to his wife or hers to him were preserved—indeed he destroyed them, so private was he about this relationship—there were discovered forty-four years after his death in a secret drawer envelopes containing locks of his wife's hair and other remembrances of her, all labeled and arranged in perfect order, but giving evidence of having been much handled.

Enormous as was his grief, he could not deny life, or, we might add destiny. Duty summoned. Friendships beckoned. A new destiny across the Atlantic called. He would soon stand with his eldest daughter on a new and shining ship bearing documents that named him Minister Plenipotentiary, with instructions to collaborate with John Adams and Benjamin Franklin in negotiating treaties of commerce with European nations. Paris awaited him with open arms—great art to be enjoyed, fine food to be relished, sparkling and brilliant conversations to be had, a front row seat on the makings of the French Revolution, and very soon, a remarkable romantic interlude.

10 Paris: City of Art and Elegance

Imagine how Paris in the late eighteenth century must have appeared to Jefferson, a man who, though of the most extraordinarily refined sensitivities and tastes, had never been in a town larger than twenty-five thousand inhabitants. Everything to appeal to him was there: a city of art and elegance, of graceful bridges and beautiful chateaus, of white boulevards, parks, palaces, river quays, shifting clouds of translucent light, the greatest book stalls in the world, the finest museums, the most elegant food and wine, and the most scintillating conversations. Paris was the market town for the arts of the world, the center for music and musicians, and the capitol for the purveying and testing of new ideas. And Jefferson arrived there as a prophet of new ideas, a much admired and much celebrated statesman and writer, the hero of the hour, a man who everybody wanted as their guest, and everyone appreciated. He wrote of France and this period of his life:

> A more benevolent people I have never known, nor greater warmth and devotedness in their select friendships. Their kindness and accommodation to strangers is unparalleled, and the hospitality of Paris is beyond anything I had con-

ceived to be practicable in a large city. Their eminence, too, in science, the communicative dispositions of their scientific men, the politeness of the general manners, the ease and vivacity of their conversation, give a charm to their society, to be found nowhere else.

In some respects Jefferson must have felt as if he had died and gone to live in a gentleman's paradise. But he was not blind to its failings. He wanted the best of the Old World to be united with the best of the New. In another letter he gives us a picture first of the worst in which he describes the French as having no happiness at home:

> Conjugal love having no existence among them, domestic happiness, of which that is the basis, is utterly unknown. In lieu of this are substituted pursuits which nourish and invigorate all our bad passions, and which offer only moments of ecstasy amidst days and months of restlessness and torment.[31]

He remembers Americans as being blessed with "tranquil permanent felicity" which gives them freedom and time for "pursuits which reason and health approve." In the same letter, however, he does allow that the European courtesy is unequaled at home:

> With respect to what are termed polite manners, I would wish my countrymen to adopt just so much of European politeness as to be ready to make all those little sacrifices of self which really render European manners amiable, and relieve society from the disagreeable scenes to which rudeness often exposes it. Here it seems that a man might pass a life without encountering a single rudeness. In the pleasures of the table they are far before us, because with good taste they unite temperance. They do not terminate the most sociable meals by transforming themselves into brutes. I have never yet seen a man drunk in France, even among the lowest of people.[32]

In this encomium we see a man dedicated to seeing only the light which he has yearned for in all his days as a member of rough-hewn colonial society: "How much I enjoy their architecture, sculpture, painting, music. . .It is in these arts they shine." For at least the first year or so, the shadows are under the table for Mr. Jefferson. For Paris of the time was also a city of six hundred thousand people, one-fifth of whom were unemployed, and many half starving. Many sullen faces, many smoldering hearts were roaming the thirteen hundred streets of Paris, as Jefferson was soon to find out. Also, beneath the beautiful manners and style of the upper classes lurked the shadowed decadence of *Les Liasons Dangereuse*, with complex erotic encounters being the obsession of the young, and Byzantine political intrigues the obsession of their elders.

But as for Jefferson's immediate experience, he became a voracious book buyer, a willing customer for fine furniture and scientific instruments, and a frequenter of the great conversational salons of the day. Jefferson's greatest friend in France was the Marquise de Lafayette, the same Lafayette who had been of enormous assistance during the American Revolution. Lafayette introduced Jefferson to everybody, especially the company of aristocrats like himself. A natural aristocrat, Jefferson felt in their company as if he had come home to who he really was. Like them he had to be surrounded by servants, for although he was the most versatile of men, he had never mastered the art of looking out for himself.

This is also the time of the *philosophes* and essayists of remarkable elegance and wit, of Voltaire and Diderot, and the creators of the great Encyclopedia—a time of new ideas concerning nature, machinery, the way things work, and even of evolution. This encyclopedia contained everything, having been compiled at probably the last time in human history when what there was to be known could still be encompassed. Jefferson's own encyclopedic mind was typical of the enlightened sensibility that produced it. At this time one person's mental equipment still was capable of having sufficient hooks and eyes to capture the clothing of nature. Today, of course, this is no longer possible. Mathematicians now theorize that the knowledge available at the time of the birth of Christ doubled by the year 1500, doubled again by the year 1750, again by the year 1800, continuing to double in ever shorter intervals. As of this writing, it is said to double every eighteen months.

Jefferson fit right in with this spirit of art and science. He even brought a huge mammoth to France to prove to the naturalist Buffon that such beasts had once roamed the Americas. As the creator of so many of the liberal ideas, especially those concerning religious freedom, he soon came to be on close footing with many of the first minds of Europe. Jefferson was, I believe, very close to what Hegel meant by a "world historical individual," which means someone whose personal passion, ideas, sentiments, and spirit correspond to the movement and turning of the time. Either out in front or behind the scenes, such individuals are the entrepreneurs of change, as if the kairos (the loaded potent time when everything becomes possible) of the age and their kairos of heart and mind utterly coincide.

Jefferson was a remarkable person who did his human homework, learning everything in sight, reflecting, totally given over to the public good, but whose personal passions corresponded to the turnings of the time. If he had been born, say, thirty years later and had come in with the rise of Napoleon, he probably would not have had that same possibility; likewise, if he come in too early, he might have been caught up in the religious embroilments of early America. Interestingly, Jefferson himself wished he had been born in a far earlier time, around 1340, when he could have been simply a family man and a farmer, as he was when home in the feudal, baronial society of Monticello. Nevertheless, Jefferson prepared himself thoroughly for the option and the opportunity to be an agent of change and always acted as if he could make a difference.

Europe and particularly France had already been seduced by the American genius of Ambassador Benjamin Franklin, whose romantic liaisons with some of the most brilliant and extraordinary women of Paris delighted the French and shocked Jefferson. One can appreciate the picture Franklin made when Jefferson went to his home the first time, sitting there with his high domed forehead and thin wispy long hair, his glasses slipping down his nose, his gouty leg up on a stool, being constantly entertained and caressed by a bevy of elegant ladies in white wigs and gorgeous gowns. Jefferson tried to be gallant when several years later Franklin passed on his position as ambassador to him, saying he wished Franklin could also pass on his winning ways with the great ladies. To this Franklin replied to the forty-four-year-old Jefferson, "You are too young, my boy, to appeal to them."

What Franklin did pass on and what Jefferson developed was a canny political gift and the ability to do the hard work of government that the French nobility were not willing to do. He hammered out an all-purpose model treaty agreement for commerce and friendship that could be presented with variations to any of the nations the United States might approach. While doing so, he reformed the outmoded language of all old treaties, and with his talent for classification, put topics under appropriate heads and subheads and generally did away with the verbiage and abstraction that haunted the age-encrusted documents of Europe. At a time in which time-honored traditions were ripe for renovation, not to say revolution, he evolved rather than revolted, which is a much more difficult task as well as a much more fruitful one.

Jefferson's great ability was to be able to set his mind free from old traditions and approach a task afresh. A most interesting and innovative note was struck in his humanitarian approach to prisoners of war. Prisoners, Jefferson said, were not to be kept in irons or restrained, were to be allowed plenty of exercise, good food, and visitors from their governments. Of even greater importance, and chastening to us today, was his insistence that, in times of war, all women, children, scholars, farmers, artists, manufacturers, fishermen—all those whose occupations were for the subsistence of humankind—should be allowed to continue in their respective employments, while their houses, farms, or goods could not be destroyed by any occupying force. And if such destruction occurred, the victims should be paid for whatever was destroyed. We know that the emperor of Prussia, the enlightened Frederick the Great, scanned Jefferson's document with great approval and subsequently endorsed it.

Jefferson proposed many other possibilities for a world in which countries could work together that were so innovative that many of them will probably not become feasible until the twenty-first century. One of these was extending full rights of citizenship to the citizens of one nation when they are in the territory of another. If Jefferson were alive today, what wonderful ideas would he have about the shaping of the coming world government and planetary society, and what persistence and dedication could he bring to the difficult task of hammering out the details! I invite the reader to consider just what he might do.

Among the other issues that deeply concerned Jefferson in his capacity as ambassador was the safety of American shipping. Realizing as a true farmer does that unless one can get goods to market, there is no point in growing them, much of Jefferson's concern was over the organized piracy centered in the states of the Barbary Coast: Algeria, Morocco, Tunisia, and Libya. Jefferson shared this concern with John Adams, then Minister to England. Not only did Barbary Coast corsairs seize any ship they encountered, they brought the sailors and others on board ship back to Barbary and made slaves of them until ransom was paid. It incensed Jefferson that countries should have to pay ransom for their citizens. He wanted to send even the tiny American navy under the command of John Paul Jones to decimate the pirate fleets. When Jefferson and Adams met with the ambassador from Tunisia to protest the action of making war upon a nation that had done them no injury, the ambassador responded that they were enjoined by the Koran to make war upon any nation that did not acknowledge its authority. And because as infidels they were sinners, their people deserved to be made slaves, and that any Mohammedan who died in the service of such righteous war was sure to go to Paradise. These sentiments echo harshly down the centuries. Given this mindset, they were never able to reach a satisfactory agreement with the United States.

During the years that Jefferson lived in France and performed his services for his country through the many nations of Europe, his daughter Martha Jefferson was attending the best convent school in Paris, the Abbaie de Panthemont, where she found herself extremely happy with the nuns and their kind mothering. It was here too that she found a more passionate spirituality than the one she knew from her father's genial agnosticism. Under the tutoring of the sisters she was becoming avid to convert to Catholicism and enter religious orders. Later on when his younger daughter, nine-year-old Polly, arrived, she also went to school there. Their father visited them often, especially at first. When the French Revolution and its disturbances began in 1789, and Jefferson was preparing to go home, perhaps only for a short time, he took them out of the school. Home was safer for them than France, and he needed to discourage Martha from her growing obsession of becoming a nun—a very aristocratic nun, but a nun, nonetheless.

Jefferson was in Europe for five years and a few months. He was busy, occupied with matters vital to the well-being of the infant United States. For much of this time he was an ambassador to the court at Versailles, attending the *levees,* in which the king and queen received visitors in bed. At the same time, he was under many pressures and much pain. His youngest surviving daughter died of the whooping cough while he was away; the second daughter, Maria, known as Polly, also contracted it but survived. Perhaps it is this that made Jefferson so adamant about bringing her to him in France, even though the relatives with whom she lived begged him to let her stay in Virginia. Polly didn't want to go; she didn't remember her father. So she was tricked into coming aboard ship, where she was enticed into playing many games until she fell asleep from exhaustion and the ship sailed. Luckily, she became tremendously fond of the captain. As another inducement, her traveling companion was her friend and quadroon slave, fourteen-year-old Sally Hemings.

Jefferson also had expenses far beyond any salary or allowance; his country, too, was severely in debt, and one of his labors involved the negotiations for new loans and favorable terms for paying old ones. Moreover, he apparently considered that the joy of his life had substantially ended—only his daughters could bring him joy. And he must have been homesick. Many writers say that his health, which was formidable at home, deteriorated in the vapors of France. He felt himself so busy that he could not find "occasion for a new acquaintance." He was forty-four years old, yet wrote, "I'm an old man."

But, as is the case with so many of us who assume that our lives are over, there came a period when life bloomed new for him. It began in the late summer of 1786; he had been in France two years. The Connecticut artist John Trumbull, who was in France making sketches of Jefferson for his painting of the signing of the Declaration of Independence, urged him to come and meet two artists who were also visiting Paris. They were Richard and Maria Cosway. Mr. Cosway was considered to be England's most gifted miniaturist; Mrs. Cosway, also a talented artist, was his favorite model and much admired for her beauty and wit.

Jefferson said he was too busy. But on this day he and Trumbull were to visit a remarkable building which housed the Paris grain market, a structure which Trumbull pronounced "a wonderful piece of architecture." Trumbull then told Jefferson that the Cosways were to accompany them. Jefferson almost refused to go—the press of business was great—but a fascinating building? A public market made beautiful? Who could resist? Certainly not the gentleman from Monti-cello. The descriptions of Maria Cosway are dazzling. Twenty-seven years old, she was married to a bright, strange, monkey-looking man almost the same age as Jefferson. She had porcelain skin, cupid lips, golden hair, glorious clothes, and an enigmatic smile. She was friend to many artists (and, reputedly, a very good friend of the Prince of Wales), had a delicious accent half-English and half-Italian, having lived in Italy with her English parents for many years, and was sophis-ticated and charming. They spent hours admiring the grain market, and being more than an amateur architect, Jefferson showed her the glories of the building. As he wrote later, though his head was describing how beautiful, beautiful the building was, his heart was saying how beautiful, beautiful this woman was.

Every one of the four had evening engagements, but the smitten Mr. Jefferson persuaded them all to change their former plans and stay together. They dined together, rode out to another part of Paris, went to see the shows with fireworks in Montmartre, then vis-ited a harpist who apparently gave them a concert. The time was late August—what Jefferson described later as a Lapland summer day. The country was beautiful; the sights were beautiful, the art was beauti-ful, and the music, Jefferson said, was so ravishing that it would allow him to break the commandment "Thou shalt not covet."

At the concert he learned that the devastating Maria was also a composer, a harpist, a singer, and a pianist. Every day there-after, for as long as the Cosways remained in Paris, Jefferson spent some part of each day with them, sometimes with Turnbull, some-times alone. Sometimes he and Maria would go sightseeing together, walking or riding through the Bois du Boulogne, back to St. Cloud, or to St. Germain, through woods and gardens, to inns and casinos, and especially, to ruins. Of one of their days together, Jefferson wrote to Maria:

> How grand the ideas excited by the remains of such a col-umn! The spiral staircase was too beautiful. Every moment was filled with something agreeable. The wheels of time moved on with a rapidity of which those of our carriage gave but a faint idea, and yet in the evening, when one took a retrospect of the day, what a mass of happiness had we traveled over![33]

Evidence exists that the Cosway marriage was not happy; she had married him because she and her mother were destitute, and Richard had settled money on her and promised to take care of her mother. Richard liked her beauty, and the fact that she was admired by so many brought him more commissions for work. They were apparently necessary to each other, but the tall gentleman from Virginia seemed to become her favorite among her many admirers. However, it was at this time that while walking with a companion (perhaps Maria), Jefferson tried to jump over a fence and either broke or badly dislocated his right wrist. The accident was painful and embarrassing. Two surgeons working on him did not help. But Maria soon wrote that she missed seeing him and hoped they would be able to be together soon. And so they were—but now she broke the news that her husband expected to return to England soon (this was early October). His notes to her, laboriously written with the left hand, tell of sleepless nights and infinite regret. The pain was in the hand and also in his emotions, but he gallantly saw them off on their journey to England. When he returned home, he began to write the "Dialogue Between My Head and My Heart," one of the most famous and exquisite love letters in all literature. It was nearly nine thousand words, all written with the left hand, while the surgeons continued to work on and further mishandle his broken right wrist. It is a poignant picture: this noble man so utterly in love, caught in the throes of hopelessness and loss of that love, nursing a fiercely aching wrist, sitting by his fireside "solitary and sad" and making himself write out his feelings in fiery but meticulous prose. The dialogue begins:

> *Head.* Well, friend, you seem to be in a pretty trim.

> *Heart.* I am indeed the most wretched of all earthly beings. Overwhelmed with grief, every fiber of my frame distended beyond its natural powers to bear, I would willingly meet whatever catastrophe should leave me no more to feel or to fear.[34]

As this dialogue is actually a letter sent to Maria, Jefferson provides an indirect appeal to her artistic ambitions and love of travel to beautiful places. The Head cautions the Heart that, even if Maria should return to Paris the following year, it would be only a short stay, and soon the wide Atlantic would part them forever. "What is to follow? Perhaps you flatter yourself they may come to America?" The Heart's answer is a masterpiece of allurement as it chronicles the glories of the American landscape:

> God only knows what is to happen. I see nothing impossible in that supposition, and I see things wonderfully contrived sometimes to make us happy. Where could they find such objects as in America for the exercise of their enchanting art? Especially the lady, who paints landscapes so inimitably. She wants only subjects worthy of immortality to render her

pencil immortal. The Falling Spring, the Cascade of Niagara, the passage of the Potomac through the Blue Mountains, the Natural Bridge. It is worth a voyage across the Atlantic to see these objects; much more to paint, and make them, and thereby ourselves, known to all ages. And our own dear Monticello, where has Nature spread so rich a mantle under the eye? Mountains, forests, rocks, rivers. With what majesty do we there ride above the storms! How sublime to look down into the workhouse of nature, to see her clouds, hail, snow, rain, thunder, all fabricated at our feet! And the glorious sun, when rising as if out of a distant water, just gilding the tops of the mountains, and giving life to all nature![35]

Alf Mapp says that this incident provides another instance of Jefferson's "tendency after an initial period of shock to fight disappointment and grief with purposeful activity." And, may we add, with the creation of a work of art. By making a work of art of his anguish, did he exorcise it?

Letters passed between Jefferson and Maria, but so did time, distance, much work, and many travels. For some months Jefferson was on a journey through Southern Europe. The physicians had urged him to go for his wrist's sake—the hand and nerves had shrivelled, and it was months before he could use his hand at all. He also went to study the land and the crops (ever the agriculturist), to meet secretly with a revolutionary from Brazil, and to admire the beauties of art, nature, and civilization, even those which were past. It should be stated that he kept a flirtatious and flattering correspondence going with several French women, and that his letters during this long journey were not written only to Maria. But it was only with Maria that he was apparently deeply in love.

Later in 1787, young Polly arrived in England and no one has satisfactorily reasoned why Jefferson did not himself come to meet her, especially since the longed-for Mrs. Cosway was also in England. Polly had been received into the Adams family in England and had become extremely attached to Abigail Adams and her children. Then a stranger from Paris, her father's maitre d'hotel, a man who did not even speak English, arrived from Paris to take her to a father she did not remember. Mrs. Adams scolded Jefferson severely for his insensitivity. Why did Jefferson act in such an uncharacteristic way? Perhaps he thought Mrs. Cosway was going to come to see him and felt he would miss her in the crossing. That's how in love he was. Later that year, Maria Cosway did come to Paris without her husband, but her time was so full and her admirers so many that she and Jefferson seemed somehow not to be able to get together satisfactorily. There are many opinions about what happened during the months she was there. They both complained to each other and to friends about not having time together and missing each other. "A fatality has attended my wishes," Jefferson wrote. When she returned in December to England, the relationship was strained and somehow broken. She sent Jefferson word that a dear and beautiful friend was coming to Paris, Angelica Church. Thereafter Mr. Jefferson referred to the two of them together—one on one arm and the other on the other, in his talk of their times together.

After leaving Europe, Jefferson never saw Maria again, but from their friendship and romance he was greatly invigorated. This testifies to the miracle of rebirth that can occur when one feels dead and finished. Somehow either one's head or one's heart is blown open by an unlooked for but felicitous experience, by sheer unexpected happenings. No matter whether this quickening happens to the head or the heart first, the other soon follows. Some of Jefferson's richest thinking emerged at that time of the greening of his heart and spirit. He was helping Lafayette and the French revolutionists understand what they called the Rights of Man. He was corresponding with James Madison over the crafting of the Constitution and the Bill of Rights. He was at this time the arbiter, the evocateur, the genius of peaceful revolution of the moment and nation-making for the future. Ultimately, of course, the call came for him to return home.

PROCESS 7
THE "DIALOGUE BETWEEN MY HEAD AND MY HEART"

In the following process we will engage in our own dialogue between our head and our heart. In the extraordinary letter that Jefferson wrote to Maria Cosway, he revealed the emotional fire of his heart and tried to justify its ways to the cool and austere logic of his head.

The head says to the heart, "Why didn't you plan this? Why didn't you look out for contingent plans and opportunities? Why didn't you realize that pleasure is only a hope ahead, but misery is always at your side?" The heart replies, "I'm not listening. I have never known such happiness. I have never known such love, such days of rapture. It was worth everything. It was worth my entire life." It is this kind of back and forth internal conversation that Jefferson records and sends to Maria Cosway.

In a larger sense, Jefferson was also writing out the perennial dialogue which haunts the human psyche. Perhaps this theme of head versus heart owes its antiquity and staying power to the fact that we humans have so great a split between the needs of our old paleomammalian emotional brain (the limbic system), our reptilian survival brain, and the creative but abstracting brain of our neocortex. Our antic disposition, therefore, moves us regularly between passion and austerity, logic and romance. Thus we sometimes feel that we contain within us divided and distinguished worlds—part of us a cold and calculating computer; part swayed by the emotions and yearnings of the moment.

TIME: NINETY MINUTES TO TWO HOURS.

•MATERIALS:
Drawing and writing materials and large sheets of paper for each participant.

•MUSIC:
Romantic music in a classical mode for the parts of this process dealing with memories or imaginings of a heartfelt nature. The very best would be the old French song "Plaisir d'Amour" as sung by Nana Mouskouri from her cassette or CD album, *Passport*. Doubtless, Jefferson knew and loved this song during his romantic interlude with Maria Cosway, and its enchantments continue to move us today. The Guide would have this song play repeatedly. Another good choice would be Respighi's *Ancient Airs and Dances*. Information on both these record-

ings is found in the listing under Area Two of Musical Selections. The later part of the process requires a tape of a heartbeat. If this can't be obtained, the Guide should sound the heartbeat on a drum.

• *INSTRUCTIONS FOR GOING SOLO:*

Tape the instructions and follow them up to the part where you begin to draw. Then just follow the instructions of the Guide in the book. In lieu of a partner, at the end of this process, read the dialogue between your head and your heart out loud.

• *SCRIPT FOR THE GUIDE:*

Would everyone please get comfortable, either lying down or sitting up, and close your eyes. In a few moments I am going to read to you from Thomas Jefferson's letter to Maria Cosway on the dialogue between his head and his heart. As you listen I want you to think about the dialogue between your own head and heart. You will begin to drift into levels of soft remembrance. Just let yourself float into your own beautiful day, that long Lapland summer day when love was new and winsome and wonderful. Being present now to that delicious time when there's such delicate exploration going on. And if there was someone who shared with you such a glorious day, invite that person here. Or if you wish to plan or imagine a glorious long day of adventure and exploration and the delight of the possibility of new life and new loving with someone, bring that person here.

And feel and be in that day. The canoe ride on the river. The walk through the woods. The grapes and fried chicken that you ate. The strawberries in the wine. The linked hands; the loving looks. The instant communion; the two minds seemingly one. The birdsong celebrating your friendship; the breeze whispering "yes" in the trees. And be there with that loved one now. And let the glorious day continue to unfold in your inner world or memory or imagination as I read part of this wonderful dialogue to you.

(The song, "Plaisir d'Amour" or some other romantic selection begins to play. The Guide now reads in a quiet voice from Jefferson's "My Head and My Heart." The reading of the text should only be background to the memories and reflections of the participants and should not dominate the process.)

Head. Well, friend, you seem to be in a pretty trim.

Heart. I am indeed the most wretched of all earthly beings. Overwhelmed with grief, every fibre of my frame distended beyond its natural powers to bear, I would willingly meet whatever catastrophe should leave me with no more to feel or to fear.

Head. These are the eternal consequences of your warmth and precipitation. This is one of the scrapes into which you are ever leading us. You confess your follies indeed: but still you hug and cherish them, and no reformation can be hoped, where there is no repentance.

Heart. Oh my friend! This is no moment to upbraid my foibles. I am rent into fragments by the force of my grief! If you have any balm, pour it into my wounds: if none, do not harrow them by new torments. Spare me this awful moment! At any other I will attend with patience your admonitions.

Head. On the contrary I never found that the moment of triumph with you was the moment of attention to my admonitions. . . .I never ceased whispering to you that we had no occasion for new acquaintance, that the greater the merits and talents, the more dangerous their friendship to our tranquillity, because the regret at parting would be greater. . . . Every soul of you had an engagement for the day. Yet all of these were to be sacrificed, that you might dine together. Lying messengers were to be dispatched into every quarter of the city with apologies for your breach of engagement. You particularly had the effrontery to send word to the Dutchess Danville that, in the moment we were setting out to dine with her, dispatches came to hand which required immediate attention. You wanted me to invent a more ingenious excuse; but I knew you were getting into a scrape, and I would have nothing to do with it. Well, after dinner to St. Cloud, from St. Cloud to Ruggieri's, from Ruggieri to Krumfoltz, and if the day had been as long as a Lapland summer day, you would still have contrived means, among you, to have filled it.

Heart. Oh! my dear friend, how you have revived me by recalling to my mind the transactions of that day! How well I remember them all, and that when I came home at night and looked back to the morning, it seemed to have been a month agone. Go on then, like a kind comforter, and paint to me the day we went to St. Germains. How beautiful was every object! the Port de Neuilly, the hills along the Seine, the rainbows of the machine at Marly, the terras of St. Germains, the chateaux, the gardens, the statues of Marly, the pavillion of Lucienne. Recollect too Madrid, Bagatelle, the King's garden, the Dessert. How grand the idea excited by the remains of such a column! The spiral staircase too was beautiful. Every moment was filled with something agreeable. The wheels of time moved on with a rapidity of which those of our carriage gave but a faint idea, and yet in the evening, when one took a retrospect of the day, what a mass of happiness had we travelled over! Retrace all those scenes to me, my good companion, and I will forgive the unkindness with which you were chiding me.

Head. Thou art the most incorrigible of all the beings that ever sinned! I reminded you of the follies of the first day, intending to deduce from thence some useful lessons for you, but instead of listening to these, you kindle at the recollection, you retrace the whole series with a fondness which shows you want nothing but the opportunity to act it over again. I often told you during its course that you were imprudently engaging your affections under circumstances that must cost you a great deal of pain. . .that their stay here was to be short: that you rack our whole system when you are parted from those you love, complaining that such a separation is worse than death, inasmuch as this ends our sufferings, whereas that only begins them: and that the separation would in this instance be the more severe as you would probably never see them again.

Heart. But they told me they would come back again the next year. . . .

Head. Very well. Suppose then they come back. They are to stay here two months, and when these are expired, what is to follow? Perhaps you flatter yourself they may come to America?

Heart. God only knows what is to happen. I see nothing impossible in that supposition, and I see things wonderfully contrived sometimes to make us happy.

Where could they find such objects as in America for the exercise of their enchanting art? Especially the lady, who paints landscapes so inimitably. She wants only subjects worthy of immortality to render her pencil immortal. The Falling Spring, the Cascade of Niagara, the Passage of the Potowmac through the Blue Mountains, the Natural Bridge. It is worth a voyage across the Atlantic to see these objects; much more to paint, and make them, and thereby ourselves, known to all ages. And our own dear Monticello, where has Nature spread so rich a mantle under the eye? Mountains, forests, rocks, rivers. With what majesty do we there ride above the storms!

How sublime to look down into the workhouse of nature, to see her clouds, hail, snow, rain, thunder, all fabricated at our feet! And the glorious Sun, when rising as if out of a distant water, just gilding the tops of the mountains, and giving life to all nature!—I hope in god no circumstance may ever make either seek an asylum from grief! With what sincere sympathy I would open every cell of my composition to receive the effusion of their woes! I would pour my tears into their wounds: and if a drop of balm could be found at the top of the Cordilleras, or at the remotest sources of the Missouri, I would go thither myself to seek and to bring it. Deeply practised in the school of affliction, the human heart knows no joy which I have not lost, no sorrow of which I have not drank! Fortune can present no grief of unknown form to me! Who then can so softly bind up the wound of another as he who has felt the same wound himself? But Heaven forbid they should ever know a sorrow!—Let us turn over another leaf, for this has distracted me.

(After reading this text, the Guide will say:)

Holding in your heart and in your head, the memories or imaginings of sweetest, life-giving love. And holding in your heart the beloved of that day. And thanking him or her for memories that last a lifetime.

Let your own heart and head soar and fly out through the night and the day, across time to the lonely American in Paris, writing by a fireside on that razor's edge between love and loss. And letting your memory of your glorious day fly out to join his memory of the days with Maria Cosway in Paris in 1786. So that the memories of love are augmented and sing through the night for all of us. And the head and heart of Thomas Jefferson are now writing to each other as they were on this night over two hundred years ago. And Tom Jefferson's head is being blown open to all kinds of thoughts and enchantments and belief and sweetness. And his heart is being opened to affirm the worth and beauty of all people.

So, Tom, Long Tom, Wild Tom, Bright Tom, Tom in Love, Tom in Thought, we call you now on this day, two hundred years later, but only an eyeblink of time in cosmic memory. We call on you so that like you, we too can encompass in our love a nation, a world, all peoples, all sentient beings. We call on you as you are now, blown open by love to the transcendence of time and space to inspire our minds so that we too can hammer out the knowings and the details to encompass the courage and sweetness of our hearts. As it was then, so it is on the same evening now, and for all time.

And this is what I would like us to do. We will begin our journey by evoking our heads. Would you all please begin to tap on your heads. And as you tap with all your fingers on your head, you can even address your head. "Hello, head. Hi, head. How're you doing, head?" Keep on tapping, tapping on the head. As you tap, I'm going to ask you to move your closed eyes all round your head. Move your eyes to the right brain; now to the left brain; now to the back of the head where the old reptilian brain resides; now to the center of the head, the site of the limbic system and the old mammalian brain. Now move your eyes to the frontal lobes of the neocortex, the most recent and most creative of your brains. Keep swinging and looping your eyes through the various parts of your head and brain, having a sense of older and newer parts of the brain being linked up as you move your eyes between them, connecting the different parts of your brain with the energy of your eyes' movement.

As you do this, continue to tap on your head. Linking the protective and survival mechanism of your old reptilian brain now with the emotional power and socialization of the limbic system of the old mammalian brain. And with your eyes swing through the brain so that your eyes are weaving circuits of new connections. You may even begin to notice the dendritic connections and sense the immense weave of interconnections between the cells of the brain, reaching out to each other in trillions of combinations. And you suddenly realize that you have an entire cosmos in your head, a universe in miniature. And you think of all the new connections and associations that you could put in that might make you more intelligent and even more complex, able perhaps to understand the range and reach of it all.

But you also sense the great swelling swamp of the emotional brain rising up and saying, "No, you don't! I'll drown you out! We don't need any more complexity than we've already got. At least pay some attention now to your heart!" And you realize that what with all these incredible interconnections, this cosmos in your head, you need the balance of your heart lest you get drowned in the too-muchness of it all. You need a dialogue between the cosmos in your head and the cosmos in your heart. So let us turn to the heart now.

(The Guide puts on the heartbeat tape here or drums the beat.)

So let us focus our closed eyes to the area around the heart, imagining that you can move your eyes within the ventricles of your heart. And at the same time tap with your hands on your heart. And as you tap your heart, imagine that your heart is the sun. Sun heart. Heart sun. Sun heart. Heart sun. Sun heart. Heart sun.

And those of you who have practiced yoga or are very limber, tap in back as well as in the front. One hand in front, and one hand in back, and tap the heart front and back. Front and back or just front in a heart beat rhythm. Bump bump. . . Bump bump. . . Bump bump. . . bump bump. . .With your eyes, continuing to look inside your heart. Seeing there the arterial flow of blood to the four great valves, the pulse of life moving through your mighty heart. Keep tapping on your heart and seeing the spiralling pattern of the deep inward heart.

And knowing the times that you have been in a paroxysm of emotion, of love perhaps, or hate, or anger or yearning, or emotional need. And knowing too how your heart has sometimes contracted so as to protect you from the storms of love or need or desire or anxiety. And yet often this contraction gave you the implosive power that allowed you to explode into action and to have the courage to be. And you realize that heart has been the great energizing instrument to put you back into life when you have despaired of life.

And now with your right hand, tap the heart. And with your left hand, tap the head. Tapping them together. And feeling in your eyes swirling through that head the incredible numbers of dendrite connections that can help you know and understand so much. And feeling in that heart the pulsing, seething vortex of the life force that gives the impulse to the knowings of the head. And knowing that the feelings of the head give the impulse to the knowing of the heart. The heart has its reason that reason cannot know. The reason has its feeling which heart cannot feel. Somewhere in the course of evolution of consciousness they come together. And that moment, that point of evolution, is now. "What, now?" complains the old limbic emotional brain. "Not now! Twenty, thirty, forty, fifty thousand years from now, maybe. But not now! Please, not now!" But if we are to survive, it is critical that we come now into congruence of head and heart. For we see on the front page of the newspaper and the television news the problem of the war between the heart of the world and the head of the world and the violent and crazy breakdown of communication that has kept the heart and head separated in the world for, lo, these many thousands of years. So the time is now to bring them together, in ourselves, and through ourselves, for the head and the heart of the world.

So would you please now, with both hands, tap on your heart, feeling it now to be the heartbeat of the world. So your heart is not just your local heart. Not Betty's heart. Not Don's heart. Not Bob's heart. Not Trish's heart. Not Barbara Jo's heart. (The Guide names the people present.) But the heart of the world. The heart of Ireland and England and South Africa. The heart of Peru and Ecuador and Columbia and Venezuela. The heart of the Andes and the Alps, the Himalayas and the Grand Canyon. Of the Netherlands. Of Australia and New Zealand. The heart of China. The heart of Iraq and of Iran and of Israel. The heart of Arabia. The heart of India, Pakistan and Bangladesh. The heart of Africa. The heart of Mozambique, of Zambia, of Egypt and Libya and Liberia. The heart of Canada, Mexico. The heart of Siberia and of the great arid tundras. The heart of Luxembourg and of Wales and, yes, of France. The heart of Italy, and let us not forget Sicily. The heart of Scotland and of Iceland. The heart of Germany. (The Guide can name more countries and areas, especially local areas if he or she chooses to do so.)

All of these countries and places are part of your heart beating the rhythms of awakening to new world, to new possibility for this planet. Feel the heart of the Earth beating within you. And your heart extending now to include the heartbeat of the solar system—of Mars and Venus, Mercury and Pluto, Jupiter and Saturn and Neptune. The heartbeat of Uranus and the newly discovered planet Chiron. Containing within you too the heartbeat of comets and asteroids. And beyond that, the heart of our galaxy with its hundred billion stars. And who knows how many planets and moons. And the heartbeat of the galaxy reaching out now to other galaxies. To the great clustering hearts of galaxies. Hundreds of billions of galaxies. Even unto the galaxies of galaxies! Do they sing to each other? Do they fall in love with each other? If it is true, as the old hermetic philosophers tell us, that as above, so below—

they do. For we know that our atoms yearn for each other, and in yearning, form new combinations and new patterns of possibilities as complex atomic linkages and the growing of molecules. So what must happen when galaxies fall in love?

(The Guide may at this point raise the volume on the recording of the heartbeat.)

And now yours is the Heart of All Being. And the loving heart of the Universe pours its radiance into your heart, and you are back here in time and space with your own heart amplified and in a state of atunement with the heart of All Being.

And now we will do the same for the head. Your hand that has been tapping your head now taps to the rhythm of the heartbeat. And your other hand taps the same rhythm on your heart. For now we will tune the head to the amplified heart. Think of your head as also containing the Earth—its continents, its nations and peoples. And within your head is the bringing down of the walls that are there between nations. For now thoughts are reaching out to each other across the seas of your mind and across the continents of your brain. The knowing of the cycles of nature. The knowing of the cultures past and present. The knowing of the constitutions, laws, and parliaments. The knowing of the sciences. The knowing of the dreams and the fantasies, the stories and the myths. Of the music and the paintings and the arts. The knowing of the great understanding and the reading of the patterns of nature by the aboriginal peoples who remember the original Plan of Being. The knowing of the human heart which can go to the lengths of God. The knowing of the Earth Herself. And feel the movement within you now of the rhythm between your head and your heart, and the head and heart of the Earth.

Global head. . . global heart. . .global head. . . global heart. . . global head. . . global heart. . .global head. . . global heart. . .And the heart and mind of the galaxy is within you also. The galactic intelligence which keeps it all together is flowing into you here and now at this little corner of the edge of the galaxy where I like to think they have set up a school for gods. A school for co-creators, where we can be trained to go out and create new planets or life forms. But for this to happen, there has to be greater communion between your head and your heart. So let the old walls come down if you wish. They have protected you to this point, but now they may be restricting you, keeping you left back in the school of evolution. Let the membranes between your head and your heart become utterly full of holes so that you are becoming whole as well as holy.

Galactic brain. . .Galactic heart. . .Cosmic mind. . .Cosmic soul. Coming together. And the two pulsing in you so that the great restrictions and inhibitions between your heart and your head are now being let down. And new linkings are happening, going back and forth, between your hands tapping the rhythm of the connection between your head and your heart. Head and heart and head and heart and head and heart. And know that the local self is no longer and never was insufficient, inadequate, inept; for your patterning, parenting, patronage is from the Cosmic Head and Cosmic Heart of which you are a very wonderful part.

Now would everybody please take a sheet of paper. And will you draw in the center of the sheet a quick sketch of your head. Draw it quickly with no details. Now from this head I'd like you to draw lines leading off from it. We will call these lines radiant beams of ideas. And these radiant beams represent the various ideas or thoughts or other considerations that occur to you right now. Or they can refer to the kinds of thoughts that you think about with your head. Some examples of these considerations might be: Am I really part of God? What will I do with my profession next year? How am I going to make a living? How will I be able to get along with my family with all these new ideas? What creative intention do I have for my life, what plan of action or project? Just draw these ideas in pictures or words and put little circles around them as they radiate out of the center of your head. You will have five minutes to do this. Begin. (Five minutes.)

Now I want you to pick up random thoughts that are coming in from around the world or the universe, from Great Mind at large. They could be coming in from other parts of the Earth. They could be coming from other dimensions, or from other parts of the galaxy. Just tune in and be there for these thoughts coming through. And then draw more radiant beams showing those thoughts, those ideas that come in. They could be shown as words or drawings. You will have five minutes of clock time to do this. (Five minutes.)

Begin to notice if the beams of ideas coming from your own life and thought are somehow interconnected with the more universal ideas that are coming through. Is there a connection? Is there a webbing between personal and universal mind and ideas at work? Can the more universal patterns help and charge the ideas of the local personal patterns? What we are learning to do is to think as Mr. Jefferson did. He was able to build bridges in his mind to connect personal interests like planting and architecture to constitutions, to the creation of nations, to new theories of governance and society. So, too, by joining personal with universal thought, you can create from the materials of your mind a new medical fellowship, or a business, or some kind of sharing of psychological resources with the former Soviet Union, or perhaps a kind of sacred theater of the heart.

As you see these connections, begin to draw them. Notice how the thoughts, both personal and universal, begin

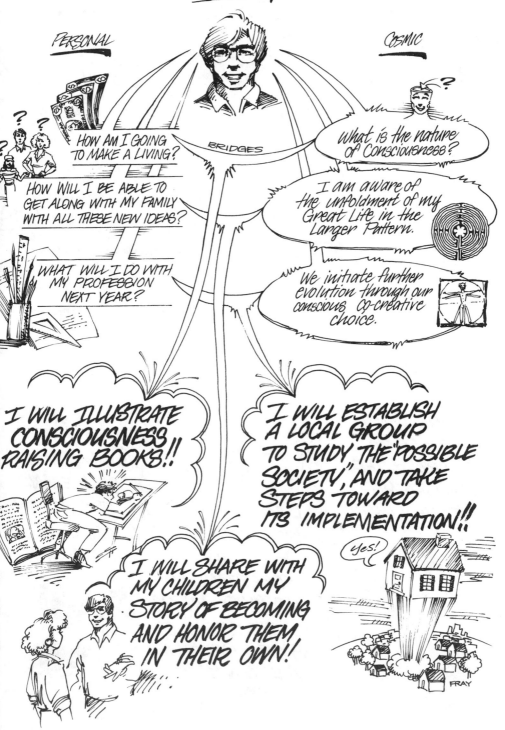

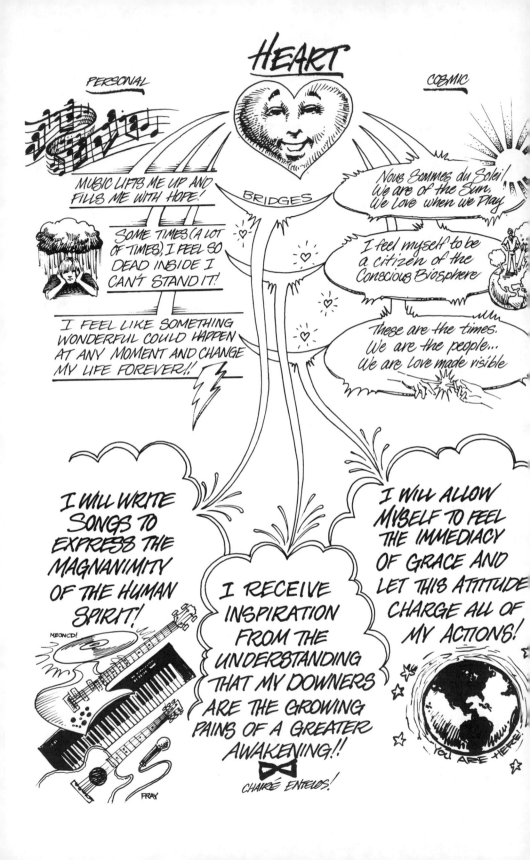

to connect to each other, leading to a strengthening column of thoughts and of patterns of creation. For what the coherent orchestral mind is able to do is to marshall all of its troops, all of its thoughts together to create something. Now you may discover that you have all kinds of allies within your individual thoughtful life and your Cosmic Thoughtful Life. For perhaps we can access the great archetypal patterns of thought and creation as well. But this we can do only if we have built up the connections between our own thought life and the Cosmic Thought Life. Then we've got a net to catch the universe.

And that is what Mr. Jefferson probably did. He so constructed the lines of communication within his own head, and ultimately with his own heart, so that he had a bridgework, a network, a mind work to catch the universe of new ideas and feelings. Otherwise we get these wild inspirations, and they go away, because we haven't got the netting to catch them and bring them home. In the next five minutes would you please draw or write some of the interconnections between universal and personal thought-life and where they seem to be going. (Five minutes.)

We're working creatively right now, but we could have looked as well at negative thoughts that obstruct. A negative thought doesn't have to be a downer. It can be a sense of absence that makes the mind work stronger. We can reframe a negative thought as a driver, a mental enzyme, a catalytic agent to drive us to reach out, to think more, to find real time to do real thought.

Now would you take another sheet of paper, please. And on it would you draw your sense of your heart in the center. And as we did with the head, would you draw radiant beams of feeling images from the heart. Heart images. Things that occur to you around your heart, around your feeling life. And draw circles around these ideas and images. And if thoughts or feelings connected with the heart come into you from the Earth or beyond, from the heart of All Being, then draw or write those also. So you're doing both this time. Drawing or writing your own feelings and those heart feelings and knowings coming in from the Heart of All Being, the heart of the planet, the heart of the universe, the heart of other dimensions.

Allow also the difficult or even negative heart feelings to come in. Make sure there are a few of them in there. But think of them catalytically. Think of them as enzymes rather than as poisons. Enzymes rather than poisons to make your heart open up. Often it is the great wounding thoughts that have caused you to be more vulnerable and available as well as more empathic and compassionate to others. Without your holy wounds, chances are you wouldn't be reaching out. But if you see them as enzymes and not as poisons, it changes the whole situation. It becomes a sacrifice of the heart; it becomes an ennoblement of the heart instead of a destruction of it. Would you draw or write all of this now for the next ten minutes. (Ten minutes.)

When you are ready, would you now draw or write on a radiant beam some issue of the heart that you wish to put forward. Some issue that involves your emotional charge that you wish to be able to put into the world as an enterprise, as a project, a relationship, a creation that you wish to commit to working on. Just as before you wrote or drew a creative thought intention, now you will draw or write a creative heart intention. You have two minutes to do this. (Two minutes.)

Now look at the connection existing between your personal feeling life and the more universal heart life, including the catalytic agents which you've thought of as poisons. Notice the connections between them and how they can work together to support your particular heart intention. You are observing the patterning of the heart, the story of the heart as it interconnects with Great Heart and your creative heart intention. This is the dialogue within the heart.

Would you now take both your pictures, and would you turn to a partner please. You will now speak first one, and then the other, of what you have learned of from the knowledge of the head and the knowledge of the heart. In other words you will have your own dialogue between your head and your heart. Your partner will be high witness to this dialogue which should last for about ten minutes. As you dialogue, you will notice the patterns of your head and of your heart. And just as Thomas Jefferson had a dialogue between his head and his heart, you are having a dialogue, and you're playing both parts. And all the while your partner is listening. Not commenting, just listening. Beginning now, you have ten minutes to use your drawings to prompt you in your dialogue between your head and your heart. (Ten minutes.)

And now let the second person begin, paying close attention to what they have drawn and written on their sheets of the nature of the dialogue between the head and the heart. You have ten minutes. (Ten minutes.)

We have been working in this long process to gain a more conscious interrelationship between our head and our heart. This can bring us to a mind and heart of many textures, of many more hooks and eyes, which in turn, will yield us incredible access to each other as well as to the universe at large. (The Guide may now lead the group in a discussion of the process.)

11 Secretary of State

After a smooth crossing of the Atlantic in the very short time of twenty-six days, Jefferson's ship ran into a solid fog bank blocking the eastern coast of the United States. Finally pulling into an inlet near Norfolk, the ship caught fire soon after Jefferson disembarked. Interestingly, the only thing that did not burn was the hold which contained the books, furniture, and other purchases Jefferson was bringing home from France, so all of his beautiful things were saved. As he left the ship, Jefferson was astonished when out of the mist came strange figures (actually the mayor and several aldermen of the city of Norfolk) greeting him as Secretary of State. In his absence he had been designated to hold that position, the most important in the country after that of the new President, George Washington.

Jefferson didn't even know what a Secretary of State was but hoped it meant a minimum of work so that he could spend most of his time back at Monticello. Unfortunately, that was not what the job entailed; rather, it assumed that he would be the chief functionary for all domestic affairs and carry all the administrative and diplomatic roles in foreign affairs.

Massive approbation and celebration greeted Jefferson on his journey home, including salutes from the Virginia legislature and everywhere the sense that this was the man of the hour, the man who would create the new America. Absence had definitely made the political heart grow fonder. On his way to Monticello, he received Washington's formal request that he assume the new position and soon knew that accepting it would mean more years of separation from his family, mounting debt, and many years of living in the acrimonious atmosphere of political life, which he hated more than anything. Yet he could not turn down a man like Washington, since the President insisted to him that his appointment was critical to the public welfare. "You are the best man for the office," the President told him, and his friend James Madison wrote him that a "universal anxiety is expressed for your acceptance." "It is not for an individual to choose his post," Jefferson finally wrote Washington, "you are to marshal us as may be best for the public good."

Much has been written of the scene of near Dionysian joy that greeted Jefferson upon his return at last to Monticello. All the hundreds of slaves thronged around his carriage, weeping and shouting, laughing and singing, unhitching the horses and pulling the carriage up the hill to the house. Then Jefferson himself was lifted out of the carriage by the black people who carried him to the house, still laughing and crying and covering him with kisses. Then all the neighbors showed up and showered him with praises and a formal memorial was held congratulating him on twenty years of extraordinary public service.

The homecoming festivities also included the marriage of his six-foot-tall, look-alike daughter Martha to her brilliant but highly neurotic cousin Thomas Randolph; the young couple was given much property by the bride's doting father. Even in the first months of her marriage—even with a new baby arriving almost every year, Martha would always write to her father, telling him that he was the first and foremost in her affections, as we know she was in his. Unlike today when we are more informal and lavish in expression in person yet more formal and circumspect in what we will say to each other in letters, in the eighteenth century you were allowed to express in writing sentiments which could not be expressed in person. One could only wonder whether Martha's devotion to her father was what drove her husband into so many desperate episodes of depression and near psychosis. Yet Jefferson was hugely affirming of his sons-in-law as well, treating them as full sons, while urging them to try harder.

Around this time, Jefferson visited the dying Benjamin Franklin, who listened to the reports of the convulsions in France with intense interest and animation. This excitement proved too much for his strength, however. But then, in a curious action, the old man forced upon Jefferson papers from his autobiography, saying "Keep them." There is some mystery about what was in these papers. Some believe that they contained an esoteric, even Masonic statement of a line of succession, some revelation about the mystical future of the United States and the world. "I will return them," said Jefferson. "No, keep them," Franklin repeated over and over again, and those were their last words to each other.

Jefferson moved to New York, then the seat of the government. Almost immediately he met his shadow, his most consistent antagonist, a man whose views were almost always diametrically opposite to his own and who himself regarded Jefferson as the shadow of the American republic. That man was Alexander Hamilton. A product of an illegitimate union between a West Indian merchant of Scotch descent and a lady who was living there at the time, Hamilton was a very pretty fellow who from his earliest days was filled with driving ambition and an abundance of erotic zeal. A splendid writer, his abilities in journalism and amorous verse had caused his fellow islanders in the West Indies to raise a fund to send him to New York's King's College. By the time he was twenty-two, his writing abilities had earned him the rank of Lieutenant Colonel on Washington's staff, but his duties were as chief writer. Washington loved him as the son he didn't have and refused to give him a military command lest he be killed. In fact, the only military experience Hamilton had was in the final great battle at Yorktown, which was a relatively easy victory.

Hamilton then married into New York Dutch aristocracy, and this assured him a successful political career. He wrote many of *The Federalist Papers* which launched the Constitutional Convention and contributed many ideas to the Constitution itself. Washington named him Secretary of the Treasury, convinced of his genius and his courage. One story about his courage tells of the time when he first faced enemy fire and couldn't stop his knees from knocking together. "Are you afraid, Mr. Hamilton?" a more experienced soldier asked. "Yes, I'm afraid," he replied, "and if you were half as scared as I am, you would run." Washington was greatly taken as well with Hamilton's eloquence, tremendous efficiency, and considerable understanding of finance and government. Nor was he alone in his regard. The great French statesman Talleyrand, who knew everybody, thought the greatest men of the epoch were Hamilton, Napoleon, and Charles Fox who was important in the British government, and that of these, the greatest was Hamilton.

Hamilton, however, did not trust ordinary people. "The public is a great beast," he once said. "Take mankind in general, they are vicious." Most people he believed, were governed by the crassest kind of self-interest, blind passion, and the basest instincts. There is no question but that he longed for some kind of return to dynastic monarchy. Indeed, he was an Anglophile, thinking the British monarchical and parliamentary system the best in the world. It was this tendency more that any other which deeply disturbed Jefferson, who believed in the public and thought that every human being had immense potential. Washington told him that both men were needed in the Cabinet to balance each other. As a member of Washington's Cabinet, Hamilton proposed an Assumption Bill, in which the federal government would assume the war debt of all the states in return for a considerable rise in taxes. Hamilton was also the author of many schemes in which members of the government made money and which helped various financiers make money as well. He created the modern banking system and the Federal Bank. With this considerable influx of money, mills and factories sprang up everywhere under Hamilton's financial management, and an era of apparent unparalleled prosperity was at hand.

All this was watched with great disheartenment by Jefferson, who saw his cherished vision of an agrarian commonwealth inhabited by men who tilled the fields gradually falling into the hands of merchants and speculators. Jefferson had enormous distrust of the growth of cities and financial power structures. In his *Notes on Virginia*, he had described great cities as "festering sores on the body politic" and had predicted that growth in disease, crime, and class struggle would accompany urban development. He greatly feared the concentration of wealth, especially in the hands of those who did not actually produce the wealth, but instead shuffled its papers— stocks, bonds, certificates, currency. Also—and this was Jefferson's greatest fear—men of business were not interested in liberty or equality. Their interest in government was solely to the degree that it could help them further their financial interests. Hamilton was utterly polarized in his view, believing that a strong nation found its finest exemplars in its industrial entrepreneurs and captains of finance and that having creditors assured a source of both energy and stability. In the same vein, while Jefferson called for diffusion of government, Hamilton was for centralization in everything.

More often than not, it was Hamilton who convinced Washington on matters of public policy, while Jefferson held the sway of public opinion. Herein lies the source of conflict between the American dream and the American reality, which has haunted the Earth ever since. The dream calls for equal opportunity and liberty, while the reality calls for more and more capital being poured into business, with the result that the rich get richer and the poor get poorer, causing tremendous frustration on the part of people and nations. Yet Jefferson had to admit that the country was prospering, while he was both personally and politically something of an idiot in financial matters. Clearly, both men believed that their positions were absolutely right. Each man was the other's shadow: Hamilton was whispered to by elite financiers, who told him, "You're right; you're right"; mad applause from the masses accompanied Jefferson. Hamilton trusted the corporation; Jefferson trusted the individual. Hamilton believed in the economy of head; Jefferson in the economy of heart. Hamilton was the champion of the industrial economy; Jefferson championed individual initiative, equality, and personal liberty.

The acrimony of this struggle between the two men was carried forth in newspapers of the day, Hamilton's mouthpiece being *The Gazette of the United States*, in which he himself wrote and published vitriolic attacks of Jefferson under the name of Catullus, calling Jefferson an enemy of the Constitution, a terrible business advisor, and a hypocrite. Jefferson's organ was the Philadelphia-based *National Gazette*, pro-French and pro-American republican democracy. It constantly caricatured Hamilton as a flunkey of the monarchy. This was, of course, the beginning of the use of newspapers as tools of polarization and over-simplification.

Meanwhile, in the middle was Washington, a man of grave dignity, prudence, and moderation, who simply could not understand such passionate outbursts, the father in some way of both men, who was at sixty aging rapidly, in poor health, and fearful that the antics of his sons would tear the republic apart. Furthermore, he was sick of politics and wanted to retire, but only if Jefferson would consent to being made President. Wise little James Madison, Jefferson's closest friend, warned the President that with respect to Jefferson:

> . . . his extreme repugnance to public life and anxiety to exchange it for his farm and his philosophy made it doubtful. . .whether it would be possible to obtain his own con-

sent; and if obtained, whether local prejudices in the Northern States. . .would not be a bar to his appointment.[36]

And so there was no one to replace Washington, and the precarious unity of the republic hung by a slender thread upon one man (which is why Washington is remembered with such awe: he was utterly irreplaceable and always the Wise Father). His role was that of the grand conciliator, who kept the polarity between Jefferson and Hamilton balanced. With Washington between them, each man had to clarify and justify his position, which resulted in better treaties, better forms of banking, better ways of solving the national indebtedness. Unfortunately, Washington did not know how to take all the poison of the conflict he was absorbing out of himself, and he got steadily sicker. We might fruitfully look at our own lives in this regard. How many of us are Hamiltonians, trying to build up the political and financial power of an organization while creating a good support system? How many are Jeffersonians, striving to create equality and an empowerment of the personal in each person? How many are Washingtons, conciliators trying to hold it all together and see a much larger picture? How many of us act at times as all three?

Jefferson desired nothing so much as to retire, but was prevailed upon by Washington and Madison not to do so. He suffered horrendous migraines during this period, lasting for weeks on end. What did Jefferson do with all this misery? He used his pain as impetus, turning it into creative endeavor, inventing a whole new system of weights and measures based on the decimal system, one of the great systems of American science. He also created the Patent Office for new inventions, helped develop the new classical style of architecture, and worked to lay out the streets of what would be the new capital at Washington City. And this was while suffering crushing headaches!

In the fall of 1792, the atmosphere of political dissension was so grave that old friends crossed the streets in order to avoid each other. The Jefferson-Hamilton conflict was projected upon the national arena. There was no problem in reelecting Washington, but for Vice President, John Adams, the Federalist party's choice, won out over Jefferson's Republican party choice of George Clinton. The aftermath of the election was massive animosity between sections of the country and between classes. People were especially taking sides on the French Revolution. Feelings mounted to fever heat, for the French Revolution was like every ball game, every soap opera, and every movie, all rolled up into one. The division was between the wealthier and the poorer peoples, and the split formed especially around the two poles of France-loving Jefferson and England-worshipping Hamilton. Jefferson was alone in the cabinet in supporting the French Revolution, for even Washington was shocked at the lengths to which the French Revolutionists were going and the degree of butchering of their opponents that was occurring. We have to realize that Jefferson had a profound sense of history and believed that support of the revolution in France would support revolution and new government everywhere in Europe and bolster the American democracy. But as with all polarizations, the sympathy towards the British monarchy and government by the financiers was gaining a great deal of ground in the light of the Jacobin atrocities. With this in mind, Jefferson wrote his belief's about the French Revolution in one of his most remarkable letters:

> In the struggle which was necessary, many guilty persons fell without the forms of trial, and with them some innocent. These I deplore as much as any body, & shall deplore some of them to the day of my death. But I deplore them as I should have done had they fallen in battle. It was necessary to use the arm of the people, a machine not quite so blind as balls and bombs, but blind to a certain degree. A few of their cordial friends met at their hands the fate of enemies. But time and truth will rescue & embalm their memories, while their posterity will be enjoying that very liberty for which they would never have hesitated to offer up their lives. The liberty of the whole earth was depending on the issue of the contest, and was ever such a prize won with so little innocent blood? My own affections have been deeply wounded by some of the martyrs to this cause, but rather than it should have failed I would have seen half the earth desolated. Were there but an Adam & Eve left in every country, & left free, it would be better than as it now is.[37]

For three months no ships crossed the Atlantic, so wild were the gales raging across the ocean. Then in April, 1793, a ship from France landed, and Americans were stunned to learn that the French had cut off the heads of their king and queen and declared war on Britain and Spain. Also arriving on the first of the ships to cross the Atlantic was a preening, brilliant, madly egotistical fellow, Edmond Genet, who was the new minister from France. To the ecstatic applause of crowds everywhere, Genet pushed the French cause, troubling the Washington government to remember their promise to be the ally of France in its troubles with Britain and asking them to fit out privateers to prey upon British shipping and to recruit troops for the seizure of Spanish-held Florida and Louisiana. Genet's presence and volatility was of considerable embarrassment to Jefferson. Here was Jefferson blithely writing that the "tree of liberty must be refreshed from time to time with the blood of patriots and tyrants. It is its natural manure." And here was Genet, the blood of kings fairly dripping off his hands, calling for a little more blood, indeed demanding it as the due of alliances which Jefferson had himself helped to set up. Jefferson tried to maintain a sneaking neutrality and a tortuous subterfuge, referring to obscure legal arguments as to why America could not help France. With immense diplomacy he managed to steer the new nation clear of granting military aid and of outfitting privateers, while still remaining a friend of France. Jefferson and Washington were both attacked for this diplomacy in the letters published by Genet. The effect of their sidestepping was to throw public opinion in the direction of the pro-British Federalists. Washington at a Cabinet meeting was so on edge that he flew into a rare and terrifying rage. As Jefferson recorded in his diary:

> He got into one of those passions when he cannot command himself. . .defied any man on earth to produce one single act of his. . .which had not been done on the purest motives. . .that, By God, he had rather be in his grave than in the present situation. He had rather be on his farm than to be made emperor of the world.[38]

On his part, Jefferson felt exactly the same way. Utterly disenchanted with the political world in which he labored, he asked to resign immediately. Only his close friend James Madison could dissuade him saying:

> I feel for your situation but you must bear it. Every consideration, private as well as public, requires a further sacrifice of your longings for the repose of Monticello. . . .you must not make your final exit from public life till it will be marked with justifying circumstances which all good citizens will respect, and to which your friends can appeal.[39]

Jefferson's response in a letter to Madison is one of the most eloquent ever written of the tortures that the private individual must undergo to carry out the impulses of history:

> To my fellow citizens the debt of service has been fully and faithfully paid. I acknowledge that such a debt exists, that a tour of duty in whatever line he can be most useful to his country is due from every individual. I have now been in the public service four and twenty years, one half of which has been spent in total occupation with their affairs and absence from my own. I have served my tour then. No positive engagement by word or deed binds me to their further service.

[Then his great psychological statement:] The motion of my blood no longer keeps time with the tumult of the world. It leads me to seek for happiness in the lap and love of my family, in the society of my neighbors and my books. In the wholesome occupations of my farm and my affairs. In an interest or affection in every bud that opens, in every breath that blows around me. In an entire freedom of rest or motion, of thought or incogitancy, owing account to myself alone of my hours and actions.

[And he continued this lament for his dead hopes, picturing himself:] Worn down with labors from morning to night and day to day, knowing them as fruitless to others as they are vexatious to myself, committed singly in desperate and eternal contest against a host who are systematically undermining the public liberty and prosperity, even the rare hours of relaxation sacrificed to the society of persons in the same intentions of whose hatred I am conscious even in those moments of conviviality when the heart wishes most to open itself to the effusions of friendship and confidence.

Cut off from my family and friends, my affairs abandoned, chaos and derangement, in short, giving everything I love in exchange for everything I hate. And all this without a single gratification in possession or prospect in present enjoyment or future wish.[40]

This ranks as perhaps one of the greatest statements ever made of the private cry of the individual who's had to go public. But, in the end, he did agree to stay in office until December of 1793.

12 A Matter of Historical Destiny

Soul sick and bone weary, Jefferson finally was able to return to Monticello in January of 1794. "Never again," he kept repeating to all who would listen, "never again" would he return to political life where jackals and wolves were in the habit of tearing at the vitals of a man's character and reputation. He plunged into farming with an ardor he said he had not known since his youth. "Instead of writing 10, or 12 letters a day, which I have been in the habit of doing as a thing of course, I put off answering my letters now, farmer-like, till a rainy day." He discovered himself to be land rich and money poor—having to borrow a hundred dollars to cultivate the two thousand out of ten thousand acres fit for agriculture. But he was so happy; he rode through his acreage every day singing French and Italian songs to the trees and vegetables and vines, hundreds of different kinds which he had imported from all over the world. He rejoiced in the opportunity to restore to productivity lands which had fallen into disuse. When news came to him about the latest triumph of his nemesis Hamilton, such as his putting down the Whiskey Rebellion (farmers who were making their own whiskey and not paying taxes) by riding into Pennsylvania and threatening the farmers with fourteen thousand troops, he was able to ignore it, and when he was asked to take on a special mission to Spain, he was able to decline. As one writer has said, "His eye was on the furrow, and he would not meddle. To Washington he wrote only of agricultural matters." [41]

There were more than a hundred slaves in the house and on the grounds of Monticello, many living in cabins on Mulberry Row near the house, others on the various farms. Most had specific roles and maintained a kind of a class system among themselves based on duties and seniority. There were body servants, valets, house servants, cooks, artisans, and field hands. There was a special inner family of slaves headed by a matriarch, the mulatto Betty Hemings, many of whose children were sired by the father of Jefferson's wife. These children were white in color, with straight hair and light eyes; they were the house servants. One, James, had been trained to be a fine French cook and was given his freedom as soon as he taught his younger brother. Another, John, was a skilled cabinetmaker and artisan. Almost all of them were eventually freed, except for Sally, who continued to have white children who looked like Jefferson, although most biographers claim they were children by Jefferson's nephews. The slaves all supported each other, sold chickens and eggs and various other goods to Jefferson, were partly salaried, and were evidently very devoted to Jefferson who, we gather, treated them as a part of an extended family, and, it must be observed, continually wrote of slavery as a millstone, a hair shirt, a fatal stain on the Old South. He took to letting his slaves escape by simply walking off the premises without pursuit.

Grandchildren were beginning to fill the house, and Jefferson became fascinated with his little grandson Jeffy, who he described as "robust as a beef" and who refused to wear shoes until his grandfather designed a pair of moccasins that could be laced on strongly. He installed cast iron stoves throughout the house so that there would be fewer colds. His daughter Maria lived with him during these years; he demanded from her unwavering love as well as incredible acts of scholarship and behavior, as he did of her elder sister. Jefferson demanded that his daughters learn all of the household arts and continuously study sciences, languages, and arts. It was as if he was always educating them to be the wife he would have wanted and couldn't have because of his promise to Martha Jefferson on her deathbed. Certainly at one time or other, his daughters fulfilled the role of perfect hostess—perfectly brilliant, perfectly knowledgeable, perfectly charming, perfectly his—so much so that Jefferson's much admiring son-in-law Thomas Mann Randolph went into terrible fits of melancholy, often bordering on madness, because of his inability to live up to his father-in-law in his wife's estimation. Martha loved these rigors that came with fatherly love, but there is evidence that Maria began to become withdrawn. To Maria at age eleven, when she had a tendency to freckle, he had written an admonishment not to go out without wearing her bonnet, "because it will make you very ugly and then we should not love you so much." Maria hated Spanish, and so he assigned her ten pages a day of *Don Quixote*. She was also made to learn to set a hen, cut a beefsteak, and make a pudding, in order to forever merit her father's affection. It would make him so happy, he once wrote her about this time, "to see that you are improved in Spanish, in writing, in needlework, in good humour, and kind and generous dispositions, and that you grow daily more and more worthy of the love of, dear Maria, yours affectionately." This attitude caused Martha to thrive as well as strive, but the younger Maria became delicate and timid, and died in 1804 at the age of twenty-six, survived by her husband John Eppes and two children, "still smothered in father-love while fearing paradoxically that her father did not love her enough."[42]

We know from Jefferson's many thousands of notations in his journals and farm books about his interests: brickmaking, nail-making, rotating crops to improve the soil. His vegetable garden extended along a thousand-foot terrace; his large collection of books on gardening were catalogued under "Fine Arts." He was always experimenting to see which plants would thrive in the American climate, planting cuttings of olive trees from Italy and France in the hope that Americans would find them a profitable source of oil. He found rice that would flourish in dry fields, and laid the basis for the Carolina rice crops. He experimented successfully with wine making and with every sort of new farm equipment, including threshing machines. He followed the progress of a ham through its many months of smoking with the passion with which he once followed the progress of a treaty. When Maria Cosway wrote him in the fall of 1794 for news of him, he waited a year before replying and then told her in a letter, "you have the power of making fair weather wherever you go." The rest of his letter is fascinating for the light it shines on his own self-conception:

> I am become for instance a real farmer—measuring fields, following my plows, helping the haymakers. Never knowing a day that has not done something for futurity. How better this than to be shut up in the four walls of an office, the sun ever excluded, the balmy breeze never felt, the evening

closed with the barren consolation that the drudgery of the day is got through, the morning opening with the fable repeated of the Augean Stable. A new load of labors in place of the old, and thus day after day worn through with no prospect before us but of more days to wear through in the same way.

And then he thought of Maria, and a geyser of poetry rose out of him:

I had but to walk out in the sun myself, tell him he does not shine on a being whose happiness I wish more than yours. Pray him devoutly to bind his beams together with tenfold force to penetrate if possible the mass of smoke and fog under which you are buried and to gild with his rays the room you inhabit and the road you travel. Then tell you I have a most cordial friendship for you, that I regret the distance that separates us, and will not permit myself to believe we are no more to meet till you meet me where time and distance are nothing.[43]

Meanwhile the Republican leaders of Congress were letting Jefferson know that he was the only viable candidate for the Presidency. James Madison was in the forefront of the movement to draft him, telling Jefferson, "It's a matter of historical destiny, Sir, that you become a candidate. I entreat you not to procrastinate, much less abandon, your historical task. . . . You owe it to yourself, to truth, to the world."[44]

Jefferson sent out hints that he might stand for office, but he would not run for it. He still proclaimed to all askers, "The little spice of ambition which I had in my younger days has long since evaporated. I am happier at home than I can be elsewhere." And yet several years later when his daughter Maria, after her marriage, showed signs of even greater withdrawal from society, Jefferson wrote to her about these years of 1793-1797—the period of his own withdrawal—of the necessity of remaining in society:

I am convinced our own happiness requires that we should continue to mix with the world, to keep pace with it as it goes. And that every person who retires from free communication with it is severely punished afterwards by the state of mind into which they get and which can only be prevented by feeding our sociable principles.

I can speak from experience on this subject. From 1793-1797 I remained closely at home, saw none but those who came there, and at length became very sensible of the ill effect it had upon my own mind and of its direct and irresistible tendency to render me unfit for society and uneasy when necessarily engaged in it. I felt enough of the effect of withdrawing from the world then to see that it led to an antisocial and misanthropic state of mind which severely punishes him who gives in to it. And it will be a lesson I never shall forget as to myself.[45]

True to his promise, Jefferson did nothing to campaign for the Presidency and lost by only three votes to Federalist party leader John Adams, becoming thereby Vice President of the United States. Since he was now totally back in politics and fairly certain that he was going to be the next President, he set about as Vice President to weaken the Federalists and to enhance democracy. One of the things he did was to strengthen the idea and practice of the political party system. Unlike Washington who hated political parties, Jefferson was one of the first great modern leaders to realize that opposition parties were essential to self-government, because they functioned as checks of the party in power: "In every free and deliberating society, there must, from the nature of man, be opposite parties, and virulent dissensions and discords; and one of these, for the most part, must prevail over the other for a longer or a shorter time."[46] The party system keeps all the people aware of the inner doings of government, since each party is certain to tell tales about the other. It also keeps the electorate vastly entertained, and, at least, in those days, engaged as concerned citizens in the government. It was critical that Jefferson come out for opposition, for the Federalists in Congress passed an anti-opposition bill, the infamous Alien and Sedition Acts, designed to stifle any agitation or criticism of the Adams administration. The law was so inclusive as to what constituted sedition that it virtually abolished the Bill of Rights. A full witch hunt went into effect—a Federalist reign of terror—in which outstanding citizens who had been born in Ireland or England and who satirized the President were convicted and sentenced to stiff fines and years in jail.

Throughout this period, Jefferson became a master strategist, keeping a low profile but helping to author bills that supported states' rights over federal ones and many, many letters and pamphlets on upholding liberty to be distributed and read around stoves in stores, taverns, and shops. He also let it be widely known that he would be a candidate for President in 1800 and that his administration would be based on supporting freedom and opportunity for all people over and against privileged financial and elitists interests. It was in his candidacy for President that he honed his ideas and became truly the voice of the people—formulating their inarticulate hopes.

You see, Jefferson had agreed to be a vehicle of history. What happens when you agree to such a role is that you begin to be given the job of formulating what is yet the inarticulate and inchoate hopes of history waiting at the threshold to enter into time. Many people may feel the pressure of such hopes moving through them, but then they come up against the problem of how to put passionate ephemera into meaningful form. Often they end up stuttering on the edge of eternity: B-b-b-b-but . . . . Having been a chronic stutterer of this variety myself, I have found something of a solution for myself and for my friends and students. It requires that you take a season, around three months, and devote part of each day to concentrating on what's trying to come through; read, write, and think about it almost constantly; have dialogues daily between your head and your heart, and stay in high expectation that the formulation will start to come. Each of us exists in a field of resonance with everybody else; at the level of psyche, all people are interconnected, and so the aspiration of the emergent human species begins to come through those who agree to be vehicles for collective consciousness. With this order of resonance, the hopes and dreams of billions of people and of millennia past and yet to come are transmitted through the air waves of the media, are born in through the thought waves of the mind field, and cascade on the shore of a receptive consciousness. After three months of deep listening, one may well, like Jefferson, craft this muchness into new forms of expression and application, but you must give the time and make the effort.

As such a vehicle of emerging new forms of self and society, Jefferson was unique in that he trusted people's judgment—not just their innate ability, but their judgment, and people came alive around him: That man trusts me! He trusts me to govern myself and to govern others. He trusts me to have a chance for life, liberty, and the pursuit of happiness. At bottom, Jefferson believed in the possible human, and he wanted to create the possible society that would bring that humanity forth. He believed that human potential could be realized best in an agricultural society, because that was what he knew and where his heart was. Ultimately, however, the form didn't matter as much as did his trust in people's judgment to know what was best for themselves. To trust the judgment of the other is to trust the entelechy, the deep core purpose and possibility of the other—and this from a man who had little direct experience with what is now commonly called the masses. Most of his supporters had never seen him or heard him speak, and if they did, one wonders what they would have made of him—this natural aristocrat with exquisite manners, this very shy gentleman who hated meeting people in large numbers, but who had devoted his life to the popular cause. What a paradox! But, as one of his biographers has noted:

He was also, in the strictest and non-invidious sense of the word, the master politician of the age. For sheer political adroitness Jefferson probably has never been excelled in America, except possibly by Abraham Lincoln, whose physical and mental resemblance to Jefferson, frequently overlooked, is startling. Like the far better known Lincoln, Jefferson had the knack of crystallizing popular ideas and aspiration in unforgettable words. Again like Lincoln, Jefferson had the priceless gift of knowing how to get along smoothly with those who were ambitious for power and prestige. And like Lincoln, Jefferson knew when and where to strike the telling blow.[47]

And so he orchestrated his political campaign with masterful artistry, knowing how to get the maximum political effectiveness through his various agents. No possible advantage was overlooked, no flank left unexposed. He wrote letters constantly to his cohorts, not only giving them strategy, but, and this is most important, inspiring their own humanity, empowering and encouraging them as human beings. This made all the difference. And so Jefferson's agents went out to the taverns and the country stores, the barbecues and the court houses, talking to all the folks dressed in homespun about the man who had spoken so deeply to their own humanity. Whenever and wherever Jefferson himself was present, there was no real campaigning done, as we understand it. As one participant at such a political nonmeeting recalled: "I never knew men more agreeable than they were. We talked and strolled and rowed ourselves in boats, and feasted on delicious crabs." Jefferson also taught his campaigners how to write intelligent and informative letters and articles on social issues for the newspapers and sent out pamphlets like Paine's "Rights of Man" to be distributed in all public places. He was re-educating the public and taking them seriously, raising their sights, and raising the level of public dialogue.

The big issue, a gigantic one, brought against Jefferson was the religious question. The Federalists of the North painted him as a non-believer and heretic who would outlaw the Bible if elected. He was accused by clergymen of robbing widows and orphans to get his property and, since this was the time when religion was firmly tied to morals, a man accused of irreligion, because he did not go to church, was automatically considered to be a moral degenerate, a thief, seducer, and villain. There was no crime and no evil with which the clergy didn't brand Jefferson from their pulpits. Jefferson's response was not to respond; he had too great a contempt for his detractors to dignify them with a reply. "I leave them," he said, "to the reproof of their own consciences." But in a letter to his good friend, Dr. Benjamin Rush, he wrote:

they [the clergy] believe that any portion of power confided to me will be exerted in opposition to their schemes. And they believe rightly; for I have sworn upon the altar of God, eternal hostility against every form of tyranny over the mind of man.[48]

The religion issue was something of a red herring, for the real issue was the war of democracy against the people of privilege, the Jeffersonian Democrats being described by the Federalists, as Henry Adams put it, in most unflattering terms:

Every dissolute intriguer, loose-liver, forger, false-coiner, and prison-bird; every hare-brained, loud-talking demagogue; every speculator, scoffer and atheist, was a follower of Jefferson; and Jefferson was himself the incarnation of their theories.

The Federalists, appalled at the idea of people without money and property winning the campaign, overlooked a critical fact that Lincoln knew very well when he said that God must love the common people because he made so many of them. Common people, that is people without much property, were by far the majority of the voters. Every time the Federalists attacked Jefferson as the leader of democracy, they identified him more strongly with the people. And so in spite of all the attacks from banking firms, commercial houses, and pulpits, from newspapers and the citadels of power, Jefferson was elected the third President of the United States by a handy majority of the popular vote. However, in the Electoral College, he came out even with Aaron Burr and the vote was returned to the House of Representatives, the stronghold of Federalist power, to break the tie. Burr might even have won had it not been for Alexander Hamilton, who urged the Representatives to vote for Jefferson on the grounds that he was a man of noble principles who could command the respect of the country, while Burr was a scandalous figure, bankrupt beyond redemption, in Hamilton's words, a man who had "formed himself upon the model of [Roman conspirator] Cataline, and. . . too cold-blooded and too determined a conspirator ever to change his plan." This action by Hamilton was a victory of patriotism over personal animosity.

The capitol had just been moved to foggy, swamp-ridden Washington, a city described ironically as "the best city in the world for a future residence. We want nothing here but houses, cellars, kitchens, well informed men, amiable women, and other trifles of this kind, to make our city perfect." Dressed very simply, the long and bony new President left his boarding house and ambled along to the Capitol in his loose gaited fashion, accompanied by a few friends, to be inaugurated. This was in stark contrast to the imperial coach and six and big parade which had accompanied John Adams' inauguration. Jefferson was making a point concerning democratic symbolism, for as he said, "the trappings of monarchy encouraged the philosophy of tyranny." He took his oath of office with two avowed enemies at either side. One of the great scoundrels of American history, Aaron Burr stood on his right as the new Vice President, and on his left, Chief Justice John Marshall, whom Adams appointed just before his term ended at midnight, and who was to be the *bete noire* of Jefferson's entire administration. Adams himself refused to be present. Of his appearance at that time, Margaret Bayard Smith, wife of the publisher of the *Washington National Intelligencer*, and herself raised a Federalist commented that she found it hard to believe that:

> this man so meek and mild, yet dignified in manners, with a voice so soft and low, with a countenance so benignant and intelligent. . .could be the violent democrat, the vulgar demagogue, the both atheist and profligate man I have so often heard denounced by the Federalists.[49]

Jefferson's speech had in part to do with what he firmly believed, that the human race had a new opportunity, that a new chapter in history had been opened. He said in the speech:

> During the throes and convulsions of the ancient world, during the agonizing spasms of infuriated man, seeking through blood and slaughter his long lost liberty, it was not wonderful that the agitation of the billows should reach even this distant and peaceful shore; that this should be more felt and reared by some and less by others, and should divide opinions as to measures of safety. But every difference of opinion is not a difference of principle. We have called by different names brethren of the same principle. We are all republicans, we are all federalists.

In this speech, too, he spoke of the ultimate laissez faire—that government is best that governs least:

> With all these blessings what more is necessary to make us a happy and prosperous people? Still one thing more, fellow citizens—a wise and frugal government, which shall restrain men from injuring one another, shall leave them otherwise free to regulate their own pursuits of industry and improve-

ment, and shall not take from the mouth of labor the bread it has earned. This is the sum of good government.

He also reminded the country that the rights of the minority were as sacred as those of the majority. He reassured the people that there would be no injustice and no persecution, and he appealed to the whole country to unite with "one heart and one mind." This was March 4, 1801, the first year in a new century. Jefferson felt the power and the portent of the year, for as he wrote Joseph Priestly right after the inauguration: "We can no longer say there is nothing new under the sun. For this whole chapter in the history of man is new. The great experiment of our Republic is new. . . ." [50]

His first term as President was one of the most felicitous in American history. It was a very feminine presidency, very nurturing in its ability to evoke and empower people. Jefferson appointed a remarkable Cabinet; among his appointees were James Madison—a tiny man with a massive intellect—as Secretary of State, and the great Swiss-born economist Albert Gallatin as Secretary of the Treasury. The Cabinet operated with remarkable harmony. Jefferson insisted that every idea should be listened to and discussed in depth. There was never an unpleasant word; rather, each of the six members considered the Cabinet meetings a most interesting and important occurrence. They knew they were creating something memorable, and the debate among themselves sharpened and deepened the possibilities. Jefferson himself wrote of this Cabinet years later that history furnished no parallel for such harmony. It also helped that the country was prospering. There was no war on any horizon; the French Revolution had run its terrible course, and Napoleon Bonaparte had picked up the spoils but as yet was not the military adventurer which he later became. Peace abroad and economy at home were Jefferson's watchwords. The national debt was being paid off by systematic payments of principal and interest. There was to be no more borrowing and, unlike the British system under Hamilton in which the legislature was given an accounting only after the moneys were spent, Congress had to pass on a very detailed budget. Jefferson also asked that America become the haven for the oppressed peoples of the world, inviting especially Italians to emigrate. My own maternal grandfather, Prospero Todaro, decided to come to America from Sicily in 1913 because a priest told him about Jefferson's invitation to Italians.

Jefferson called back U.S. diplomats, not wanting to mix the young country in European machinations and follies. He wanted only commissioners for commerce to serve abroad. Napoleon, however, was on the rise and needed money for his dynastic ambitions, and there was a large chunk of America called Louisiana, a region of almost a million square miles, so big that all of Western Europe, including Scandinavia could be fitted into it. Napoleon had acquired

Louisiana, New Orleans, and the Floridas through a secret treaty with Spain. Because of the immense French presence in his backyard, Jefferson's dreams of isolationism were over; such a stance would mean eventual war with France. In a historic treaty in 1802, concluded because the U.S. bluffed on how much money it had, Jefferson was able to purchase Louisiana from France for fifteen million dollars. Out of the Louisiana Purchase were eventually created the states of Louisiana, Arkansas, Colorado, North and South Dakota, Iowa, Kansas, Minnesota, Missouri, Montana, Nebraska, Oklahoma and Wyoming—in all, the biggest real estate deal in history. And here was a wilderness paradise filled with immense natural wonders and incredible resources, inhabited at that time by many thousands of Indians and a handful of whites. It was the backbone upon which American wealth was built, with the Mississippi running right down the middle of it.

So as President, Jefferson had doubled the territory of the United States, not by war, but through purchase, an achievement rarely occurring in human history. However, many Indians were displaced. No President in history entertained so many legations of Indians. To the many who came, Jefferson expressed his wish that they settle down and become an agricultural people, telling them that their diet would improve and that they could live on big farms. Of course, telling a wandering people to become agricultural was, in our terms, quite frankly pretty shaky, and by the time Andrew Johnson became President, the promise turned to carnage and the great decimation of the Indian peoples of the nineteenth century had begun. That Jefferson's policies contributed to this tragedy, by attempting to change the nature of a people's relation to the land, is another of his shadows. Jefferson's actions were predicated on the assumption that a human being can and should own the land, and that if the people who dwelled on the land before seem not to share that belief, then it made good sense to buy or claim or steal the land from them, or to get them to own land as well. Jefferson's other shadow, of course, was the assumption that one can inherit and benefit from ownership of other human beings and his inability to trace a clear way through to the eradication of this admitted and much-bewailed iniquity. In thinking about these shadows, we might fruitfully ask two questions of ourselves: First, how do these two shadows continue to weigh upon and infiltrate our lives and what can we yet do about them? And second, what are the questionable assumptions that we live under today which are so thickly a part of our lives as both individuals and citizens that we cannot see them, and for which our descendants will sit in judgment upon us?

These difficulties aside, Jefferson's entire first term was one of remarkably positive and creative happenings, marred, however, by the fact that the Vice President, Aaron Burr, shot and killed Alexander Hamilton in a duel, and the Federalist press continued a virulent and constant attack and besmirching of Jefferson. They were actively libelous, but Jefferson refused to strike back. He regarded his situation as a test of freedom of speech, and regardless of how awfully the newspapers abused this freedom, he felt that it was vital to democracy that this freedom not be stopped. Personally we know that he suffered deeply from the poisoned print that came his way in the name of freedom. Still he wrote: "If I try to stop this, even though it's directed against me, it will stop the freedom of the press. We cannot stop the freedom of the press."[51]

Jefferson was very democratic in his manners and diplomatic protocol. One example that ultimately had bad results is the Merry affair. The British Ambassador, a Mr. Merry, came once to dine with Jefferson. Merry was resplendent in a uniform decked with gold braid and topped with a tricornered hat. Jefferson greeted him wearing rumpled clothes and down-at-the-heels shoes, and with his shirt undone. Normally at such an event, the guests were seated in order of precedence at a rectangular table, but Jefferson had a round table where everyone had to sit pell-mell. Instead of taking Mrs. Merry's arm and escorting her in, Jefferson took Dolly Madison, who was his official hostess, to sit down by his side, and allowed the other guests to scramble to find their own seats. Of course Merry and the other visiting statesmen were appalled.

What did Jefferson, age about sixty, look like at this time? We have a description from an Irish poet, Tom Moore, who hated Jefferson but was nevertheless fair and graphic in his description:

> He's a large man. In fact, I never met a man of loftier stature. He has a noble face with a Scottish-Irish cast of feature, and with curly hair of reddish tint, although greatly mixed with gray. His mouth is large and firm set, while his nose is of the true Scottish type and unusually wide at the nostrils. As to his eyes, I would say they are a grayish and light blue tint mixed and steely in expression. His brow is broad and wide and very free from wrinkles. His whole appearance denotes a man of vigorous actions, and did I not know he was President of the United States, I would judge him to be a gentleman of landed property with all the inclinations of a fox-hunting squire.[52]

Jefferson was also a very friendly man, who used dinners, at what was reputedly the best table in Washington, as the way to provide a mellow atmosphere in which to deepen discussion between opponents. When he came to the beginning of the election year for his second term, there was virtually no challenge, and he was reelected by an overwhelming majority. Taxes had been repealed, the national debt virtually gone, enormous territory had been acquired, and unbounded public confidence was the rule of the day.

Unfortunately, this period of felicity was the calm before the storm. The bad days began with Jefferson refusing Burr's bid for the Vice Presidency after he had slain Hamilton. Even though Burr pleaded with Jefferson to give at least one word of approval to ease his entry into New York politics, Jefferson could not do this, deeply distrusting the man. Then Jefferson's daughter Maria died at the age of twenty-six, and he was plunged into a state of intense grief which lasted for some time. He wrote to a friend at this time in grief and bitterness: "Others may lose of their abundance, but I, of my want, have lost even the half of all I had. My evening prospects now hang on the slender thread of a single life," meaning, of course, his daughter Martha.

The disgruntled Burr approached any enemy of Jefferson he could find plotting for a way to destroy Jefferson and the country. He even approached the British minister Merry, still very angry about Jefferson's dinner table slight, and offered him half a million dollars if he would detach the western states from the union. Burr actually tried to raise an army to do this, but Jefferson was able to intercept and stop the plot. When Burr came up for trial, he argued brilliantly in his own defense, and since John Marshall, another avowed enemy of Jefferson, was the judge, Burr was acquitted. Despite this, Jefferson said, "there is no one in the United States who is not satisfied with the depth of [Burr's] guilt." Indeed, Burr had to disguise himself as a common sailor to flee the country, because many Americans wanted to lynch him!

The real problems of Jefferson's second term came from abroad. Napoleonic France and England were locked in a struggle to the death for supremacy in Europe using shipping blockades as a weapon. Eighty percent of America's six million people lived along the Atlantic coast; thus any blockade impacted the country tremendously. Both French and British ships interfered with American shipping and commerce. Further, the British were fond of boarding American ships and impressing the seamen into British service if they had anything remotely like a British accent. On the other side, Napoleon referred to the American flag as a silly, striped piece of bunting and declared this country not worthy of consideration. Jefferson's response was the equivalent of "a pox on both your houses"; he put into effect an embargo on all European goods, most of which came from France and England. In his agriculturally romantic way, he wanted to make America self-sufficient as well as isolate her from the ills of Europe. Such a stance might have been fine for an earlier century. But in an age of invention and opportunity, with growing intercultural interaction, and with fast sailing ships that could cross the Atlantic in a mere twenty to twenty-six days, Jefferson's policy of embargo spawned fury, more than a few bankruptcies, and the growth of a spectacular smuggling business. The world, too, was changing rapidly, with many nations moving into an era of adventurer politicians who sought to amass great empires of worldwide reach. England, Holland, and France were all expanding their control through trade and influence.

Jefferson became subject to constant bitter attack and criticism. He remarked that the office of the Presidency "brings nothing but unceasing drudgery and daily loss of friends." He knew it was time to retire and let a younger man take over. At the inaugural ball of his successor, little James Madison, Jefferson was the happiest person there, full of jokes, laughter, and much good humor. Jefferson enchanted all the guests, while Madison looked like he was under a dark cloud, which, in fact, he was.

At last Jefferson could return to Monticello—in fact, he went as quickly as he could, riding home through terrible weather in a state of utter joy. "I am supremely happy in being withdrawn from these turmoils," he announced. He was now in the harvest time of his life. As one commentator has beautifully described it:

> His life had been full and fruitful. He had experienced some defeats and many triumphs, and his name, he knew, was imperishably linked with the story of his country. He had doubled the territory of the United States, and had welded from loose and scattered materials, a powerful political party. His ideals on liberty were graven into the law of the land, and his measures—the coinage for example—were among the permanent institutions of the country. He had achieved all this by means of peace and persuasion. As he wrote the Papal Nuncio in 1816, "I have the consolation that during the period of my administration not a drop of blood of a single fellow citizen was shed by the sword of war or of the law.". . .the years of struggle and turmoil had given him an immense reservoir of moral strength. Time, like fire, having purified whatever weaknesses lurked in his character, he could face the opinion of his contemporaries and the judgment of history with equal serenity. Well past middle age, he was now that most rare of human species, a balanced and harmonious man capable of viewing the world with detached compassion and serene wisdom. Few men in history ever achieved such philosophical balance and spiritual harmony as did Jefferson in his later—his postpolitical—years.[53]

Jefferson became the Sage of Monticello, an American Saint who provided the model for what human beings could be. Everybody came to visit him, and he exhausted his financial resources putting them up. It was not unusual for there to be seventy visitors at a time coming round to occupy his beds, eat his food, and try to get some of his conversation. He turned no one away, and many of those who enjoyed his hospitality wrote accounts of him, which is why there are so many on record. Still, he was able to be on his horse managing his estates for many hours a day, and his many activities kept him, in his own words, "as busy as a bee in a molasses barrel." He played constantly with his grandchildren, read as much as he could, often the ancient writers, and was devoured by correspondence. He kept inventing things—a wonderful new plow, dumbwaiters, weather vanes, butter refrigerators. A marvelous description of Jefferson at this time has come down to us from Margaret Bayard Smith:

> There is a tranquility about him which an inward peace alone could bestow. His tall and slender figure is not impaired by age. His white locks announce an age. His activity, strength, health, enthusiasm, ardor and gaiety contradict. His face owes all its charm to its expression and intelligence. His countenance is so full of soul and beams with much benignity. His low and mild voice harmonizes with his countenance rather than his figure. But his manners—how gentle, how humble, how kind! To a disposition ardent, affectionate and communicative, he joins manners timid even to bashfulness.[54]

Jefferson himself said at this time in a conversation with the same Mrs. Smith:

> The whole of my life has been a war with my natural taste, feelings and wishes. Domestic life and literary pursuits were my first and my latest inclination. Circumstances and not my desires led me the path I have trod. And like a bow though long bent, which when unstrung flies back to its natural state, I resumed with delight the character and pursuits for which nature designed me.

And so Jefferson was back in the world nature designed him for, even though he had led an utterly other kind of life.

Perhaps the most heartwarming thing that happened to Jefferson during these years is that at the age of sixty-eight, he received a letter from seventy-six-year-old John Adams telling him of his continuing love and asking him to forget the miserable frivolities of politics that had kept the two estranged. Thus began a precious correspondence between the two elder statesmen. The letters were affectionate and filled with mutual regard and the renewal of their transformational friendship; hundreds of letters passed back and forth between the two old gentlemen, filled with rich remembrances and often radically inventive ideas about everything. In his first letter to Adams, Jefferson referred to their earlier work together as: "Laboring always at the same oar. . .we rode through the storm with heart and hand, and made a happy port." [55] Adams wrote, "You and I ought not to die before we have explained ourselves to each other." [56] In characteristic fashion John Adams wrote plaintively to Jefferson: "Who shall write the history of the American Revolution? Who can write it? Who will ever be able to write it?" Jefferson, for his part told him that he liked "the dreams of the future better than the history of the past." [57]

In his last years Jefferson turned to a reconsideration of religion and even created his own Newer Testament by cutting out just the words that Jesus had said and arranging them in chronological and subject order. The result was a gospel of higher ethics about the oneness of God and his perfection, the perfectibility of humans, and the assurance that loving God and your neighbor as yourself was the essence of the entire preachment of Jesus. From his mid-seventies through to the end of his life, Jefferson also put energy into the creation of the University of Virginia. He knew there had to be a place of higher education where young people's minds and spirits could be formed. Jefferson designed and laid out the campus; he taught the brickmakers and the carpenters. In all weathers, he was seen to call for his horse Eagle, mount up, and ride down to Charlottesville to help build the University. He was also instrumental in convincing the Virginia legislature to fund the University.

Finally, when he was eighty-one, Jefferson had a moving, poignant meeting with Lafayette. When Lafayette's carriage stopped outside the portico of Monticello, Jefferson descended the steps. He could barely walk, while Lafayette himself was lame. Jefferson's grandson recalls what happened: "As they approached each other, their uncertain gait quickened itself into a shuffling run, and exclaiming, 'Ah Jefferson!' 'Ah Lafayette!' they burst into tears as they fell into each other's arms." Hundreds of people witnessed the scene; there was not a dry eye among them. The two old men spent two happy weeks together discussing the past, present, and future of the world: slavery, South America, democracy, Europe, life, and their coming deaths.

In the last years of his life, Jefferson was again plagued with terrible financial worries. Over $40,000 in debt, he was afraid he would lose Monticello. His troubles were ended temporarily when several states voted to pay off his debts. This was, perhaps, the greatest tribute he received, a vindication of his faith in the goodness of people. Unfortunately, after Jefferson's death, Monticello did pass out of the hands of the family because of debts, not to be restored to them until 1924. But Jefferson himself died happy, thinking that Monticello was saved.

Near the end, Jefferson was invited to attend the fiftieth anniversary of the signing of the Declaration of Independence on July

4th, 1826, but wrote that he was too weak to do so. Still, he wanted to stay alive until that date. And sometime after midnight, although nearly dead, he asked, "Is this the Fourth?" and the people gathered around said, "Pretty soon." The moment he died, around noon on that July 4th, hundreds of thousands of people were celebrating the fiftieth anniversary of the Declaration. At the same moment, ninety-one-year-old John Adams, also dying in his bed up in New England, said "Thomas Jefferson yet survives," and with those words, he too died.

After Jefferson was buried, a gray obelisk was placed over his grave. Engraved on it are these words that he himself chose for his epitaph:

Here was Buried THOMAS Jefferson
Author of the Declaration of American Independence
of the Statute of Virginia for Religious Freedom
and Father of the University of Virginia

This was all he wanted to be remembered for—not the Presidency, not any of the accomplishments of his brilliant political career. To Jefferson's humble words we might add, a man who despite all inclinations to the contrary, agreed to be the vehicle through which a new image of human possibility could enter into time. In this way, and for all time, Thomas Jefferson yet survives!

PROCESS 8
VISITING THE POSSIBLE SOCIETY, WITH MR. JEFFERSON AS GUIDE

TIME: FORTY-FIVE MINUTES.

●*MATERIALS:*
Writing and drawing materials and journals.

●*MUSIC:*
Music from Area One.

●*INSTRUCTIONS FOR GOING SOLO:*
Follow the instructions on tape, giving yourself plenty of time for envisioning the possible society.

●*SCRIPT FOR THE GUIDE:*
We are about to embark on a process of creating a visionary society. With Mr. Jefferson as our guide, we will enter a world beyond space and time to visit such an optimal society of the future. We will then travel to a visionary Monticello from which we will be able to observe ourselves and others hammering out the details for creating a better society in our own era.

If you wish, sit closer together and reach out to one or two other people so that everybody is linked up, and we can begin our travels as a society of connected individuals.

(Note to those traveling solo: imagine that you have a number of good friends traveling with you. Try to sense the touch of their hands in yours.)

Now let us to begin with breathing as one. Together everybody inhale. . . .And exhale. . . . And inhale. . . . And exhale . . . . Breathing in rhythm together, continue to inhale slowly and deeply . . . . And exhale slowly and completely . . . . And continue to inhale and exhale slowly and deeply in the same rhythm together for the next minute or so . . . . (One minute).

And begin to feel, now that you are interconnected, you are the entire country of America. You feel as if you are a vast and varied landscape, over which there is brooding a great presence. And you are not only this country, you are also everyone within this country. You are. . .

—A new baby being born in Des Moines, Iowa.

—A Navaho woman making a pot of Spider Woman, placing bits of coral and turquoise in a wonderful circular theme.

—You are also a quiet grove of redwood trees, backlit with God's own lighting, the sun, a temple made by nature for the repose and the silence of the human soul.

—You are also great waters reaching toward the shore, bathing the shores.

—You are great rivers, mountains, lakes.

—You are traveling herds of bison, deer, painted ponies.

—You are also an aged, homeless woman wandering the streets of Sacramento, stockings ragged around your ankles, spewing a weird mind salad of seemingly unconnected verse.

—But you are also a wise woman now in your nineties in Wisconsin, interpreting the dreams of women and of nations.

—You are an Iraqi computer programmer in Boston; your wife has just had a new baby. Torn by your desire to remain true to your homeland, you feel a fierce unbidden pride in the place your adopted country is occupying in the conscience of the world.

—You are also an actor whose children are the roles he's played, many and varied, memorable and stirring, an actor who is different and therefore unforgettable.

—And you're lying on the bed, your skin turning yellow because cancer is spreading through your body as a result of AIDS. Your friends and loved ones gather around. And you are also those friends and loved ones, honoring you. And the light of another world seems to be shining from you. And you both hold onto life, and seek new life elsewhere.

—You are also a wizened, wise-cracking tarheel from the Carolinas, concerned about the tobacco crop. You are aware of the controversy around tobacco and yet you cannot imagine what else there is to grow, and you are holding your land against the incursions of the city folk.

—You are also a fisherman in southern California out catching tuna in large nets. Your conscience has been struck by your child coming home from school and telling you about dolphins. You are working very hard to free several dolphins who have gotten into your net, knowing that you will lose part of your catch, but feeling that you are saying yes to the Earth, called to a higher morality by what you're now doing.

You are all of these people and places and more. You are America.

And stored in your unconscious, your psyche, are the hopes and dreams, not just of several hundred years of immigrants, but the hopes and dreams of millions of people over thousands of years for that Western Land Beyond The Waters where there will be an opportunity previously thought to exist only in Paradise. And you are that rising tide of unconscious resource—the psyche of America yearning to rise again.

And you look up, and brooding over it all is Thomas Jefferson, in one or another of his ways of being. Is he Long Tom, Planter Tom, Thinker Tom, Philosopher Tom, President Tom, Tom the lover, the artist, the architect, the writer, the inventor? And he beckons you forward. And you see him or sense him in one or another way. He beckons you toward a kind of tunnel that appears to be a kind of space and time warp. And you follow him into the tunnel that will lead you eventually to a society that is a Possible Society of the future.

As you follow him, years fall away. The years remaining in the 1990's (the Guide names these: i.e., 1995, 1996, etc.). Follow Tom. Hear the echoing of his slippered footsteps. . . 1996 . . . 1997. And as you follow him, you go deeper and deeper into an inner state of trance or vision . . .1997. . .1998. The year 1999. The year 2000. Now you follow him down these corridors of time to the year 2001 . . .2010 . . .2020. Following his retreating back down the corridors of time future. Going deeper and deeper. Going deeper into the visionary world and into the minds of the Great Artists and Archetypes creating this visionary world of 2020. . .2030. . .2040. Following him.

Following his tall beckoning figure . . .2050. The year 2055 . . . 2060 . . .2070. Going deeper into this inward state that carries you deeper into this visionary realm of the future society . . .2080 . . .2090 . . .2100. Following him to the year 2110. . .2130 . . .2140. Following his beckoning figure . . .2150. Going deeper and deeper into the inner world, as you go deeper and deeper into this place . . .2170 . . .2180 . . .2190 . . . 2200. Following him now, through this great tunnel of time, to the year 2210. Going deeper and deeper into the visionary world as your follow him to this Possible Society, this visionary place . . .2220. Following him now into the year 2230 . . .2240 . . . 2250. . .2260. Following him. . .2270 . . .2280. . .2281 . . . 2282 . . .2283 . . .2284 . . . 2285. . .2286 . . .2287. And you see that the light in the tunnel has become a light at the end opening out—upward and out . . .2288 . . .2289 . . .2290.

And you are at the threshold. And you are passing out of the tunnel . . .2295. And you are now out of the tunnel and into the world of 2295. And you are walking around, led by Tom, into this world. And in your deep visionary mind, connected with the coding of the optimal society, you see a vigorous, exciting, but real society, which has its problems, but which has remarkable and humane ways of dealing with these problems: perhaps, problems of technology; of keeping the planet alive; of having to reorganize or redesign human beings genetically; of tremendous responsibility for inner and outer space and for evolutionary governance. Moving in this world, now, sensing it, feeling it. Touching it. Tasting it. Seeing it. Hearing it. Exploring this world now. Going to its schools. Looking in on its families and social units. Observing its technologies. Noting its laws and how it governs itself. Seeing what the people look like. How they dress. What they sound like. Can you understand their language, or has it changed too much? Are the tastes different? The smells? Have a meal in one of their restaurants and see how the food has changed. What kinds of art and architecture do they have? What kinds of music? You are in that world of the future.

I will give you about six minutes of clock time, equal subjectively to all the time you need—it may seem to be weeks or months—to be in this world of the optimal but altogether feasible possible society. Be there now, with Mr. Jefferson. Explore it. Talk about it. Interact with him. Let him introduce you to some of the people who live there. Be there now, and discover as much as you can. (Six minutes.)

(After six minutes or so, the Guide will say:)

And now following Mr. Jefferson, he leads you to a place that seems to be a meta-Monticello, a Monticello of the visionary realms. And you climb a mountain, a very small mountain, going up and around and around and around, up this mountain. And the atmosphere changes perceptibly. And you realize that you are no longer in 2295. You are moving into a world which is outside of space and time, but you carry with you the vision of the optimal society of the future.

And you see or sense a beautiful neo-classical building, perhaps not unlike some of the capitol buildings, perhaps not unlike Monticello itself. Its art form is of the once and future times. And you enter into a Visitors' Gallery. And you look down. And down below you see yourself with other friends of yours, or people perhaps that you do not yet know in the twentieth century, working to hammer out the details that will create an optimal society in your own time.

But as you watch yourself work in many ways—it may be working in a school; it may be working on yourself to manifest your own possible human; it may be working with your friends and colleagues on a variety of projects to better society; it may even be working on your Declaration of Interdependence—you see that surrounding you, almost like a penumbra of light, is a Divine Architect for whom you are the chosen art form. And this Divine Archetype, this Beloved Spiritual Presence, is there working in you and through you to help hammer out the details of the new society. You are not just caught in the plodding everydayness of it all. You are also being continuously sourced and re-sourced by the Great Envisioner, who helps you to access the many possible patterns of a better society as well as the practical details as to how to go about creating it.

And Mr. Jefferson is up there in the Gallery with your observing self, saying, "Look, my friend, look at how much you are able to do in making it all happen. And how deeply befriended you are by the Great Ally and Artist from the Deep World. And please know that I too am still about to help and inspire you in your endeavors. For your era is as important and critical as was my own. And what I was able to do and what you yet can do can make a profound difference in the way that the world goes. And so open you visionary eyes and ears and see how you yet may go about making your world better in terms of both the vision of the possible and the specific details as to how it can be done."

And as Mr. Jefferson says these words to you, it seems that you have a close-up lens on how this can happen. You are able to observe yourself and your friends back there in the late twentieth century and early twenty-first century helping to make the world work, hammering out the details as it were. And if you find yourself getting stuck or confused, or the vision ceases, you can ask Mr. Jefferson or your guiding Divine Architect to help illumine your vision so that you will be able to see more clearly how it can be done. It especially helps to dialogue with Mr. Jefferson about these things, for he is still full of bright ideas on making society work. And you will continue to see this vision and to hammer out its details for the next five minutes of clock time, equal subjectively to all the time that you need. (Five minutes.)

Now begin to follow the beckoning figure of Thomas Jefferson out of the Visitors' Gallery of the visionary Monticello, down the hill into the optimal society of 2295, knowing that you can always return to it if you wish. Entering now the tunnel of time, and following Mr. Jefferson to the years 2290, 2280, 2270, 2260, 2250, 2240, 2220, 2210, 2200. Continuing to follow the tall figure of Thomas Jefferson back through time. 2170, 2140, 2100, 2190, 2080, 2070, 2060, 2050, 2040, 2030, 2020, 2010. The year 2000. 1999, 1998, 1997. (The Guide takes the participants to the present year.)

And now here at the present year the tunnel ends, and you find yourself stepping out into present space and time. You thank Mr. Jefferson for the journey and say goodbye to him. He bows and smiles, shakes your hand, and walks away. Remembering now all that you have experienced, you begin again to breathe slowly and deeply, becoming more and more awake. Coming now to full waking consciousness, squeeze the hands of the persons next to you, if you are still holding on to them. Continuing to breathe more quickly now, drop hands, stretch your fingers, arms, legs, and feet. Clap your hands, and open your eyes.

And back now into your usual time and space, would you please take up your writing and drawing materials and record what you have seen of the future society of the year 2295 and what you have seen of your own role and actions in creating an optimal society here and now. You will have twenty minutes to make this record. After that time, we will take turns sharing what we have discovered.

NOTES

[1]Saul K. Padover, *Jefferson* (New York: New American Library, Mentor Book, 1970), p. 7.

[2]Alf J. Mapp, Jr., *Thomas Jefferson: A Strange Case of Mistaken Identity* (Lanham, MD: Madison Books, 1987), p. 5.

[3]Jefferson to Martha Jefferson, May 28, April 7, 1787, in *The Family Letters of Thomas Jefferson*, ed. Edwin A. Betts and James A. Bear (Columbia, MO: University of Missouri Press, 1966), pp. 34, 36.

[4]Ibid., Thomas Jefferson to Thomas Jefferson Randolph, p. 362.

[5]Thomas Jefferson, *Notes on the State of Virginia*, ed. William Peden (Chapel Hill, NC: University of North Carolina Press, 1955), p. 162.

[6]Jefferson to John Page, December 25, 1762, *The Papers of Thomas Jefferson*. Vol. I-III to date, ed. Julian P. Boyd (Princeton: Princeton University Press, 1950-1982), I, pp. 3-6.

[7]Ibid., I, p. 11.

[8]Padover, p. 20.

[9]*Thomas Jefferson's Garden Book, 1766-1824, with Relevant Extracts from His Other Writings*, ed. Edwin M.Betts (Philadelphia, 1944).

[10]This is the conclusion of Fawn Brodie in her biography, *Thomas Jefferson, An Intimate History* (New York: Bantam Books, 1975). It is also the conclusion of many black and female scholars. Certainly, during his lifetime and especially during his presidency, Jefferson was constantly accused by political opponents of consorting with Sally Hemings, and many ribald songs were written to that effect. Dumas Malone, however, author of the definitive six-volume study of the life of Jefferson does not accept this conclusion. He writes that Sally Hemings' children were by other fathers, one of whom was a nephew of Jefferson. So we may never know what the truth of the matter is. But as Edwin Weeks summed up the issue in the *Atlantic Magazine*, "Does it really matter?"

[11]Quoted in Mapp, p. 68.

[12]Quoted in Padover, p. 27.

[13]Mapp, p. 90.

[14]For a full account by witnesses of this event, see Moses Colt Tylor, *Patrick Henry* (Ithaca, NY: Great Seal Books, 1962), pp. 147-149.

[15]Thomas Jefferson to William Small, May 7, 1775, *The Papers of Thomas Jefferson*, Vol. I, p. 165.

[16]Thomas Paine, *Common Sense and the Crisis* (New York, 1960), p. 27.

[17]John Adams to Timothy Pickering, August 6, 1822, in John Adams, *Works*, ed. C. F. Adams, 10 vols. (Boston, 1856) II, p. 514, n.

[18]Thomas Jefferson to Henry Lee, May 8, 1825, *The Writings of Thomas Jefferson*. 10 vols., ed. Paul Leicester Ford (New York, 1892-1899), X, p. 343.

[19]*The Papers of Thomas Jefferson*, I, p. 427.

[20]Ibid., I, pp. 317-318.

[21]*The Autobiography of Thomas Jefferson*, with an Introductory Essay by Dumas Malone (Boston, 1948) p. 35.

[22]Quoted in Fawn Brodie, p. 147.

[23]Abigail Adams to John Adams, November 12, 1775, *The Adams Family Correspondence*, ed. Lyman H. Butterfield (Cambridge, MA, 1963) I, p. 324.

[24]Quoted in Fawn Brodie, pp. 126-127.

[25]Quoted in Padover, pp. 41-42.

[26]Ibid., pp. 43-45 passim.

[27]Ibid., p. 50.

[28]Mapp, p. 160.

[29]Marquise de Chastellux, *Travels In North America, 1780, 1781, and 1782*, ed. Howard C. Rice, Jr. (Chapel Hill, NC, 1963), II, p. 46.

[30]Henry S. Randall, *The Life of Thomas Jefferson*, 3 vols. (Philadelphia, 1865), I, p. 383.

[31]Jefferson to Charles Bellini, September 30, 1785, *The Papers of Thomas Jefferson*, VIII, pp. 568-569.

[32]Ibid., p. 568.

[33]Quoted in Fawn Brodie, p. 260.

[34]Thomas Jefferson to Maria Cosway, October 12, 1786, *The Papers of Thomas Jefferson*, X, p. 444.

[35]Ibid., p. 456.

[36]Quoted in Padover, p. 88.

[37]Fortunately Jefferson was far more circumspect about his revolutionary feelings in public than in a number of private letters. This particular one is found in the Library of Congress: Thomas Jefferson to William Short, March 23, 1793, *Thomas Jefferson Papers*, Library of Congress, Series I, Reel 17.

[38]Quoted in Padover, p. 99.

[39]Quoted in Mapp, p. 325.

[40]Ibid., p. 326.

[41]Donald Jackson, *A Year at Monticello - 1795* (Golden, CO: Fulcrum, Inc.) p. 26.

[42]Ibid., p. 36.

[43]Ibid., pp. 85-86.

[44]Padover, p. 103.

[45]Thomas Jefferson to Maria Jefferson Eppes, March 3, 1802, *Family Letters*, ed. Betts and Bear (Columbia, MO: University of Missouri Press, 1966), p. 219.

[46]Quoted in Padover, p. 107.

[47]Padover, pp. 113-114.

[48]Thomas Jefferson to Benjamin Rush, September 23, 1800, *Thomas Jefferson: Writings*, ed. Merrill D. Peterson (New York: The Library of America, 1984), p. 1082.

[49]Margaret Bayard Smith, *The First Forty Years of Washington Society* (New York, 1906), p. 5-6.

[50]Thomas Jefferson to Joseph Priestly, March 21, 1801, *The Writings of Thomas Jefferson* (Ford VIII), p. 22.

[51]Padover, p. 143.

[52]Ibid., p. 146.

[53]Ibid., p. 159.

[54]Margaret Bayard Smith, p. 79.

[55]Quoted in Dumas Malone, *Jefferson and His Time: The Sage of Monticello* (Boston: Little, Brown, 1981), p. 96.

[56]Ibid., p. 106.

[57]Ibid., pp. 224, 200.

PART 3

Helen Keller & Annie Sullivan

INTRODUCTION

Sometimes I feel sightless and senseless. Sometimes—too often if the truth be told—I look out through the hazy portholes of my mind's body and detect only occasional glimmerings of who or what is out there. I yearn to know, and I know that my yearning is not enough. The world is mute, and time seems a vast conspiracy of silence. I look inward, and the inhabitants of that arcane and beautiful country flash by like shy comets. Who are they, I wonder, and who or what is their place in the order of things? And who or what are you sitting there reading my musings? Do you muse in like manner, I wonder? Are we together a museum of lonely musing pieces stammering our frustration on the edge of eternity? What key is needed to unlock the coding; what hand tapping the alphabet of creation into our outstretched palms is near to awakening that all-but-forgotten memory of who we are, and what it's all about?

And so we turn to the story of Helen Keller and Teacher, of Annie Sullivan and Phantom, of the Golden Child of Southern gentry and the gritty, tormented orphan of the poorhouse. This unlikely duo were utterly necessary to each other; their story renews our hope as it devastates our emotions. In this rare partnership is seen a higher design, the hand of God tapping out a code to break the silence of the universe, to bring us into conversation with the stars and with that most unknown and defiantly hidden and uncommunicative of all beings—ourselves.

In studying the story of Helen Keller and Annie Sullivan, we receive hints about the workings of grace, glimpses of the larger intention and possibility of ourselves. We also learn that it is no easy path; indeed it is the hardest path of all—the path of moving from the darkness into—not light—light is for those rare moments in which we go skinny-dipping in eternity—but rather into what Helen Keller came to know—an illumined and transfigured darkness. And in the midst of the illumination, lest we think that we can cross a bridge into unstoppable glory, there is life more abundant and more filled with challenge, chaos, catastrophe, and sheer human worry and concern. Helen and Annie, after their triumph resplendent with spirit, nevertheless inherit the whirlwind: accusations of fakery, humbug, plagiarism; infestations of mean spirits; forms and fears of victimization by con artists; promises of support and then subsequent withdrawal of support; incessant and voracious appeals for help; fevers and congestions, rheumatisms and lumbago; marriage and proposals of marriage, shattered hearts; the lecture circuit; promises of movie riches; the need to turn to vaudeville for money to support themselves and then being made objects of ridicule for having to work in vaudeville sandwiched between jugglers and trained pigs; accusations from conservatives about Helen's support of the Women's Suffrage movement, the Civil Rights movement, the Socialist Party; betrayal or seeming betrayal by close friends; endless fund-raising and exhausting trips and appeals for support for programs for all handicapped persons; and almost always, especially in the earlier years, worry and concern about how they were going to support themselves and where the next piece of money for them to live on was going to come from. The miracle is that in the midst of all this and through all of this, Helen's spirit kept growing brighter, more sensitive of the possibilities of others, more appreciative of the sheer, staggering glory of being alive.

I met Helen once. I went to one of the great public schools of the world, P.S. 6 in New York. Our teachers, some of whom had been taught by John Dewey, were offering to special classes experimental programs in multi-modal education. We learned mathematics by dancing, studied the Native Americans by preparing and eating Indian foods and building teepees, and, most important, we were taken to meet the great elders of the times. I was about eight or nine when I was taken across the river to meet Albert Einstein, who I remember as being extremely vague and as having a great head of hair.

That same year our teacher, Miss O'Reilly, took us to meet Helen Keller. Before we got on the bus to go somewhere in the East 60's, she read us the powerful passage in which Helen Keller writes that for the first six years of her life, she had no concepts whatsoever; her mind was muddy and closed off. Finally her teacher, Annie Sullivan, in a fit of frustration, pulled her out to the ivy-covered well house, pumped a cool, clear something into one of her hands, while she spelled W-A-T-E-R over and over again into the other.

. . .I stood still, my whole attention fixed upon the motions of her fingers. Suddenly I felt a misty consciousness as of something forgotten—a thrill of returning thought; and somehow the mystery of language was revealed to me. I knew then that "w-a-t-e-r" meant the wonderful cool something that was flowing over my hand. That living word awakened my soul, gave it light, hope, joy, set it free! There were barriers still, it is true, but barriers that could in time be swept away.[1]

As Miss O'Reilly continued to read to us from Miss Keller's autobiography, I too could feel sweet strange things begin to wing themselves over my mind. It was almost, but not quite, like an awakening to what I had long forgotten. With Helen however, the awakening was complete. The word *water* dropped into her mind like the sun into a frozen, winter world, and she learned the names for thirty things before the end of that day.

With this preparation, Class 4B got on the bus. Miss Keller was radiant, utterly radiant! I had never seen anybody in my entire life so full of joy. To be in the same room with her was to be in a space so filled with presence it was like being exposed to an electrical charge. She must have been sixty-eight or sixty-nine at the time—very beautiful, a big woman, about five foot eight or so. She spoke to us in an awesome voice, which has been described as the voice of a pythoness, an oracle. She had never heard speech since the age of nineteen months, so her inflections were all over the place.

I remember being so deeply moved that I knew I had to speak to her. I didn't know what I wanted to say, I just knew that I had to speak to her. When we were asked if there were any questions, I raised my hand. Normally the companion who was with her—it was Polly Thomson—would tap out the questions for her, but children who wanted to talk more directly to her were allowed to go up to Miss Keller to ask their question. I remember that she reached out to me and put her entire hand over my face. It seems to me now that the center of her palm was on my lips; the rest of her hand and fingers were reading my face and expression. Still I didn't know what to say, so I just blurted out what was in my heart, "Why are you so happy?"

She laughed, and laughed, and laughed, and then she said in that awesome voice of hers, "My child, it is because I live each day as if it were my last, and life in all its moments is so full of glory."

Her hands lingered on my face for a moment, and again I felt as if I were lifted into radiance, and some kind of a charge passed between us. I was never again quite the same, and I will never forget her. She was certainly in my experience the most illumined human being I ever met. Despite living in a world of utter darkness and no sound, she operated on many, many more levels and with many,

many more senses than anyone else I have ever known.

How did the glory come to be? It came through an incandescent partnership. Helen and Teacher met because of their incredible woundings, and both became avatars of divine events in the lives of each other and for the world that met them.

13 Fingers Upon My Palm

Nineteen years after the death of Annie Sullivan in 1936 at the age of seventy-five, Helen Keller wrote, "To this day, I cannot command the uses of my soul, or stir my mind to action without the memory of the quasi-electric touch of Teacher's fingers upon my palm."

Teacher was the daughter of Irish immigrants, at that time, the outcast social group in the Northeast. "No Irish need apply" was the sign in too many factories and store windows. Her early life was a New England version of Dickensian horrors: her mother buried early in a potters' field grave; her father a raving drunk for whom she kept house in a dilapidated cabin, but who nevertheless regaled her in his heavy brogue with the rich language and vibrant tales of Irish folklore. He also filled his daughter with hatred for landlords, and all uppity folks.

The extremes of poverty and personal handicaps finally brought the nearly blind Annie and her crippled little brother Jimmy to the state poorhouse in Tewksbury, Massachusetts. There they were abandoned to a world of shadows, crowded with the misshapen, the diseased, and the maniacal. Their only toys were the rats, and they lived in a room in a house of rotting corpses, where bodies were kept until the ground thawed enough to swallow them. One night Annie awoke suddenly to reach out to her much-loved little brother and found instead empty space. Trembling she made her way to the dead room and felt among the corpses until she found his cold body under the sheets. She flung herself on the body, covering it with kisses, for he was "the dearest thing in the world, the only thing I had ever loved." Shortly after Jimmy's death, someone gave her an Agnus Dei to wear around her neck and told her that it held the body of Jesus. She broke open the silken covers to see (she was nothing if not curious), and the priest berated her with the words, "You have wounded the body of the Lord." This outraged the nine-year-old Annie, who declared that she was finished with confession. This harsh priest was replaced by a much kinder one; Father Barbara took an interest in her and declared that he would take her away from this place. She had already had two operations on her eyes; the priest took her to have another, which somewhat relieved the piercing pains and extreme light sensitivity, but left her vision still so dim that she remained on the record as officially blind. The priest talked with her and found a place in Boston where she could live, doing light kitchen work; but her eyes made life difficult, and she was subjected to two more operations at the city infirmary. When she was released, the family in Boston refused to have her back, and the friendly priest had been transferred to another location. So back she went, protesting and screaming, to Tewksbury, this time to a ward with younger women who had suffered every conceivable outrage and disgrace and discussed them in the coarsest and vilest terms. Fifty years later, when Nella Braddy Henney was interviewing her for her biography, she said, "I was not shocked, pained, grieved or troubled by what happened. Such things happened. People behaved like that. . . .It was all the life I knew. Things impressed themselves upon me because I had a receptive mind. Curiosity kept me alert and keen to know everything."

In the course of wanting to know everything, she had a narrow escape from being knifed by a young insane boy, only to be told by her fellow inmates: "Serves you right. He should have cut your heart out." Somehow from someone she had learned that there was somewhere a school for the blind; she was desperate and determined to get out of Tewksbury and go there, and she could talk of nothing else. "She'll be walking out of here some day on the arm of the Emperor of Penzance," her acquaintances declaimed.

One day an investigating committee arrived to inspect the premises—many gruesome stories had made their way across the state about the goings on at Tewksbury. She followed the group from ward to ward, finally screwing her courage to the sticking place just as the men were at the gate: "Mr. Sanborn, Mr. Sanborn, I want to go to school!" That cry rips through us still. The response was not immediate, but soon afterward, a woman appeared who informed her she was to go to school.

The school was the Perkins Institution for the Blind, and she entered as a charity case, a child from the poorhouse with two calico dresses and with the words of advice from the women she left behind ringing in her ears. "Keep your head up, you're as good as any of them." "Don't tell anyone you came from the poorhouse." "Don't ever come back to this place. Do you hear? Forget this and you will be all right."

She was received with official pity, which hurt her so badly that she later remembered it in words that pierce us: "The essence of poverty is shame. Shame to have been overwhelmed by ugliness, shame to be a hole in the perfect pattern of the universe." Annie seemed to be of two minds about her Tewksbury experience. In one she felt that she had not been besmirched by it, because the child mind has "immunities that prevent it from being harmed." The other expressed itself in "the conviction that life is primarily cruel and bitter. . . .I doubt if life or for that matter eternity is long enough to erase the terrors and ugly blots scored upon my mind during those dismal years from 8 to 14."

When Annie got to Perkins, she immediately ran smack into the ghost of Samuel Gridley Howe, the mind and master of Perkins, who had just died. An Olympian spirit, he had joined Lord Byron in the Greek Revolution and Lafayette in Paris during the 1830 Revolution, finally leaving his life of overseas adventures when Lafayette told him, "Reserve yourself for the service of America, young friend." Upon his return, he was invited to run the newly organized school for the blind in Boston and immediately launched an intensive investigation to find the best methods and the finest teachers to accomplish them. He also managed to marry the most brilliant and fascinating of America's eligible aristocratic women, Julia Ward, suffragette and author of "The Battle Hymn of the Republic." The combination was unbeatable. Although later in life, when asked how Dr. Howe was, Julia Ward Howe answered, "I really can't tell you, because as I'm neither deaf, dumb, nor blind . . . I really see very little of my husband, dear Dr. Howe." Julia Ward Howe later became the focus of many of Annie's public barbed remarks against the rich and powerful, and both women were wickedly witty to and about each other whenever the occasion arose.

Howe had made phenomenal progress with a blind and deaf woman, Laura Bridgeman, reaching her sealed mind through words raised up in highly tactual print, upon actual objects, like a key and a spoon. In this manner many everyday objects were labeled and their names learned. Howe continued working with Laura week after week until, as he wrote, "The truth began to flash upon her. Her intellect began to work. She perceived that there was a way by which she could herself make a sign of anything that was in the mind, and show it to another mind, and at once her countenance lighted up with a human expression; it was no longer a dog or a parrot—it was an immortal spirit seizing upon a new link of union with other spirits." [2] Howe also chanced upon the use of an alphabet of simple movements of the fingers to be tapped into a person's palm. It was a system created by a group of Spanish monks who used it as a means of speaking to each other without having to break their vow of silence. Howe's work with Laura achieved international renown, and the Perkins Institute became the place where every European of distinction had to visit. Charles Dickens wrote glowingly of the place in his "American Notes" and of the enormous progress made by Laura Bridgeman. It was his remarks that Helen Keller's mother Kate Adams Keller chanced upon one day, which started the process by which twenty-year-old Annie, newly graduated from Perkins, came to Alabama to work with Helen. When Howe died, he selected his son-in-law, Greek-born Michael Anagnos as his successor. A man of great personal warmth, Anagnos was an extraordinary organizer, fundraiser, and promoter of educational innovation, who was able to apply Howe's methods in many cases. Fourteen-year-old Annie came in to the school illiterate for all intents and purposes. In the first few weeks, "Big Annie," as she was mockingly known, did very badly, and everyone made great fun of her. But within a few months she was way ahead of her more tutored schoolmates. Her early experiences with the cruelty of her classmates both scarred her and spurred her on to greater efforts. She felt herself to have more life experience than both her peers and her teachers and was feared as a brilliant heckler and deflater of anyone's ego who crossed her own. She was also an injustice collector, and her spitfire temperament nearly got her thrown out of the school on more than one occasion.

Only the appreciation of several teachers who understood the bifurcation of Annie's mind—one side as undeveloped as a small child's, and the other astonishingly mature—helped her past the danger zone. Several more operations made it possible for her to read with her eyes, and she quickly devoured as much poetry and fine literature as she could find. She graduated as valedictorian, delivering an earnest and thoughtful speech on human potentials. It was considered so splendid a statement that the Boston newspapers quoted it in entirety. It is a remarkable expression, not just for its originality and gracefulness, but for its prophetic announcement of what would be her path in awakening a dormant soul:

> . . .And now we are going out into the busy world, to take our share in life's burdens, and do our little to make that world better, wiser and happier.
>
> We shall be more likely to succeed in this, if we obey the great law of our being. God has placed us here to grow, to expand, to progress. To a certain extent our growth is unconscious. We receive impressions and arrive at conclusion without any effort on our part; but we also have the power of controlling the course of our lives. We can educate ourselves; we can by thought and perseverance, develop all the powers and capacities entrusted to us, and build for ourselves true and noble characters. Because we can, we must. It is a duty we owe to ourselves, to our country and to God.
>
> All the wondrous physical, intellectual and moral endowments, with which man is blessed, will, by inevitable law, become useless, unless he uses and improves them. The muscles must be used, or they become unserviceable. The memory, understanding and judgment must be used, or they become feeble and inactive. If a love for truth and beauty and goodness is not cultivated, the mind loses the strength

which comes from truth, the refinement which comes from beauty, and the happiness which comes from goodness. . . .

The advancement of society always has its commencement in the individual soul. It is by battling with the circumstances, temptations and failures of the world, that the individual reaches his highest possibilities.[3]

Meanwhile in Tuscumbia, Alabama, the dormant soul that was Helen was raging like a wild animal, knocking over anything that got in her way, constantly filthy, constantly soiling herself, indulged to the point of outrageousness, snatching with her filthy hand gobs of food from the plates, as she made her way around the table of her elegant and genteel family. Before her illness at nineteen months, Helen had been an unusually bright child—walking well and already gifted with a phenomenal memory and a capacity for speech and mimicry. She had been the recipient of constant affection and approbation and was already quite a full little person before the mysterious fever struck which took away her eyes and her ears. With these senses gone, her mind sealed over, descending into the mud of all creation and waiting there until the hand would come that could pull her out again. She tells us that she lost concepts and language, becoming a "phantom" of herself, a hideous gibbering ghost, not unlike the dead shades in Homer's underworld who have lost their spirit of understanding. To quote Helen about herself, "Her body was growing, but her mind was chained in darkness as the fire within the flint." Nevertheless, in spite of her "two-fold solitude," the little Phantom had some sixty signs that she had invented and that were perfectly understandable to those who were close to her. If she wanted bread and butter she would make the motions of spreading butter on bread. If she desired ice cream she would mime the turning of the handle on the freezer and shiver a little. But when she could not make herself understood, she threw increasingly violent tantrums. It particularly bothered her when she was standing between two people who were talking to each other. She too would move her lips, but upon getting no response, would grow wild with rage. Little Helen's chief companions were a little black girl, Martha Washington, and Belle, an old setter dog. Together, Helen and Martha explored the tactile world of the Keller plantation, kneading dough, pulling flowers off the climbing vines, cutting off each other's hair.

As mentioned, Mrs. Keller already was intrigued by the work of the Perkins Institute through what she had read of it in the account of Charles Dickens. But the actual coming of Annie from the Institute to the household was initiated by Alexander Graham Bell, the great inventor, whose wife was deaf and who spent much of his life in service to those who dwelled in a world of silence. Bell suggested that

Captain Keller write to Anagnos. When the job and its compensation (board, washing, and twenty-five dollars a month) were made clear to him, Anagnos recognized that Annie was the person who might be able to fill it. She prepared by studying again the Laura Bridgeman case and visiting Laura for many hours. Laura herself made a dress for the doll the Perkins Institute girls sent with Annie for Helen.

After a terrible journey taking many days with any number of unnecessary changes of train, Annie arrived in Tuscumbia, on March 3, 1887, utterly exhausted, with eyes sore from a recent operation. But what a different world she entered once she got off the train! Honeysuckle perfumed the air, everywhere fruit trees were weighed down with blossoms, and, best of all, Mrs. Keller, young and highly cultivated, met her with great Southern courtesy and appreciation. "This is a good time and a pleasant place to begin my life's work," Annie thought, as they entered the narrow lane leading to the house.

In describing their actual meeting in *The Story of My Life*, Helen wrote: "I felt approaching footsteps. I stretched out my hand as I supposed to my mother. Someone took it, and I was caught up and held close in the arms of her who had come to reveal all things to me, and more than all things else, to love me." [4]

Annie's account, given about a year later, was even more interesting. She said that she ran up the porch steps when she saw Helen standing by the porch door, with one hand stretched out as if she expected someone:

> Her little face wore an eager expression, and I noticed that her body was well formed and sturdy. For this I was most thankful. I did not mind the tumbled hair, the soiled pinafore, the shoes tied with white strings—all that could be remedied in time, but if she had been deformed, or had acquired any of those nervous habits that so often accompany blindness. . .how much harder it would have been for me! I remember how disappointed I was when the untamed little creature stubbornly refused to kiss me and struggled to free herself from my embrace. I remember, too, how her eager, impetuous fingers felt my face and dress and my bag which she insisted on opening at once, showing by signs that she expected to find something good to eat in it. [5]

The next few days and weeks were the most critical in Annie and Helen's life together and laid the foundation for the extraordinary partnership and learning experience that was to follow. Grueling contests of will punctuated their encounters, for Annie thought that the greatest immediate problem was how to discipline and control the wild and willful Helen, who would lie on the floor kicking and screaming when Annie refused to allow her to grab food in her usual way from her plate. Helen would pinch; Annie would slap; Helen would throw things; Annie would wrestle her into her clothes. The incident that became the basis for the well known table manners scene in *The Miracle Worker* was richly described by Annie Sullivan in a letter following that grand debacle:

> I had a battle royal with Helen this morning. Although I try very hard not to force issues, I find it very difficult to avoid them.
> Helen's table manners are appalling. She puts her hands in our plates and helps herself, and when the dishes are passed, she grabs them and takes out whatever she wants. This morning I would not let her put her hand in my plate. She persisted and a contest of wills followed. Naturally the family was much disturbed, and left the room. I locked the dining-room door, and proceeded to eat my breakfast, though the food almost choked me. Helen was lying on the floor, kicking and screaming and trying to pull my chair from under me. She kept this up for half an hour, then she got up to see what I was doing. I let her see that I was eating but did not let her put her hand in the plate. She pinched me, and I slapped her every time she did it. Then she went all round the table to see who was there, and finding no one but me, she seemed bewildered. After a few minutes she came back to her place and began to eat her breakfast with her fingers. I gave her a spoon, which she threw on the floor. I forced her out of the chair and made her pick it up. Finally I succeeded in getting her back in her chair again, and held the spoon in her hand, compelling her to take up the food with it and put it in her mouth. In a few minutes she yielded and finished her breakfast peaceable. Then we had another tussle over folding her napkin. When she had finished, she threw it on the floor and ran toward the door. Finding it locked, she began to kick and scream all over again. It was another hour before I succeeded in getting her napkin folded. Then I let her out into the warm sunshine and went up to my room and threw myself on the bed exhausted. I had a good cry and felt better. I suppose I shall have many such battles with the little woman before she learns the only two essential things I can teach her, obedience and love.[6]

The family was confused and appalled by these confrontations, so Annie convinced them that she and Helen should move away during this difficult period, specifically to a little house a quarter of a mile down the road. Only by isolating them together, Annie felt, could the necessary bonding and obedience occur. Annie was certain that obedience was the gateway through which knowledge and even love could enter the mind of this child. Pity and making allowances for Helen's handicaps had no place in Annie's belief system. Human beings, whatever their condition, should be given every opportunity to live as normal people and to live and learn what others learn.

Slowly but surely Annie taught Helen how to imitate hand signs for spelling the names of a number of objects, but Helen could not make any connection between the spelling and the objects symbolized by the sequence of gestures. Her wild bouts of fury and recalcitrance continued. Then, one week after they had moved into the small house, Annie wrote to one of her teachers at Perkins:

> My heart is singing with joy this morning. A miracle has happened! The light of understanding has shown upon my little pupil's mind and behold, all things are changed. . . . She lets me kiss her now, and when she is in a particularly gentle mood, she will sit in my lap for a minute or two. . . .It now remains my pleasant task to direct and mold the beautiful intelligence that is beginning to stir in the child's soul.[7]

The mystery of love had been born between the two, and from that moment on, the growth in both of their gifts was nothing short of phenomenal.

Two weeks after this event, one of the most famous educational breakthroughs in human history occurred. Helen still could not understand what Teacher was spelling into her hand with the finger movements. Finally in frustration, Annie took Helen over to the ivy-covered pumphouse and placed her hand under the spout. And the miracle of W-A-T-E-R occurred. Helen left the well house eager to learn. . . everything! Now everything had a name, "and each name gave birth to a new thought. As we returned to the house every object which I touched seemed to quiver with life." Annie's letter to Mrs. Hopkins confirms the miracle. She wrote:

> She has learned that everything has a name and that the manual alphabet is the key to everything she wants to know. . . .Helen got up this morning like a radiant fairy. She has flitted from object to object, asking the name of everything, and kissing me for very gladness. Last night when I got into bed, she stole into my arms of her own accord and kissed me for the first time, and I thought my heart would burst so full was it of joy.[8]

In the great breakthrough of the soul's awakening, however or whenever it occurs, that which has been sealed, that which has been forgotten, suddenly opens up, and the energy of that knowing pulses out and encompasses all within one's purview. Helen and Annie were required to tell the story of this moment thousands of times, and each time they rehearsed it, even on the vaudeville stage, it was as if that miracle happened again, and Helen's soul grew that much more every time it was told.

People often say to me, "Why do you keep telling your story about your religious experience at six?" I answer, "Because it's important to me, that's why." Daily life has its ways of sealing us up and putting us back to sleep. Telling our important stories keeps them current and allows us to act out again our own awakenings. I believe that everyone wakes up at least once in their life. What makes Helen's breakthrough so wondrous is that it was kept alive and current, through its many retellings. In our own ways, we are as closed and as sealed off from the world—sighted and sensed as we are—as she was. Our own moments of awakening prove it. But Helen kept awakening and awakening until she achieved an incredible state of aliveness. Her miracle experience stood over her as a kind of guiding mantra—a pattern and a call, a deep song of becoming to be sung to whomever would listen.

PROCESS 9
THE SOUL'S BIRTHDAY: TELLING OUR OWN MOMENT OF OPENING AND EXPERIENCING HELEN'S

What was your soul's awakening? If you could remember or catch just a glimpse of it, you may well be able to call it back. It's as if each of us is given at least one such moment as an act of grace from Somewhere or Someone. But because we do not treasure it and repeat its telling, we often lose it. How much better than celebrating a birthday would it be if we could celebrate the day of the moment of our awakening, even if we do not remember exactly when and where it was and what year. By celebrating it, we bring the eternal into time.

TIME: FORTY MINUTES.

•*MATERIALS:*
None.

•*MUSIC:*
None.

•*INSTRUCTIONS FOR GOING SOLO:*
This is the one process in the book that does not lend itself to going solo. Please get some good friend to do this process with you.

•*SCRIPT FOR THE GUIDE:*

Would you all turn to one other person, preferably not a person that you know very well. You can know your partner, but you should not be familiar with the details of his or her life story. And would you please face each other.

In this process we are going to be drawing upon the incident in the life of Helen Keller when Annie Sullivan tapped W-A-T-E-R into her hand, and suddenly she awoke out of her stupor to become the remarkable person that she was. Everybody awakens at least once in their life, even if they fall right back to sleep again. But through the rest of their days, there is always that memory of awakening.

This is what I'd like you to do. With your partner will you decide who will be the first person to tell the story about the time that he or she awoke to a larger life, a fuller sensibility or understanding of things. Even if you don't quite remember the incident, it's still there.

And now will you who are about to tell the story of your awakening please take one of the hands of your partner into your own. And into that hand, without speaking, just draw patterns, tap remembrances, press in stories, senses, whatever. Although you are talking, it is not in words. You're talking by tapping, by patting, by communicating the story of your waking up purely by the movement of your hand in the hand of your partner.

You may do whatever you like with the hand. You can tap into it. You can press it. You can draw pictures and patterns in it. You can put a good deal of emotional feeling into it.

Both of you have your eyes closed, but the story will be told just by the tapping and the interacting with the hand of the other. Please begin.

(The Guide will observe when the participants have finished. It should be at least five to ten minutes.)

Change roles now and let the other person now tell his or her story of awakening in the same manner, taking the partner's hand and tapping into it. (Five to ten minutes.)

Now very quietly, would the one who is now telling the story into the hand tell the story in words. But keep on tapping into your partner's hand as you continue to tell the story in words.

And you who are listening, hold the field and empower that story so it can endure, yes, for the rest of the speaker's life. And the person who is listening should also tell what he or she felt in the other person's story when it was told in the hand. Eyes closed. Begin. (Five minutes.)

And after this person is finished, then let the other person tell his or her story in words, again tapping it into the partner's hand. And you who are now the listener tell the speaker what story or pattern or feeling you heard in your hand. (Five minutes.)

When you're both finished, come to silence please. And bring your two hands together with your partner's two hands. Gently touch hands. And you will take that overlighting story of Helen and Annie that has empowered so many and it will empower your own story and your own awakening.

And you will feel that story as if it is happening now for the first time, and it is amplified and extended between your hands, rippling through the whole of your being.

And let this day be the beginning of the raising again of your bright intelligence, told and remembered in each other's hands and in each other's spirits, holding for each other the promise that this re-memberance is the time in which you again come out of the dark place where you have been hidden and that you move into a life that knows no real obstruction, but in which you are called into levels of knowing, into powers of usefulness, into patterns of co-creation.

For the story of Annie and Helen is your story, and your story is that bright and shining story that says, "It is beginning again! It is beginning now! This is the day of my soul's awakening. This is the day of my soul's awakening. This is the day of my soul's awakening."

SO BE IT.

And opening your eyes now, look with eyes that see more than eyes usually see into each other's eyes. Opening your eyes and seeing with eyes that know more than eyes—eyes of the inward looking as well as eyes of the outward looking—the miracle of seeing and the greater miracle of deep seeing.

And touching now with the hands that feel, with the hands that are deeper than feeling, the hands that know inner feeling. The miracle of the hands feeling.

Into Thy Hands I commend my spirit. Into each other's hands you invest with trust an important part of your life. Herein we gain what other times and other cultures have known, but which many of us have lost since print and media gained the dominance. This is the importance of the kinesthetic knowing of hands knowing hands; the power and primacy of communication in touch.

Teacher wrote a poem when Helen was just a child called "Hands" that speaks so deeply of these things. Let me read it to you now:

Hands

Understanding hands.
Hands that caress like delicate green leaves.
Hands, eager hands.
Hands that gather knowledge from great books,
*   Braille books.*
Hands that fill empty space with liveable things.
Hands so quiet, folded on a book.
Hands, forgetful of the words they have read all
*   night.*
Hands asleep on the open page.
Strong hands that sow and reap thought.
Hands tremulous and ecstatic listening to music.
Hands keeping the rhythm of song and dance.

14 Bright Days and Storm Clouds

The story of Helen and Annie from the very beginning is the story of the mystery of love and the unfolding of the latent self. The deeper I get into this story, the more I am aware that if each of us got a fraction of what Annie gave and Helen got, those latencies, those blinded inner eyes and inner senses, those veils that separate us from the larger reality within and without us would be lifted. There is such a difference between this mystery and what Dr. Howe did with Laura Bridgeman; true, he turned her into a functioning being, but one who was fussy and who did not much like to be touched. Annie with her ebullient, abundant heart, and above all, with her great beneficence of loving teaching hands, brought Helen to life and made her bloom. Their relationship was an archetype of the meta-teacher/student relationship, a joining of hearts which reveals and lifts both student and teacher into a higher state. The Sufis teach the tradition of The Friend—The Friend being God—the One who is reflected in the soul of the human friend and who through love and cherishing calls us into fullness. But the story of Helen and Annie is also an incredible practicum on how this calling forth can be accomplished. When the mystery of a love and commitment which unlocks all potentials is combined with expert teaching, the results are formidable, if not miraculous.

Annie kept the fascinated faculty and President Anagnos of the Perkins Institute abreast of Helen's progress and her teaching methods almost on a daily basis. She wrote:

> It is a rare privilege to watch the birth, growth and first feeble struggles of a living mind; this privilege is mine; and moreover, it is given me to raise and guide this bright intelligence. . . .My mind is undisciplined and full of slips and jumps. I need a teacher quite as much as Helen. I know that the education of this child will be the distinguishing event of my life, . . .if I have the brains and perseverance to accomplish it.[9]

Although they interspersed their lessons with outdoor walks and forays into nature, Helen's mind was consumed by ceaseless activity, as if she were trying to make up in a few weeks what had been lost for six years. "I feel as if I had never seen anything until now," Annie wrote about these walks, "Helen finds so much to ask about along the way." Helen could not be kept from thinking. She began to spell the moment she woke up. If Annie wouldn't talk to her, she would spell words into her own hand, carrying on the liveliest conversations with herself. Helen was fascinated by plants. Like her, were they able to skip, hop, fall, bend, and climb? She was a walk-plant, she declared to Annie. Everything, especially out of doors, presented itself as an original idea, to be understood from the freshest possible perspective. "Indeed, everything that could hum, or buzz, or sing, or bloom, had a part in my education," she writes. This already tells us a great deal about what education should be. A child can't just sit there in a rigid posture behind a desk—with a great divide between the self and the rest of the world—learning "concepts"; the child has to be among that which hums and buzzes and booms and sings and blooms.

Under Annie's guidance, Helen's enormous powers of retention and her prodigious memory began to emerge. Her memory and retention became so developed because they had to be—they were all she had. Moreover, Helen had no distractions, living as she did in a world of utter internalization. Her only diversions were the things of the world and of nature, and she met these in an utter incarnational relationship. She not only saw the buzz, she buzzed with it; she not only felt the plant, she became a walk-plant. Through the limited senses she had, she became what she beheld, and when you become what you behold, you do not forget a thing.

Little Helen was very fond of gentlemen. She would make friends much sooner with a man than with a woman, and would always kiss them as she would not with a lady. Remarking that she and her mother were the only women that Helen would allow to caress her, Annie said that it was because Helen saw many more men than women, and they always made much of her.

A purity and sweetness of nature also began to blossom in Helen, which all found astonishing. A few years later, when Helen was the toast of New York cultural and literary society, the writer Laurence Hutton remarked of her:

> We felt as if we were looking into a perfectly clear fresh soul, exhibited to us by a person of more that unusual intellect and intelligence, freely and without reserve. Here was a creature who absolutely knew no guile and no sorrow; from whom all that was impure and unpleasant had been kept. . . . She was a revelation and an inspiration to us. And she made us think and shudder, and think again. She had come straight from the hands of God, and for fourteen years the world and the flesh and the devil had not obtained possession of her.[10]

She was very much her own being, and to others she seemed to be of an angelic order—a bodhisattva come to Earth.

A very important part of Helen's education was learning how to play. Annie was herself naturally very playful, and she was the first to see that playfulness was a key to learning. In her book *Teacher*, Helen writes:

> One of Annie Sullivan's first procedures was to teach Helen how to play. She bestowed a faculty-shaping element without which either study or skillful work is hardly possible. Helen had not laughed since she became deaf. When she had learned obedience and some patience, Teacher came into the room one day laughing merrily, throwing out breezes of glee. She put the child's hand on her bright face spelling, "Laugh." Then gently tickled her into a burst of mirth that gladdened the hearts of the family. She did it again and again, after which she guided Helen through the motions of romping—swinging, tumbling, jumping, hopping, skipping and so forth—suiting her spelled word to each act. In a few days, Helen was another child, splashing radiant joy and oh! the marvelous frolics she and Annie had! The overflowing, bursting gladness, the exultation beyond utterance, the animation of new discoveries that wrapped Helen like light! Romping with Helen, Teacher felt herself transported to the Country of Fairy where the gift of constructive play which she had not known in her own childhood was conferred upon her.
>
> Thus, by all kinds of movements, exercises and games, Helen was stimulated to ask the names of those different actions and pursue knowledge through the ever-springing flames of Teacher's finger spelling. And the witchery of that spelling was unforgettable. Teacher's fingers positively twinkled in Helen's hand while they played Hide and Seek or bounced balls or gamboled with kittens and puppies.[11]

Teacher also kept pigeons. When they were let out, she and Helen would both chase them, and Helen would feel the air from their wings and conceive the glory of flight. Eventually, the pigeons got over their shyness and would light on Helen's arms.

After several months with Annie, Helen had begun to shine with that radiance of spirit that would characterize her for the rest of her life. The door to her mind opened, the spirit shone unrestricted and untrammeled in a manner few had ever seen before or since. In the first Christmas since her mind opened, she proved how loving her spirit had become. During the whole Christmas season in Tuscumbia, she went visiting around from place to place feeling the toys of the other children and laughing with glee at what they received. Upon finding a child who had not been given a present, she was at first very troubled, but then her face became radiant, and she spelled into Annie's hand, "I will give Nellie mug." The mug had been the present she had received that had pleased her the most, yet she gave it to the child in a manner that expressed not self-denial but a loving sympathy and openheartedness.

Helen began learning other languages almost immediately. When a French word was tapped into her hand, she was enchanted by the idea: "Teach me French," she insisted. Then she found out about Latin, and so had to learn that language too. By March of 1890, she was also learning to speak, much to Annie's discomfort. "The voices of deaf children are not agreeable to me," she said. Because they started with pronouncing syllables and not with actual voice production, Helen never really spoke naturally. Her voice as a child was described as that of a Pythoness—the loneliest sound one ever heard, like waves breaking on the coast of some desert island.

What about twenty-one-year-old Annie's needs? She had always greatly enjoyed the company of men, had in fact been something of a flirt and continued to be so, but as she writes from that time:

> My work occupies my mind, heart and body, and there is no room in them for a lover. I feel in every heart-beat that I belong to Helen, and it awes me when I think of it—this giving of oneself that another might live. God help me make the gift worthwhile! It is a privilege to love and minister to such a rare spirit. It is not in the nature of man to love so entirely and dependently as Helen. She does not merely absorb what I give, she returns my love with interest, so that every touch and act seems a caress.[12]

In her autobiography Helen writes of this:

> My teacher is so near to me that I scarcely think of myself apart from her. How much of my delight in all beautiful things is innate, and how much is due to her influence, I can never tell. I feel that her being is inseparable from my own, and that the footsteps of my life are in hers. All the best of me belongs to her—there is not a talent, or an aspiration or a joy in me that has not been awakened by her loving touch.[13]

She added in a letter a few days later:

> To have a friend is to have one of the sweetest gifts that life can bring, and my heart sings for joy now; for I have found a

real friend—one who will never get away from me, or try to, or want to.

The next year, 1888, saw the utter triumph of Annie and Helen. Anagnos devoted most of his annual report of the Perkins Institute to the case, calling it unique in human history, and presenting Annie as one of the towering educators of all time. He quoted extensively from Annie's letters and observations to support his statements. It was in this report that Annie was first described as a "miracle worker." Between Anagnos and Alexander Graham Bell, who was also spreading the news of the miracle worker and her charge, the two were becoming very famous very quickly. Reporters showed up night and day to be duly and unceremoniously kicked out by Captain Keller, and newspaper articles were full of praise and astonishment. An affectionate father-daughter relationship was growing up through the mails between Annie and Anagnos. This letter of May 3, 1888, reflects the warmth of their relationship as well as Helen's own description of the way that Annie had her increase her vocabulary while playing.

Dear Mr. Anagnos—I am glad to write to you this morning, because I love you very much. I was very happy to receive pretty book and nice candy and two letters from you. I will come to see you soon, and will ask you many questions about countries and you will love good child.

Mother is making me pretty new dresses to wear in Boston and I will look lovely to see little girls and boys and you. Friday teacher and I went to a picnic with little children. We played game and ate dinner under the trees, and we found ferns and wild flowers. I walked in the woods and learned names of many trees. There are poplar and cedar and pine and oak and ash and hickory and maple trees. They make a pleasant shade and the little birds love to swing to and fro and sing sweetly up in the trees. Rabbits hop and squirrels run and ugly snakes do crawl in the woods. Geranium and roses jasmines and japonicas are cultivated flowers. I help mother and teacher water them every night before supper. . . .I am tired now and I do want to go down stairs. I send many kisses and hugs with letter.

Your darling child
Helen Keller[14]

By the time that Helen and Annie went to Boston for their first visit, they were the toast of the town. Helen's impact on sensitive and thoughtful people was intense and immediate. Her presence with its bright and lively gaiety and charm beguiled everyone. As Joseph Lash observes, "It was difficult to resist Helen. Her passion for doing good, her sympathy for all living creatures, the unbreakable conviction that was mirrored in her very mobile and expressive little body that everyone was as good and loving as she was, made sophisticated men and women believe she was a direct emanation of the Lord." [15] Listen to the poem written to her at that time by Edmund Steadman, a poet of considerable renown of the time:

> *Mute, sightless visitant,*
> *From what uncharted world*
> *Hast voyaged into Life's rude sea*
> *With guidance scant;*
> *As if some bark mysteriously*
> *Should hither glide, with spars aslant*
> *And sails all furled!*
>
> *In what perpetual dawn,*
> *Child of the spotless brow,*
> *Hast kept thy spirit far withdrawn. . . .*
> *Pity thy unconfined*
> *Clear spirit, whose enfranchised eyes*
> *Use not their grosser sense?*
> *Ah, no! Thy bright intelligence*
> *Hath its own Paradise,*
> *A realm where to hear and see*
> *Things hidden from our kind.*
> *Not thou, not thou - 'tis we*
> *Are deaf, are dumb, are blind!* [16]

Then there was the utter obsession of Anagnos for the two. Anagnos, a fiftyish widower, immensely affectionate, was clearly in love with the idea of both of them together. In the Helen Keller story, he had acquired for a time a supreme outlet for all his enthusiasms; moreover, the pair's fame was making the Perkins Institute the paramount place in the world for the treatment of the handicapped. The school was becoming the citadel of human promise, governed by a benign and Olympian Greek—Anagnos. But as was the case with Zeus, there were tremendous clouds on the horizon, and thunderbolts soon to fall on his unusual children.

At the tender age of eight or nine, Helen was already becoming the focus of fundraising—a role that would haunt her till the end of her days. It was the classic American scenario: a former pariah who becomes a worshipped wonder and then becomes a "cause" for fundraising. Is it any surprise that Helen turned eventually to socialism? However, Helen also had a passion for doing good.

Imagine this child of the South, deeply affectionate, with the most intense sympathy for everyone, and with the absolute conviction that everyone was as compassionate and virtuous as she was. Because she was so bounded, she had no boundaries. Her face was a miracle of expressiveness—so much so that you understand why the most sophisticated people began to believe that she was a direct emanation from God—Christ come back as a blinded, muted child. Most of all, Annie believed this; having given up her God, she had found the Holy Child.

The difference in temperament between Annie and Helen was noted by all, most of all by Annie herself. "Sometimes I look at the child and wonder how she can be so patient and sweet tempered when I am ready to devour my best friend." Annie also oscillated between periods of self-importance and self-abasement that drove her sponsors wild with annoyance.

The bright days of Helen's awakening and discovery of and by the world were ending. Storm clouds now began to gather. In spite of all their successes, a rift opened between Annie's service and love to Helen and her loyalty and sense of belonging to the Perkins Institute, to which she had been contributing her reports of Helen's progress. She seemed to feel that the school was taking all the credit for Helen's accomplishments, which, in fact, it was. Annie resented her teaching being seen as a mere extension of Dr. Howe's methods. She knew that there was a vast difference between Dr. Howe spending an hour or two a day with Laura Bridgeman and her total, twenty-four hour a day devotion to Helen. Moreover, Dr. Howe had not felt that bond of love with his student which gave Annie as teacher so many ideas of how to interact with her willing pupil. Annie felt that she had developed her own unique teaching method, even though it had sprung out of techniques originated at Perkins. Feeling as she did overlooked and under appreciated by the Boston establishment, Annie gave newspaper interviews which gave the impression that her methods were so radically innovative as to have left those of the Perkins Institute and Dr. Howe far behind. Be this as it may, Annie's stance angered and antagonized the formerly benign and all-accepting Mr. Anagnos. This growing bitterness was increased to the point of no return by the Frost King episode.

Out of love for Anagnos, Helen wrote a story for him for his birthday. In it she told how King Frost first came to paint the autumn colors in the trees "to comfort us for the flight of summer." Filled with rich sensory imageries of sound and sight, the story began with the Frost King sending some of his excess supply of beautiful and precious stones of many colors to his friend and neighbor Santa Claus in order that he might "buy presents of food and clothing for the poor, that they might not suffer so much when King Winter went near their homes." The Frost King sent his mischievous fairies with jars and vases filled with the stones on their errand to Santa. However, they caught the spirit of play instead and hid their jars amidst the oaks and the maples. Meanwhile, Mr. Sun melted the rubies and other jewels, and the trees ran with the colors of the melted gems—gold, crimson, and emerald. King Frost was furious when he found out about it, but when he saw the marvelous colors of the trees, his anger left him, for he had been taught a new way of bringing good things into the world. Helen concluded her story with the words, "From that time, I suppose, it has been part of Jack Frost's work to paint the trees with the glowing colors we see in the autumn; and if they are not covered with gold and precious stones, I do not know how he makes them so bright, do you?"

Everyone was astonished by the ingenious and beautiful imagery and could not understand how someone unsighted could conceive of such pictures. So beautiful was the story and so touched was Anagnos that he included it in his annual report. However, another magazine was given first rights on the story, and it was published immediately. A week later the Virginia *Gazette for the Blind* published excerpts from a children's book by Margaret Canby which included a story titled "The Frost Fairies." In facing columns the Gazette showed that phrase for phrase, paragraph for paragraph and sometimes word for word, Canby's story and Helen's were remarkably alike. "Comment is unnecessary," the *Gazette* editor wrote.

Immediately a fire storm began at Perkins. Was Helen a fake? Was the school a victim of duplicity? Had Helen been primed with this kind of material all along? A lot of the blame fell on Annie who was accused of knowingly trying to palm off the Frost King story as Helen's own. We think now that what actually had happened is that Margaret Canby's story had been read to Helen in Boston by Mrs. Hopkins, the house mother at Perkins, and not by Annie at all. The story had settled in Helen's mind, as all stories did at this time, and became to her like paintings to which her intensive imagination gave life and color. Also that autumn Annie had taken long walks in the woods with Helen, spending many hours describing the fall foliage to her. These descriptions of the fall colors together with the beautiful story so imprinted her inner life that they became entirely her own unconscious lifelike experience. Moreover, as flooded with language as she was, patterns of words simply stuck in her mind. Helen writes of this incident:

> I thought then that I was "making up a story," as children say, and I eagerly sat down to write it before the ideas should slip from me. My thoughts flowed easily; I felt a sense of joy in the composition. Words and images came tripping to my finger ends, and as I thought out sentence after sentence, I wrote them on my braille slate. Now if words and images come to me without effort, it is a pretty

> sure sign that they are not the offspring of my own mind, but stray waifs that I regretfully dismiss.[17]

Upon learning that she had unconsciously plagiarized, Helen was astonished and grieved.

> No child ever drank deeper of the cup of bitterness than I did. I had disgraced myself; I had brought suspicion upon those I loved best. And yet how could it possibly have happened? I racked my brain until I was weary to recall anything about the frost I had read before I wrote "The Frost King"; but I could remember nothing. . . .[18]

What did the enlightened minds at Perkins do? They put Helen, a child of eight or nine, on trial, by herself, her beloved teacher sent out of the room, to determine whether or not she had plagiarized. It was by all accounts a very cruel trial. The atmosphere in the trial room was both hostile and menacing, filled with officers of the Perkins Institute (decayed human turnips, as Mark Twain later referred to them) cross-examining the little girl, their questions loaded with doubt and suspicion, as they tried to force her to confess to remembering having had the Canby story read to her. Helen didn't even know the meaning of the word *plagiarism* and was so seething in shock and sorrow that she could barely answer them. Despite her statement of not being aware of the Canby book, Annie was, of course, blamed for feeding Helen images from the book. In the end, Anagnos declared the evidence to be inconclusive and said that Helen should not be considered guilty. But although Anagnos professed to understand the whole incident, after it, he made great efforts to avoid Helen and Annie in spite of many, many letters and attempts at reconciliation on the part of Helen. The child who had known only warmth and affirmation had suddenly again become an outcast. For many months afterward, Helen fell into a slough of despondency and lassitude, experiencing a profound sense of guilt and wrongness—not so much for herself but on Teacher's behalf. For many years thereafter, Helen rigorously reviewed anything she wrote, plagued by the ghost of the chance that she would again plagiarize without realizing it.

The Frost King episode was not the only storm. It was at this time, too, that what would be a lifelong critique of Annie and her methods was beginning, led, ironically, by the man who professed to be her most loving father, Anagnos. Let us look into the nature of this critique both then and through the years, for it casts light on the relationship of the teacher and the taught, the evoker and the evoked, the midwife of latent sensibilities and the new being who comes to term under the teacher's hands.

Annie, the Archetypal Teacher, was also intensely human, moody, driven, wounded by her past experience, fiercely demanding that Helen prove herself more capable, more talented, more everything than anyone with normal senses could possibly be. Many questions have been asked about her methods. Some have accused her of turning Helen's mind to literature and determining that she be a "seeing" child without considering that she might have other means of development equally worthwhile. There are outright accusations of cruelty and abuse; indeed in reading *Teacher*, which was written in 1955, it is difficult not to bewail some of the things done to the child Helen and remembered with poignancy and shame by the adult. But Helen's shame was based for the most part on the sense that she had somehow disappointed her beloved Teacher. (Who among us does not feel sadness that we have been unable to fulfill the expectations of a dearly loved guide?) As Helen wrote:

> There had been no one else on record who regarded a deaf-blind creature (I use the word literally, a creature of circumstances) as capable of attaining normality to more than a small degree, and behold, there was Annie Sullivan soaring on the fiery wings of that dream! How she conceived it and why she persevered all her life towards that goal she called "perfection" I do not know, but from bits of talk I caught on her fingers I know that in her mind there were lovely visions, now radiant, now dimmed through disappointment, of "an angel child," "a maiden fair and full of grace," "a young woman pleading the cause of the unfortunate with a natural voice," and other images whose nonrealization makes tears start to my eyes.[19]

This book was the least successful of Helen's books among the reading public perhaps because of its many purple passages. Helen's writing depended on her memory of poetic turns of phrase and ideas of the beauty of words often of the far more sentimental nineteenth-century authors, and therefore seems to present her as much more sentimental than she ever in fact was. Indeed, as we will see, there are few people in history who have ever worked harder or with more unstinting fervor than Helen Keller did for the cause of the unfortunate.

Certainly Teacher created controversy; even in the early days, Anagnos would write her commanding her to let Helen develop naturally and play more instead of studying so much. Annie responded to such commands as most of us would, though she certainly followed his suggestions much of the time. Helen says that Teacher was never a schoolmarm but was rather "a lively young woman whose imagination was kindled by her accomplishments with little Helen to unique dreams of molding a deaf-blind creature to the full life of a useful, normal human being."

Throughout their lifetimes, people were inclined occasionally to think that Helen was a creation of Teacher's. Numerous studies and critiques have been made of Annie's erratic temperament, her demanding devotion to perfection, and her unceasing insistence on Helen's acquisition of an understanding and skill that could be recognized as those of a person of cultivation, intellectuality, and *belles lettres*. (Annie was still the child of the Irish poor proving herself worthy to the English and new English gentry.) Perhaps in the long run these questions and criticisms have proved worthwhile. Certainly between them, these women pulled our attention and focus to the nature of fearful disadvantage; and through them we have learned more about the nature of the brain and its powers of compensation. Further, the nitty-gritty reality of their story takes it out of the realm of fairy tale and into realms which are at once mythic and almost too human to bear.

Some of us go into wishful thinking concerning the relationship—witness one writer who discussed how much better it would have been for Helen had William James been her teacher and trained her in the value of perceiving things instead of words. One is tempted to add that the world would have been much better off had Annie not been subjected to nine operations and the consistent threat of blindness and had not been a victim of raw and aching poverty, deprivation, humiliation, and heartbreak. Annie's critics decry the fact that Helen used the words for colors and verbs having to do with knowing what those words meant, which would have been impossible unless Annie had force fed them to her. Neurological and psychological tests seemed to show that Helen was not highly gifted in the acuity of her remaining senses, suggesting that Annie served as a kind of living prosthesis to Helen's remaining sensory world.

All her life Helen was expected to prove somehow that she existed in her own way and to submit to "tests" that proved or disproved what she said. Needless to say, much of what was "discovered" proved damaging and hurtful to both Helen and Teacher. But when it implied criticism of Annie, it was doubly, triply painful to Helen.

PROCESS 10
THE FROST KING STORY IN OUR LIVES

Helen Keller was deeply wounded over the incident of the Frost King story. Think of little Helen, ingenuous, without a trace of guile, trusting and affectionate, suddenly being called a fake, a plagiarist, a dupe of Annie Sullivan, and virtually being brought to trial for her innocent actions. It was only the loving support and understanding of Annie Sullivan and the Keller family that brought her through this crisis of personal wounding, making her ultimately stronger and more compassionate to the failings of others.

It is probable that each one of you reading these pages has had a Frost King story in your lives—a time in which you too have been wounded and humiliated by being wrongly seen and blamed. Chances are you may continue to bear the scars of that sorrow and that shame to some degree even today.

In this process, working in partners, we tell each other our Frost King stories. Then we each become the representative of those who perpetrated the wounding which our partner received. But we also move toward forgiveness, understanding, and empowerment. Finally, we rename each other in the fullness of who and what we are.

TIME: ONE HOUR.

• MATERIALS:
A cleared room or other fairly large space. It also helps for this process to provide subdued lighting or candles.

• MUSIC:
Dark, evocative music like the first half of Vangelis' *Ignacio*. For the part in which we rename each other, some stirring celebrational music like "Eric's Theme" from *Chariots of Fire*, by Vangelis.

• INSTRUCTIONS FOR GOING SOLO:
This is a process in which it is better to have a partner. However, if that is not possible, then read the instructions given below carefully before you begin. Prepare the music and allow yourself to become centered, relaxed, focused. It is important that you physically walk backward with your eyes half-closed as instructed, speaking your Frost King story as you walk. Then sit and write, letting your journal be your partner, and write the words of empowerment. Also, be sure to dance your own renaming, saying, "I rename myself. . . ."

SCRIPT FOR THE GUIDE:

I would like each one of you to get a partner, preferably someone whose life you do not know in detail.

Sit together and listen as I explain what we are about to do. As in all of our work together, it is essential that you honor the privacy of what you may hear from each other. As you explore the role of what we are calling the "Frost King" story in your life, remember that wounding, betrayal, and humiliation often become the way through which we grow into greater life. This is one of the reasons why all great myths and tales of people living at their edges have betrayal and humiliation at the center of the story.

Now you will each take turns remembering and speaking of your own particular "Frost King" story, and then being renamed. Thus one person will be the one to tell his or her story, while the other will be the guide and take his or her partner through the entire process before reversing roles.

Before we begin, let me read to you from an example drawn from the transcript of Jean Houston demonstrating this process with a participant at Mystery School.

Jean: I will begin by placing my hands on your shoulders. Would you please close your eyes for this part of the process. Now, as the music plays, I will gently walk you backwards. (Music plays. Jean guides the man by placing her hands on his shoulders as he walks backwards.) And now, I am going to ask you about the time in your life when you had a Frost King episode. I will not encourage or discourage you. I will certainly not do psychotherapy or offer my condolences. Instead, I will be there utterly as High Witness to your story. And after you have told me your story, I will stand in for all of your accusers as well. What is your Frost King Story?

Man participant: I have a number of them but my major Frost King story, the one that really wounded me, occurred about ten years ago. I was in charge of production at a large theater complex in the Midwest which was famous for the excellence of its repertory theater. I took my job very seriously and had won a number of awards. All in all I was proud of the job I was doing. And I especially worked at creating an atmosphere and environment in which the artistry of the artists—directors, actors, set designers—could flourish, while the efforts of the production and PR people would be appreciated. But there were a number of co-workers who evidently didn't like my efforts, people I respected and relied upon. And I began to have a sense that something was wrong because people stopped looking at me, and conversations stopped abruptly when I came into a room. And I suspected that I was being discussed in special meetings to which I was not invited. But there was no way that I could discover what was going wrong or defend myself.

And after I came back from a business trip, there was this long letter that had been written by my co-workers to a supposed expert in my field who was asked to judge my work and say what was wrong with it and how to fix it. And I was furious because things had been going on behind my back about stuff that concerned me. And. . .listen to my voice. Even after ten years, I am still hurt.

Jean: Now, I want you to put your hands on my shoulders. And you are going to tell me the truth of your situation, and what was then is now. But this time open your eyes and look into mine.

And you guide me and walk me backwards as you speak to your accusers, whom I now represent.

Man participant: I would like you to know that it was unfair. And I felt both enraged and deeply wounded by your needing to go behind my back to complain about work I was very proud of. Now in the world of the theater, we try to work together, artists, producers, designers, stage managers, public relations people. And I know it's hard, and it is sometimes not easy to respect as equally important other people who are not artists but who are doing valuable jobs. (I'm speaking here to a particular set designer who really shafted me.)

Jean: Speak to me as if I were that set designer.

Man participant: I am the representative of everyone working in the theater, not just you. Also a very important part of my job is to fill those seats with people who are hungry to be present at the enactment of a play. And the fact that you are the designer does not mean that you are the one who did the play, or the one who created the play. Nobody is trying to take away your credit for what you've done. Your work is excellent. But there is credit to be shared by others. And the true enactment of this work is in working together. And I am deeply pained and I carry still the scars of my work being criticized so cruelly behind my back and never having had the chance to say straight out—I'm not the kind of artist that you are. I have different kinds of talents. And my job is different from yours. And I want you to hear that now.

Jean: I see it, and I understand what happened to you. But also I now am able to see you in your fullness, to appreciate you more richly. I hear you now, and I thank you for telling me your story. I understand and am deeply sorry for the wounding you received. But I see you now in your fullness.

Because these tales of our woundings tend to be reverberated through time, don't they? And the longer you hold onto the scars of wounding, the more you may attract a similar pattern of wounding, re-living variations of your Frost King story over and over again.

But if there can be this moment in which a listener can understand and appreciate the breadth and depth of the shame and wounding, then perhaps the wounding is unveiled and no longer put away to fester. This often then allows the energy stored in the memory of wounding to be released in love, forgiveness, and understanding. This energy then becomes the power behind greater personal development and even transformation. When we are humbled, we are made into humus, rich earth from which new plants of consciousness can grow.

(After reading from this transcript of an example of Mystery School proceedings, the Guide will say:)

Would you decide please between you, who is to be the first to tell the Frost King story and who is to be the first guide and listener. The person who is remembering a Frost King episode will have eyes closed. The guide will have eyes open.

Will the guide and listener now please place his or her hands on the rememberer's shoulders. Now guide, start to gently walk your partner backwards, turning whenever you need to avoid a wall or obstacle.

(The music begins here.)

You who are guide and listener are also High Witness. Please remain centered throughout the walk, maintaining a loving and supportive silence. Commentary and discussion, no matter how caring, only dilutes the power of the experience. Will you who are guide now ask the question of your partner, "What is your Frost King story?" You will have ten minutes for the first story. (Ten minutes.)

Will you who have just told your Frost King story now place both your hands on your partner's shoulder. And you who have been guide and listener will now become the representative of the one or ones who willingly or unwillingly were the cause of the shame and humiliation of your partner. You become the one who had been the betrayer, the accuser at the trial, the jury. But this time you will give a different verdict, one of understanding, compassion, and deep seeing.

And with eyes open now, the teller of the story will look into the eyes of the guide and gently walking them backward, speak the things you did not say at the time, your feelings of being wronged and unnecessarily wounded. Say exactly what was going on as you saw it. You are proclaiming your higher innocence, with eyes open. (Three to five minutes.)

Now will you who are the guide speak your understanding of your partner's wounding. And then speak words of seeing them fully and of honoring them. Say to them words to the effect that "I see you as whole and wholesome. I see you as full of knowledge of the human soul. I see you as full of wonder and all possibility." Be as imaginative as you can in your seeing and speaking, "I see you as a beautiful valley which the storm clouds have left." Speak the words in your own style to honor and empower your partner whose painful story you have just been witness to. (Two minutes.)

Coming now to a natural ending. Now we will reverse roles. And the person who was the guide becomes the rememberer. The rememberer becomes the guide.

(The Guide for the group repeats the instructions above for the second speaker. When both partners have finished, the Guide will say:)

All woundings however painful often have consequences for good. They open us to new dimensions of ourselves. As a result of the Frost King episode, Helen and Annie both became more conscious, and Helen learned to appreciate the depths and originality of her own mind. One might say that they were spurred on by this incident to greater mindfulness and true originality.

I would like each pair of partners to take each other by the waist and just spin for a few moments in one direction. (Twenty seconds.) Now stop. And let the partner who had first told his or her story say, "As a result of this situation having happened, I was spurred on to. . . ." And tell the consequences for good or other kinds of growth or exploration that resulted. (One minute.)

Now would you take each other by the waist again, but this time spin in the opposite direction. (Twenty seconds.) And stop. And will the other partner now say, "As a result of this situation having happened, I was spurred on to. . . ." And give the answer. (One minute.)

By now you each have received interesting and enlightening information from each other. And now I want you to tell each other how in the light of what you have just explored you would like to be renamed. For example, you might want to name yourself as Strong Heart, or Thundering Mind, or Spirit Dancing, or Merry Man, or whatever rises up in you. It may be one name or many. Consider these as spirit names, names for your soul, or for who and what you really are. Share some of these names back and forth now. Be sure to listen carefully to these names, for you will be re-naming each other with them shortly. (Two to three minutes.)

All right. Now we will move together around the room, dancing with each other to the celebrational music we will be playing, and as you dance, say "I name you Soul of Courage; I name you Lady of High Integrity," or whatever are the names your partner wishes to be called. This is a ceremony of renaming done as a dance.

I see you! I name you! Begin!

(Celebrational music is now played. At the end of the process the Guide will say:)

Renamed. Reseen. You now may live beyond your Frost King.

SO BE IT.

15 The Threshold and Beyond

As time passed, Annie began to shepherd Helen through a series of schools to prepare her for entrance to Radcliffe College. You can just picture it, can't you? See Annie spending hours in classrooms further ruining her eyes by reading ahead in subjects to help Helen learn Latin, Greek, German, mathematics, history. See the male teachers of these prep schools so utterly fascinated with Helen that they gradually try to wean her away from Annie, demanding to take charge of her education themselves. Listen as they echo Anagnos' charges that Annie was preventing Helen's autonomous and independent development into a self-reliant girl. The pressure builds on Helen to succeed, succeed, succeed—to do in academic subjects what she has already done to transcend her own handicap. At the same time, Annie is being baited, her integrity impugned, jealousies raging in the silence around Helen's head about who should be her teacher.

You can understand how it would happen. Imagine Helen looking at you with those radiant eyes which seem to see into your very soul. Listen to her speak with that oracular voice, making statements that go right to your heart. Consider the effect! She is very pretty too, with charming manners. She is speaking to you in the voice of another time and place, and what she is speaking is your soul's own truths. But next to her is her protector, Teacher, a spitfire who is looking daggers at you, and possibly whispering barbed wires.

In the midst of this, Helen passed with honors an array of subjects that today would be considered impossible—indeed no candidate ever in the history of Harvard and Radcliffe had ever scored higher in English, and this with only three year's preparatory time. What was going on here?

Helen's secret, if it can be called one, was her utter focus and attention to the subject she was studying and her ability to incarnate, to body forth what she learned. She truly became what, in her mind's eye, she beheld. In spite of all the complaints about her lack of independence in spirit, she was in essence radically autonomous—able to travel in spirit to distant times and places and to exist within the field and the feelings of these domains. In her imagination, she could travel anywhere. She wrote to Anagnos about being in Greece with him, and her description was generally accurate in feeling and kinesthetic sensibility. The same happened when she studied history. She could "visit" a place or a time, and then write about it with passion. She was never bored; all her lessons were like play because she experienced them on so many levels. She herself said that she was limited by only two senses, but in fact, all the other senses—known and unknown—woke up in her to a degree virtually unique in human history. She was given to the extrasensory perceptions that earlier cultures perhaps had known, and what she gained through her exquisitely refined kinesthetic sense gave her access to the hologramatic feel of things. Thus for Helen learning was an act of meeting—of radical inception rather than perception.

Helen was admitted into Radcliffe in 1899. We see her riding vigorously through the streets of Cambridge in tandem on a bicycle built for two. We see her swimming and winning races and being a formidable opponent in chess and checkers. But still she is unable to join the other girls in the subtle pleasures of an early twentieth-century girls' college—gossip, small escapades, rich pleasures of community. Her separation from the other girls was inevitable.

> I have had moments of loneliness when the girls have passed me on the stairs and in the lecture-rooms without a sign. I have sometimes had a depressing sense of isolation in the midst of my classmates. There are times when one wearies of books, which after all are only symbols of the spirit, and when one reaches out to the warm, living touch of a friendly hand. But I understand perfectly how the girls feel. They cannot speak to me and they do not see the light of recognition in my face as we pass. The situation to them must be strange and discouraging.[20]

Also the slow pace of the learning from books took so much time. The books on the reading list had to be transcribed into Braille or into a print-raised text. Helen had to jot down in Braille the lectures she remembered from the classroom when she got home. During all the lectures, Annie was spelling out with selective rapidity what the lecturers were saying, and sometimes Helen followed with her other hand in a print-raised book the text to which the teacher was referring. Fine points were often lost, but the gist of every lecture was communicated. With transcriptions of lectures, extra reading, homework, translations from Latin, French, and German, and themes required to be written almost every day in English, there was little time left over for extracurricular activity. Helen echoed the complaint of every college student from time immemorial:

> I used to have time to think, to reflect—my mind and I. But in college there is no time to commune with one's thoughts. One goes to college to learn, not to think, it seems.

You are the best writer of freshman English we have ever encountered, her teachers told her, but we want your own your original thoughts, not what you have digested from other sources. Perhaps as Lash suggests, Helen feared that her lack of sight and sound had prevented her from experiencing anything that would provide an interesting subject; perhaps she remembered the torments of accusations of plagiarism. At any rate, she reports "a strange vacancy in mind and heart":

> In my heart there seems to be no feeling—only a void; a vacuum, waiting to be filled by a rush of fresh spiritual life.

She became more and more concerned with the nature of the something that she lacked in her heart and fell into agonies of self-reproach. Here is one of her themes that she did not submit:

> Again tonight I feel the emptiness of heart and the utter want of something essential to self-improvement that often depresses me. What is that something I lack? I repeat this question often, but in vain. Self-reproach sweeps down upon me each time I reflect on this subject. I deny none of the charges of my conscience, they are all too true. I know I am not brave, or strong or resolute; in fact I regard myself as a failure in all that is highest and noblest in a woman. Not only have I strayed from the way of truth; but I have not performed my duties fully enough or utilized the precious opportunities that have offered themselves. Even the tender impulses that have stolen into my soul and made me weep have vanished into indifference. . . . Once this melancholy would have filled my heart with bitterness and despair; now it is a constant trouble which I forget in my enthusiasm over something beautiful or my anxiety not to disturb the people I live with and love.[21]

The disparity between her felt private failures and her public plaudits weighed on her heavily. Moreover, she felt keenly the pressure of having to produce brilliance on demand: "I am also discouraged about writing. . . .I find it a burden, not a pleasure, and at times I HATE it." What writer has not experienced the same ghastly and hopeless sense of blankness and emptiness when faced with the command "Write!" She felt, however, ideas beating upon her brain like caged birds, but which would not yet sing themselves into words. Yet as she studied harder and harder, she found her moral will developing strongly within her. Here was her course of study at Radcliffe: French, German, English composition, Milton, government, economics, history, Shakespeare, Elizabethan literature, English literature of the nineteenth century, English Bible, and the history of philosophy. But with all of this, college turned out not to be the "universal Athens" that she had hoped it would be: "There one does not meet the great and the wise face to face; one does not even feel their living touch. They are there, it is true; but they seem mummified." [22]

Perhaps it was the spiritual wasteland of her studies that all the more inflamed her ardor for social justice. Helen, in the throes of late adolescence, was at this time full of the passions that bespeak that stage when true belief and ideology gains precedence over the shadings and subtleties of the more mature mind. Helen's special situation only accentuated her sense of the ethical polarities; she felt moved by either moral outrage at injustices done, or moral sympathy towards those unfairly treated. The world was seen as a conflict between light and darkness, but to Helen, the signals coming to her through her other senses were full of ambiguity and uncertainty— shadows that she could not experience, and therefore hardly felt at all. Not seeing any light, which itself is woven with shadows, she was a champion for a light that was vaunted but unequivocal. As she wrote at this time:

> I can find no middle course between love and hatred, cruelty and kindness, truth and falsehood, or any of the great, inconvertible opposites that are excellent or compatible with enlightened self-interest or the principles of a genuine civilization. A middle course is really a compromise with evil.

Helen embodied this stance for her entire life. It was the basis for the powerful positions she took in helping women, the handicapped, the less fortunate, the laborer. No reconciler, no compromiser was she! How different in this was she from Teacher who, in her own self, discovered the bold interweaving of good and bad qualities. Knowing herself to be filled with empathy, high ideals, loving solicitude, and a passion to serve, Annie, with her antic disposition, could still write about herself in a letter to a beloved friend, "I would much prefer to have people despise me as they certainly would if they guessed how full of distrust and contempt my heart is toward my fellow beings. I know it grieves you to hear me speak this way and doubtless it will hurt you still more to have me write it, but I want you to know just how detestable I am. I find people hateful and I hate them." [23] Despite this, to a very great extent, it was Teacher who imbued Helen with the concepts of right and wrong; this and her other manifold gifts had so endeared her to Helen that Helen simply could not recognize Teacher as anything other than wholly loving and wholly good.

Seven years before her admission to Radcliffe, Helen had been introduced to Mr. John Hitz, Consul-General for Switzerland, and friend of Alexander Graham Bell. Mr. Hitz became one of her most devoted and important friends; he visited Helen and Annie often, spent six weeks with them every summer, learned Braille so that he could write to Helen and she could read his letters, gave her a gold watch with an open face so that she could read the time. In *My Religion* Helen wrote that she loved him next best to her teacher. And it was he who gave her her first taste of Emanuel Swedenborg's world of inner light, gifting her with a copy of *Heaven and Hell* in raised letters. Of this gift she writes in *My Religion*:

> Impelled only by the curiosity of a young girl who loves to read, I opened that big book and lo, my fingers lighted upon a paragraph in the preface about a blind woman whose darkness was illumined with beautiful truths from Swedenborg's writings. She believed that they imparted a light to her mind which more than compensated her for the loss of earthly light. She never doubted that there was a spiritual body within the material one with perfect senses, and that after a few dark years the eyes within her eyes would open to a world infinitely more wonderful, complete, and satisfying than this. My heart gave a joyous bound.[24]

The fact that for Swedenborg, an eighteenth-century Swedish scientist and visionary, there was no condemnation of other religions and their beliefs and no afterlife hell for the unbeliever appealed enormously to Helen's sense of what religion could be. Instead, in *Heaven and Hell*, she found that "'Jesus' stands for Divine Good, Good wrought into deeds, and 'Christ' divine Truth, sending forth new thought, new life and joy into the minds of men; therefore no one who believes in God and lives right is ever condemned."[25]

With its emphasis on the many dimensions of reality and the availability of higher worlds to the seeking and contemplative mind, the Swedenborgian New Church and its beliefs led Helen into passageways and labyrinths where Teacher could not go. Certainly its emphasis on the life in the supernal and imaginal realms and the joy perceived there at the same time that one lives on the Earth shone warm on Helen's heart and no doubt helped her attain an even greater depth of spirit and loving capacity. Here was a belief and a practice that addressed the inner senses and the inner universe. With its central doctrine of the ever-near presence of God in this world and the understanding of God as divine love, divine wisdom, and, most especially, as power for use, Helen had found a faith that gave her a freer and more complete universe than the fragmented one she met with her limited physical senses and her even more limited traditional Christian beliefs.

Not content with her normal course of study at Radcliffe, in her sophomore year Helen, urged on by Teacher, signed a contract to write the story of her life in five installments for one of the leading women's magazines. She was persuaded that much of it was already written, at least in part, in her compositions and that it would be easily possible to complete the rest. Indeed, the first part was easy and went well, but the next installments were tougher. Rescue arrived in the person of a young Harvard instructor, who had proved a brilliant scholar during his undergraduate career, and who was a good writer as well. His name was John Macy. Not only did John help edit and organize the installments of Helen's life story, he also cleverly negotiated the book rights, and then helped get the book written. The book included Annie's letters to Mrs. Hopkins describing the time of her teaching young Phantom (Helen had apparently forgotten much of it), but Annie refused to talk about her own early life, especially the days at Tewksbury. The book, published in March, 1903, received great critical acclaim, but did not immediately sell in the large numbers that their publisher had hoped. The letters by Annie were mentioned by at least two reviewers as adding to the richness of the book. Across the Atlantic, the reception was equally warm and vigorous. Queen Victoria wished to see Helen should she visit England. The Duke of Westminster requested and received a picture of Miss Keller and Miss Sullivan and kept it on his desk.

But there were quibbles and quarrels from Anagnos and others at Perkins, who wanted to claim their share of Helen's education, but who had not answered Macy's request for fuller information until very late. Again there were questions about who had written the book. Others fumed, how dare she use second-hand impressions, which they must be, since she had no capacity to see or hear, yet claimed in her descriptions to have seen and heard. A serious critic in *The Nation*, reprinted in the *New York Post*, iterated the tired point of view that "All her knowledge is hearsay knowledge. . . .if she could only realize that it is better to be one's self, however limited and afflicted, than the best imitation of somebody else that could be achieved!" All this was in spite of the fact that Helen was very clear about her alternate modes of perception in passages such as the following in which she contrasts city and country knowings:

> People who think that all sensations reach us through the eye and ear have expressed surprise that I should notice any difference, except possible the absence of pavements, between walking in city streets and in country roads. They forget that my whole body is alive to the conditions about me. The rumble and roar of the city smite the nerves on my face, and I feel the ceaseless tramp of an unseen multitude. . . The children who crowd these grimy alleys, half-clad and underfed, shrink away from your outstretched hand as if from a blow. Dear little creatures, they crouch in my heart and haunt me with a constant sense of pain. There are men

and women too, all gnarled and bent out of shape. I have felt their hard rough hands and realized what an endless struggle their existence must be—no more than a series of scrimmages, thwarted attempts to do something. . . .

What a joy it is to feel the soft, springy earth under my feet once more, to follow grassy roads that lead to ferny brooks where I can bathe my fingers in a cataract of rippling notes, or to clamber over a stone wall into green fields that tumble and roll and climb in riotous gladness! [26]

Helen wrote in her autobiography of the innate memory of the earth that everyone who is earthborn feels. Neither blindness nor deafness can rob one of this gift of memory of the green earth and murmuring waters from past generations. And then there is the most marvelous perception of all—the ability to grasp in toto works of art, as well as human souls, through one's fingertips. She derived great pleasure, she wrote:

from touching great works of art. As my fingertips trace line and curve, they discover the thought and emotion which the artist portrayed. I can feel hate, courage, and love, just as I can detect them in living faces. . . .

The hands of those I meet are dumbly eloquent. The touch of some hands is an impertinence. I have met people so empty of joy, that when I clasped their finger tips, it seemed as if I were shaking hands with a northeast storm. Others have sunbeams in them, so that their grasp warms my heart. It may be only the clinging touch of a child's hand but there is as much potential sunshine in it for me as there is in a loving glance for others. [27]

The semi-accusations of Helen's critics were answered clearly and emphatically by many people, including John Macy and Helen herself. Many other reviewers recognized that the greatness of Helen's accomplishment was proof of Annie's gift—which some called "genius." At any rate her autobiography became and still is a classic, and Annie's letters are read by teachers with appreciation, understanding, and gratitude.

With the publication of this first major and successful book, the financial picture shifted for Annie and Helen, and they had time and money to indulge themselves somewhat. John Macy's friendship and assistance had quickly became indispensable; in fact within the first few months of his working with them, he and Annie had fallen in love. Macy did his best to take care of Annie's health; both eyes and feet were troubling to her, and he saw to it that she had medical care for both. The few surviving letters we have of Annie to Macy prove to us again that even the finest and highest things have a price that must be paid. When she and Helen joined their lives and fates and formed that incandescent partnership, of necessity the individual accomplishments each might have made were sacrificed, and one of these was Annie's life as a writer. Consider the beauty of these passages from her letters: "The sense of being at home comes to me so deeply when I am near you," she wrote to Macy, "that I am always a little shivery when you leave me, as if the spirit of death shut his wings over me, but the next moment the thought of your love for me brings a rush of life back to my heart." And in another letter written some nine months later, in February, 1903, while Macy was away in New York: "there are many lonely hours when I move with the careless majesty of a sometime goddess amid the ruins of joys that have been."

Later that year Teacher bought a house (for $2700) in Wrentham, Massachusetts; they lived in it until 1917. Meetings with President Theodore Roosevelt, with Mark Twain (who adored Helen practically above all other beings—her complete goodness, he often said, kept him from total despair over the nature of the rest of the human race), visits with friends among the blind and deaf communities, with other friends, and with her mother kept Helen busy, as did her already extensive correspondence and her heartfelt attempts to do some good for the handicapped. Her main point was that the handicapped should receive education so that they could work and feel themselves to be productive members of the society. To this end she willingly offered her testimony before legislatures and spoke at the openings of places like New York's Eye and Ear Infirmary. And like all writers, she yearned for something to do besides writing: "Every line I write is forced out at the point of the bayonet." But her next writing for publication was an essay on the "goodness of life" called "Optimism." In it we find the beginnings of Helen's philosophy of the existence of an ideal, archetypal realm from which inspiration for this world is to be drawn:

> If I am happy in spite of my deprivations; if my happiness is so deep that it is a faith; my testimony to the creed of optimism is worth hearing. . . . A deaf-blind person ought to find special meaning in Plato's Ideal World. These things which you see and hear and touch are not the reality of what is, but imperfect manifestations of the Idea, the Principle, the Spiritual. . . .

From her habitation in this Ideal, archetypal realm, Helen saw the plan for the unfolding of future society and the coming turmoil of the new twentieth century:

Out of the fierce struggle and turmoil of contending systems and powers I see a brighter spiritual era slowly emerge—an era in which there shall be no England, no France, no Germany, no America, no this people or that, but one family, the human race, one law, peace; one need, harmony; one means, labor; one taskmaster, God.[28]

By the time of her graduation from Radcliffe, Helen was sounding the trumpets for work for women as well as for the deaf and the blind and deploring with vigor her nation's expenditures of so many millions of dollars for war and war engines, more in those days, she tells us, than twice what was spent for public schools. Those close to her recognized—some more slowly than others—that Helen was to be an "unconquerable liberal." In her speech to the Radcliffe alumnae, she said:

There are harsh customs to be made sweet with love; hearts in which a kind, tolerant brotherly love must be awakened; time-hallowed prejudices that must be overthrown. One evil that must be checked is the ignorance of the learned who have never learned the simple, honest language of the heart, which is the most vital of all.

What a scene her graduation from Radcliffe must have been: a company of musicians in the balcony, the graduates singing Mendelssohn's "Spring Song," everyone coming on stage capped and gowned. Each graduate is congratulated, and then they call for Helen. She comes to the platform, tall, erect, grave-looking. The audience is hushed. She mounts the platform with Annie guiding her on one arm, bows to the college secretary, and approaches the president. Bowing again, she stretches forward her hands to grasp the diploma. The applause turns to an ovation as *Cum Laude* is added to her degree, with a Special Excellence in English.

Soon after commencement, she gave a speech in which she said:

College has breathed new life into my mind and given me new views of things, a perception of new truths and of new aspects of the old ones. I grow stronger in the conviction that there is nothing good or right which we cannot accomplish if we have the will to strive. The assured reality and nearness of the end of my school days fills me with bright anticipations. The doors of the bright world are flung open before me and a light shines upon me, the light kindled by the thought that there is something for me to do beyond the threshold.[29]

After graduation Annie and Helen lived in their new house at Wrentham. By this point John Macy was virtually one of the household—making bookshelves, clearing Helen's path so that she could walk farther into the fields, cleaning out the barn. Visitors sometimes came to check out the truth: was Miss Sullivan the housekeeper or was she the brains? Was Miss Keller a dupe or a *wunderkind*? Many who came to question remained to praise. About this time, a Helen Keller Day was held at the St. Louis Exposition celebrating the 100th Anniversary of the Louisiana Purchase under the presidency of Thomas Jefferson. (Can't you imagine those two benign and luminous beings meeting—two visionaries tapping social transformation into each other's hands?) Her words to the thousands who crowded in to see and hear her included, "God bless the nation that provides education and opportunity for all her children."

During all this, Teacher was waffling about marrying John, who had been trying to persuade her to say yes for a year, even though he knew well what it would mean. Annie hesitated, citing her volcanic moods, the fact that she was ten years older than he, the fact that she was Catholic, even though a long-forsaken one, and he was Protestant. They did not seem to have worried much over the fact that he was a heavy drinker. Even here, there are many versions of the story and many conjectures. Some say that John really loved Helen and wanted to marry her, but because of Teacher's feelings, he had to marry Annie in order to be near Helen! Whatever the case, the letters show that the two agreed to marry in May, making careful arrangements for Helen's continuing happiness and security. She was to live with them; they would all work together, and John promised to stay with Helen and care for her in case Annie should die before either of the others. And so Annie and John were married, and the two went off to New York for a boat trip to New Orleans.

The honeymoon included a visit to Helen who was then at home in Alabama, and together, they made their way back north. The next period was marred only by the death of Anagnos and the painful memories which were evoked when the eulogies seemed to ignore the role that Annie played in Helen's education. Insults and threats were traded, and no doubt old wounds were opened, but Helen was soon embarked upon a new project, writing the very successful *The World I Live In*. Her essays made it clear that imagination held the key for her life, while also describing how her three remaining senses helped to compensate for the two that she lost. The most important sense for her was touch: "If I had to make a man, I should certainly have put the brain and the soul in his fingertips." It was here too that she spoke so eloquently about smell, the "fallen angel" of the senses, but also "a potent wizard that transports us across thousands of miles and all the years we have lived." "The sense of smell," she wrote, "has told me of a coming storm hours before there was any sign of it visible. I notice first, a throb of expectancy, a slight quiver, a concentration in my nostrils. As the storm nears my nostrils dilate, the better to receive the flood of earth odors which seem to multiply and extend, until I feel a splash of rain against my cheek. As the tempest departs, receding farther and farther, the odors fade, becoming fainter and fainter, and die away beyond the bar of space." [30] Helen's genius for detecting the sheer archaeological dig of life through smell is apparent. She recognized "an old fashioned country house because it has several layers of odors, left by a succession of families, of plants, of perfumes and draperies."

Helen's new book was acclaimed by many, including the great William James, who called it one of the classics in psychology. ". . . you have told so much truth about human nature which nobody had suspected. Evidently sensations as such form the relatively smaller part of the world we mentally live in, relations being the things of most interest. . . .The sum of it is that you're a blessing & I'll kill any one who says you're not!" Helen wrote this book in high spirits and halcyon days, part of the pleasure coming from the collaboration of the devoted and helpful John Macy.

Subsequent years brought money problems and the death of old friends, including her beloved John Hitz. Hitz had gone to Union Station in Washington, D.C., to meet Helen and her mother. He pressed Helen's hand in great happiness, tapping into her hand that she was the beloved daughter of his heart, and then a few moments later, he collapsed and died. His was a sore and piteous loss.

The death of Mark Twain was also felt keenly. As Helen described him later: "He entered into my limited world with enthusiasm just as he might have explored Mars. Blindness was an adventure that kindled his curiosity. He treated me not as a freak but as a handicapped woman seeking a way to circumvent extraordinary difficulties." At their initial meeting when she was in her early teens, she had run her hands through his wonderful white mane, caressed his face, and declared him quite handsome. Mark Twain himself was quite overcome by the meeting, and kept returning again and again to have his hair ruffled. It was a love affair of soul at first sight and first touch. They beatified each other. She softened his cynicism and gave him new ideals of human virtue, while he offered her a comical and canny view of the world. She would laugh until the tears came as she listened with her fingers to his lips to his wild and wooly tales of life on the Mississippi. When she wrote about her shame and guilt over the Frost King affair in her autobiography, he responded to her in a manner calculated to reduce all guilt and raise all laughter: "Oh, dear me, how unspeakably funny and owlishly idiotic and grotesque was that 'plagiarism' farce! As if there was much of anything in any human utterance, oral or written, *except* plagiarism. . . .For substantially all ideas are secondhand, consciously and unconsciously drawn from a million outside sources, and daily used by the garnerer with a pride and satisfaction born of the superstition that he originated them."

Most telling and most wonderful to me is the letter Mark Twain wrote to Helen of the meaning and uniqueness of their friendship, "which has subsisted between us for nine years without a break and without a single act of violence that I can call to mind. I suppose there is nothing like it in heaven; and not likely to be until we get there and show off. . . .I often think of it with longing, and how they'll say, 'there they come—sit down in front!' I am practising with a tin halo. You do the same. . . .You are a wonderful creature, the most wonderful in the world—you and your other half together— Miss Sullivan, I mean, for it took the pair of you to make a complete and perfect whole."

As Helen's contacts and knowledge of the world widened, her social and political agenda was also expanding. As an advocate for the handicapped, Helen soon began to be aware of the need to demand help from the state as well as from private individuals. Then her interest shifted from concern with work opportunities for the blind and the deaf to statistics that showed that a great many babies were made blind because of the mother's infection with venereal disease. She, therefore, began to demand that newborns receive that drop of silver nitrate that would prevent their blindness. Not long after this campaign, she and John joined the Socialist Party. Helen was already a suffragist, but now she gathered her opinions and desire for social justice and turned them fully to the cause of the people and against the many who took cruel advantage of their fellows. At that time, many were turning to socialism as offering a viable and practical path through the morass of social evils. The dialectical philosophy of Marx and Engels appealed especially to intellectuals who appreciated their historical sweep and neo-Hegelian critique of economics as determining the body, mind and souls of millions.

In addition to their care for the downtrodden, the trio of Helen, Annie, and John were experiencing more of their perennial financial troubles, but still Helen turned down a pension of $5000 per year from Andrew Carnegie. She did it gallantly, declaring that she wanted to make her own way, but adding that she could not accept money from one of the men whose only goal had previously been the acquisition of a huge fortune. Soon she was writing that the ill-treatment of the blind goes hand in hand with the ill-treatment of all workers everywhere: "We know now that the welfare of the whole people is essential to the welfare of each."

Her political voice was loud and clear (and many of her friends and family found themselves dismayed). In the days and months before the presidential election of 1912, she was eager to join the great fray. John finished and published one of the classics of criticism, *The Spirit of American Literature*, and was shortly afterward invited to Schenectady to serve as executive secretary to the mayor; Walter Lippman had resigned and recommended John as his successor. The city thought that Helen was coming too, and with much public fanfare, the mayor offered to give her a place on the newly created Board of Public Welfare. Helen was much excited by the prospect of having an actual city with which to try out her social philosophy, and tentatively accepted the offer. In the end, however, troubles between Annie and John sent John to Schenectady alone.

By now, John and Annie had been married seven years, and their relationship was suffering. Annie had never liked housekeeping, though she was a good cook, and she must have been feeling the strain. She gained weight, and her moods went through wild swings. The mood swings made John drink; and his drinking caused further mood swings. Too, Annie was politically a conservative—or rather a pessimist about the nature of humankind—and could not have been hopeful about the causes John and Helen were espousing so gleefully.

By contrast, Helen declared in interviews that her life was just beginning; now she would have the opportunity to begin to "help all mankind." This made her eager to do more work on her voice. Charles White, a specialist at the Boston Conservatory of Music, was eager to help, and after his work with her, Helen was able to speak with greater clarity and make herself understood by many people. In *Teacher* Helen says that in the early years, when Annie tried to teach her how to speak melodiously and expressively, they had not realized, until White illustrated it, that they had tried to "build up speech without voice production." White's work on voice production with Helen continued for three summers. By the end of this time, Helen's speech was understandable to most in the audiences she addressed.

The summer months of 1912 were spent with John away in Schenectady, and with Helen continuing to work on her voice production while taking care of the ailing Annie. John did not stay away for long. Apparently bored and frustrated in Schenectady because, as he complained, "A socialist administration within a capitalist society cannot do anything essentially socialistic," John suggested that Helen embark on a lecture series about socialism and about work for the handicapped. But before any firm plans could be made, Teacher underwent major surgery, and John was forced to resign and return to Wrentham to be with Helen and Annie as she recovered. No one knows the nature of the surgery, except that it nearly killed Annie.

At this time there were strikes and furor at the mills and factories around Massachusetts and New York. The IWW was active, and Helen was eager to give her support, especially to labor organizer Big Bill Haywood. She sent a gift of $87.50 to support the women engaged in the strike. Lash tells us that "her participation in the socialist movement gave her a sense of comradeship with millions throughout the world." Her concern had widened from a sense of communion with the handicapped to an overarching care for the disadvantaged and for laborers all over the world. What with workers' rights, the women's suffrage movement, and her advocacy of centers for teaching and assistance to the blind and deaf, Helen was busy. The national election held at this time brought in Woodrow Wilson as President of the United States. On this, too, Helen had an opinion. Wilson was "a man of sincere character and unusual moral force," she wrote, "but capitalism was still king," and nothing was going to be said or done about the deplorable living and working conditions of America's laborers. She spent a good deal of time visiting labor shantytowns and factories, and she would come back angrier than ever.

It was just on the verge of World War I when Helen and Teacher began their fifty-year career on the lecture circuit. They made a wonderfully entertaining pair. Annie had a phenomenal voice, beautiful and melodious, but she also had a wry, wicked, complex sense of humor. Their lectures were an extraordinary partnership of two minds working in tandem. Their message, delivered in rich and impassioned prose, was one of hope and optimism and the glory of human possibilities. Their work together showed an utter unity of spirit, mind, and love. As usual, however, what Helen said was received joyously by some and denied by others. Who was writing her speeches? Who was influencing her judgment? And then poor Teacher once more came under attack as an avowed Marxist, though she was nothing of the kind. In fact, she and John went at it hammer and tongs whenever the subject of Socialism was raised between them, which had to have been often. John did influence Annie, true, but only in ways which followed her long-held sympathies and beliefs. As a friend of John's wrote, "Fancy anybody doing anything to that mind against that will!"

The spring of 1913 saw John off to Europe alone, on his first real vacation. Annie and Helen went on with their speaking engagements. John's trip was paid for by Helen as a last effort to save Teacher's marriage; she was only able to provide the money because she at last said yes to the Carnegie pension. She agreed to accept the money after a horrendous experience that occurred while on the lecture circuit when she found herself in a hotel room in Maine with a terribly ill Teacher, not able to call anyone or go out and find someone to help. Helen's willingness to help John with money went on for many years, even after his painful separation from Annie. John, by this time a serious alcoholic, began to write a series of paranoid, accusatory letters about Annie to Helen. Helen's replies to John answering his accusations are painful to read:

> You say you can 'never explain to me what life with Teacher has been.' I remember that in spite of many hard trials in the past we have had happy days, many of them, when we three seemed to feel in each others handclasp a bit of heaven. Have you forgotten it all that you say such bitter things about my teacher, about her who has made my darkness

beautiful and rent asunder the iron gates of silence? Have you forgotten all the sunshine, all the laughter, all the long walks, drives and jolly adventures, all the splendid books we read together. . . .Have you forgotten that at times, when we had all been impatient, you would say to me: 'If we were not a trouble to each other, we could not love as we do.'

I know how imperious, changeable and quick-tempered Teacher is. I have suffered just as much from those failings as you have: but my love for her has never wavered, never will. Perhaps she owes her success to some of those very failings. You know—you have often told me as much—that the education of a deaf-blind child is a tremendous strain upon the faculties and the health of a teacher, and that only a few can stay with such a child more than a year or two. Only Teacher's splendid vigor has made it possible for her to stick to her colossal task during twenty-six years. Think of it! [31]

Over and over she appealed to him to remember what love is. No matter what he says or feels now, and how misjudging he is of Teacher and her motives, she will not forget that she loves him; no matter how hurt she feels over what she considers his injustice to Teacher, she still remembers the happy days with joy, and she still thinks of him with love.

As for Teacher, she was utterly broken, devastated by the fact that John's love had turned so sour, fearful of going insane with grief, yet pulling herself together before each public appearance with Helen, knowing that those who have come to hear the story are not to blame for what has happened in her personal life. Annie seemed full of schemes to try to win John back—at least partly because her hopes and dreams for Helen's life depended on John to be carried out. For his part, John was filled with loathing and distrust of Annie and felt himself betrayed by her. Lash points out that all the men that turned against Annie and tried to deny her her place in Helen's life eventually ended up calling her a humbug and a fake. This is the one thing that Helen would allow no one to say about Annie. With all this going on, what a miserable and dark time it must have been for those poor travelers on that exhausting lecture tour.

But when the autumn came and the two returned to Wrentham, John was there with them. His apartment in Boston had burned, destroying his possessions as well as those of Annie and Helen which were kept there. John pitched in around the house, and they had more money to keep things up and to hire a maid as well as a cook and a houseboy. They also bought a motorcar. War had broken out in Europe, and Helen felt herself to be, if anything, on the German side. It was, after all, the land of Beethoven, Goethe, Kant, and Karl Marx. She continued lecturing, and Helen tried to stay neutral on the war; John worked on his book, *Socialism in America*. While preparing for their lengthy 1915 tour, they brought in a new assistant, Polly Thomson, a young Scottish immigrant. Polly became a devoted friend for the rest of Helen's life. By the time they began the tour, John had moved out again. This trip was well attended, and Helen and Annie met many new friends as well as old ones. To Dr. Maria Montessori, Helen said, placing her hands on her shoulders and speaking with great distinctness: "Blessed are the feet of her who comes across the seas with a message of liberty to the children of America." Maria Montessori in turn said of Annie to Helen, "She is the creator of a soul, but you had the soul to be created."

At the San Francisco Panama-Pacific Exhibition, a Helen Keller Day was proclaimed, and Teacher was presented a medal. In accepting the medal, Annie gave an extraordinarily potent and compelling statement of her educational philosophy. Her words remain as valid today alas, as they did then. Pointing to Helen, she said:

> Here is no dazzling personage, no startling circumstance. A young woman, blind, deaf and dumb from infancy, has, through the kind of education that is the right of every child, won her way out of darkness and silence, has found speech and has brought a message of cheer to the world. . . .
>
> What she has accomplished without sight and hearing suggests the forces that lie dormant in every human being. . . .If Helen Keller, lacking the two senses that are usually considered the most important, has become a writer of ability and a leader among women, why should we not expect the average child, possessed of all its faculties, to attain a far higher ability and knowledge than the schools of today develop? Many realize that there is something radically wrong with a system of eduction that obviously does not educate.
>
> Every child begins life as an eager, active little creature, always doing something, always trying to get something that he wants very much. Even before he can utter a word, he succeeds in making known his desires by cries and grimaces. . . .
>
> Our educational system spoils this fine enthusiasm. . . .Our schools. . .kill imagination in the bud. They uproot the creative ideals of childhood and plant in their place worthless ideals of ownership. The fine soul of the child is of far greater importance than high marks, yet the system causes pupils to prize high grades above knowledge, and he goes from the schools into his life work believing always that the

score is more important than the game, possession more praiseworthy than achievements.[32]

The war in Europe had begun, and the actions by the Germans had changed American minds and sympathies. Helen remained true to her pacifist beliefs, but she no longer had an easy way, through John, to get news of what was really happening. However, she spoke out against American preparedness as a method for munitions makers to turn a handy profit and for America's greedy capitalists to wrong American workers. She spoke out in places that shocked opponents of her position, who, of course, claimed that she had no way of knowing what was going on anyway. Still, Helen maintained her position, which was clear and undefiled no matter what its ramifications. She made sweeping claims that the movement for national defense was a plot of J. P. Morgan, that World War I was largely a banker's and munitions makers' plot, and that the American workers had nothing to defend anyway. Even friendly newspapers that had adored her said of her, "Why should the so-called Labour Forum be permitted to use the pathos of her personality to promote a propaganda of disloyalty and anarchy?" Nevertheless, her stirring speeches met with wild ovations. By now for Helen, even the Socialist Party was moving too slowly, seemingly more interested in theoretical discussion than in actions, so Helen became an IWW member. "I don't give a damn about semi-radicals," Helen said.

As her interviews grew in pugnacity and anti-government remarks, she found herself identifying with other martyrs of the spirit:

> I feel like Joan of Arc at times. My whole being becomes uplifted. I, too, hear the voices that say "come," and I will follow no matter what the cost, no matter what the trials I am placed under. Jail, poverty, calumny—they matter not. Truly He has said, "Woe unto you that permit the least of me to suffer."

She seemed to be courting martyrdom. Incredible was the range of her fury and the violent uncompromising views uttered by this gentle woman. It was a miracle she was not arrested for them. Take, for example, her comments on President Teddy Roosevelt to newspaper reporters following a lecture:

> He is the most bloodthirsty man in the United States. When he is not dreaming of plunging this country into war and shedding the blood of men, he is writing books about his own prowess in shedding the blood of animals.

When pressed further about who she would deem the most blood-thirsty man in Europe, she answered with a smile described as sweet and filled with womanly warmth, "The Czar. I know you expected me to say the Kaiser, but the Kaiser has never turned his cannon upon his own people as the Czar has done. The Kaiser never massacred the Jews. Put Rockefeller in with Roosevelt and the Czar. He has a greater blood guilt if not greater bloodthirst [than Roosevelt]."

It's interesting to learn how Helen managed to speak before so many large audiences. Her formal lecture was almost always non-political and followed a fixed form. Annie went onto the platform first and told about the education of Helen; then leading Helen onto the stage, she first accustomed the audience to Helen's unusual voice. She had Helen repeat slowly sentences that Helen read with her fingers from Annie's lips. Then Helen slowly said the words of the hymn *Abide With Me*. By this point the audience was expected to be used to her voice. Helen then gave her main speech, which she called her "Message of Happiness." This was a series of anecdotes and morally uplifting ideas full of hope and the possibility of goodness in the world. Even the most astute audiences apparently had difficulty following her vocal inflections, but they certainly admired her courage and willingness to present herself to them. A question period followed, and people always wanted to know her political beliefs and espousals. By the time of the Presidential campaign in 1918, even the antifeminist Wilson had declared that it was time for women to have the vote, but that was still ahead. Demands fell upon Helen that she present a Chautauqua series on Preparedness for Peace, which she did.

However, two things happened that made every other concern fade into the background. Teacher was sick again, they feared with consumption, and Helen fell in love.

From the start Helen had always been interested in the idea of love. One day, not long after coming to Tuscumbia, Annie Sullivan had spelled into Helen's hand, "I love Helen." Helen recalled in her autobiography the wonderful conversation that followed:

> "What is love?" I asked.
> She drew me closer to her and said, "It is here," pointing to my heart whose beats I was conscious of for the first time. Her words puzzled me very much because I did not then understand anything unless I touched it.
> I smelt the violets in her hand and asked, half in words, half in signs, a question which meant, "Is love the sweetness of flowers?"
> "No," said my teacher.
> Again I thought. The warm sun was shining on us.

"Is this not love?" I asked, pointing in the direction from which the heat came. "Is this not love?"

A few days later when the sun came out after the clouds and rain had finished again Helen asked, "Is this not love?" to which Annie replied:

> "Love is something like the clouds that were in the sky before the sun came out. . . .You cannot touch the clouds you know; but you feel the rain and know how glad the flowers and the thirsty earth are to have it after a hot day. You cannot touch love either; but you feel the sweetness that it pours into everything. Without love you would not be happy or want to play."
> The beautiful truth burst upon my mind—I felt that there were invisible lines stretched between my spirit and the spirit of others.[33]

That Helen would actually ever "fall in love" was anticipated by her genial and fatherly friend, Alexander Graham Bell. In *Midstream*, Helen describes how one day, in 1900, after they had been talking for some time of poetic and philosophical things, Dr. Bell paused for a long time, and then said:

> "It seems to me, Helen, a day must come when love, which is more than friendship will knock at the door of your heart and demand to be let in."
> "What made you think of that?" I asked.
> "Oh, I often think of your future. To me you are a sweet, desirable young girl, and it is natural to think about love and happiness when we are young."
> "I do think of love sometimes," I admitted; "but it is like a beautiful flower which I may not touch, but whose fragrance makes the garden a place of delight just the same."
> He sat silent for a minute or two, thought-troubled, I fancied. Then his dear fingers touched my hand again like a tender breath, and he said, "Do not think that because you cannot see or hear, you are debarred from the supreme happiness of woman. . . ."
> "Oh, but I am happy, very happy!" I told him. "I have my teacher and my mother and you, and all kinds of interesting things to do. I really don't care a bit about being married. . . ."
> "I know," he answered, "but life does strange things to us. You may not always have your mother, and in the

nature of things Miss Sullivan will marry, and there may be a barren stretch in your life when you will be very lonely."

"I can't imagine a man wanting to marry me," I said. "I should think it would be like marrying a statue."

"You are very young," he replied, patting my hand tenderly. . . .[34]

The man who won her devotion was twenty-nine-year-old Peter Fagan, a former assistant of John Macy's who later became Helen's secretary. It began one evening when Helen, then thirty-six, was sitting alone in her study in a despondent state. Peter came in and sat down beside her, taking her hand and holding it in silence. Then he began to talk to her with the greatest of tenderness, telling her how much he loved her. He told her that if she would marry him, he would be her life partner and help her through all the difficulties of her life including reading to her and helping her with her books. Needless to say, he was socialist. Their romance continued with passing notes back and forth in Braille. Helen describes herself as being enchanted: "His love was a bright sun that shone upon my helplessness and isolation. The sweetness of being loved enchanted me, and I yielded to an imperious longing to be part of a man's life. For a brief space I danced in and out of the gates of heaven, wrapped up in a web of bright imaginings." Peter did not want Helen to tell her mother or Teacher about their love for each other, for Teacher was ill, and he felt that he had to win Mrs. Keller's approval by evidence of his devotion to Helen. Nonetheless, it appears that soon Peter and Helen were planning to elope, and he had obtained a marriage license. This was duly reported in the *Boston Globe*, whereupon Mrs. Keller, who saw no possibility of married life for her daughter, went into a perfect fury and did everything she could to dissuade Helen from going through with it. Whenever Peter would come to the house, he was unceremoniously thrown out by Mrs. Keller.

In a comic opera adventure, Mrs. Keller then tried to remove Helen from the scene of the romance by taking her home to Alabama by way of a boat that stopped at Savannah and then by train to Montgomery. Fagan was evidently on the boat, and so Mrs. Keller pulled Helen off it in order to upset the scheme Peter had hatched, with Helen's consent, to abduct her on the way from the boat to the train, at which time they would elope to Florida and be married by a minister friend. Though this initial plan was foiled, Peter was not to be derailed. One morning in Montgomery, Helen's sister saw her talking to a strange man on the porch. He was spelling into Helen's hand with great excitement. Mildred sent out the alarm, and her husband came down with a shotgun and threatened to shoot Peter. Though he pleaded his love and desire to marry Helen, he was run off the premises. A few nights later Helen had packed her bag and waited on the porch all night for Peter, who never came. Helen wrote of this: "The brief love will remain in my life, a little island of joy, surrounded by dark waters. I am glad that I have had the experience of being loved and desired." [35] She also wrote a poem about the loss of physical loving and of the motherhood never to be hers:

> *What earthly consolation is there for one like me*
> *Whom fate has denied a husband and the joy of*
> *   motherhood?*
> *At the moment my loneliness seems a void that will*
> *   always be immense.*
> *Fortunately I have much work to do.*
> *More than ever before, in fact,*
> *And while doing it, I shall have confidence as always,*
> *That my unfilled longings will be gloriously satisfied*
> *In a world where eyes never grow dim, nor ears dull.* [36]

Teacher did not know of Helen's poignant attempts at elopement. She was attempting to recover her health and spirit under the tropical sun in Puerto Rico and was in high good humor. She detected none of Helen's sorrow, writing, "Dear, I do want to get well for your sake. You do need me still. This separation is teaching us both a number of things, is it not?" It was during this time that they were forced to give up the house in Wrentham; perhaps the only pleasant news was the fact that the doctor who had diagnosed consumption in Annie had mistakenly read the report of another patient. So what Annie got was a nice long vacation in Puerto Rico, from which she came back full of energy.

In fact their next adventure, after being reunited and moving to a new house in Forest Hills, Long Island, included a trip to Hollywood and the making of a movie about Helen's life story. Helen reported that she enjoyed meeting the stars, but that Teacher was shy and restrained with all but Charlie Chaplin. At a dinner party he would talk with no one else but she, telling her the story of his life and all his marriage problems. Finally he asked her, "Do you think I'm disgusting?" "Yes," she replied. "Any one who would have so many custard pies thrown in his face is disgusting." They soon became fast friends. The motion picture was a pastiche of tableaux from Helen's life, the earlier scenes remarkably close to what was performed in Gibson's play *The Miracle Worker*. However, the later scenes (in which Helen tirelessly but a little woodenly played herself) were much along the lines of almost operatic symbolism: a fierce battle staged before the cave of Father Time between Knowledge and Ignorance for the control of Helen's mind. For the love interest they brought in Odysseus and had Helen shipwrecked with him on Circe's Island (this to express her love of Greek myths). One scene had her flying alone in an airplane; another showed her as the Mother of Sorrows touching huge crowds of the maimed and the diseased; and for the grand finale, Helen, dressed like Joan of Arc, was ushered into the convocation of the leaders of the world where she urged them to bring the war to a close. This scene was cut out on the absolute demand of Helen and Annie, and instead the picture ended with Helen on a huge white horse, blowing a trumpet and leading thousands of shipyard and factory workers, people of all nations, towards "deliverance." This scene gave the movie its title, *Deliverance.*

The reviewers loved it, calling it an educational picture in the highest sense and "one of the most compact photo plays ever filmed, each flash upon the silver screen being filled with action that has meaning." Alas, in the era of Charlie Chaplin and Tom Mix, the public was not interested in higher meaning, and the film was not a commercial success. Helen and Annie were near destitute as a result of participating in this picture.

They continued to struggle to support themselves with lecture tours, and from 1920 to 1924 by going on the vaudeville circuit because it offered a chance of making more money than either writing or the lecture circuit. It was also easier on the two travelers since it involved their staying in one place for a week, instead of being always on the go. They found themselves on the "bill" sandwiched between acrobats, monkeys, horses, dogs, and parrots, but their act was dignified, and people loved it. Helen, surprisingly, loved it too. The vaudeville audiences were always warm, and enthusiastic—full of the smells, the vibrations, and the pulse of life. Backstage, the other actors shared their trade with Helen, performing special acts for her, letting her feel their costumes, having her play with their trained animals, teaching her magic tricks, and telling her all the secrets of their wild parties. Helen, by her own words, "enjoyed it keenly." [37]

But with Teacher's health and vitality steadily declining, there were more doctor's bills than income. They sold their car, lost the little help they had, and mortgaged the house to the hilt. In the midst of this, Helen received a very serious marriage proposal from a fine, wealthy man, which she carefully rejected, after giving him the thorough and thoughtful reasons as to why she could not marry. She and her suitor wrote wonderful letters back and forth, in which she described in great detail what was required just to keep her going and which expressed her fear that the life of her husband would have no reality apart from care of her. She also wrote of her strong physical passions, which, she admitted, would have led her to marry had she not turned them into a generalized affection for everyone. In essence, she transubstantiated her high quotient of eros into an "enormous sympathy" and a great deal of hard work.

In 1923, when Helen was forty-three, she embarked upon what she later called her life work, full-time helping of the handicapped. When she joined the American Foundation for the Blind, she was asked to soft-pedal her politics—which she did since she understood that unless she did so, she would not be in a position to appeal to people of all political positions. Still, toning down her beliefs seemed to her the height of idiocy, yet it worked. "PURSES FLY OPEN TO HELEN KELLER" was the kind of headline that greeted her public appeals. "What does it look like?" Helen asked when all who intended to sign contribution pledge forms were asked to wave them over their heads. "Like the fluttering of birds," she was told. In ecstasy, Helen reached out and embraced and kissed everyone within reach.

This is not to say that Helen enjoyed all this money raising. "Oh my, what a strenuous business this beggar's life is!" she lamented. "Mendicants at the door of plenty" was another phrase she used. She and Annie were constantly in public, had to see an endless flow of visitors, and answer stacks of mail. Annie hated it, boiling over into a volcano of resentment fed by the fires of her earlier life. Being the Master Teacher that she was, this public life was denying Annie her true bent. This would have been the time to write her magnum opus as she had long since wanted to do; it would have been part autobiography, part treatise on the training of the handicapped. The pair faced not only the general public but spoke before legislatures and congresses, spurring on government and private groups all over the country to greater efforts for the blind and handicapped, presenting the picture of any human being as full of merit and usefulness and infinitely educable. Helen herself had become an archetype of the possible.

On their travels Helen met someone for whom she felt the deepest sympathy—a soulmate almost. It was, tellingly enough, the great plant breeder and mystic Luther Burbank. He was the man who was able to mix and match plants, coaxing from them nature's secrets, because he talked to them. Helen met him coming down the path in his magic garden in Santa Rosa, California. He guided Helen's hands over leaves and blossoms, including the spineless cactus he had developed. Helen wrote of him:

> He has the rarest of gifts, the receptive spirit of a child. When plants talk to him, he listens. That is why they tell him so many things about themselves. Only a wise child can understand the language of flowers and trees. Mr. Burbank feels the individuality or genius of the plant—that something which invents, changes, urges and adds and drops characteristics as the plant advances. So he encourages the plant to put forth the best of which it is capable. In the same way, he says, every human being should be given a chance to grow in freedom and develop his powers according to the inner law of his nature.[38]

With Burbank, Helen felt that she had come, perhaps, closest to the person who was like herself, though not handicapped. Like her, he, too, had a profound sense of the natural process of unfolding what is there in the entelechy of a plant, a human being, or a culture.

Annie's sight was now down to about ten per cent of normal vision. Even with the $2000 dollars a month they received from the American Foundation for the Blind, their circumstances were straightened. Given these problems and the fact that Helen's publishers wanted her to resume her writing career, they decided to go off the road for awhile to work on writing projects. *The Story of My Life* was still selling, but it was only the story of Helen's life up to the Radcliffe years. The public, which had been seeing so much of Helen, wanted to know more about her recent life, and so Helen embarked upon her book covering the years from 1904 to 1927 to be called *Midstream*.

PROCESS 11
RELEASING TENSION IN THE TONGUE/THE ECOLOGY OF DEEP SPEECH

Many people feel that they have difficulty speaking, Helen Keller most of all. And yet her voice could speak glories. Hearing her speak was like listening to the voice of creation itself, pronouncing the world into being.

In this long and complex process in two parts, we will discover the voice of creation. First we will perform a psychophysical exercise largely designed by Robert Masters to release the tension in the tongue.[39] The tongue is one of the most common sites of chronic unconscious muscular tension. Tensions in the tongue are likely to contribute to tension in other parts of the face, including the muscles of the jaw. Among the detrimental effects can be impairment of speech, interference with breathing, and, following from this, inhibition in thought and expression.

In the myths of many lands and many peoples, the world began when the god or great spiritual principle gathered up his/her resources and spoke or uttered the sounds of creation. "In the beginning was the Logos, the Word," is a sacred pronouncement told in varying ways the world over. These scriptural or mythic statements are then generally followed with the statement that humans are made in the image of the Creator, and therein lies a tale. For what separates us from even the most advanced of other species is our capacity for speech and for creation—"how like a God" human beings are, as Shakespeare observed. The linguistic structures of our brain are very large and could be thought of as logos lasers. These are embedded in the neocortex which, with its enormous powers of reflection, self-awareness, and conscious orchestration of other functions, allows for the integration and conscious orchestration of the simpler systems of the earlier neural structures of the brain to its own higher purposes. It is thus that the logos factor can recruit the brain's powerful but more primitive operations for acts of creativity.

So first we will release the tongue and then we will learn how to use the logos laser of creation to express a deeper ecology of speech such as Helen Keller must have known.

TIME: NINETY MINUTES TO TWO HOURS.

• MATERIALS:
None.

- ## *MUSIC:*
  None.

- ## *INSTRUCTIONS FOR GOING SOLO:*
  Put this entire process on tape, taking care to allow yourself appropriate pauses to do the exercise.

  (Note to the Guide: Please allow sufficient time after each instruction for the participants to do the process indicated. It will be clear from the instructions given below where those pauses are.)

- ## *SCRIPT FOR THE GUIDE:*

  ### *PART ONE:*
  ### *RELEASING TENSION IN THE TONGUE*
  To begin, sit in a comfortable position, holding the head reasonably erect. Scan your tongue, the whole surface of it, insofar as you can. Sense its position in relation to the roof and to the floor of your mouth. See whether it touches your teeth in the front. Do you find that your tongue is in the middle of your mouth or is it closer to the left cheek or to the right cheek?

  Sense the bottom of your tongue, the top of it, how wide it is, how long it is, how thick it is. See whether you notice any tension in it and whether it seems to change as you examine it. Does it get any wider or bigger? Are you more aware of the inside of your mouth as you bring the tongue more fully into your awareness?

  Now, with a good deal of focus and attention, please run the tip of your tongue over the inside of your lower teeth a few times. Go as far from left to right and right to left as you can. And then, just for a moment, run your tongue over the tops of the lower teeth. Then over the cutting edges of the upper teeth and the insides of the upper teeth, as far to the left and as far to the right as you can.

  Continue to stay very focused as you next run your tongue over the outside of the upper teeth, between the teeth and the upper lip, going from left to right as far as you can. Do the same with the lower teeth, running your tongue between the teeth and the lower lip. Do each of the movements at least ten or fifteen times. Stop.

  Now press your tongue against the roof of your mouth. Press hard and hold it there for a while. Breathe normally as you do it. Relax, let go, and then press again. Relax, and then press your tongue against the floor of your mouth.

Do it in such a way that as your tongue presses, your mouth opens. You should be pushing your lower jaw down with your tongue. Push it down as far as it will go. Do this several times.

Now press your tongue against the roof of the mouth so that you have the feeling that you are pushing the mouth open. Do this several times.

Now close your mouth and see whether you feel any tension in the jaw or the facial muscles. Then yawn deeply several times. Try to be aware of your tongue as you yawn. Is it difficult to keep track of the position of your tongue when you are yawning? Now just open your mouth several times to see how wide you can open it without any strain. Stop and thrust your lower jaw forward so that your lower teeth come out in front of your upper teeth and lip. Do this several times.

Try opening your mouth again to see if it opens wider now, and then flick your tongue from left to right a few times. Flick it in and out between your lips, like a snake, several times. Then lie down on your back and rest.

As you rest, try to become aware of the tongue again, whether it is positioned in the mouth differently than it was when you were sitting. Is it farther back in the mouth now and farther away from your teeth? How about the distances between the tongue and the roof of the mouth and the tongue and the floor of the mouth? Are they the same as before or different? Is the tongue generally in the middle of the mouth? Try to remember how it was when you were sitting up and compare that with how it is now.

If you can't remember, sit up for just a moment and see how the tongue lies. See whether it is closer to the floor of the mouth and to the teeth and notice any other differences. Then lie down again and examine it. Are you becoming more clearly aware of the tongue than you were before?

Now roll your head from side to side several times and see what happens to the tongue. See whether, when you roll the head to the right, the tongue goes to the right side, and when you roll the head to the left, the tongue goes to the left without any effort on your part. Roll your head way over to the left and observe where the tongue goes. Then way over to the right, again observing where the tongue goes.

Do this with your eyes open and with your eyes closed. See whether that makes any difference. Do it with the eyes open, and look as far to the side as you can. When you look to the front, focus as far away as possible. When you look to the right side again, look as far as you can. Does that make any difference in the movement of the tongue as compared to what it was when you did it with your eyes closed?

Pull your chin down toward your chest as far as it will go easily. Close your mouth and rest a moment. Then just move the tongue from left to right. Move it toward the left cheek, then toward the right cheek, back and forth like a pendulum, breathing freely as you do it. Now run your tongue, from right to left, over the outside of your upper teeth, between the teeth and the lip, then over the outside of the lower teeth, between the teeth and the lip.

Next, use your tongue to explore the inside of your mouth for a time. Go everywhere you can with it. Sense the difference between the way the front of the teeth feel to you and the way the back of the teeth feel, the difference between the roof and the floor of the mouth, and how the insides of the cheeks feel.

Try it first with the jaw closed tight, then with the mouth open a little. Still exploring with the tongue, open the mouth wide. Then close it tightly once again, continuing to move the tongue around. Does the tongue feel a little cramped now, maybe even a bit claustrophobic in such a narrow space?

Now yawn deeply several times, observing the tongue as you do it. Take a little rest. Observe how the tongue lies. Do you notice any difference in its width? In its length? If your tongue was far back behind the teeth when you began, it should be considerably longer and wider now that the tension has gone out of it. If your tongue was just a bit back from the teeth when you first lay down, it may now want to poke out between the teeth somewhat.

Now, sit up again. Stick your tongue out a little and hold it there with your teeth to mark how far out it extends. Then stick it out just a little more, again biting down gently with the teeth to measure your progress. Keep doing this, sticking your tongue out a little farther each time. Extend it, hold it, then extend it a little more.

When you've gone as far as you can, retract your tongue and repeat the process, breathing normally as you do it. See how many little extensions you can make, whether you can extend it ten times, fifteen times, or twenty times, putting it out just a little farther each time. All your movements should be light and gentle.

Now stop and retract your tongue. Then stick it out as far as is comfortable. Keeping your tongue rigid, move it in circles. You should be circling with your whole head. You can imagine that you're using your tongue to push the hand of a clock around the dial. First turn the hand clockwise around the dial; then turn it counterclockwise.

Stop and move your tongue in and out of your mouth, using your lips to sense what the tongue feels like. Try to do it so that the tongue doesn't scrape over your teeth. First sense primarily the top side of the tongue and the upper lip as you move it in and out. Then sense the lower side of the tongue and the lower lip. Compare the great difference between the top of the tongue and the bottom of the tongue. Then sense both the top and the bottom simultaneously as the tongue goes in and out.

With the tongue still protruding, move it from side to side, from one corner of the mouth to the other. See whether you can sense the difference between the top and the bottom of the tongue as clearly when it goes from side to side.

Dart the tongue in and out between the lips several times, scraping the teeth very gently as you do it.

Now move the tongue in an oval over the gums, between the teeth and lips. Circle round and round in one direction, in the other direction, and then stop.

Now, get down on your hands and your knees for a moment. Look at the floor and sense how the tongue hangs. Open your mouth and let the tongue dangle. Does it dangle like a dog's tongue, or like a panting tiger's? Raise your head up and down a few times with the tongue hanging out. See whether it touches the lower lip when the head comes up and the upper lip when the head goes down.

Shake your head from side to side a few times, and see if you can let the tongue swing freely as your head moves. Then stick it out and pull it in a few times while looking at the floor. Can you see your tongue as it comes out of your mouth? Watch it as it appears and as it retracts.

Move your tongue from side to side and note whether you can continue to see it. Make clockwise and counterclockwise circles with your tongue, still looking at it if you can. Then just move the tongue in and out again.

Sit back down and observe once more how your tongue lies in your mouth. Does it seem wider, flatter, and longer? Are you more clearly aware of the inside of your mouth and lips now? See if you can sense clearly where your lips touch each other. Open and close your mouth several times. Your mouth should open very easily now.

Lie down on your back and roll your head from side to side several times. Do this a number of times with your eyes closed and a number of times with your eyes open, going way over to one side and then the other. Try it with your arms folded on your chest, and see whether the tongue goes easily and naturally from one side to the other. As you move your head from side to side, consciously increase the speed and movement of the tongue inside the mouth. The tongue should move easily and without compulsion, like a very fast pendulum.

Stop. Dart your tongue in and out of your mouth like a snake or lizard does, and see whether it moves very quickly now. Move it back and forth between the corners of your mouth, and see how quickly that goes.

Sit up and stick your tongue out several times, noticing the difference in your sensing of the top and the bottom of the tongue. Does the tongue go out more easily and farther now? Is it more relaxed? Retract your tongue and note now how it lies on the floor of the mouth. Is its tip just behind the teeth now? Does the tongue seem wider than before? Get up and walk around a little and continue to make your observations. Keep the tongue clearly in your awareness and resolve to remember what you are now sensing.

PART TWO:
THE ECOLOGY OF DEEP SPEECH

As noted earlier, many people have great difficulty in speaking and in expressing themselves, Helen Keller especially. Because she was deaf and blind by the time she was nineteen months old, she could never speak normally, but still she managed to express everything. Her voice transcended its limitations and could speak glories. And with our new freedom of tongue we will shortly do likewise.

Move your jaw now and notice that with the relaxation of the tongue, the jaw has become relaxed as well. Not only your jaw, but your throat is also freer. And, as we will soon discover, so is your capacity for speech, for voice production and for a powerful use of the linguistic structures of your brain. It is a fascinating discovery that different positions of tongue and palate give very different personalities, just as different accents give different personalities. By doing tongue exercises and releasing the tongue, you may even discover within yourself the persona of a Creator. Because we are speech-producing beings, the part of the left hemisphere responsible for language, the logos laser, is huge. It occupies so large an area that it influences us profoundly in all the ways that we think, dream, act, relate to our world. According to the ways that we use it then, it can either open us to glory or keep us caught in a narrow and inhibited grammar of experience. As you begin to activate that palate and tongue, you create a transcendental tongue that plays upon the palate like Franz Liszt could play upon the piano with his transcendental fingers, defying scales and arpeggios. You become able to release a grammar of deep experience not available to the usual condition of your inhibited tongue and speech patterns.

As you begin to release the tongue, the logos laser in the brain will release new concepts and thoughts and ways of seeing the world. Utter glory will pour out of your mouth, as it did with Helen Keller. If you keep your palate and tongue available for incandescence, you can begin to speak for your entelechy, your high self, and perhaps even begin to acquire the persona of your entelechy. Your entelechy can speak through you. The preparation of the tongue also prepares the way for the ecology of deeper speech. What follows is a practice for deeper speech which includes the calling of creation.

We will begin by uttering with our newly-released tongues our own names until our name changes or becomes our own true name. We will discover there is always a truer name behind our name. It may, in fact, even be the one we were given, but we cannot find its power until we work with it, as we now will do.

Will everybody please stand up. What I want you to do is to utter your own name in a full lively manner until your name or your sense of your name changes and becomes a true name. Experiment with many different positions of your tongue and mouth in uttering your name. Begin now uttering your name. (Five minutes.)

Now would you please utter your name as if you're calling creation into being. And as you do this you may discover that your name may change or it may remain the same. Begin. (Two minutes.)

Keep it going and stay standing, but now let your hands also move out and start creating and fashioning things—planets, trees, elephants, jungles, roller skates. As you say your name, let the hands move out and fashion and create. The name itself may change. (Two minutes.)

In the ancient Vedic scriptures of India, Lord Pahapati, the Creator of the world, after he rises out of the golden Cosmic Egg, offers the sacred injunction, "Bouse, Bouvack, Savar," conjuring up Earth/Bouse, Air/Bouvack, and Sky/Savar. You can try it now, uttering the words "Earth, Air, Sky. Earth, Air, Sky. Earth, Air, Sky." Keep uttering these words which call up creation, fashioning with your hands earth, air, and sky as you do so. You are calling up creation. Call it up. You're calling the latency of creation into being. Continue to call up "Earth, Air, Sky," until the words change to new words or to the very sounds of creation. (Two minutes.)

Now would you please face a partner, and as you continue to call up the sounds of creation, would you please tap into each others hands the energy and feeling of what you are calling into being. And also have the sense that you are calling up and tapping at the same time the fullness of the life of the other into being. Begin. (Two minutes.)

Stay with your partner as I briefly speak to you. In the American Indian tradition, the Maidu Indians say that at first there was only water, and the coyote said, "Let the surf become sand!" and it did. About the many things of the world Coyote said, "Let there be!" And, lo, they each and every one came into being on the vibrations of his voice. Since everything is vibrations in different frequencies and qualities, this is not so strange is it? And in another Native American tradition, the god Nichon of the Gros-Ventra Indians of Montana fashioned a circle of mud just wide enough for him to stand on. Stepping on this circle of mud, he closed his eyes and demanded, "Let there be land as far as my eye can see." And when he opened his eyes once more, the surrounding water had gone down, and the land was there.

In a sense, when you have nothing, and you are in a crisis of reality where you have no-thing before and behind and around you, when the world seems naughted, and you, the term in the middle, seem lost, then you rise up out of your mud place and start proclaiming what it really should be!

Now we are going to stand on our own mud pile, and still facing our partner, but moving a little ways back from each other, we will proclaim the things we need for our own better life using the ancient words, "Let there be. . . ." Be very specific in what you proclaim for your life, such as "Let there be a useful job! Let there be health! Let there be further education! etc." And have a sense as you proclaim these things that they are out there waiting for you to pull them in by virtue of your incarnate word, your logos laser. Begin now. "Let there be. . . ." (Two minutes.)

Keep proclaiming, but this time add all your senses to your proclaiming of creation, so that you smell it, you touch it, you taste it, you are it. Let there be! I mean, really feel yourself identified with what you want there to be. That's what Helen Keller did. In all likelihood, that's what Emily Dickinson did as well. They incarnated their sense of the possible reality, Emily because she was always reinventing the world; Helen because she needed to invest so much more of herself into any perception and intention owing to her deafness and blindness.

Keep on expressing your wishes. Let the words tumble and burst out of your throat—burst out like gold from your throat. (Two minutes.)

Your words have the greatest possible effect, your real words, your words of juiciness and of power and of intentionality. And this is true and ever more true when the words are spoken simultaneously with images and movements. If you just declare, "abundance and happiness," that's not going to do much for you. Such a declaration still needs juice. In order to bring it in, you call it out of the Realm of Pattern. The word becomes flesh or opportunity or profession or relationship or even abundance. After you've experienced the power of this, you will know yourself to be a logos laser. You have to be an incarnate word. That means you've got to not just talk it. You've got to be it, to express it, to think it, to chew it up, to spit it out. You've got to feel its energies humming within you. For we are at that phenomenal place of co-creativeness, trying to retrain the dramatic stuff within ourselves for the dramatic universe which demands of us the co-creation of a better world. We can no longer lose, as we have for too many years, the incarnational power of the word. Yes, it's true that a lot of words have degenerated into noise and jargon or just a stream of uninspired sound.

And that is why we take on people like Thomas Jefferson and Emily Dickinson and Helen Keller who each, in his or her own way, found the power of the word and word creation. And do not think that the world has not been made immensely richer because they each took on their own unique re-creation of their world.

Now for the final part of the process, we will partner creation by first becoming the parts of creation. Like Helen who often sounded like birds or winds or trees or monkeys or seas lapping on shores—so various were her voices—we will do likewise. With sound and gesture we will imitate or incarnate the members of creation calling. We will begin now as an animal, any kind of animal that you feel drawn to. Become that animal now, cat or dog, lion or elephant, bear or deer, but being that animal with all its ways of movement and soundings. And as that animal, move around the room and call in the spring.

Now become a monkey, a really curious monkey calling to other monkeys to see what it has found in a tree. Now be the tree itself calling. Now be the wind calling, calling the Earth to its fullness. The sun calling. The moon calling. The stars calling. All early human beings calling. People from ancient civilizations calling. Find yourself speaking an ancient language. Now calling in English or your native language the Earth and the seasons into being. Use juicy, succulent language to call the Earth into being.

Now call your life as you really need it to be into being. Call this time with words. Let your mouth become filled with imagery and metaphor by the passion of your words. Use your hands and use your body as you do this. Try calling your life by using the words of someone like Helen who is deaf and blind, so that the images would have to come from other sensory realms. (One minute.)

Now use the full apparatus of you multi-sensory knowing to call again your life as you need it to be into being. Be it. Incarnate it. Let it be. Bring it in. (One minute.)

Now you will partner creation. Feel creation as a presence or as an energy field by your side or surrounding you. Take creation by the arm or follow alongside or be embraced by the presence of creation. Keep your logos lasers open during this, and keep on talking about what you need to bring into time. Partner creation, and let creation begin to partner you. The door is open. The Great Continuum between the realities is present and available to you. The door is open. We meet. We meet.

Feel yourself partnered by creation. And let creation speak through you too. Creation uses your tongue and mouth and speech, but you will use his/her/its version of tongue and mouth and speech as well. You speak and co-create together. You bring in a time and a place that you in your local life did not imagine. Feel it, and be it. Feel it, and be it. Feel it, and be it. You and the powers of creation together.

And finally gather all your vocal resources to let a call, which is a co-creative sound coming from you and creation, to rise up from your lips. Whether words or sounds, let that call sound now! Let that call, that co-creative sound rise! And bring it to silence.

And let it be utterly internalized as well, so that the great call continues within. And the door is now open. But it is up to you to keep it open, as Helen kept it open, as Emily kept it open, and as Thomas Jefferson kept it open. Because they knew, as now you know, that together with the spirit of creation and creativity, you re-invent the world.

SO BE IT.

16 The High Claims of My Spirit

Now off the road and prepared to spend time writing, Helen was contacted by the Swedenborg Foundation, who wanted a well-known person to write a book about the religion. As a labor of love, Helen detoured from her autobiographical book *Midstream* to prepare such a manuscript. The book that resulted is a fascinating account of the need for a religion of the inner worlds by a person with Helen's handicaps.

Is it any wonder that Helen came to honor and practice a religion that, far from asking her to prove her existence, allowed her to accept and enjoy utterly the existence of another world, another sun, a parallel reality? Its founder, Emanuel Swedenborg, was an eighteenth-century scientist, astronomer, and mineralogist. He had written many books and invented much of the field of mineralogy; the development of modern engineering owes a good deal to some of his early inventions. After this remarkable career in the practical world, he turned to the inner life and, at the age of fifty-six, began to have visions of an inner world which he saw as vividly as one did the outer world. The world of his vision was an after-death world, full of different kinds of beings—angels and archangels. Swedenborg also saw principles of correspondence between the inner imaginal world and the outward world. He saw, for example, that everything had its archetype or ideal form and wrote about these correspondences and about the ability to travel to other realms and have out-of-body experiences. Helen, of necessity, was a genius at out-of-body experiences. Not only would she go traveling, but she'd know what was there. She would be talking to somebody, and then she'd say, "Excuse me. I have to go to the Alps." Two minutes later she'd come back, having fully been to the Alps and able to describe what she saw and what happened during her visit. Her natural attraction to Swedenborgian religion is best expressed for me in this passage from *My Religion*:

> All about me may be silence and darkness, yet within me, in the spirit, is music and brightness, and color flashes through all my thoughts. So out of Swedenborg's evidence from beyond earth's frontier I construct a world that shall measure up to the high claims of my spirit when I quit this wonderful but imprisoning house of clay.[40]

In the same passage, Helen spoke of the dimness of the senses that tell us so little of the abundant life around us. Given this, she wrote:

Why cannot the soul with equal freedom go forth from its dwelling place and, discarding the poor lenses of the body, peer through the telescopes of truth into the infinite reaches of immortality? At all events this gives a key to Swedenborg's other-world records.[41]

Helen had already discovered for herself that we have other senses than those of the body, and her development of them gave her an access to a wider, deeper universe. I think that Swedenborg too saw another world, but what he saw was filtered through the acculturated lenses of his Judeo-Christian/Swedish tradition. Sufis, too, speak of the ability to enter imaginal worlds, but the ones they describe generally belong to the world of Islamic culture, just as descriptions of the inner world of Hindu yogis are often filled with the sights and sounds of the subcontinent of India. In the same way, Swedenborg's other world was an eighteenth-century Scandinavian version of these deeper realities.

We tend to assume that sense impression is so victorious over the mind's knowing that it takes prodigies of concentration to get rid of it. But Helen, so continuously thrown back within her thoughts and imagination, was always enjoying the inward contemplation of, say, the outward garden and flowers, or the pulse and rhythms of the music she was listening to by holding a radio in her embrace, or even of the person with whom she was conversing. All she had to do, she said, was move a little way away from the correspondences that others were telling her about, and she was in an autonomous and equally real inward world—a world like that which Swedenborg, through his particular lenses, also enjoyed.

During his twenty-seven years of inner seeing, Swedenborg had produced 127 volumes crammed with finely detailed descriptions of the life, landscapes, and psychology of the other world, and with conversations with its angels and other spirits. The constant discourse and learning to be had in this vast dominion—the ease of communication as well as comprehension to be found there—appealed enormously to Helen. Here is her description of the collectivity of mind and learning in the other world:

According to all Swedenborg's testimony, after death we are like travelers going from place to place, making the acquaintance of all kinds of interesting objects, meeting all sorts of people, and receiving something from each individual on the way. We observe, judge, criticize and listen to words of wisdom or folly. We drop an opinion, take up another, sift it and test it in our mental crucible. From each new experience we extract finer kinds of knowledge and those truer intellectual concepts which are the property of all. On earth man lives apart, though not alone. And the most wonderful thoughts that he has known through lack of listeners have never been said. But in the other life it is different. All live together and learn together.[42]

For Helen life in Swedenborg's other world seemed in ways not unlike Helen's own—one of unending education (but without any requirement for fundraising) and filled with all kinds of jobs and service to be enjoyed as people rose through education to angelic status, gaining new powers and nobler tasks. And here was Helen, with her own theology of inner striving to angelhood. She said:

> There are said to be three kinds of angels to which one aspires—those whose task is protection, those whose job is to originate ideas, and those who can through extraordinary empathy bring their minds and souls within another so to enhance their powers for quick and direct action.[43]

Helen was particularly charmed as to how the congregation of this spiritual universe was hologrammatically interrelated—bound together in one magnificent system of uses so that each spiritual being contributed his or her abilities to the whole and became more and more responsive to receiving the abilities of others. (Helen would have loved botanist Rupert Sheldrake's theory of morphogenetic fields which offers a scientific explanation of how new habits and patterns of learning are communicated through a field of resonance.) Helen extended this Law of Use to this world and to improving education, so that each person was seen as unique and as uniquely useful and was educated to that end by specializing in either mental, practical, or spiritual services. The heaven life of Swedenborg, in Helen's view, served as a great pattern and object lesson for this life.

Above all the Swedenborgian realm was a world of love and communion of the heart. Helen wrote, "I believe that when the eyes within my physical eyes shall open upon the world to come, I shall simply be consciously living in the country of my heart." But she added words that tell us that she had often visited there already:

> My steadfast thought rises above the treason of my eyes to follow sight beyond all temporal seeing! . . .How real is the darkness to one who only guesses in the shadows of earth at an unseen sun! But how well worth the effort it is to keep spiritually in touch with those who have loved us to their last moment upon earth![44]

Helen realized that the other world is not so much *other* but *within*, prompting us so much the more to act, to love, to hope against hope, and resolutely to tinge our surrounding darkness with the hues of the indwelling heaven here and now. If we act as if heaven is here, we insert our active imagination into the void between the worlds, and the inner world rises to our call.

Swedenborg's doctrine of *reliqua* also appealed strongly to Helen. By this, Swedenborg referred to the "remains" of the love, truth, and beauty of the spiritual universe that is still there in child-hood—the "trailing clouds of glory," as Wordsworth expressed it, with which all children enter this world. Helen expressed the notion slightly differently: "heaven ensphered him like the sunshine," she wrote. These remains although often forgotten in maturity are never-theless stored up capabilities in the holy places within us, the psychic meeting ground for the mortal and immortal. In the agony of life, these hidden remains become once again active. In Helen's case they burst through as if they had never been hidden, after the larger universe, through Annie's fingers, began tapping out its rhythms of awakening into her hand. We can compare Helen's case to the modern example of Stephen Hawking, one of the greatest minds in modern physics, imprisoned in a body wracked by bilateral amyotrophic sclerosis. His Swedenborgian universe would be a scientific one; he, no doubt, listens through the lenses of science past his affliction to the other universe. His interest is also in conversing with the stars, but his vehicle is the structure of physics, through which he is able to tune in to the other world.

Does one ever see completely through the veil separating us from the other world? Perhaps, we do—in childhood, before the patterns of culture are set in the brain. The same sort of clear seeing occurs, of course, in mystical experiences, in which the brain/mind may be in macrophasic wave resonance with All and Everything, and it's as if all cultures and conditions dissolve and you are one with the One. In between childhood and such mystical experiences, however, we tend to see the other world only through whatever our lenses are—be they scientific, cultural, or related to our particular religious tradition.

Finally it is Swedenborg's notion, greatly expanded and much more deeply understood by Helen, that our limitations and seeming afflictions give us the grit to hone our lenses to see into the deeper universe, to reach our highest possibilities. She saw her handicaps in this light not as punishments or misfortunes but as the opportunity for training and refinement of the soul. In every limitation we have a choice, and in this choice lies the power of creation; we can choose to be crushed, or we can choose to convert our trials into new forces for good. It is the same with our spirits, she tells us. We grow as we discern more fully the amplitude of possibilities inherent in every daily contact. Our experiences are cups of poison or cups of life depending on what we choose to put into them—how we choose to frame them, to use a modern idiom.

Helen used herself as an example. Her major access to the outer world was through imperfect and limited touch, but she turned it into a depth-reaching faculty—touch that had been internalized and refashioned by an inner process of spiritualization so that even the distant stars seemed to be at her very door, and strong bonds were felt and known between heaven and earth, now and eternity, God and human. This internalized touch, then, became a new sense, at once speculative, intuitive, and reminiscent. It connected an objective physical world to an objective spiritual world. As Swedenborg explained the correspondence: just as the physical world is perceived by sensory apparatus that is of the same substance as the sensory world, so the spiritual world is perceived by sensory apparatus that is of the same substance as the spiritual world. Helen had to make use of both kinds of "touch" to make sense of either world, or of both.

The fact that Helen had such intense perceptions of the spiritual realm was the key to her belief in the Swedenborgian philosophy. It was not so much that she adopted Swedenborg's vision, but that she found in its philosophy the closest approach to her own experience. As she wrote:

> I cannot imagine myself without religion. I could as easily fancy a living body without a heart. To one who is deaf and blind, the spiritual world offers no difficulty. Nearly everything in the natural world is as vague, as remote from my senses as spiritual things seem in the minds of most people. I plunge my hands deep into my large Braille volumes containing Swedenborg's teachings, and withdraw them full of the secrets of the spiritual world. The inner, or "mystic," sense, if you like, gives me vision of the unseen.[45]

We well remember the story of how the word *water* dropped into Helen's mind like the sun into a frozen winter world. It was the same with regard to the Swedenborg teachings, for now it was as if light came where there had been no light before; the intangible spiritual world became a shining certainty. Just as her mind widened and thoughts raced after her comprehension of the hand movements for *water*, so her mind widened to include a larger and richer and fuller universe—one that could be known and journeyed into with feeling and intuition and heartfulness. Recalling her first awakening, Helen wrote:

> The world to which I awoke was still mysterious; but there was hope and love and God in it, and nothing else mattered.

Is it not possible that our entrance into heaven may be like this experience of mine?

The essence of Helen's religious sensibility was expressed in what is, perhaps, one of the greatest statements of the human spirit:

Truly I have looked into the very heart of darkness, and refused to yield to its paralyzing influence, but in spirit I am one of those who walk the morning.

The book on religion finished, Helen launched again into *Midstream*. The writing and researching of it was an agony. Imagine how laborious was the process of recovery and review. "Hammering out ideas without being able to see what one is doing is one of the most exasperating trials of blindness," she wrote. Then there was Annie, almost totally blind, going through the files with heavy, double-lensed glasses. And with John no longer present with his wonderful sense of structure and style and his trenchant but accurate blue pencil, the work of writing was more difficult than it ever had been. Helen also experienced the constant emotional pain of reviewing years that had been rich, but also incredibly painful. Fortunately, Helen's extraordinary retention and memory not only helped her recall details of what had happened but also to flip through the Braille text of what she had written to locate passages she was asked about.

When *Midstream* appeared, it proved to be very popular, though, of course, the same old criticisms were raised about her use of imagery she could not possibly have experienced. Her answer to these critics was vivid and to the point: "When eyes are blind, the mind seeks new ways of seeing. My fingers look not with two eyes but with ten eyes, and the whole body is alert to perceive and hears the voice of life." We might describe her critics as "sense arrogant": How dare you try to think you know anything about the world, they seemed to say, since you don't have the five senses that we do!

With the improvement of techniques of diagnostic measurement, both physical and psychological, many became interested in the manner and degree with which Helen met the world. There was much criticism of Annie, saying that she had essentially designed Helen, but there was more serious and sensitive work done by those who were asking deep questions of Helen as to how she really sensed the world. What was the actual form of her perception? Nella Henney Braddy, a close friend and editor of *Midstream* as well as the eventual biographer of Annie Sullivan, was present when Teacher decided to test Helen on the nature of her perceptions.[46] Imagine being in their home in Forest Hills, New York when the following scene took place:

Teacher asks her, "When the word for *horse* is said, Helen, what do you feel? What do you see?"

Helen's response is kinesthetic, "His long face." She shapes the air with her hands. "His big form." Then her hands form more precise shapes. "His short hair, his mane, his tail, if he has a tail."

"What color?" Teacher asks.

"Well, that depends on what I am told," replies Helen. "But by the twitching of his ears and the way his tail switches back and forth I can tell you about the spirit of this horse."

Teacher and Nella confer for a moment and then say, "What do you get from the concept of *city*?"

"Long streets," Helen replies. "Tramping feet, smells from windows, tobacco, pipes, gas, fruits, aromas, tiers upon tiers of odor. Automobiles. A whir that makes me shiver, a rumble. It seems to have no shape, but to be a concentrated mass of vibrations coming down upon me. New York—dense imprisoning sensation. Feeling the gloom of narrow streets. Traffic is wearisome, depressing. Weighed down with vibrations."

"*House*. What about *house*?"

"Some houses are friendly," she comments, "and hold out their arms to me."

Teacher says, "Give me an example."

"Gretchen's little house."

"Well," Teacher says, "that's five times the size of ours." It seems small to Helen because it contains so many objects she can touch.

Teacher and Nella ask what her *friends* mean to her. "A touch of the hand, the footstep, the feel of the face and the skin." She's very sensitive as to the mood that people reveal as they spell into her hand, whether they're pleasant, receptive, or disagreeable. She is only too aware of how the sighted shrink from contact with the blind. "I am very conscious of irritability."

"Who is the most irritable person you know?" Teacher asks.

"Let me think," Helen stalls, but it is evident that she does not want to answer.

"What about me?" Teacher goads her.

"You are surely irritable," Helen replies, "but faults are not so much faults in some people as they are in others."

She built up her ideas of color "through association and analogy." Pink is "like a baby's cheek or a soft Southern breeze." Gray is "like a soft shawl around the shoulders." Yellow is "like the sun. It means life and is rich in promise." Brown appears as two kinds. One is "warm and friendly like leaf mould." The other is "like the trunks of aged trees with worm holes in them, or like withered hands." Teacher's favorite color, lilac, "makes me think of faces I have loved and kissed." The warm sun brings out odors, and she thinks of red. Coolness also bring out smells, but is green. The quivering of soap bubbles brings to mind the sense of a sparkling color.

Helen's world was "a workable correspondence." [47] Was it any wonder then that she was so drawn to the Swedenborg faith with its emphasis on the nature of the correspondence between this and the other world—everything in this world having a richer, deeper correspondence in the other, but with many more angelic modes of perception in use?

Helen also greatly enjoyed music. Caruso sang the aria of the blinded, chained Samson into her hands, and everyone who was in the room wept. She would go into transports of ecstasy as she held the radio close to her when a magnificent piece of music was being played. She could always distinguish the different instruments, but not one composition from another, but that didn't mean that her appreciation was any less. Once after holding the radio as the New York Symphony Orchestra played Beethoven's *Ninth* she reported in a letter of appreciation to the orchestra that she had "spent a glorious hour last night listening over the radio. . . I could actually distinguish the cornets, the rolls of the drums, deep-toned viols and violins playing in lovely unison."

Tactile stimulation became the occasion for vivid fantasy. She was constantly reinventing the world that she received through her limited lenses. Geometric shapes became metaphors for the divine. Listen to what she said of shapes and forms:

> How does the straight line feel? It feels, as I suppose it looks, straight—a dull thought drawn out endlessly. It is unstraight lines, or many straight and uncurved lines together, that are eloquent to the touch. They appear and disappear, are now deep, now shallow, now broken off or lengthened or swelling. They rise and sink beneath my fingers, they are full of sudden starts and pauses, and their variety is inexhaustible and wonderful.[48]

Ernst Cassirer, the great German philosopher who investigated the mythic matrix of political states and symbols, and Walker Percy, the novelist and essayist, both noted that the symbolic sense was higher than the naming sense. Both observed that the symbolic sense worked in Helen as an intellectual revolution—the principle of symbols providing a principle of universal applicability which encompassed the whole field of human thought. Before the shock at the water pump, she had been a good responding organism. After the shock, she acted, in Percy's phrase, like a "rejoicing symbol-mongering human." [49] Intellectually, she went directly from names into symbolic thought. Once this leap was made, all the principles and correspondences became available, and Helen joined as few in history ever had the personal-particular to the personal-universal with its broadening contexts and more comprehensive formulations.

The content of Helen's speech, as we have noted, was bookish, embellished, beautiful. Having never heard ordinary speech, having never heard "an ungrammatical or an ignoble word," her speech was literary in the extreme, giving the listener an impression of goody-goodyism and sweet sentimentality which the experiences of her life belied. What she did see, however, was the larger pattern of things, the Pattern That Connects, the inspiration and higher forms of things beneath their surface. As a symbolic, Platonic thinker, Helen always saw the higher possibilities. The universals, whether they be of love, goodness, nobility, work, relationship were ever before her inward senses, guiding her actions and thought in all things. She was truly a citizen of a universe larger than our aspiration and more complex and beautiful than all our dreams. Living in the extended universe as she did, she had awakened the Real world as few in history ever had.

17 Violet Shadows

By the mid-1930s, Annie was descending into darkness. One of her eyes had to be removed, and the other was so clouded with cataract and so thin from amateurish operations that there was not much that could be done for it. She and Helen traveled to Ireland to get the scents and sounds of Annie's ancestors. Of this Annie wrote:

> The bogs influence me strangely. The weird rocks on the hillside watch me, and their expression is intense. I find myself waiting for them to speak to me, and deep down in my soul I know their message will break my heart. The long violet shadows call to me to follow them over the rocks and cliffs down, down, to the sea, whose cruel white hands will drag me from the light and the warm sun forever. . . .There is always the ghost of an emigrant ship in the Irish mind.[50]

Back in the States, Helen and Annie were offered honorary doctorates by Temple University, but Teacher, tormented by her recurrent feelings of inadequacy, declined, writing Temple University President Charles Beury that "It is a valuation to which I do not consider my education commensurate. All my life I have suffered in connection with my work from a deficiency of equipment." However, when Helen explained to the audience at the award ceremony why Annie had refused the honor, the audience rose and demanded by acclamation that Annie accept the degree.

Annie was by now old beyond her years, "infinitely sickened of many things," and even a triumphant tour of Eastern Europe was faced with regret. Clearly she was getting ready to die. Everything had come too late for her, and she was constantly haunted by the sense that her life had been a failure. While in Scotland Annie received a telegram telling her of John's death. "Now my heart is full of withered emotions," she wrote at this news. "My eyes are blinded with unshed tears. Today only the dead seem to be travelling. I wish I was going his way." For all her bitterness and pain, she summed up her agonized remembrances of their relationship with poignancy and beauty:

> Three thousand miles away his body, once so dear, lies cold and still. The dreadful drama is finished, the fierce struggle that won only despair is ended. . . .

> I have been homesick many a year for his arms. Perhaps it was wrong to look too deep within. Now he is dead.

> How often he read immortal verse and taught me to understand the shining soul of it! Love is ever in flight, it gleams and goes, it is the irised wing of a fugitive dream, but imagination once kindled is the life of the spirit, and lives forever.

Then she writes about their relationship:

> What dreams! What tremulous expectations! What clouds of suspicion, of jealousy! What amazing cruelties of looks and tones and sudden denials! There is more pain than joy in the most passionate love—pain and waste for a brief ecstasy. But one glances away, and all is gone—all that golden abundance of beauty and joy, of hope, of excitement and adventure. . . .

> As I write them down years and years afterward, my heart leaps to the whisper of a name, a touch, the first kiss that lives in every kiss. Those vanished golden hours, those warm, loving hands and lips murmuring shy words which are the sweet blossoms of life's springtime are gone past recall. Gone? No! they flash before me more real than the realities of mature years.

Her final lines are tremendously moving:

> Now I wait for death—not sad, not heroically but just a bit tired. To love and succeed is a fine thing, to love and fail is

the next best, and the best of all is to fail and yet keep on loving.[51]

It was the middle of the Depression, and Helen's hold on the public conscience was as deep as ever. Her appeal was not due only to her ceaseless efforts at bringing in new legislation for the handicapped and her constant service and labor for the blind and deaf, for women, for laborers, and for just about anyone else whose possibilities had been thwarted. It was also the freshness of her mind and her indomitable will that won over many. She always had radically new ideas and new things to say, and she would take up a cross for anyone in need or cross the continent to persuade a recalcitrant legislature or public official. She handed over to the Foundation for the Blind any prize money that she won for her efforts, like the $5000 award from the Pictorial Review in 1932, meant for her private use—no mean sum in those days of enforced poverty.

An article written by her for the *Atlantic Monthly* had a phenomenal influence on peoples' views of themselves and pulled many out of the psychological depression brought on by the economic Depression. The article was titled "Three Days to See," and it caused many people to realize how well off they were. In the article Helen wrote about what she would want to see if she was miraculously given three days of sight. The first day, she wrote, "I should want to see the people whose kindness, gentleness and companionship have made my life worth living." On the second day, she would arise in time to see the dawn and spend her time in the museums which contained "the condensed history of the earth and its inhabitants," seeing with her eyes the many objects she had touched with her hands. The third day she would make the rounds of the city to get a sense of "the workaday world of the present." She concludes the article: "I who am blind can give one hint to those who see—one admonition to those who would make full use of the gift of sight: Use your eyes as if tomorrow you would be stricken blind."

By 1936 Helen was nursing Annie who was now virtually blind, racked with many disorders, and in the throes of a bitter despair. "I am trying so hard to live for you," Annie said to Helen after one collapse. Her final messages were jotted down as they were recited in her last moments of lucidity. Here are Polly's notes describing Teacher's last words and actions:

> Good-bye, John Macy. I'll soon be with you, good-bye, I loved you.
>
> I wanted to be loved. I was lonesome—then Helen came into my life. I wanted her to love me and I loved her. Then later Polly came and I loved Polly and we were always so happy together—my Polly, my Helen. Dear children, may we all meet together in harmony.

My Jimmy [her brother who died], I'll lay these flowers by your face—don't take him away from me. I loved him so, he's all I've got. She took the bed clothes and threw [the] bucket of flowers out of there.

Teacher was complimenting nurse and nurse said, "Oh, you are playing to the gallery." Teacher threw her head back smiling and said, "I've play-acted all my life and I shall play up till I die!"

Polly will take care of Helen. As the years go on her speeches won't be so brilliant as what people will think [sic] but my guiding hand won't be there to take out what should be taken out.

Thank God that I gave up my life that Helen might live. God help her to live without me when I go. [52]

And she died.

Everybody came to her funeral. Alexander Woollcott, who declined to be a pall bearer because of a sense of personal unworthiness, wrote of the funeral:

I think everyone at the funeral felt immeasurably impoverished, but one and all were stricken most by the tragedy of Helen parted from Teacher after fifty years. All of us [were] heart-sick at the mere thought of that unimaginable separation. Surely all eyes in the church were riveted on the sight of Polly Thomson and Helen Keller following the coffin together, the tears pouring down Miss Thomson's cheeks. And just as the two of them passed the pew where I sat, I saw the swift, bird-like fluttering of Helen's hands—saw and with a quickened heartbeat knew what I had seen— Helen—think of it—Helen comforting her companion. [53]

The bishop of the National Cathedral in Washington made Annie the first woman to be honored by burial in a sepulchre in the National Cathedral on her own merits. Later, Helen was entombed there as well.

Annie's last real statement a few weeks before she died was captioned by Helen, "Teacher sets sail with this message." This was the message:

Helen Keller's development suggests to me that the loss of one or more faculties may, by way of discipline, drive the handicapped person to deeper levels of will-power than is required of normally equipped human beings. I have no doubt whatever that most people live in a very restricted sphere of their potential capacities. They make use of only a small portion of their possible powers and of the resources of their minds. It is as if, out of all their physical furnishings, they should use only a fraction of each sense. When the complete destruction of one or more senses creates an emergency, we see how much greater our resources are than we supposed. May not deafness and blindness be a way of getting at latent functional possibilities? [54]

This passage speaks profoundly to the commitments of my life. For years I have investigated the mystery of why people fail to use their full powers. As director of The Foundation for Mind Research, I have sought clues to this latency in many fields—history, literature, anthropology, psychophysiology, as well as research into the nature of brain and consciousness. Using various techniques, ancient and modern, I have guided thousands of research subjects and close to a million seminar participants on journeys both physical and mental. The evidence of this work clearly suggests that in the human being as he or she presently exists, a great many abilities and ways of functioning have been distorted, inhibited, or altogether blocked. Although the causes and effects vary widely from person to person and from culture to culture, it appears that very few of us have escaped serious crippling. To be human in this time is to be handicapped. In this we are all Helen Keller! But unlike Helen most of us agree to our limitations and live out a life that is much less than we have the demonstrated capacity to be. The history of genius, creativity, and the turned-on mind give us time and again stories of people who are handicapped in one or another way, but who, by virtue of their limitations, go deeper into that vast and beautiful storehouse of alternatives that is the body-mind system. Often as in the case of Helen, they bring back natural powers of astonishing range and usefulness. They bring evolutionary latencies into the light of day. In the course of our research at the Foundation, we have explored ways to unshackle these natural powers in adults and to prevent their initial inhibition in children. Our experiments persuade us that ordinary people, given opportunity and training, can learn to think, feel, and know in new ways, to become more creative, more imaginative, and to aspire within realistic limits to a much larger awareness, one that is superbly equipped to deal with the complex challenges of modern life.

Such statements may sound utopian—the fancies of a lobbyist for Atlantis—but nothing is more urgent today than our need to overcome the psychological constraints of tribalism, nationalism, and ecological mayhem. Time is warping, space is shrinking, and we have entered a period of global interdependence in which the human species may not survive if we retain our lethal habits of consumption, aggrandizement, paranoia, and manipulation. The human species may end in a blaze of blinding light if we continue to restrict its mind, thwart its potential, refuse its willingness to be prepared for life in a universe larger than its aspiration, more complex than all its dreams. It is time to educate ourselves to the web of kinship and fellow feeling necessary on this endangered planet—to awaken all those dormant potentials that were not necessary to humankind in its role as conqueror of nature and other people. We are challenged, as never before, to achieve a new humanity and a new way of nurturing the species to realize its genius in harmony with nature and each other. The vision of this new humanity is given to us by Helen Keller. Her handicaps were but the most dramatic and poignant statement of our own; her capacity with the help of Teacher to transcend these and put in their place a vast new range of human potential gave us new maps to the strange and wonderful territory that is called being human.

"Never have I trodden the stones and thorns of personal disaster as I am doing now." So Helen wrote to friends who urged her to stay with them rather than go home to the house in Forest Hills after Teacher's funeral. In another letter she tried to "believe that. . .'time is a great healer' and to wait until my blinding sorrow breaks to let in the radiance of the Life Beyond."

Soon after Annie's death, Helen sailed to Scotland with Polly to visit Polly's brother, a minister. He took very good care of the pair, but Helen was numb, numb. Not having those fingers speaking into her hands, it was as if a part of her had died. But in spite of her overwhelming grief, Helen poured herself into new projects, such as learning to manipulate a new Braille writer to tackle her ever more voluminous correspondence. Polly was a wonder, but she was not Teacher. In Scotland Helen heard the shocking news of the King's abdication because of his love for Adela Wallace Simpson. Helen's response is quite revealing of what she valued: "Many persons have a wrong idea of what constitutes true happiness. It is not attained through self-gratification but through fidelity to a worthy purpose." Helen's whole life, of course, was commitment to worthy purpose. And if anything, with the death of Teacher, her emotional fire for making the world work better grew even more intense. The whole world of the blind and handicapped continued to call on her. She was invited to visit both France and Japan and again urged to do whatever she could to bring relief to the soldiers and sailors who had been blinded in the war. Of course, she went and did what she could. While in Paris, she visited the famous statues by Rodin. The museum allowed her to touch everything. As she ran her hands over *The Thinker*, she said, "He's not thinking. He's trying to think. In every limb I felt the throes of emerging mind." She later added that it reminded her of "the force that shook me when Teacher spelled

'Water.'" A famous sculptor, Gutzon Borglum, who was being honored at the time, escorted her through the museum and later said, "I shall never forget that hour with Helen Keller. . . .From it I learned that the soul, over and above the body, has eyes." Helen was deeply moved, when seated beside her at dinner, the sculptor said that Teacher had been a kind of sculptor too—"your Praxiteles, breathing life into your sense-shut faculties."

About this time, Helen was also asked to write a journal of her life without Annie. She faithfully wrote in her journal every day, though it was very painful, and she sometimes bewailed the agreement to do so. The journal revealed the ways in which Helen worked to surmount her intense grief and sense of incalculable loss, but being so strong-willed and determined, she was able to stay active in a remarkable range of projects and concerns. Her sense of independence was growing, and her ideas and opinions were, if anything, becoming more finely etched with her own unique personality. When the journal was published, it was greeted with warmth and happiness, for it seemed that more and more of the real Helen Keller had emerged in its pages. Her brave words showed the world that though grief-stricken, Helen was still herself, still determined to express herself freely and to run her own life, with the assistance of her companion Polly Thomson.

Though Helen accepted the invitation to visit Japan, there were many considerations about the trip. What should her speeches say? Worries about her speeches kept her working some days from five in the morning until ten at night. In preparation for the trip, Helen received counsel about friendship and goodwill from President Roosevelt. She visited thirty-nine Japanese cities and gave ninety-seven lectures to overwhelmingly enthusiastic audiences, beginning with thousands of children waving American and Japanese flags as she stepped off the boat in Yokohama. She met the princes and princesses and all the officials of the Emperor's court. Her talks and the onward and upward bent of her personality and life seemed to soften the long-held Japanese view that the gods had given people their handicaps as part of their karma. Her influence brought about the founding of clinics to work with the deaf and blind, many of which have been maintained to this day. After Japan she and Polly went on to Korea and Manchuria (Japan had just attacked China). She was relieved when the trip ended. "I do not know whom I feel more sorry for," she said upon her return, "— the long enduring shamefully insulted Chinese dying by the thousands for freedom they are beginning to understand, or the Japanese millions staggering under the heaviest taxation in their history." As a souvenir of her trip, she brought home an Akita puppy—the first of the breed to enter America. This large kindly dog was raised for over two thousand years to guard the Buddhist temples and continues to treat its owner as if she or he were a Buddha! I have an Akita, too, for which I have Helen to thank. Of course, when he bows to me in the morning, it is a bit disconcerting.

When she returned to America after this exhausting journey, she was admitted to Mayo Clinic, where her gall bladder was removed. By this time Nella Braddy Henney had become deeply necessary to Polly and Helen. Nella was essential for her editorial abilities, her public relations skills, and her care of many other details that were overwhelming the pair.

There ensued a number of unpleasant and painful political maneuverings involving the Foundation for the Blind. In spite of her constant efforts in their behalf, her endless money-raising speeches, and trips to Washington and to wealthy potential donors, Helen felt they were using her in a crass and inhuman way, commercializing her name and limitations. One such furor had to do with the project of talking books. The supporters of the project wanted to make it the major fund raising campaign of the Foundation and for this, they needed Helen's help. Helen waffled a long time, for while she was willing to write and ask others to support the project, she could not herself support it because the campaign, as she wrote, "appeared to me untimely when people both blind and seeing were crying out for practical help in the problems of daily life."

There is no question but that providing practical help came about in part because of the growing affection and affinity between Helen and Franklin and Eleanor Roosevelt. Mrs. Roosevelt and Helen had long been part of a mutual admiration society. They were sisters under the skin, tall strong women, looking somewhat alike, whose hearts and minds were totally honed to the most sensitive awareness of the problems and potentials of others. There was, in spite of their vast experience among many people and social issues, a kind of ultimate innocence in both, an absurd yet holy belief that goodness was innate in everyone, despite the most awful appearances to the contrary. President Roosevelt also appreciated Helen enormously. Perhaps he caught his wife's affection for her; perhaps it was because he too was seriously crippled as a result of contracting polio. "Anything Helen Keller is for, I am for," he announced. And in the course of their mutual activities in the service of the handicapped, this certainly proved true.

Helen's heart ached for the deaf-blind, whom she called "the loneliest people on earth," but by working with the Roosevelts and speaking before government committees, she managed to raise the public and political awareness to the whole range of problems and opportunities facing the handicapped. Thus measures and bills were passed, such as the Social Security Act, which now, as a result of her efforts, included the blind in its provisions, and the Wagner-Lewis bill, which would assist state commissions for the blind with matching funds. Writing to her close colleague at the Foundation for the Blind, Major Moses Migel, Helen wrote of Roosevelt that "The blind of America have cause to bless him. He has done more for their well-being than any other President of the United States. . . .Some people criticize President Roosevelt severely, but when all is said, he has made a nation's concern the problem of the underprivileged."

Though Helen continued her work for the Foundation, she determined to give herself time and space to work on another project, a book about Teacher. By this time a kind and gentle man named Herbert Haas had joined the household. Teacher had cared for him greatly and had left Helen and Polly in his hands. He managed the household, repaired all broken appliances, took care of the garden, drove the car, and often tended whoever was ailing. He became a close friend to Helen, learning the manual language so as to speak with her, playing dominoes and checkers with her, and seeing that she got sufficient exercise by taking her out on walks and hikes. All who knew him considered him to be a blessing dropped from heaven. To Helen, he was a member of the family.

Politics also continued to call Helen. She was anguished about the Civil War in Spain ("it is proud tears that I shed for the masses who are giving their lives to create a more enlightened and civilized nation"), furious that one of her books had been added to the famous book-burning night of the Nazis, and deeply saddened by France and Britain's "perfidy" to Czechoslovakia. She was heartsick when she heard that the Jewish Institute for the Blind in Vienna had been closed by the Nazis and the inmates driven into the streets to beg or starve. At the same time, she was deeply touched by the drive toward a homeland in "Palestine" by Europe's troubled Jews. "I have long felt that their problem can be solved only if they have a homeland where they can develop unmolested their peculiar genius in religion, art and social justice," she wrote in her journal in January, 1937. She also felt that the Jews deserved this nation, for her biblical studies convinced her of their right to Palestine, since they "held the land long before an Arab invader appeared. . . .What have the Arabs done to develop Palestine?" Helen was nothing if not outspoken and controversial in many of her opinions.

In the midst of the world's travails and her personal sorrow, she sold the house in Forest Hills and prepared to move into one on land given to the Foundation for the purpose of creating a home for Helen by the pharmaceutical tycoon, Gustavus Pfeiffer, who owned the worldwide Warner-Hudnut concern. Helen and Polly named the house and its gardens and shrubs Arcan Ridge, after one of Teacher's favorite places in the Scottish Highlands.

Another abiding and exciting friendship began in these years with the luminous American stage actress Katharine Cornell. Cornell was noted for playing the major classical roles for women; she traveled the country bringing great theater and acting to every city large enough to have something like a stage. As much as anyone, she elevated the dramatic tastes of the American public for live drama and did much to help establish repertory and regional theater. Helen had always loved the theater, and now with the friendship of the elegant and aristocratic Miss Cornell and her entourage, the worlds of the theater opened to her completely. Helen would sit in the first row, with her hand on the stage, listening to everything that was happening through one hand while getting a tapped out play by play of the action in the other. Helen also enjoyed the slightly libertine ambience of Miss Cornell's establishment. Once, while visiting her at her summer home in Martha's Vineyard, Cornell proposed that they all go swimming and warned Helen that she always swam in the nude. Helen rose to the occasion, replying that since she did not have the pleasure of seeing, she would wear a bathing suit. Katharine Cornell and her manager Nancy Hamilton remained among Helen's most constant and reliable friends, always providing in addition to their warm friendship occasions for amusement and for meeting interesting people. From them, Helen learned one of the great untold secrets of the planet—theater people are among the most generous and supportive in the world. The great actress even hitchhiked from her home in the Vineyard to be with Helen when Herbert Haas died.

The War was moving ever closer. Helen was making trips on behalf of the Foundation for the Blind to persuade states of their obligations to consider the handicapped, especially the blind, but she wished desperately for some war-related work, and sadly, it came. American soldiers were being wounded in battle in large numbers. Nella Braddy suggested that Helen might pay her part of the debt all Americans owed to the soldiers by visiting them to "find out for yourself what you can do for them." Soon Helen was visiting hospitals and centers for the wounded across the country. She paused only to campaign actively for Roosevelt's reelection. Upon attending his inaugural, she tenderly touched the face of the exhausted and ailing President who would die before finishing this term in office, reporting that "Upon his worn face shines the heroic ambitions of Hercules to subdue the beasts of greed and deliver the world from robber states. . . .He trusts the progressive tendencies converging toward a nobler goal."

Helen had also taken to writing constantly about her concern that Black blind people receive government assistance so that they could live in a way "worthy of their human dignity and courage in the face of fearful obstacles." But it was her visits to thousands and thousands of war wounded, whom she cherished in her own light-giving way—often holding and kissing them as a mother would—that became for her "the crowning experience of my life." Imagine the battered, destroyed young fellows, held within the tremendous charge that was Helen Keller! Here is how Helen described what happened during one such visit:

Often it was not verbal encouragement that was asked of me but a kiss or the laying of my hand on a weary head. This always made me feel as if I were partaking of a sacrament. A patient, appealingly young, came up to rest his head on my shoulder and was silent for a minute, evidently bracing himself for a new try at life. A drop of sweetness stole into my grief over the paralyzed as they tried to put their wasted arms around me, not always successfully, but their wish was a benediction I shall treasure forever.

A boy of 18 on his way to the operating table said he knew he would come through all right after I had embraced him. Another to whom I wished speedy recovery after an operation said, 'I don't want your wishes but your love,' and seemed cheered by my assurance that he had it. Another soldier, obviously dying, held my hand as if I had been his mother. One said, 'My, I have not had a kiss like that in years. My mother used to kiss me that way.' [55]

After the war ended and Roosevelt died, Helen engaged herself to take a Foundation-sponsored tour of the European hospitals and centers for the blind that had been destroyed by the war and to visit wounded veterans overseas. This time, she flew across the Atlantic, visiting England, Paris, Rome, and Athens. On this trip, she finally visited the Parthenon—a long yearned-for source of many imaginary scenes of glory. As she touched the columns of the Temple of Athena, she said, "How interesting. They are meant to see out from, not to be looked at." Whether consciously or unconsciously known, Athena—always the Goddess of those who live life fully and at its edges—was a guiding archetype for Helen. Refusing to brook any whiny nay-saying, Athena helps her beloveds in the human world, even in the midst of the most daunting of obstacles, to develop those qualities of mind, body, and spirit that help them chart new ways of being.

In her book about Teacher, Helen described the journey up to the Acropolis as a personal metaphor for her life with Annie: As she walked it, it "symbolized the difficulties Teacher and I had overcome together and I was spiritually strengthened to ascend a metaphorical Acropolis in my work for the blind. As we had gone from one camp of the life-wrecked blind to another, a mountain of suffering had been laid upon me. I knew that to bring them back to self-help and usefulness would require years of unremitting endeavor. I felt the uniqueness of the tragedy that confronted me, but the thought of Teacher's perseverance spurred me on." [56]

While in Rome, Polly and Helen received word that the house at Arcan Ridge had burned, and with it, its contents, including the manuscript about Teacher that Helen had been working on for twenty years in spare moments. Also lost were all their books, letters, treasures, gifts, and papers. "But from the moment I grasped the fullness of our disaster, I experienced life triumphant over the narrowness of my bodily existence—mighty life, seeing and hearing life, the creation of the spirit. This inner life surged and expanded within me." After this latest loss, she began to relive in spirit the countless devastations of the war, the bombs, the concentration camps, the battles, the agony of Europe's blind and newly blind, the harrowing accounts of the veterans who were mutilated by every kind of fire. Her heart burned with the determination to give her life in the service of the great light that she believed was there to help brighten and "exalt" human life.

Though Helen declared that old age was just another limitation to overcome, at the age of sixty-eight, she was wearing down. She was not as fast on the uptake when spelling was being tapped into her hands, would more and more often be found dozing at her desk, and even wear the expression that deaf people sometimes do when they are pretending to understand. Still, she had grand ideas for projects and travels. Another world tour was planned—to teach, to inspire, to evoke the possibilities of transforming the perception of what it meant to be handicapped, and to set up schools for the handicapped. As Polly and Helen set out for Australia, Nella wrote to Polly: "Helen is one of our saints. It hurts to be a saint. Just now it hurts more than ever and what hurts us who are on the sidelines is that there is nothing we can do. All we can say is that we are with you and God help you!"

On this trip, Helen and Polly traveled to Australia, to New Zealand, and back to Australia. Then at General MacArthur's invitation, she returned to Japan to visit the blind, to assess Japanese homes for the blind, and to advise the Japanese government how best to meet their needs. Her visits to Hiroshima and Nagasaki, she said, "scorched a deep scar in my soul." She determined to "do what lies in my power to fight against the demons of atomic warfare and for the constructive uses of atomic energy." Midway through the tour, Polly suffered an alarming attack of high blood pressure, and the rest of the tour was canceled. The pair came home and checked into the Mayo Clinic. The word from the doctors was that both of them needed to slow down, especially Polly. There was a report that Helen was so terrified of having to live without Polly, that she asked Polly to provide her with some pills that would allow her to follow in case Polly died.

For a time they did take it easier. Their life, as always, included worries about money and staffing needs for the house. Helen wrote many articles, and Nella criticized them freely. Within a few months Helen and Polly took another trip to Europe to spend time with old and new friends and to visit Michelangelo's sculptures. The sculptor Jo Davidson describes this encounter of Helen with Michaelangelo:

A moveable scaffold was set up so that Helen could pass her hand over the sculptures of Donatello and Michaelangelo. I have seen these sculptures before but never so intimately as when I watched her hands wandering over the forms, peering into the slightest crevices, into the most subtle undulations. She exclaimed with delight as she divined the slightly open mouth of the sighing young 'St. John the Baptist.'

We who were below were transfixed as Helen contemplated Michaelangelo's 'Night' and 'Dawn.' And when she came upon the 'Madonna and Child' she discovered the 'Suckling Babe,' she threw her arms around the group and murmured: 'Innocent Greed.' [57]

Their return was marred by the death of their old and indispensable friend Herbert, who had devoted his life to them for many years.

Helen's life work of the soul had become the deaf and blind of the world, and she responded to this knowing by leaving in 1951 for South Africa, where she addressed scores of institutions and schools as well as speaking at forty-eight different meetings and receptions. Everywhere her message was about the failure of white society to redeem the blind and the deaf of color because of racial prejudice. This, she said to her abashed audience was "an offense against humanitarianism which life never forgives." Wherever she went, it was the Black people especially who recognized her contribution. The Zulus gave her a title *Homvuselelo*, meaning "You have aroused the consciences of many."

Life at home was full of problems—by this time, Polly was someone that people put up with because they loved Helen. She had become curt, rude, and infuriating. Domestic assistance was impossible to come by because of Polly's overbearing behavior. A perfectionist, she would snipe at household help until they would leave in fury. Visits to Montgomery and Helen's sister's family were equally troubled as they had hardened into hidebound Southern conservatives who couldn't care less about Helen's interests and horizons.

The two ladies were feeling lonely and unprotected, Polly especially believing they had few friends left. They set off traveling again, this time to Egypt and to Israel. In Israel, Helen became furious when she heard about a Village for the Blind that the Israelis had set up. "You must not segregate the blind," she said. "You must break up the village and give them the opportunity for a normal life." The Israelis did what she said. One of her colleagues at the American Foundation for the Blind declared that it was this hard-nosed understanding of the needs of blind people and the willingness to demand it for them that made Helen a professional in the care and treatment of the handicapped. On their way home Polly and Helen flew to Paris to celebrate the 100th anniversary of the death of Louis Braille. Helen called this giant "the Gutenberg of the blind." She herself was made a Chevalier of the Legion of Honor and accepted in "faultlessly grammatical French."

Back home, work began on a documentary of Helen's life. Unfortunately, the film showed too much of the triumph and not enough of the continuing struggle—the long, long hours spent over the mail, the long, long hours composing speeches, memorizing them and practicing them. Nella expressed these concerns to Helen. As always, her views were sharp, clear, and upfront—if not necessarily kind. Trips to Latin America and proposed trips to the countries Helen had not visited spurred them on, though friends noted that Helen's senses were weakening. Her hands now needed to be warmed before she could read with them. But there were positive things. The documentary about Helen's life titled *The Unconquered* was a critical success and won an Academy Award. Everyone was pleased about it, but it was not a commercial success. Now Helen was hard at work—and painfully—on her book about Teacher. Writing about their life together and about Teacher's life required a great expense of spirit and anguish, but her friends felt this to be one of Helen's finest works. As usual Helen and Polly were planning a trip—this one to India and Pakistan. The book about Teacher came out, but it did not sell well, partly because it was too soft to be a tribute to the toughness that was Annie Sullivan. But soon came the script for *The Miracle Worker*, which Nella liked but which she feared that Polly and Helen might not. Helen was impressed by the author William Gibson, but as Nella feared, she had problems with the script. For one thing, Helen said, Teacher would never have told about her Tewksbury experiences to her family, let alone want them to be known by the public at large. So far as we know, Helen never saw the play performed.

After yet another tour to Scandinavia and Iceland, Helen was home again, this time to have her foot operated on. As she was recovering and at home by herself, Polly suffered a cerebral hemorrhage. After that event we have mostly the words of Nella Braddy to tell us what went on, and they are not generous to Polly. Sometime in this period Helen turned more and more inward, and Polly grew more and more frantic about anyone else having real contact with Helen. The entire question of *The Miracle Worker* came to a head in a fight between Nella and Helen's trustees, and finally Helen repudiated Nella, though Nella never knew why. She suspected that Polly had fed her lies about Nella's activities. The whole episode was profoundly human and deeply dismaying, with everyone thinking they knew best what needed to be done for Helen and for others in her life. When Polly died, Helen, already much withdrawn into an inward life, seemed unswayed by much of the carrying on. She was convinced that Polly and Teacher had a bright new life in heaven. Other friends did their best to keep Helen informed about the world outside her silent darkness.

One bright spot came with the dedication of the Anne Sullivan Macy Memorial Fountain at Radcliffe, and the Helen Keller Garden that surrounded it. Helen was about to make a formal speech, when she suddenly announced that she had not seen the garden, and until she had done so, would not speak. The situation was explained to the president of the alumnae, and while the audience sat and waited, Helen, the president, and her friends went to the garden and the fountain. Helen knelt and felt and smelled the flowers and the fountain and spelled out the word "Water." What else, in fact, was there to say? "Water. Water. Water. Water."

She died quietly. Her last few years, she just communicated more and more with the inward world, until she finally stepped across the frame a week short of her eighty-eighth year, in 1968. And now she steps back and forth with us.

PROCESS 12
JOURNEYING WITH HELEN IN THE INWARD AND OUTWARD WORLDS

TIME: FORTY-FIVE MINUTES.

- ## MATERIALS:
  None.

- ## MUSIC:
  Soft background music from Area One like Deuter's *Ecstasy.*

- ## INSTRUCTIONS FOR GOING SOLO:
  This process lends itself wonderfully well to the solo voyager. Put the script for the Guide on tape with appropriate music. Make sure that you give yourself plenty of time and pauses to experience each direction.

- ## SCRIPT FOR THE GUIDE:

  So many millions of people the world over have continued to honor and affirm the life and work of Helen Keller that in some sense her spirit exists. Millions have read books about her, seen the movies and plays like *The Miracle Worker* which dealt with her early life with Annie Sullivan, or are familiar with the work of the various institutes influenced by her which help people with visual or hearing disorders. But most of all, her bright spirit rises up even beyond these familiarities and calls us into a world of grace. In this she is immortal, and now, to conclude our adventure with Helen and the other great Americans, we will visit this immortal, imaginal realm. In doing so, we will be honoring and experiencing something of her own belief system in which she was influenced by the teachings of Swedenborg. She believed deeply in the inner world, the "world of the morning," and it is to this world that we will travel with her.

  To begin, would everyone please look at the picture of Helen Keller in this book. Look at the picture, and then close your eyes and internalize its details. Then pass the book over to someone else so they can do the same. (The Guide gives the participants time to do this.)

  Would you please lie down now and make yourself comfortable. Close your eyes and breathe slowly and deeply. . . . And as you breathe, will you accept for the duration of the process that Helen Keller's spirit and presence will be with you. Imagine or see her now coming toward you, her wonderful smile, her face luminous with love and grace, her sensitive hands.

Behind your closed eyes, see or imagine her figure filled with light, filled with energy and charge. Her hands are extensions of her soul. So feel those charged, expressive, communicating hands beckoning you, beckoning you past the passageways in the Heart of Darkness, into the Morning.

You sense her communicating to you her wonderful knowings of which she wrote, "Truly I have looked into the very heart of darkness and refused to yield to its paralyzing influence." And into your heart comes the rest of what she is communicating to you: "But in spirit I am one of those who walk the morning. I invite you, my friend, to walk the morning with me. To rise out of your paralysis of heart or mind or courage, and to walk the morning."

And you put out your right hand. And gradually you sense her hand on yours. Oh, it may be very subtle at first, almost like butterfly wings, or the most delicate of electrical pulsations. But feel it you do. And with her hand in yours, you begin to follow her. And she is tapping so subtly into your palm the experience of her morning, the experience of her inner realm. And feeling in your palm the charge of her experience as she leads you on this walk of the morning into the immortal and celestial realms where spirit and service are one and where light is all. . . . And as she taps this message into your palm, feel yourself encircled by the light coming from her radiant presence. And listening with your palm now, feel the experience of Helen's realms of morning. . . . And allowing yourself to tap back to her something of your experience of her experience, because she loves the give and take of communication. . . .

And Helen reaches out to you now, and she touches your eyes to fill you with inward seeing. And you know your eyes to be good for inward seeing. And her rare colors and forms and dimensions begin to pulse through your inner eyes. And you are given eyes with which to see, as Helen did, as her spiritual teacher Emmanuel Swedenborg did, the inner universe.

And she touches your ears, and you are given deep inner hearing. And you feel that warmth and electrical tremor around your ears as you are given deep inner hearing with which to hear the beautiful sounds of the inward realms.

And she touches your lips and your tongue, and you are given the gift of deep inward speech, that you may have the capacity for deep inward communication and conversation.

And she touches your nose, and you are given the knowledge of deep inward aromas, the scents and smells of the inward realms.

And she takes your hand, caresses your hand, and you are given the gift of deep inward tactile and kinesthetic knowing.

And she touches your mind, and you are given the gift of deep inner intelligence. And suddenly there seems to be a kind of inward sun that is also perceived and known. You can feel its heat. You know its radiance. And you realize that as you walk the morning with her, you have passed into the domain of your own inward realm.

What do you sense there? What do you see? Is it persons? Is it angel-like beings? Is it beings of light? Is the landscape different, and the music, and the art? Do they have a different culture there as Swedenborg and Helen suggested? Or is it quite an ordinary world like your own? Know that whatever or whoever is there, you are perceiving through the unique lens of your own inner perceptions this inward universe.

And Helen is there with you all the time. And since she has led you here, you feel the desire to communicate with her the nature of this realm, your own personal immortal realm. And now you become the leader of this walk through the morning. So knowing how subtle is her sense, how delicate and potent her willingness to understand, you give her a guided tour of your immortal realm, pressing into her palm what you see and feel, experience and know, so that her delighted spirit may catch fire with your spirit. . . . And now where you are in this inward realm, you notice that nearby is a frame. And through the frame the world seems misty, ambiguous. For what you see through the frame is the outward world—what you have thought of as the ordinary world. And you look at this ordinary life and world, but from the point of view of the other side of the frame. And you see how the regular or ordinary world seems to an inhabitant of the Deep World. And you and Helen share knowings about the nature of that ordinary reality. She says, "My dear, it's so easy to go back and forth. We merely step through the frame." So with her hand in yours, you step back across the frame into this world. But you're carrying with you the magic of the other world, which is able to transcend the boundaries of space and time.

And you take her on a journey of your present life. You show her your friends, your loved ones, your work. But you see it with her hand in yours. So what you see is the endless opportunities and beautiful possibilities in each encounter, in each event. Perhaps you take her to some event in your life that you would like to show her. Or perhaps you will take her to your life of a few days ago. Carrying the magic of the Other World, the world beyond the frame, perhaps you take her to an event of tomorrow. But living each moment as if it were your last, you see it in its fullness, as Helen taps her sense of glory and wonder of your life into your hand, and helps you see it in fullness. Perhaps it's a scene around your kitchen table. It can be something very simple. But Helen is in this world with you now, helping you see its possibilities. . . .

Introduce her to your children, or to your husband or wife, or friends, or to your work day. And let her wonder and delight fill you with her own. And if you have not yet done so, bring her to meet your most dearly loved one in this time, or your most dearly detested one in this time. And with this person's permission, ask Helen to touch her face, his face, with those God-knowing fingers, those oracular fingers. And watch as Helen discovers the miracle of the face of this one. And feel that one you love the most, or detest the most, opening the truth of his or her face and character to Helen's knowing and so tender fingers. . . .

And after a while Helen says to you, "But, my friend, it is so easy to go back and forth once you know that the universe is One." And taking you by the hand, she guides you back through the frame between the worlds into that inner world. And this inner world may seem changed now because you have seen it as part of a continuum with your everyday world. And you look again at this inner world. And you sense senses that perhaps you didn't even know you had in your ways of knowing it. And you sense as mystics and poets throughout the centuries have the correspondences and the partnerships that are there in this inner world for every part of your outer world. You wonder with the philosophers like Plato whether in this inner world are held the optimal forms, the ideal expressions and patterns for your outer world. And you know that you are free now, free, to know these ideal forms, to have them as guidelines, as patterns, as transcendent object lessons.

And there in this place also dwells the Beloved of your soul, the godself within, your partner in the depth world, that one who loves you into being, who is sending his/her/its influence and corresponding teachers, events, opportunities to call you into greater life, finer living. But here in this inner realm you have a clearer, richer, more available partnership with the Beloved of your soul.

And Helen laughs with joy as she brings your hands together with that beloved Teacher and Friend. And she suddenly spells out in your hand W-A-T-E-R. And you see the water of this inward world. And Helen puts your hand in the water of this inward world. And then she spells L-O-V-E. And then you notice something wonderful. The water is flowing through the frame and it is flowing into this world. And Helen steps through the frame with you, and she puts your hand in the water in this world. And she spells W-A-T-E-R. And then L-O-V-E.

And you know that these deep Waters of Life flow back and forth, from this world to the next. And from that Depth World to this one. And Helen invites you to drink of these waters. So you drink now of these waters of spirit and wisdom. And the wonder and knowledge that this water of life holds courses through you, opening you to a sense that the universe is one.

And Helen says to you in her heart's language, "From this moment, my friend, you will be always able to take my hand which is so willingly offered to you, and to cross into the inner world. There you will find the correspondences for the outer world, but perhaps in a more perfect, more harmonic form." So that you may then go back into the regular world following this great stream of living water from one realm to the other, bringing the Waters of Possibility, the Waters of Creation, the Waters of a more hopeful, better life, community, relationship, governance, culture, art, medicine, science, spirituality, from this realm, the Realm of Pattern and Possibility, into your realm, the realm of expression.

And hold your hand out again so you can feel her tapping in it, W-A-T-E-R. W-A-T-E-R. W-A-T-E-R. And she also communicates to you, "I am so happy to get involved again and to bring these wonders and possibilities that I know in my spirit's life to help you bring them into time through this courseway, this stream of living water."

So knowing that you have your friends—Helen and the Beloved of the Soul—in this deep inner world that holds the great patterns of co-creation, you thank Helen and embrace her. She loves to be embraced. And you feel her embracing you. And you step across the frame. You wave at her. She waves at you. And you gradually, at your own pace, stand up with your eyes half-closed. And you come back into this world. Eyes half-closed. Don't open them until you really get here. And yet you continue to see her there, waving at you from the world behind the frame. Wave back at her. May you continue with Helen. May you continue to walk the morning with her. May you continue to learn, may you continue to grow. She also for you can be Teacher.

NOTES

[1]Helen Keller, *The Story of My Life* (New York: Doubleday, 1954), p. 36.

[2]Quoted in Joseph P. Lash, *Helen and Teacher: The Story of Helen Keller and Anne Sullivan Macy* (New York: Delta/A Merloyd Lawrence Book, 1981), p. 18.

[3]Quoted in Lash, pp. 40-41.

[4]Helen Keller, *The Story of My Life*, p. 35.

[5]Quoted in Lash, pp. 52-53.

[6]Letter in Helen Keller, *The Story of My Life*, p. 248.

[7]Quoted in Lash, p. 56.

[8]Quoted in Lash, pp. 57-58.

[9]Quoted in Lash, pp. 60-61.

[10]Quoted in Lash, p. 202.

[11]Helen Keller, *Teacher* (New York: Doubleday, 1955), pp. 44-45.

[12]Quoted in Lash, p. 81.

[13]Helen Keller, *The Story of My Life*, p. 47.

[14]Ibid., pp. 129-130.

[15]Lash, p. 101.

[16]Ibid., p. 105.

[17]Helen Keller, *The Story of My Life*, p. 63.

[18]Ibid., p. 64.

[19]Helen Keller, *Teacher*, p. 54.

[20]Quoted in Lash, p. 273.

[21]Ibid., p. 279.

[22]Helen Keller, *The Story of My Life*, p. 88.

[23]Quoted in Lash, p. 245.

[24]Helen Keller, *My Religion* (New York: The Swedenborg Foundation, Inc., 1960), pp. 46-47.

[25]Ibid., p. 48.

[26]Helen Keller, *The Story of My Life*, pp. 103-104.

[27]Ibid., p. 106; pp. 109-110.

[28]Quoted in Lash, pp. 322-323.

[29]Quoted in Lash, p. 331.

[30]Quoted in Diane Ackerman, *A Natural History of the Senses* (New York: Random House, 1990), p. 44.

[31]Lash, p. 420.

[32]Quoted in Lash, pp. 442-443.

[33]Helen Keller, *The Story of My Life*, pp. 40-41.

[34]Helen Keller, *Midstream: My Later Life* (New York: Greenwood, 1968), pp. 133-134.

[35]The description of this romance appears, greatly edited, it seems, by editor Nella Braddy in *Midstream*, pp. 177-182.

[36]Lash, p. 468.

[37]Helen describes her life in films and vaudeville in *Midstream*, pp. 186-215.

[38]Ibid., pp. 566-567.

[39]The first part of this process dealing with releasing tension in the tongue is adapted from one that Robert Masters and I offer in our book, *Listening to the Body* (New York: Delta, 1978), pp. 137-145.

[40]Helen Keller, *My Religion*, pp. 66-67.

[41]Ibid.

[42]Ibid., p. 102.

[43]Ibid., pp. 105-106.

[44]Ibid., p. 110.

[45]Ibid., p. 157.

[46]Some of Nella Braddy's remarkable observations on this are to be found in her book *Anne Sullivan Macy* (New York, 1933).

[47]Some of these descriptions are offered by Nella Braddy in her foreword to *Midstream*. See especially pp. xvii to xxii.

[48]Quoted in Lash, p. 600.

[49]See, for example, the interesting reflections on Helen's awakening to symbolic forms in the water incident in Ernst Cassirer, *An Essay on Man: An Introduction to a Philosophy of Human Culture* (New Haven: Yale University Press, 1944). Also see Walker Percy, *The Message in the Bottle* (New York: Farrar, Straus & Girou, 1975).

[50]Quoted in Lash, pp. 622-623.

[51]Ibid., pp. 645-646.

[52]Ibid., pp. 657-658.

[53]Ibid., p. 659.

[54]Ibid., p. 658.

[55]Ibid., pp. 719-720.

[56]Helen Keller, *Teacher: Anne Sullivan Macy* (New York: Doubleday, 1955), p. 29.

[57]Ibid., p. 756.

MUSICAL SELECTIONS

*T*he following listings are suggestions and are drawn from music that we have used successfully in the teaching and practice of this work. The reader should feel free to use his or her own favorites, while trying to keep within the mood of the applicable area. Some of the selections from one area can be used in the two other areas at the Guide's discretion. Area I represents music that has been found to be particularly powerful as background music. It is also effective for guided imagery and meditation and during evocation of altered states of consciousness. Area II is evocative music and is meant to stimulate and enhance the process itself. Area III represents music that has a celebratory character and is often used to accompany the conclusion of exercises and processes. The music listed below, as well as tapes of the actual Mystery School sessions from which the material in this book was drawn, is available from:

Wind Over the Earth, Inc.
1688 Redwood Avenue
Boulder, CO 80304
1 (800) 726-0847

AREA I:
BACKGROUND MEDITATIVE MUSIC

Don G. Campbell, *Crystal Meditations* (The Art of Relaxation C-9517).

Coyote Oldman, *Tear of the Moon* (Coyote Oldman).

Constance Denby, *Novus Magnificat* (Hearts of Space HS 11003-4).

Chaitanya Hari Deuter, *Land of Enchantment* (Kuckuck 11081-4).

Chaitanya Hari Deuter, *Ecstasy* (Kuckuck 11044-4).

Kay Gardner, *A Rainbow Path* (Ladyslipper L3C 103).

Gregorian Chants, *Officinum Tenebarum* (Celestial Harmonies 13022-4).

Abbess Hildegard, *A Feather on the Breath of God, Sequences and Hymns by Abbess Hildegard of Bingen* (Hyperion Records).

Alan Hovhaness, *Mysterious Mountain* (RCA AGLI-4215).

Keith Jarrett, *Koln Concert* (ECM 810067-4).

Georgia Kelly, *Ancient Echoes* (Heru Records).

Kitaro, *Silk Road* (Canyon 051-052).

Daniel Kobialka, *Dream Passage* (LiSem Enterprises OK 101).

Daniel Kobialka, *Timeless Motion* (LiSem Enterprises OK 102).

Ottmar Liebert, *Borrasca* (Higher Octave HOMC-7036).

Melissa Morgan, *Invocation to Isis* (Kicking Mule KM-414).

R. Carlos Nakai, *Journeys: Native American Flute Music* (Canyon CR-613-C).

Ottorino Respighi, *Ancient Airs and Dances* (Mercury 434304-2).

Mike Rowland, *The Fairy Ring* (Sona Gaia Productions).

Satsang Fellowship, *Song of the Golden Lotus: The Mantric Music of Swami Kriya Ramananda.*

Therese Schroeder-Sheker, *In Dulci Jubilo* (Celestial Harmonies 13039-2).

Therese Schroeder-Sheker, *Rosa Mystica* (Celestial Harmonies 13034-2).

Tony Scott, *Music for Zen Meditation* (Verve 817209-4).

John Serrie, *And the Stars Go with You* (Miramar MPC-2001).

Spiritual Environment, Shamanic Dream (Nightingale Records 321).

Michael Stearns, *Planetary Unfolding* (Sonic Atmospheres CD-307).

Michael Stearns, *Chronos* (Sonic Atmospheres CD-312).

Eric Tingstad/Nancy Rumbel, *Legends* (Narada Lotus NC-61022).

Eric Tingstad/Nancy Rumbel, *Homeland* (Narada Lotus ND-61026).

Vangelis, *L'Apocalypse Now* (POL 31503).

Rob Whitesides-Woo, *Heart to Crown* (Serenity 005).

Rob Whitesides-Woo, *Miracles* (Serenity 002).

Rob Whitesides-Woo, *Mountain Light* (Serenity 70018-4).

Henry Wolff/Nancy Hemings, *Tibetan Bells II* (Serenity 006).

AREA II:
EVOCATIVE MUSIC

J. S. Bach, *Brandenburg Concertos—Volumes I & II* (COL 42274 and COL 42275).

Samuel Barber, *Adagio for Strings* (RCA AGLI-3790).

Chaitanya Hari Deuter, *Ecstasy* (Kuckuck 11044-4).

Empire of the Sun (soundtrack) (Warner Bros. 25668-4).

Field of Dreams (soundtrack) (Novus 3060-4-N).

Kay Gardner, *A Rainbow Path* (Ladyslipper LRC 103).

Robert Gass and Wings of Song, *Extended Chant Series: Heart of Perfect Wisdom, Kalama, Shri Ram, Om Namah Shivaya, Alleluia* (Spring Hill Music 1012, 1011, 1013, 1005, 1006).

Al Gromer Khan, *Mahogany Nights* (Hearts of Space 11020).

Philip Glass, *Koyaanisquatsi* (Antilles 422-814042-4).

The Gyoto Monks, *Freedom Chants from the Roof of the World* (Rykodisc RACS-20113).

Mickey Hart, *At the Edge* (Rykodisc RACS-10124).

Hildegard of Bingen, *A Feather on the Breath of God* (Hyperion CDA 66039).

Jean Michel Jarre, *Oxygene* (NTI 824746).

Jean Michel Jarre, *Equinox* (Polydor 8294556).

Magnum Mysterium, *Collection of Sacred Music* (Celestial Harmonies 18.45012).

The Mission (Virgin 905676-2).

Mendelssohn/Bruch, *Violin Concertos* (Capital 69003).

Nana Mouskouri, *Passport* (Philips 830764-2).

Nana Mouskouri, *Why Worry* (Polydor 830492-4).

Nana Mouskouri, *Ma Verité* (Philips 826391-4).

Nana Mouskouri, *Libertad* (Mercury 826799-4).

Nana Mouskouri, *Tierra Viva* (Mercury 832958-4).

NASA Voyager II Space Sounds, Miranda (Brain/Mind Research).

Olatunji, *Drums of Passion* (COL CK8210).

Carl Orff, *Carmina Burana* (COL 33172).

Francis Poulenc, *Concerto for Organ* (Angel S-35953).

The Rustavi Choir, *Georgian Voices* (Elektra/Nonesuch 79224-4).

Camille Saint-Saens, *Symphony No. 3* (RCA ATLI-4039).

Jean Sibelius, *Finlandia* (Phillips 9500140).

Smetana, *My Country* (DGG 2707054).

Smetana, *The Moldau* (COL 36716).

Jeffrey Thompson, *Child of Dream* (Brain/Mind Research).

Taise, *Wait for the Lord.*

Tchaikovsky, *Violin Concerto in D* (Angel-EMI 32807).

Vangelis, *Heaven and Hell* (RCA LPK1-5110).

Vangelis, *Ignacio* (Barclay 813042-2).

Vangelis, *Ode* (POL 1473109).

Vangelis, *Opera Sauvage* (Polydor 829663-4).

Vangelis, *L'Apoloclypse Des Animaux* (POL 831503-2).

Vangelis, *Direct* (Arista AC-8545).

Vangelis, *Chariots of Fire* (Polydor 825384-4).

Vivaldi, *Gloria* (Electra 45248).

Paul Winter, *Missa Gaia/Earth Mass* (Living Music LMC-0002).

Zuleika, *White Pavillion.*

AREA III:
CELEBRATORY MUSIC

Anugama, *Exotic Dance* (Nightingale Records NGH CD-311).

Enya, *Watermark* (Reprise 26774-4).

Hooked on Classics, *Volumes I, II, III* (K-Tel NU 6113, NU 6893, NU626).

Jean Houston/Howard Jerome, *You are More* (Wind Over the Earth).

Nusrat Fateh Ali Khan, *Qawwal and Party* (Real World #991300-2).

Nusrat Fateh Ali Khan, *Mustt Mustt* (Real World #91630-2).

Daniel Kobialka, *Timeless Motion* (LiSem Enterprises DK 102).

Eric Kunzel and Cincinnati Pops Orchestra, *Pomp & Pizazz* (Telarc 80122).

La Bamba (soundtrack) (Slash 25605-4).

Brent Lewis, *Earth Tribe Rhythms* (Ikauma COM-3300).

Perles Du Baroque (Arion Records ARN 436342).

Smetana, *The Moldau* (COL 36716).

Paul Simon, *Graceland* (Warner Bros. 9 25447-4).

Paul Simon, *The Rhythm of the Saints* (Warner Bros. 26091-4).

INDEX

QUEST BOOKS
are published by
The Theosophical Society in America,
Wheaton, Illinois 60189-0270,
a branch of a world organization
dedicated to the promotion of the unity of
humanity and the encouragement of the study of
religion, philosophy, and science, to the end that
we may better understand ourselves and our place in
the universe. The Society stands for complete
freedom of individual search and belief.
In the Classics Series well-known
theosophical works are made
available in popular editions.